European in...

Peter Raedts is Lec...
Institute at Utrechu...

RICHARD RUFUS
OF CORNWALL
and the Tradition of
Oxford Theology

PETER RAEDTS

CLARENDON PRESS · OXFORD
1987

Oxford University Press, Walton Street, Oxford OX2 6DP

Oxford New York Toronto
Delhi Bombay Calcutta Madras Karachi
Petaling Jaya Singapore Hong Kong Tokyo
Nairobi Dar es Salaam Cape Town
Melbourne Auckland

and associated companies in
Beirut Berlin Ibadan Nicosia

Oxford is a trade mark of Oxford University Press

Published in the United States
by Oxford University Press, New York

British Library Cataloguing in Publication Data
Raedts, P. G. J. M.
Richard Rufus of Cornwall and the tradition
of Oxford theology. —(Oxford historical
monographs)
1 Rufus, Richard
I. Title
230'.092'4 BX4705.R7285/
ISBN 0-19-822941-0

Library of Congress Cataloging in Publication Data
Raedts, P. G. J. M. (Peter G. J. M.)
Richard Rufus of Cornwall and the tradition of
Oxford theology.
(Oxford historical monographs)
Bibliography: p.
Includes index.
1. Richard Rufus, of Cornwall, d. ca. 1260.
2. Theology, Doctrinal—History—Middle Ages, 600—1500.
3. Catholic Church—Doctrines—History. I. Title.
BX1749.R53R34 1987 230'.2'0924 86-18268
ISBN 0-19-822941-0

Typeset by Joshua Associates Limited, Oxford
Printed and bound in Great Britain by
Biddles Limited, Guildford and King's Lynn

IN MEMORY OF MY FATHER

Preface

THE encyclical *Aeterni Patris* (1879) did much to foster the study of medieval theology and philosophy. It also had one rather damaging side-effect in that it concentrated most intellectual effort on the man whom Pope Leo XIII called 'inter scholasticos Doctores omnium princeps et magister', Thomas Aquinas. No one doubts that Aquinas was a towering genius, nor that his systematic introduction of Aristotelian concepts into theology was a highly original achievement. But to lavish so much attention on one man must distort the historical perspective. For a long time Aquinas was regarded as the man in whom medieval scholarship had reached its pinnacle, who had absorbed all previous learning and built it into his own synthesis. His *Summa* was compared to a Gothic cathedral because of the perfect integration of all the parts. It was less emphasized, if not forgotten, that there had been many schools of thought, both before and after Aquinas, and that many theologians had been hardly influenced by him, nor he by them. Another consequence of this preoccupation with Aquinas was that later medieval theology was not sufficiently valued on its own merits, but usually described as a falling-away from the high standards set by Aquinas. Both Scotus and Ockham, to mention only its two most important representatives, have often been called the destroyers of the medieval synthesis.

Now times have changed. The bias towards Aquinas has given way to a more balanced approach. Scholars see more clearly now that Aquinas's contribution to medieval thought was not in all respects as original and as final as an earlier generation had thought it to be. Moreover, it is also dawning upon us that the admiration for his work rests on the presupposition that the highest goal the human mind can reach is a system in which perfect harmony between all the constitutive parts is achieved, in Aquinas's case the harmony between the natural and the supernatural, between faith and reason, based on the idea that the present universe is the best of all possible worlds and reflects God's eternal Being in time. Someone who is less interested in harmony and more concerned about the sheer fortuity of human existence might find Scotus far more original and palatable, especially where he argues that the present universe is only one of many possible worlds, thereby testifying to the radical contingency of man's existence and God's unpredictable but loving freedom.

As a consequence scholars now pay more attention to the many traditions of medieval thought and give more credit to the originality of later medieval thinkers like Scotus and Ockham. This also implies that attention is no longer focused exclusively on Paris. Both Scotus and Ockham received most of their education in the Franciscan convent at Oxford, where theology had been taught ever since, in 1229, the Franciscans had asked Robert Grosseteste to lecture to their students. From that time theology had been taught at Oxford for more than fifty years of which we as yet know very little. Grosseteste and Scotus have been studied, but in between there is a gap. Some very valuable work was done by Callus, Little, and Pelster, but their research necessarily consisted mainly of unearthing and identifying manuscripts.

The purpose of this book is to make a beginning with the bridging of this gap. Richard Rufus of Cornwall is a good starting-point. He is the first Franciscan theologian at Oxford whose works have survived. He was also, in a certain sense, a pupil of Robert Grosseteste and used much of the Bishop's work in his own commentaries. He did not, however, share many of Grosseteste's insights or concerns. On the contrary, with him a new tradition of theology gets off the ground, and it will be my contention that in his teaching he foreshadowed some of the revolutionary ideas, later to be voiced in the Oxford schools, about the contingency of the universe and the unlimited freedom of God. This work is a historical study, which, for the present purpose, means two things. First, I felt it to be necessary once again to go over works attributed to Richard and to determine which of them were authentic. Too much was attributed to him once he had been rediscovered by Pelster in 1926. Secondly, I was more interested in the question why Richard Rufus or Robert Grosseteste held certain opinions, and from what attitude, or outlook, or mentality—to use a fashionable word—they sprang, than in the question what the exact content of their ideas was. I know that the one is not really possible without the other, and I have tried to be as meticulous as possible in describing their opinions, yet the emphasis of a historian should be on the why, leaving the what to philosophers and theologians, who are much better equipped to deal with ideas in the abstract.

A work of this scope can never be finished without the help of many people. I am most grateful to the late Richard Hunt, who suggested that

I concentrate on Richard Rufus. In the course of my work I received valuable help from Maura O'Carroll, Richard Rouse, the late James Weisheipl, and especially from Osmund Lewry, whose diligent scholarship saved me from many oversights. I am most indebted to Vincent Quinn and Penelope Bulloch, librarians of Balliol College, Oxford, for making two of their manuscripts available to me over a period of several years. Many other librarians have helped, but I will always remember particularly the staff of Duke Humfrey's Library, whose unfailing courtesy and patience made my work much easier. In the last frantic stages I was ably assisted by Gillian Barnard, who typed the last draft of the manuscript, and by Paul Edwards, who corrected my foreigner's English. This book first saw the light as a thesis in the Faculty of Modern History at Oxford, so that much revision was needed before its publication. I greatly profited from the remarks of my examiners, Jeremy Catto and Alexander Murray. I honour the memory of Beryl Smalley, who was unable to be my examiner but, in the last weeks of her life, wrote a long, critical letter to me instead. All her remarks have been incorporated in this revised version. In a later stage of the revision my present colleague, Ferdinand de Grijs, pointed out several theological errors and inaccuracies. I had invaluable help from Henry Mayr-Harting in preparing the text for this edition. All the remaining errors in judgement and language are mine only. I would never have been able to embark on this project without the generous permission of my religious superiors, the two successive Provincials of the Dutch Jesuit province, Hans van Leeuwen and Gregory Brennink-meijer. My province, in the person of the treasurer, Clemens Brennink-meijer. They also provided the means to spend such a happy and fruitful time at Oxford. In all the years I worked on this book the Jesuit community of Campion Hall, Oxford, and my present community of De Breul, Zeist, gave me the brotherly support I needed. Last of all I thank my former supervisor, Sir Richard Southern. It is told of some of the great Jewish teachers that they spoke with such love about the Law that one could hear the melody of the Song of Songs in their voice. I often heard that melody when he talked to me about medieval man and showed me how in the dry discussions of scholastic theologians yet another episode was being enacted in the eternal struggle of Jacob with the angel, of man with his God. My father died one week after I had been accepted as a Probationer B. Litt. student at Oxford. He saw the joy of the beginning but not the end. To his memory I dedicate this book.

Utrecht, 24 November 1985 P.R.

Contents

Conventions   xiv

Sigla   xv

List of Abbreviations   xvi

1. Sources for the Life of Richard Rufus of Cornwall   1

PART I. THE WORKS OF RICHARD RUFUS OF CORNWALL   15

   The Process of Rediscovery   17

2. The Commentary on the *Sentences*   20
   (i) Oxford, Balliol College, MS 62 (= B)   20
   (ii) The Origin of the Commentary   25
   (iii) The Question of Its Author   30

3. The Abbreviation of Bonaventure's Commentary on the
   Sentences   40
   (i) Manuscript Tradition   40
      (*a*) Vatican City, Bibliotheca Apostolica Vaticana, MS lat.
           12993 (= V) and Assisi, Biblioteca comunale, MS 176 (= A)   40
      (*b*) Vatican City, Bibliotheca Apostolica Vaticana, MS
           Borghese 362 (= Bo)   44
      (*c*) Berlin (West), Staatsbibliothek Preussischer Kulturbesitz,
           MS Cod. theol. qu. 48 (= Be)   45
   (ii) The Abbreviator and His Work   47

4. Disputed Questions   64
   (i) Assisi, Biblioteca comunale, MS 138 (= As)   64
   (ii) Toulouse, Bibliothèque municipale, MS 737 (= T)   81
   (iii) Naples, Biblioteca nazionale, MS VII. C. 19 (= N)   85
   (iv) Paris, Bibliothèque nationale, MS lat. 16406 (= P)   86
   (v) London, British Library, MS Royal 8 C. iv (= L)   91

5. **Other Works Ascribed to Richard Rufus**   94
   - (i) A Commentary on Aristotle's *Metaphysics*   94
   - (ii) A Paris University Sermon   105
   - (iii) A Collection of Logical *Abstractiones*   107
   - (iv) Conclusion   113

PART II. RICHARD RUFUS OF CORNWALL AND ROBERT GROSSETESTE: A STUDY IN THEOLOGICAL OUTLOOK AND TRADITION   115

    The Extent of Richard's Indebtedness   117

6. **The Dispute on Method in Theology**   122
   - (i) Robert Grosseteste and the Tradition of the Fathers   122
   - (ii) Richard Rufus and the Demands of the New Age   137
   - (iii) Conclusion   150

7. **The Work of the Six Days**   152
   - (i) Creation: Biblical Study or Natural Philosophy?   152
   - (ii) The Origin of the Animal Soul   160
   - (iii) The Nature of the Human Soul and the Problem of Substantial Change   169
   - (iv) Allegorical and Physical Light   181
   - (v) The Eternity of the World   187
   - (vi) Conclusion   199

8. **Free Will in God and Man**   201
   - (i) The Problem of Free Will   201
   - (ii) Robert Grosseteste on Free Will in God and Man   203
   - (iii) Proofs of the Existence of Human Freedom of Will   207
   - (iv) Free Will in Relation to the Capacities of the Soul   210
   - (v) Freedom in God and Man   215
   - (vi) Conclusion   220

9. **The Reasons for the Incarnation**   222
   - (i) The History of the Question   222
   - (ii) Robert Grosseteste: The Completion of the Universe   225

Contents

(iii) Richard Fishacre: The Divine Pedagogy   231
(iv) Richard Rufus: The Redemption from Sin   234

Conclusions   241

Bibliography   254
  (i) Manuscript Sources   254
 (ii) Printed Sources   255
(iii) Secondary Works   257

Index   267

Conventions

QUOTATIONS from manuscript sources are in the classical Latin spelling, except that *e* is always used for *ae*, since this change is the only consistent deviation from classical spelling in the later Middle Ages. In quotations from printed sources I follow the spelling used by the editor. In references to manuscript sources I use a and b for recto and verso. If a page is divided into two columns, I use A and B for the first and second columns of the recto-page, and C and D for the first and second columns of the verso-page.

When a printed source is mentioned in the text the reader is usually referred to a critical edition. An exception has been made for the books of the Bible and the works of Aristotle and Thomas Aquinas. References to specific editions of the latter two have only been included when absolutely necessary, such as in the case of quotations from the *Aristoteles Latinus*. Only these specific editions are listed in the bibliography.

Translations from the Latin have been kept to a minimum. In the first part the Latin has been quoted to enable the reader to judge for himself on questions of authenticity. In the second part the illustrative texts are usually in Latin to give the reader a flavour of the theological language used by Richard Rufus and Robert Grosseteste. I have always tried to give a clear indication in my own writing of the content of the quoted passages.

Sigla

A	Assisi, Biblioteca comunale, MS 176
As	Assisi, Biblioteca comunale, MS 138
B	Oxford, Balliol College, MS 62
Ba	Oxford, Balliol College, MS 57
Be	Berlin (West), Staatsbibliothek Preussischer Kulturbesitz, MS Cod. theol. qu. 48
Bo	Vatican City, Bibliotheca Apostolica Vaticana, MS Borghese 362
C	Oxford, Corpus Christi College, MS 293B
D	Oxford, Bodleian Library, MS Digby 24
Di	Oxford, Bodleian Library, MS Digby 2
L	London, British Library, MS Royal 8 C. iv
N	Naples, Biblioteca nazionale, MS VII. C. 19
Ne	Oxford, New College, MS 285
O	Oxford, Oriel College, MS 43
Ox	Oxford, Bodleian Library, MS Lat. theol. c. 17
P	Paris, Bibliothèque nationale, MS lat. 16406
Pr	Prague, Library of the Metropolitan Chapter, MS M. lxxx
T	Toulouse, Bibliothèque municipale, MS 737
V	Vatican City, Bibliotheca Apostolica Vaticana, MS lat. 12993
Va	Vatican City, Bibliotheca Apostolica Vaticana, MS lat. 4538

List of Abbreviations

AFH	*Archivum Franciscanum historicum*
BGPh(Th)MA	Beiträge zur Geschichte der Philosophie (und Theologie) des Mittelalters
CC	Corpus Christianorum
CSEL	Corpus scriptorum ecclesiasticorum Latinorum
EHR	*English Historical Review*
FS	*Franciscan Studies*
FnSn	*Franziskanische Studien*
Gross. *Hex.*	Robert Grosseteste, *Hexaemeron*
Gross. *Lib.*	Robert Grosseteste, *De libero arbitrio*
MS	*Mediaeval Studies*
PL	Patrologiae cursus completus, Series Latina
RS	Rolls Series
RThAM	*Recherches de théologie ancienne et médiévale*

CHAPTER I

Sources for the Life of Richard Rufus of Cornwall

RICHARD RUFUS OF CORNWALL is one of the many medieval figures of whose life we know almost nothing. He disappears completely behind the works he left, and many details about his life can only be inferred once his works have been established and studied. Even so he hardly emerges as an individual whose life we could follow and whose preoccupations we could distinguish; he remains a cipher, a link in the chain of theological evolution at Oxford.

Contemporary evidence about his life comes from three sources: from the chronicler of the coming of the Franciscans to England, Thomas of Eccleston, from the letters of Adam Marsh, and from the writings of Roger Bacon. And they only inform us about his life as an academic theologian. It is only in a source from the eighteenth century that we find details, previously unknown and probably unreliable, about his earlier life, such as that he was born in Cirencester in Gloucestershire.[1] Richard would probably have been forgotten completely but for the fact that Roger Bacon saved him from oblivion by violently attacking him in the *Compendium studii theologie*, thereby giving him a moderate amount of notoriety, enough to keep later scholars mildly puzzled about the question what this Richard had done to deserve such a venomous attack. Bacon denounces Richard as one of the worst and most stupid authors of errors:

The one I knew best was the worst and most stupid of them all. He was the inventor of these errors. His name is Richard of Cornwall, very famous among the stupid masses, but the wise thought he was absurd. And he was rejected in Paris for the errors he had invented and promulgated, while lecturing there on the *Sentences* solemnly from the year 1250 onwards, after he had lectured on the *Sentences* at Oxford. From that time, 1250, on, therefore, most people

---

[1] [A. Parkinson], *Collectanea Anglo-minoritica, or, a Collection of the Antiquities of the . . . Gray Friers* (London, 1726), p. 79; the source of this interesting piece of information is not disclosed.

persistently followed this master in his errors, and it has mainly weakened Oxford, where all this nonsense started.[2]

This man so famous among the stupid masses, entered the order of the Franciscans at a moment of crisis:

The fifth [lecturer at the Oxford convent] was Richard [Rufus] of Cornwall, who entered at Paris at the time that Brother Elias disturbed the whole order. During that disturbance, while the appeal was pending, he firmly and devoutly made his profession. Afterwards he lectured on the *Sentences* 'cursorily' at Paris, where he was considered a great and admirable philosopher.[3]

The time that Brother Elias troubled the whole order must refer either to the events of 1238–9, leading to the deposition of Elias of Cortona as General of the Franciscans, or to the troubles around the translation of the body of Francis in 1230. The former date is suggested by another reference to Richard Rufus, made by Eccleston:

After these people Brother J. of Reading, abbot of Osney, entered, who left us examples of great perfection. After him Master Richard Rufus also entered; he was very famous in Oxford as well as in Paris.

The date of entry of John of Reading is well known: it was a few days before the beginning of Michaelmas 1235.[4] This seems inconsistent, however, with another passage in Eccleston's account, where he says:

Then several other, most reliable brethren of English origin, who had entered in Paris, came to England. I saw them, when I was still a secular. [Among them] was Brother Richard Rufus, an excellent lecturer, who afterwards went

---

[2] Roger Bacon, *Compendium studii theologie*, iv, ed. H. Rashdall (British Society of Franciscan Studies, iii, 1911), pp. 52–3. It has been a common mistake to read *priusquam* for *postquam*, based on an earlier edition of the *Compendium* in E. Charles, *Roger Bacon: sa vie, ses ouvrages, ses doctrines* (Paris, 1861), p. 415. Then the translation would be something like: '. . . while lecturing there on the *Sentences* solemnly, before he lectured on the *Sentences* at Oxford from the year 1250 on'. On the basis of this mistake many establish a wrong chronology of Richard's life, e.g. that he taught at Paris before 1250, and even was a regent master there after John of Parma's departure: thus H. Felder, *Geschichte der wissenschaftlichen Studien im Franziskanerorden bis um die Mitte des 13. Jahrhunderts* (Freiburg i. B., 1904), p. 225 n. 3; P. Mandonnet, 'Thomas d'Aquin, novice prêcheur (fin)', *Revue thomiste*, viii (1925), 512, assumes that Richard was one of the masters hit by the condemnation of 1244; M.-M. Davy, *Les Sermons universitaires parisiens de 1230–1231* (Études de philosophie médiévale, xv, 1931), pp. 141–3, credits Richard with a sermon preached in 1230 on the same grounds. On the authenticity of this sermon see below pp. 105–6.

[3] Thomas of Eccleston, *Tractatus de adventu fratrum minorum in Angliam*, xi, ed. A. G. Little (Manchester, 1951), p. 51.

[4] Eccleston, *De adventu*, iii (ed. Little, p. 18 and nn. *p* and *q*).

to the Curia as representative of France with Brother Haymo, zealous to reform the order against Brother Elias.[5]

If it is true that Richard Rufus accompanied Haymo of Faversham to Rome, then, obviously, he cannot have entered in 1238. It was in that year that Haymo went to Rome to see what could be done to prevent Elias from creating further havoc in the order, and it is unlikely that a novice woud be admitted to the high counsels of his brethren so soon. Besides, Thomas himself entered around the year 1233. So, if he saw Rufus as a Franciscan, while himself still a secular, Rufus must have entered before 1233. There is a snare, however, in this argument. The reading *Ricardus* is not entirely certain; one manuscript of Eccleston's chronicle has *Nicolaus* instead. At first Little was inclined to take the latter as the correct reading. Later he decided against it and accepted *Ricardus* despite the problems it causes.[6]

I am inclined to accept 1238 as the date of Richard's entering the Franciscan order. As Bacon says, he lectured on the *Sentences* at Oxford about 1250. It seems to me that a gap of twenty years between joining the order and the still quite modest position of *baccalaureus Sententiarum* is too wide, whereas 1238 ties in nicely with the fact that about nine years of study were required for a young theologian at Oxford before he was given leave to start his lectures on the *Sentences*.[7] This entails the admission that the person who accompanied brother Haymo to Rome was not Richard, but Nicholas Rufus. And although in textual criticism, if a choice has to be made, the more difficult reading is usually preferred, there are good reasons here for choosing the easier way out. The first two remarks about Richard Rufus, quoted from Eccleston, have much in common: in both the emphasis is that Richard was first of all an admirable scholar, well known at Oxford as well as at Paris. The third seems to deal with a different type of person: an administrator, a man who in 1238 took part in an important mission, crucial for the future of the order. And such a man would not, twelve years later, be reduced to lecturing on the *Sentences* and working for his degree in theology.

It is most likely, therefore, that Richard joined the order in Paris in

[5] Ibid. vi (ed. Little, pp. 29–30 and n. i).

[6] He still took *Nicolaus* for the correct reading in A. G. Little, 'The Franciscan School at Oxford in the 13th Century', *AFH* xix (1926), 841 n. 10. He explains his change of mind in 'The Lamport Fragment of Eccleston and Its Connexions', *EHR* xlix (1934), 299.

[7] Little, 'Franciscan School', p. 825.

1238, probably as a student in arts. By then he may even have been a master of arts, but that is not certain. Although Eccleston calls him *magister*, that title does not necessarily sum up his qualifications upon entry. John of Reading is called *frater* in the sentence before, a title which could hardly apply to his position as abbot of a grand monastery. As a novice Richard returned to England, where he made his profession. Eccleston further tells that upon his return to England he put in an appearance in the provincial chapter held that year at Oxford.[8] There he told an amusing story, how a friar in Paris had had a vision, in which he had seen how St Francis humiliated some learned scholars by praising a simple 'laicus sed contemplativus' and telling them that 'knowledge puffeth up, but charity edifieth' (1 Cor. viii. 1).[9] At first it seems odd that a novice entertained the fathers of the chapter, but considering the fact that this chapter was convened to confront a grave crisis, the participants must have been eager to hear the latest news from Paris, even if it was carried by a novice. And Richard's story certainly fitted the mood of the moment, an intense resentment against Elias, who had betrayed the spirit of true poverty and simplicity.

Richard spent the next years hidden away, probably studying theology and preparing for his degree in the Oxford faculty. The next we hear of him is in a letter of Adam Marsh. In 1248 the Minister General, John of Parma, visited England on his personal inspection tour of the order. When he left, he gave a letter to Richard Rufus, permitting him to go to Paris to continue his studies in theology there.[10] Richard did not avail himself of this permission immediately, but stayed at Oxford.

The reason for Richard's hesitation to move becomes clear from another letter of Adam Marsh: he had weak health. In one of his frequent reports to the Provincial, William of Nottingham, Adam

---

[8] A. G. Little, *Franciscan Papers, Lists and Documents* (Manchester, 1943), p. 209.

[9] Eccleston, *De adventu*, xi (ed. Little, pp. 51–2); this story only in one MS. Nevertheless it may be further evidence for the entry-date 1238. According to Little, *Franciscan Papers*, p. 209, there was no chapter at Oxford around 1230; if, then, it is true that Richard returned as a novice and spoke at the chapter, he must have entered around 1238. Caution, however, remains necessary, because our knowledge of the earliest provincial chapters is extremely sketchy.

[10] Adam Marsh, *Letters*, ccv, ed. J. Brewer, *Monumenta Franciscana*, i (RS, 1858), pp. 365–6. Adam wrote this letter much later, when Richard had decided to go to Paris after all. At the end of this letter he encloses a copy of the document which the Minister General had given to Richard 'in suo recessu'. John of Parma's visit to England took place in 1248, see J. Moorman, *A History of the Franciscan Order from its Origins to the Year 1517* (Oxford, 1968), p. 113.

writes that, after a consultation had been held with John, the papal legate, the warden of the Oxford convent, Thomas of York, and Richard himself, the conclusion had been reached that because of the many dangers to his health, it would be better for Brother Richard to stay at Oxford and complete the normal course of studies. They would send an apology to the General, and Richard would also come to London to talk matters over with the Provincial himself.[11]

Thus Richard stayed at Oxford and duly proceeded, as every student in theology had to do, to give his course of lectures on the *Sentences*, around the year 1250 according to Roger Bacon. Apparently it was then that he taught all the errors which caused Bacon's wrath to descend upon him. The reasons for Bacon's fury are difficult to understand. As will be pointed out later, the reasons he gives himself are far from satisfactory: he accuses Richard of making fundamental logical errors, but on all the points mentioned Richard represents the majority opinion among the philosophers of the day and not the beginning of some dangerous innovation.[12] Some scholars have suggested that Bacon bore Richard a personal grudge. But this is a rather hazardous conjecture, since the chronology of Bacon's life is notoriously uncertain; some even suggest that he may never have been in Oxford at all.[13] The precise cause of Bacon's anger remains a matter of speculation.

The reconstruction of the next episode in Richard's life depends on the chronology of two letters of Adam Marsh to the Provincial, William of Nottingham. The first of these letters can be dated; it begins with an extensive report of Thomas of York's inception on 13–14 March 1253 and a description of the conflict between the friars and the university which preceded this event.[14] At the end of that letter Adam mentions that Richard of Cornwall needs a secretary and that,

[11] Marsh, *Letters*, clxxxiv (ed. Brewer, p. 300). Little, 'Franciscan School', p. 842 n. 1, thinks that Richard first had permission from the General to go to Paris and subsequently was ordered to go, because Adam speaks of an 'indulgentialis littera' in the first case, and of a 'mandatum' in the second. This seems rather far-fetched; in a certain climate of religious obedience even a permission might be taken as an order. Moreover, precision often seems the victim of rhetoric in Adam Marsh's letters.

[12] Bacon, *Compendium*, iv (ed. Rashdall, p. 52); see also pp. 31–4.

[13] Little, 'Franciscan School', p. 842; S. Easton, *Roger Bacon and His Search for a Universal Science* (Oxford, 1952), pp. 95–7. The late Father J. Weisheipl once expressed his doubts about Bacon's stay at Oxford to me in a personal conversation.

[14] Adam Marsh reports that Thomas of York's inception took place in the two usual phases: 'Inceptionis vespere in crastino Beati Gregorii, feria quinta, et ipsa inceptio dispensatione feria sexta proxima sequente expeditae sunt in Domino', Marsh, *Letters*, cxcii (ed. Brewer, pp. 348–9.)

in his opinion, Brother Thomas Bacon of Nottingham convent not only is the right man for the job, but is also willing to do it:

> I implore you, Father, that with your usual courteous foresight in the Lord you will see to it that our beloved brother in God, Richard of Cornwall, a man who is in no need of intercession or recommendation to Your Paternity's shrewd experience, will get the help of a competent secretary to assist him and help him with his writing. Brother Thomas Bacon of the Nottingham convent is not only suitable, it seems, but also willing to take on the task.[15]

The second letter, which is undated, deals exclusively with the problems of Richard Rufus. Something has happened which has disturbed Richard to such an extent that he has decided to avail himself of the General's permission to go to Paris after all, and to leave Oxford immediately:

> A few days ago the aforementioned Brother R., because he found himself in a state of utter confusion, came to the irreversible decision that he wished to transfer to the province of France, availing himself of the permission given to him by the Minister-General some time ago. God willing, he desires to stay in Paris for some time.

Adam does not make clear what had happened, but Richard must have been in a pretty bad state. His mental condition is described as 'angustiae desolatio' and Adam begs the Provincial, if talking does not help, to allow Richard to go to Paris and to give him a companion to help him with his books.[16] Adam was clearly a little vexed with Richard's sudden decision to quit. Although he continues to press Richard's cause in two further letters to the Provincial, he writes in one of them that his patience has been sorely tried:

> If human reason yields to God's Providence, I think that I should be glad and generously bear with Brother R. of Cornwall's irrevocable intention [to leave for Paris].[17]

Little assumes that the letter in which Richard's sudden decision to leave for Paris is announced was written before the letter in which Adam asks the Provincial to find Richard a secretary. He sees the recommendation of Brother Thomas as a possible secretary to be a further elaboration of the request to provide Richard with a com-

---

[15] Ibid.

[16] *Letters*, ccv (ed. Brewer, pp. 365–6); this is the same letter as quoted on p. 4 n. 10.

[17] *Letters*, cc (ed. Brewer, p. 360); cf. cxcix (ed. Brewer, pp. 358–9).

panion on his journey.[18] This reconstruction leaves Little—and later Easton—with the problem of how to explain Richard's sudden collapse and flight. Both try to forge yet another link between Roger Bacon's attack on Richard and the latter's sudden departure for Paris: Richard was so distressed about Bacon's accusations that he could not possibly stay in the same house any longer.[19] The same problem arises as before: all depends on Bacon's presence in Oxford at the time. Moreover, I can see no indication of an impending departure for Paris in the letter first quoted, where Adam recommends Brother Thomas Bacon as a possible secretary. If Little had been right, one would have expected at least a hint that Brother Thomas was to go abroad with Richard.

Hence it seems more plausible to assume that Adam first wrote to ask a secretary for Richard, and later on to announce Richard's intention to leave for Paris.[20] This alternative sequence of events also admits an explanation for Richard's sudden change of mind which depends less on conjectures. From Adam's description it looks as if Richard suffered some sort of nervous breakdown. And in the proposed sequence of events this breakdown occurs some time after Thomas of York's inception. It might well be the case that Richard found it impossible to stomach the fact that Thomas of York had been appointed lecturer and regent master in his stead. The letter in which Adam asks for a secretary for Richard is also the letter in which he makes a report about Thomas of York's inception. All seems well with Richard then. Somewhat later Richard suddenly decides to leave. I suggest a connection.

There can be no doubt that Adam Marsh had been pushing Thomas of York. He had written about him to Robert Grosseteste twice, drawing the bishop's attention to the young man's great qualities.[21] Later on he urgently advised the Provincial to appoint Thomas of York to the important post of lecturer to the Oxford convent

---

[18] Little, 'Franciscan School', p. 842.

[19] Ibid.; Easton, *Roger Bacon*, pp. 95–7.

[20] This chronology is also accepted by A. Callebaut, 'Alexandre de Halès O.F.M. et ses confrères en face de condamnations parisiennes de 1241 et 1244', *La France franciscaine*, x (1927), 265.

[21] Marsh, *Letters*, xxvi and lxx (ed. Brewer, pp. 114, 176); Thomas also figured in a letter of Adam to the Bishop of Roskilde, viii (ed. Brewer, p. 91); three letters of Adam Marsh to Thomas of York are preserved in the collection, ccxxv–ccxxvii (ed. Brewer, pp. 392–6), whereas none to Richard Rufus; a close co-operation between Adam and Thomas appears in two letters they wrote together on behalf of the lapsed Franciscan Hugh Cote, clxxxix and cxcvi (ed. Brewer, pp. 340–1, 352–3).

'for his brilliancy of mind, for his linguistic skills and for the virtuous restraint, with which God has endowed him'.[22] Adam was clearly very much taken with the young man.

Richard may well have felt overtaken by this clever youth of whom his superiors thought so very highly, so much so that they were prepared to risk a conflict with the university to get him into the chair of lecturer to the Oxford Franciscans as soon as possible. The university objected to anyone incepting in theology who had not fulfilled the statutory period as a regent master in arts and had not given a course of lectures either on the Bible, or on the *Sentences*, or on the *Histories* of Peter Comestor.[23] From the university's point of view Richard was much better prepared for the job. He had been an arts student at Paris, probably even a master of arts, and had given his course of lectures on the *Sentences*. From the university statute which was drawn up as a result of the quarrel, and from Adam Marsh's report, it may be inferred that Thomas of York had done neither.[24] Thus, Thomas must have been considerably younger than Richard. But despite all this the Franciscans wanted Thomas to incept immediately without finishing his course, and they were prepared to take the protest of the university in their stride.

To be pushed out by a younger and probably more talented man, who is being lionized by his superiors, is always a bitter experience, and certainly in enclosed religious communities like the Franciscan convent at Oxford feeling in such matters can rise very high. Therefore, it seems a possibility that the state of utter confusion to which Adam so delicately refers was the pangs of jealously felt by Richard, when he saw the promotion to high office of a younger—and in the eyes of his superiors more promising—brother, elected to incept in his stead, although he was the better qualified.

It is a hypothesis. There are two additional points, however, which fit it quite well. The first is that, since Richard had lectured on the *Sentences* around 1250, the time for his inception must have been drawing very near in 1253. The second is that Adam Marsh, who had never recommended Richard in one of his letters before, now suddenly felt called upon to praise him highly and to emphasize how sorely the brethren were going to miss him: he writes to the Provincial:

[22] *Letters*, cxcviii (ed. Brewer, p. 357).
[23] *Statuta antiqua universitatis Oxoniensis*, ed. S. Gibson (Oxford, 1931), p. 49.
[24] Ibid.; Marsh, *Letters*, clxxxviii and cxcii (ed. Brewer, pp. 338, 346–9); Little, 'Franciscan School', pp. 823, 840, comes to the same conclusion.

You know . . . how agreeable the presence of our dearest brother Richard of Cornwall is to all your sons . . . It is well known that his upright life and clear knowledge, his affectionate piety and honest opinions, his skilful teaching and subtle reasoning assure him of our faithful friendship.[25]

This outburst of sudden enthusiasm only seems to underline that Richard, somehow, has been fobbed off with a consolation prize. There is the argument that the brethren are going to miss him, always a last resort. And the fulsome praise is not quite honest, as other letters testify to Adam's impatience with Richard's whims.

Such being the case, Richard may well have felt that perhaps it would be better for his own peace of mind and for good relations within the Oxford community, if he were not to go on living there under the same roof as his rival, but to beat a dignified retreat and avail himself, despite his ill health, of the General's permission to go to Paris to let matters rest for a while. Apparently he did not spend his time in idleness. Both Bacon and Eccleston report that he lectured on the *Sentences* once more at Paris, although they do not agree about the status of the lectures: Bacon thought he lectured *solempniter*, Eccleston thought *cursorie*. They also brought him the recognition which he had not received at Oxford; in Paris he was considered a great and admirable philosopher.[26]

In 1256 his fortunes changed. The lecturer to the Cambridge convent, William of Melitona, was summoned back to Paris to be chairman of the commission to complete the unfinished *Summa 'Alexandri'*. In Cambridge he was succeeded by Thomas of York.[27] And now Richard's turn came; he succeeded Thomas as fifth lecturer to the Oxford convent. The years in Paris had borne fruit. For three years he had lived in the same house as the greatest of all early Franciscan theologians, Bonaventure, and had made himself thoroughly familiar with his commentary on the *Sentences*. Back in Oxford he used his position to introduce his students to the teaching of Bonaventure by composing a careful summary of this masterly commentary with additions of his own, thus bridging the gap between the Paris and Oxford tradition.[28] From then on Richard disappears in the dark of history. The last we hear of him is in November 1259, when

[25] Marsh, *Letters*, ccv (ed. Brewer, p. 365).
[26] Eccleston, *De adventu*, xi (ed. Little, p. 51).
[27] Little, *Franciscan Papers*, pp. 134–5.
[28] For proof of the thesis that the abbreviation is a result of the second Oxford period see below, pp. 62–3.

he was bequeathed a habit by Martin de S. Cruce, master of the hospital of Sherbourne near Durham.[29]

Posterity has not dealt kindly with his memory. As far as we know he is quoted just once in a theological treatise, in Roger of Nottingham's *Introitus ad Sententias*, which dates from the middle of the fourteenth century. He is mentioned there as author of a commentary on the *Sentences*.[30]

As an author he is also mentioned in a completely different fourteenth-century source, the catalogue of the library of the Sacro Convento in Assisi, composed in 1381 by Brother John Ioli. The relevant entries are:

Primus. et secundus. fratris magistri riccardi de cornubia anglici. ordinis minorum. Cum postibus. Cuius principium est. Secundum hugone(m) de sancto victore. in libro de sacramentis. parte prima. duplex est opus creatoris. Finis vero. Quibus se non possit exuere. Explicit liber secundus. In quo libro: omnes quaterni sunt. xx. F.

Compillatio. iiijor. librorum sententiarum. [   ] secundum fratrem magistrum riccardum ruphi. de anglia. ordinis minorum. facta parisius. Cum postibus. Cuius principium est. Cupientes. Totali libro. premictit magister prologum. Finis vero. Hoc non est per executionem: sed notificationem pnu [   ] In quo libro: omnes quaterni sunt. xxiiij. N. +.[31]

---

[29] Little, 'Franciscan School', p. 845. In Adam Marsh's letters another Richard of Cornwall appears (Marsh, *Letters*, xxxiv (ed. Brewer, p. 135); he was a subdeacon recommended to Bishop Grosseteste for a prebend. Since from internal evidence it can be proved that this letter was written in 1248, it must be a different Richard. Th. Tanner, *Bibliotheca Britannico-Hibernica* (London, 1748), p. 627 n. *a*, also mentions several clerics called Richard of Cornwall, all different from the friar theologian.

[30] E. Synan, 'The *Introitus ad Sententias* of Roger of Nottingham O.F.M.', *MS* xxv (1963), 274; see also below, p. 34.

[31] C. Cenci, *Bibliotheca manuscripta ad Sacrum Conventum Assisiensem* (Il miracolo di Assisi, iv/1–2, 1981), i. 292–3, 303. A third entry with possible reference to Richard Rufus can be found in this catalogue (i. 290): 'Primus super sententias. magistri fratris riccardi. de mediavilla. ordinis minorum. Sine postibus. Cuius principium est. Quia secundum hugonem. in prologo libri de sacramentis. Finis vero. vivit et regnat deus. per omnia secula seculorum. Amen. In quo libro: omnes quaterni sunt. novem E.' Alessandri, in his edn. of *Inventario dell'antica biblioteca del S. Convento di S. Francesco in Assisi compilato nel 1381* (Assisi, 1906), p. 103 indicates that a later hand—he thinks Sbaralea's—has deleted *Mediavilla* and written *Cornubia* on top of it, probably because he had seen the similarity of the incipit with that of the work ascribed to Richard of Cornwall quoted in the text. If the incipit is right, the work cannot be Mediavilla's. F. Pelster, 'Zu Richardus Rufus de Cornubia', *Zeitschrift für katholische Theologie*, xlviii (1924), 628 says, wrongly, that according to Alessandri, this work is still in Assisi.

Except for another short reference in a fifteenth-century library catalogue in Siena, to be discussed later, this is, so far, all the material handed down to us from the Middle Ages.[32]

Richard Rufus figures somewhat more prominently in the encyclopedias drawn up by antiquaries between 1500 and 1800, eager to scrape together all the remnants of the past they could lay their hands on. Unfortunately they did not find anything other than the scant information from Eccleston, Bacon, and the Assisi catalogue, all of which have just been discussed. Leland only uses Eccleston and tries to establish a relation between Richard and a Carmelite, called Geoffrey of Cornwall, who lived, in fact, much later.[33] Bale generally transcribes what he has seen in Leland. On his journeys through England, however, he also came across a commentary on the *Sentences* by the Franciscan Richardus le Ruys in Norwich cathedral library, the *incipit* of which was: *Materia divinarum scripturarum*.[34] He adds that he has never come across that name anywhere else. Nevertheless he is able to supply his readers with a short biography of this Richard, whom he accuses of being unorthodox, and giving up the tradition of Scripture commentary for fashionable sophistry. This seems a resonance of Bacon's complaints about Richard Rufus.[35]

All later learned authors combine these four sources of information—Eccleston, Bacon, the Assisi catalogue, and Bale's discovery in Norwich cathedral library—in different ways. At the end of the sixteenth century Rodulphius discussed Richard Rufus on the basis of the Assisi catalogue only, inferring from there that a distinction had to be made between Richard Rufus, who taught at Paris, and Richard of Cornwall, who taught at Oxford.[36] This mistake was copied by Willot in his survey of Franciscan scholars.[37] Possevino, Pits, and Wadding also take over this distinction. Since they have studied Bale's reports of his travels, they end up with three different Richards: Rufus, Cornubiensis, and Ruys.[38]

---

[32] See below, p. 61.

[33] J. Lelandus, *Commentarii de scriptoribus Brittannicis*, ed. A. Hall (Oxford, 1709), p. 279 (c. 264). [34] See also below, p. 19.

[35] J. Bale, *Scriptorum illustrium maioris Brytanniae . . . catalogus* (Basle, 1557–9), ii. 81, 153. See also J. Bale, *Index Britanniae scriptorum*, ed. R. Poole and M. Bateson (Anecdota Oxoniensia, Medieval and Modern Series, ix, 1902), p. 338.

[36] P. Rodulphius, *Historiarum seraphicae religionis libri tres* (Venice, 1586), f. 333b.

[37] H. Willotus, *Athenae orthodoxorum sodalitii Franciscani* (Liège, 1598), pp. 314, 316.

[38] A. Possevinus, *Apparatus sacer ad scriptores . . . conscriptos* (2nd edn, 2 vols, Cologne, 1608), ii. 324, 326; J. Pitseus, *Relationum historicarum de rebus Anglicis* (Paris, 1619), pp. 348, 895, 898; L. Wadding, *Scriptores ordinis minorum* ed. J. Sbaralea (Rome, 1806), pp. 207–8.

Anthony Wood offers a different combination; he merges Richard Rufus, the 'Paris' theologian, with Richard Ruys. He also introduces a new mistake by identifying Richard of Cornwall, the 'Oxford' theologian, with a prebendary and chancellor of York (1227–44) of the same name. He regards this Richard of Cornwall as the person denounced by Bacon.[39] Parkinson, the first historian of the English Franciscans, seems to have consulted Eccleston directly, since he mentions Richard's alleged journey to Rome with Brother Haymo of Faversham, which is not discussed in any of the earlier works. He also saw Willot, Pits, and probably Leland, and so has a triple Richard as well.[40] As we have seen, he has it from an unknown source that Richard Rufus was born in Cirencester.

Tanner was the first to restore some order: he merges Richard Rufus and Richard of Cornwall into one person, and he clearly distinguishes this man from the homonymous prebendary of York. He does not discuss Richard Ruys.[41] Sbaralea, who revised Luke Wadding's catalogue, was the first to make some independent enquiries into the subject. He visited the library of the Sacro Convento in Assisi and consulted the catalogue of 1381, where he found the two—or three—entries about Richard. Although this new enquiry did not lead to a revision of the mistake about the three Richards,[42] Sbaralea did find a new work of Richard, the abbreviation of Bonaventure's commentary on the *Sentences*, now preserved partly in the Vatican library (MS lat. 12993) and partly in the Biblioteca comunale, Assisi (MS 176). He wished to ascribe this work to Richard Ruys, since in his chronology Ruys was the only one of the three who flourished after Bonaventure.[43]

To clarify the relations between these antiquaries, I finish with a diagram showing the lines of influence:

[39] A. Wood, *Historia et antiquitates universitatis Oxoniensis* (2 parts in one vol., Oxford, 1674), i. 72, 85, 96. In the English edition: *The History and Antiquities of the University of Oxford*, ed. J. Gutch (2 vols., Oxford, 1792–6), i. 211, 241, the passage about Ruys has been omitted.

[40] [Parkinson], *Collectanea*, pp. 28, 31–2, 58, 79, 173.

[41] Tanner, *Bibliotheca*, pp. 627–8.

[42] A. G. Little, *The Greyfriars in Oxford* (Oxford Historical Society, xx, 1892), p. 142 n. 1, established once and for all from one of the reliable MSS of Eccleston that Richard Rufus and Richard of Cornwall were one and the same person.

[43] J. Sbaralea, 'Supplementum et castigatio ad scriptores ... a Waddingo ... descriptos', in L. Wadding, *Scriptores*, part ii, pp. 633, 635. The German antiquary J. A. Fabricius, *Bibliotheca Latina mediae et infimae aetatis* (6 vols., Hamburg, 1734–46), vi. 215, 238, limits himself to references to the learned works discussed in the text.

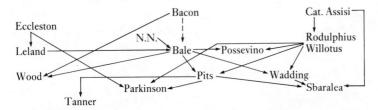

Sbaralea was the last scholar of the antiquarian type to make any new discoveries. It was not until the revival of interest in scholastic philosophy in the late nineteenth and early twentieth centuries, which caused a new generation of scholars to dig deeper into the past than the antiquaries had done, that something more than the bare name of Richard Rufus and a few uncertain incipits were retrieved. Strenuous efforts have since been made to establish a more reliable biography and to recover Richard's theological works. And it is on the solid foundations of that critical work, mainly done by Little and Pelster, that I shall be building these pages.

PART I

The Works of Richard Rufus of Cornwall

The Process of Rediscovery

THE scholastic revival brought to light the names and works of many previously unknown medieval theologians, and also new works of well-known scholars. Richard Rufus of Cornwall is a good example of how such a search takes place and of its success. Whereas in 1924 not a single work of his was known to be extant, by 1940 two commentaries on the *Sentences*, a dozen or more disputed questions, a sermon, and other bits and pieces had been attributed to this once forgotten Franciscan. Most of this new research on Richard Rufus profited considerably from the huge enterprise, which took place in the years between 1920 and 1948, to establish a critical text of the *Summa 'Alexandri'*, an encyclopedia of early Franciscan theology. Some of the finest Franciscan and other scholars roamed through all the main libraries of Europe to recover and identify the evidence of Franciscan theological activity in the years before 1250. Sometimes, however, the suspicion arises that in the excitement caused by the many new findings, too much anonymous material was identified too quickly and that the name of Richard Rufus has perhaps been bandied about too much. The purpose of this part, therefore, is to submit all the works attributed to Richard Rufus to a new enquiry, to sift new evidence that has come up since the first search, and to establish a new canon of Richard's works.

The search for the lost works of Richard Rufus started from the data supplied by the 1381 catalogue of the Sacro Convento in Assisi and by Bale. As seen, they do not amount to much more than three incipits: 'Secundum hugone(m) de sancto victore. in libro de sacramentis. parte prima. duplex est opus creatoris'; 'Cupientes. Totali libro. premictit magister prologum'; and 'Materia divinarum scripturarum omnium sunt opera restaurationis humane'.[1] Unfortunately the incipit: 'Cupientes. Totali libro' is extremely unhelpful, since it is one of the beginnings of Bonaventure's commentary on the *Sentences* and of countless abbreviations thereof.

Little has suggested that the *Sentences* commentary preserved in Balliol College library, MS 196, might represent Richard's lectures in

[1] See above, pp. 10–11.

Paris and also one of the works described in the 1381 Assisi catalogue.[2] The incipit is:

Toti operi libri sententiarum premittit magister prologum suum, ubi primo ponit causas allicientes eum ad scribendum, secundo ponit utilitates huius operis, illius *horum* . . .   (f. 4a)

Gründel agrees that it represents an early abbreviation of Bonaventure's commentary, but he puts no name to it.[3] Looking through the manuscript myself I could discover no structural similarities with Bonaventure's commentary; for instance, the *divisio textus* is completely different. The commentary seems of much older date than the late 1250s; it keeps very close to the text of Lombard, limiting itself to an exposition of the text without elaboration in the form of disputed questions. A typical example of this occurs in i. 32:

Post hec queri solet. Postea cum ex predictis constet quod filius non est sapiens a se nec de se, sed a patre et de patre, cum sit sapiens sapientia genita que a genitore est, querit magister utrum filius sit sapiens seipso vel per seipsum. Et respondet duobus modis.   (f. 55a)

The author always uses formulas like *querit magister*, *respondet*, never *respondeo*, or *hic quero*, nor does he introduce new problems and questions into the text. This points, in my opinion, to an origin in the first quarter of the thirteenth century and not to a work of Richard Rufus or any other mid-century theologian.

Another work with the *incipit* 'Cupientes' that is often mentioned in this connection is Todi, Biblioteca comunale, MS 33. To establish a connection with Richard Rufus here is all the more attractive, since it is attributed to a certain William Rufus in the modern catalogue of the library.[4] This ascription, however, seems to be spurious; Alszeghy, who saw the manuscript, describes it as an abbreviation of the first book of Bonaventure's commentary in a rather loose manner and remarks that he has not been able to discover the name of William Rufus anywhere in the manuscript.[5] Since I had no access to the

---

[2] Little, 'Franciscan School', pp. 844–5. A detailed description of the MS in R. A. B. Mynors, *Catalogue of the Manuscripts of Balliol College Oxford* (Oxford, 1962), pp. 195–6.

[3] J. Gründel, *Die Lehre von den Umständen der menschlichen Handlung im Mittelalter* (BGPhThMA xxxix/5, 1963), pp. 566–8.

[4] L. Leonii, *Invantario dei codici della comunale di Todi* (Todi, 1878), p. 16. The full incipit on the same page: 'Cupientes aliquid de penuria etc. premictit hic magister totali libro prologum'.

[5] Z. Alszeghy, 'Abbreviationes Bonaventurae. Handschriftliche Auszüge aus dem Sentenzenkommentar des hl. Bonaventura im Mittelalter', *Gregorianum*, xxviii (1947), 482.

manuscript myself, I can venture no final opinion, but it seems unlikely that this manuscript could represent one of the lost works of Richard Rufus. Alszeghy discovered no similarity between this abbreviation and the much longer one, now preserved in the Vatican and Assisi, which is definitely a work of Richard Rufus, as will be established later.[6] And it seems unlikely that Richard started out to abbreviate Bonaventure twice.

The third effort to recover one of Richard Rufus's lost works started from Bale's discovery in Norwich cathedral library of a treatise beginning with the words 'Materia divinarum scripturarum'. Stegmüller ventured the opinion that this treatise might be identical with a short work found in Oxford, Bodleian library, MS Bodley 681, pp. 149–80.[7] In the summary catalogue it is described as a short treatise on the Trinity.[8] The incipit is: 'Que sit materia divinarum scripturarum. Materia divinarum scripturarum omnium sunt opera restaurationis humane' (p. 149). A closer scrutiny of this work reveals that it is an excerpt from Hugh of Saint-Victor's *De sacramentis Christianae fidei*, consisting of a summary of the prologue (pp. 149–53), and the chapters I. i. 1 (p. 153), I. ii. 5–14 beginning (pp. 153–60), I. iii. 1–27 (pp. 160–80), ending imperfectly on p. 180.[9]

The problem in starting the search for lost works of Richard Rufus from this angle is clear. The incipits are not specific enough to go upon; they are the beginning of two very popular works, Hugh's *De sacramentis* and Bonaventure's *Sentences* commentary. And even the first incipit is very common: most questions on the nature of theology in this era start off by quoting Hugh's distinction between the works of creation and of re-creation. This road, then, almost certainly leads to a dead end. Much more promising was the discovery of F. Pelster of an anonymous commentary on the *Sentences* in Balliol College library which dated clearly from the middle of the thirteenth century and originated in Oxford. To this work we must now turn.

---

[6] See below, pp. 47–61.

[7] F. Stegmüller, *Repertorium commentariorum in Sententias Petri Lombardi* (2 vols., Würzburg, 1947), i. 356 (no. 727).

[8] F. Madan and H. Craster, *A Summary Catalogue of Western Manuscripts in the Bodleian Library at Oxford* (7 vols., Oxford, 1895–1953), ii/1, 445. In the index (vii. 411) Richard Rufus is mentioned as a probable author of this treatise.

[9] Hugh of Saint-Victor, *Liber de sacramentis Christianae fidei* (PL clxxvi, cols. 183–229A).

CHAPTER 2

The Commentary on the *Sentences*

THE first work to be ascribed to Richard Rufus, and also the most important, is a commentary on the *Sentences* preserved completely in only one manuscript, now at Balliol College, Oxford. A fragment of this commentary (ii. 1–8) can also be found in London, British Library, MS Royal 8 C. iv, which will be discussed later.[1]

(i) *Oxford, Balliol College, MS 62 (=B)*

This manuscript contains a commentary on the first three books of the *Sentences*. It is outstanding for its extremely careful organization: all the quires are numbered, the headline of every page consists of the number of book, distinction, and column. Even more striking is the numbering of the lines in every column: every fifth line has a number (from 5 to 55) put in the space between the columns. The manuscript came to Balliol College as part of the gift of William Grey, Bishop of Ely (1454–1478) (f. 5b). The work is ascribed to James of Viterbo in the same inscription in which the gift is mentioned.

i + 251 ff. + i, a single English hand of the middle thirteenth century.

Inc. Proemium: Cum venisset una vidua pauper misit duo minuta quod est quadrans (Mark xii. 41–4). Laudanda creatoris humilis et pia benevolentia que non quantum sed ex quanto affectu quis offerat sue maiestati attendit . . . (f. 6A)

Prologus: *Cupientes* etc. Hec summa dividitur in 2., in prologum et executionem. Prologus 8 habet partes. In prima insinuat quod modicus opus arduum presumpsit . . . (f. 7C)

i: *Veteris ac nove legis* etc. Incipit executio magistri. Que dividitur secundum ipsum magistrum in duas partes. Quarum prima est de rebus que non sunt signa . . . (f. 12C)

---

[1] See below, pp. 91–3. Balliol College, MS 62, was first identified as a work of Richard Rufus of Cornwall by F. Pelster, 'Der älteste Sentenzenkommentar aus der Oxforder Franziskanerschule', *Scholastik*, i (1926), 50–80.

ii: *Creationem rerum* etc. A principio dictum est a magistro
            quod primo tractat de rebus scilicet in tribus primis libris,
            in quarto de signis. De rebus autem tripliciter
            ... (f. 103C)

iii: *Cum venit igitur plenitudo temporis* etc. De quo sit hic liber
            tertius patet et prius habitum est. Et habet hec prima
            distinctio partes 5; 2ª incipit ibi: *Diligenter*... (f. 193A)

Exp.:   ... licet nulla essent de eis scripta vel promulgata vel
            recepta. Et hec sufficiant de tertio libro et continet 5
            sextarios tantum. (f. 252D)

The manuscript is clearly of university provenance; the division into
pecie is sufficient indication for that. The numbering of the lines on a
page is a very rare feature; it occurs only in a very limited number of
manuscripts, which all originate in Oxford around the middle of the
thirteenth century.[2] More puzzling is the question in what stage of the
university book production this manuscript has to be fitted.

Pollard distinguishes five stages in the academic book-making
process: the author's autograph, the apograph, the stationer's
exemplar, the *pecie*, and the *pecia* copies.[3] To begin with the end, the
present manuscript cannot have been a *pecia* copy, since it is characteristic of this sort of manuscript to have the *pecia* marks in the side
margin and not in the top or bottom margins. In other words the
quires do not coincide with the *pecie*.[4] In this manuscript, however,
they do coincide: every quire represents a *pecia*. The scribe himself
uses the words *pecia* and *sextarius* or *quaternus* indiscriminately to refer
to the same thing:

Explicit liber secundus. Et continet 8 pecias quarum prima continet 10 folia et
dimidium et precedens est finis primi libri. Sex autem pecie sequentes sunt
sextarii integri. Hec autem ultima pecia non est nisi quaternus cuius sex folia
et dimidium sunt scripta et non amplius. Amen. Deo gratias. (f. 192B)

The *pecia*-marks are to be found at the foot of the verso of the last folio
of each quire in the following form: 'I, 2us, 3us, 4ª pecia, ... 1ª pecia 2i
libri, 2ª pecia, 3ª, ... 1ª pecia 3 libri, 2ª pecia, ...'. In the same place the

[2] A. G. Little and F. Pelster, *Oxford Theology and Theologians* c. A.D. 1282–1302
(Oxford Historical Society, xcvi, 1934), p. 61; confirmed by Richard Rouse and Maura
O'Carroll.
[3] G. Pollard, 'The *Pecia* System in the Medieval Universities', in M. Parkes and
A. Watson (eds.), *Medieval Scribes, Manuscripts and Libraries, Essays... N. R. Ker* (London,
1978), pp. 151–2.
[4] Op. cit., p. 152.

catch-word of the next *pecia* is given. There are no *pecia* marks at the beginning of a quire. The fact that quire and *pecia* coincide is sufficient proof that Balliol MS 62 is not a *pecia* copy.

Neither is it a collection of *pecie* hired out for copying and later bound together in one manuscript. Characteristic of this sort of manuscript is the tattiness of the quires. According to Pollard they are internally worn, rubbed, folded, or patched, understandably so, since they must have gone through many hands. No attention has been paid to the decoration and spaces for initials have usually been left blank. They were working instruments, used by many, and, therefore, neglected.[5] The Balliol manuscript makes just the opposite impression: it bears no signs of wear and tear. It is beautifully written and carefully, if sparingly, decorated (see ff. 6A, 12C, 103C, 193A). It is not at all a working copy but a fair copy kept on the shelf.

On the other hand the manuscript does not represent the author's autograph. On f. 128C the scribe writes in the margin: 'Look here for two corresponding signs in the script of the master, which I have forgotten.' And on f. 127C the author explains that the world was created 'in mense nisan'. The scribe comments 'sic in exemplari', thus giving away that he did not understand the word *Nisan*, but thought it was a mistake of the author's. Had the author been writing this passage himself, one would have supposed that he knew what he was talking about, even though it is true that, in fact, he borrowed this piece of information from Grosseteste's *Hexaemeron*.[6]

So the manuscript could be either an apograph or an *exemplar*. For both there are some indications. Pelster thought that it was the former, a fair copy used by the stationer as the standard for further multiplication.[7] Pollard observes that he has never seen such an *exemplar*.[8] Nevertheless the careful division of the manuscript into *pecie* and especially the summing-up of the number and size of the *pecie* at the end of each book, one example of which has been quoted,[9] point more in the direction of an origin in the stationer's shop. Another indication that the manuscript served as a model for further copying is that many

[5] Op. cit., p. 153. Bruce Barker-Benfield kindly drew my attention to a fine example: Oxford, Oriel College, MS 64, a collection of medical works.

[6] Gross. *Hex*. I. x. 2, p. 65.

[7] Pelster, 'Ältester Sentenzenkommentar', pp. 70–1.

[8] Pollard, *'Pecia* System', p. 158.

[9] See above, p. 21. Further examples are to be found at the end of books i and iii of the commentary: 'Et hec de primo libro sufficiant. Et sunt in universo 8 sextarii et 1 folium et dimidium' (f. 103B). 'Et hec sufficiant de tertio libro. Et continet 5 sextarios tantum' (f. 252D).

corrections are not just given but also discussed. For example, on
f. 34A the scribe writes in the margin next to a passage which he thinks
out of place: 'I think that this should be put after the objection: *Equalia
etiam sunt*'; the said objection follows a few lines later. Sometimes he
corrects an obvious mistake, e.g. in i. 39 he writes 'Plotinus' in the text
and gives what he found in the original in the margin: 'Prothinus in
exemplari' (f. 89C). He must also have checked references, as is clear
from a passage where the author forgets to mention from what work of
Hugh of Saint-Victor he is quoting: '. . . de qua dicit Hugo parte 7 c. 31
. . .'; the scribe puts in the margin: 'De hoc nescio ubi' (f. 174B). Sometimes he explains an obscure word, e.g. in a quotation from Ambrose's
Hexaemeron, where the expression 'pisce silvio' occurs; the scribe
explains in the margin that it is a small fish (f. 247B). Such careful and
reasoned corrections would only be justified if the book were to serve
as a model for future copyists.

On the other hand, the marginal notes on the flyleaves seem to point
to a use of the book within the confines of a religious house rather than
a stationer's shop. Ff. lb and 253a are covered with notes for sermons
and stories that may have been used to illustrate sermons as well. A
pencil-note on f. 5b announces 'Memorandum accommodasse tres
pecias super librum Top. Laur. Cornub.' Lawrence of Cornwall was
an Oxford Franciscan of the last third of the thirteenth century.[10]
These notes could indicate that the book was kept in the library of the
Oxford Franciscan convent. And if the author is a Franciscan, as will
be proved later, then it could be an apograph.[11] An apograph is,
according to Pollard, a manuscript that, though it does not represent
the author's own writing, originated in the close surroundings of the
author. Examples are manuscripts which have the author's own
corrections, or fair copies made by the author's secretary, or copies
taken from the author's dictation, or presentation copies.[12] In this case
there is undoubtedly a close link between author and scribe, as can be
concluded from the remark about the corresponding signs in the
script of the master. What is peculiar, however, is the summing-up of
the number and size of the *pecie* at the end of each book. Descriptions
of this sort are usually to be found only in *exemplaria* at the stationer's,
since the wages of the copyist he hired depended on it.[13] The place of

---

[10] Mynors, *Catalogue*, p. 43. For this paragraph I am much indebted to the illumi-
nating remarks of Jeremy Catto.

[11] See below, p. 30.   [12] Pollard, '*Pecia* System', p. 151.

[13] Pelster, 'Ältester Sentenzenkommentar', p. 71; S. Patterson, 'Paris and Oxford
University Manuscripts in the Thirteenth Century' (B.Litt. thesis, Oxford, 1969), p. x.

the present manuscript in the book-making process, therefore, could have been somewhere between the stages of apograph and *exemplar*: a fair copy of the original text, though not kept in a stationer's shop and thus not an *exemplar* in the usual sense, but kept in the library of the Franciscans in Oxford for future copying and reference.[14]

This setting would also account for the curious use of another type of correction that appears frequently in the text: the *va—cat*. There seems to be no uniform use of *va—cat*s; it is different in every manuscript. Destrez mentions one use of the *va—cat* in *pecia* copies: to delete irrelevant passages that scribes put in to fill empty spaces in the text, so that the reader would not suppose that a section was missing.[15] There is no evidence of such a use in this manuscript. Most of the *va—cat*s occur in the answers of the author himself, more especially in those sections where he expresses a highly personal opinion. A good example is the question what the common property of the three persons of the Trinity is that is indicated by the word *persona*. The author mentions the two usual answers, that it is either the incommunicability (*privatio*) or the subsistence (*distinctio*), and then proceeds to give some personal reflections on the subject, which have been suppressed completely by a *va—cat* (f. 65A–B). Another interesting example is the question whether the angels were blessed before the fall:

Et si queris quantum et quid habuerunt de beatitudine VA respondeo secundum illud supra: nescio, sed in tantum beati, quantum acceperunt de cognitione et amore Dei CAT [In the margin:] Responsio huius habetur plane libro de correptione et gratia. (f. 113C)

It is also striking that the contents of many *va—cat*s are rather similar. Most of them occur in questions in which the concepts of *persona* or *hypostasis* are discussed (ff. 28B, 65A–B, 65B, 66A–B, 66D, 211C, 211D). They are not later corrections of the author's; from the colour of the ink it is clear that they were all written in at the same time as the manuscript was produced. Thus they must have appeared in the script of the master that the scribe was copying. If the assumption that the

---

[14] The terminology in the book-making process is apparently not as fixed as Pollard assumes. The scribe of Balliol MS 62 often refers to the *exemplar* when making corrections. Pollard thinks that the word *exemplar* is used either for the stationer's fair copy or for the collection of *pecie* ('*Pecia* System', p. 152). If he is right, the present MS is either a *pecia* copy or a collection of *pecie*, both of which possibilities are excluded. In this case it must be the author's text: 'scriptum magistri'.

[15] J. Destrez, *La Pecia dans les manuscrits universitaires du XIII*e *et du XIV*e *siècle* (Paris, 1935), pp. 38–9.

MS was kept in the library of the Franciscan convent at Oxford is right, then an explanation for these curious corrections suggests itself. The scribe could have copied the master's own text, not only the version the master wished to have published, but also first drafts, rejected answers, and other material he would want to keep on record but not divulge. If this is true, the manuscript has a double function: fair copy and filing-system. That would make sense in the setting of a theological library, less so in a stationer's shop.

Another question concerning the manuscript is whether it represents a work of the master himself or a *reportatio* of his lectures, made by a disciple. There is no doubt that it is the former, as a remark in the middle of f. 211D confirms: 'Et quedam que scripsi de hiis in primo libro distinctione 1a in fine, ad presens retracto.' This remark also reveals that, although the work must have been based on a course of lectures, in its present stage it was conceived as a written work. Nevertheless it does not have the smooth roundedness of commentaries like Aquinas's or Bonaventure's; many of the arguments are jotted down in a few words rather than worked out, the questions are not all treated in the same way, sometimes the objections are left out, sometimes the authorities or the arguments from reason, sometimes there is a double answer. It is a work in which the grinding of the thought processes behind it is still audible; it leads the reader straight into the heart of a theological workshop. The questions of placing it in time and finding its author become all the more pressing.

(ii) *The Origin of the Commentary*

The commentary must have been written in the years between 1245 and 1250. This precise dating can be deduced from the evidence in iii. 39, where the author discusses the possibilities of dispensation from an oath. As an example of such a dispensation he mentions the Papal dispensation from the oath of fidelity to the Emperor Frederick II, after the Emperor had been excommunicated at the Council of Lyons in 1245. In that sentence he implies that Frederick is still alive:

Potest enim in hiis papa absolvere, cum viderit universali ecclesie prodesse, sicut absolvit nunc a fidelitate Friderici. (f. 251D)[16]

---

[16] V. Doucet, 'Commentaires sur les Sentences. Supplément au répertoire de M. Frédéric Stegmüller', *AFH* xlvii (1954), 161.

Since Frederick II died on 13 December 1250, the important news of his death must have reached Oxford by February 1251 at the very latest. The author could have commented, of course, on the third book before starting on the first or the second. The requirement for young theologians, as it was laid down a few years later, was to lecture about a book of the Bible, or the *Sentences*, or the *Histories*; no order was indicated.[17] In this case, however, the author seems to have lectured on each book in the given order; there are several passages where he refers the reader to his remarks in previous books:

Et secundum hec omnia non videtur mihi quod virtus sit nunc ex nihilo creata, sed ex ipsa vi anime per operationem Spiritus Sancti ad actum educta. Hec tamen omnia sine preiudicio et assertione a me dicta sunt. Et habes de hiis libro 1 distinctione 14 G.   (ii. 26, f. 170D)

Queritur in principio de virtute in genere, quid ipse sit et de eius subdivisione. Et habes plures definitiones eius libro 2° distinctione 27ᵃ B. Habes etiam in eadem distinctione A secundum Augustinum quod virtus est bona qualitas mentis.   (iii. 23, f. 224A)

Et hec omnia sine assertione et absque preiudicio de contributione dicta sint. Et quedam que scripsi de hiis in primo libro distinctione 1a in fine ad presens retracto.   (iii. 12, f. 211D)

The quotations also show that the references to earlier remarks have not been introduced by the scribe, but are the work of the author. It may be safely assumed, therefore, that the author duly proceeded from book i to book ii to book iii. And since the remark on the oath of allegiance to the emperor Frederick is at the very end of the third book, the author must have finished the work by the end of 1250.[18] He also planned a fourth book, however, as is clear from a short reference in the question, whether Christ would have died, even if he had not been killed: 'Et de isto ad presens omitto, nam de hoc tractatur 4° libro distinctione 43' (f. 200D).

[17] 'Statuit vniversitas Oxonie, et, si statutum fuerit, iterato consensu corroborat, quod nullus in eadem vniversitate incipiat in theologia nisi prius rexerit in artibus in aliqua vniversitate, et nisi legerit aliquem librum de canone Biblie, uel librum sentenciarum uel historiarum, et predicauerit publice vniversitati'. This is one of the clauses of the statute, drawn up on 12 Mar. 1253, the day before and in connection with the inception of Thomas of York, *Statuta* (ed. Gibson, p. 49). Bonaventure, for example, did not lecture on the *Sentences* in the given order; see B. Distelbrink, *Bonaventurae Scripta . . . critice recensita* (Subsidia Scientifica Franciscalia, v, 1975), p. 5.

[18] This date effectively excludes the 15th-c. attribution of the commentary to James of Viterbo, OESA, born *c*.1255, who taught at Paris from 1293 onwards (f. 5b).

To determine the place where the commentary originated, we have to rely on internal evidence. The main manuscript was written in Oxford in the middle of the thirteenth century, and the relationship between the manuscript and the author was fairly close. It is more than likely, therefore, that the work's origin must be sought in Oxford as well.[19]

Another clear indication of Oxford provenance is that in many of the questions Robert Grosseteste and Richard Fishacre are the main opponents. In the treatment of the work of creation the author relies almost completely on Grosseteste's *Hexaemeron* and on Fishacre's use of the same work.[20] And the same is true for the question on the causes of the Incarnation; the first part exists of a summary of Grosseteste's argumentation in *De cessatione legalium*, and at the end Fishacre's point of view on the matter is also referred to.[21] Another example is the prologue, where the author discusses the nature of theology:

Oxford, Balliol College, MS 62	Robert Grosseteste, *Hexaemeron*
De subiecto ergo primo ait Hugo de Sancto Victore quod materia divinarum scripturarum omnium est opus restaurationis humane ... (f. 6D) Alii aliter, scilicet quod hoc subiectum sit Christus integer, Verbum scilicet incarnatum cum corpore suo quod est ecclesia. Et est Christus unus triplici unione, prima, qua ipse unus est in persona, Deus et homo; secunda qua ipse unus est in natura cum ecclesia per assumptam humanam naturam; tertia, qua ipsa Ecclesia unitur ei per condignam perceptionem in sacramento eucharistie illius carnis quam assumpsit de virgine.	Omnis scientia et sapientia materiam habet et subiectum aliquod, circa quod eiusdem versatur intentio ... Istud subiectum a quibusdam putatur Christus integer, Verbum videlicet incarnatum cum corpore suo quod est ecclesia.... In hoc namque uno ... videntur aggregari aliquo modo iste unitates ... videlicet qua Verbum incarnatum est unus Christus, unus videlicet in persona Deus et homo, et qua ipse est unus in natura cum ecclesia per assumptam humanam naturam, et insuper qua ecclesia reunitur ei per condignam assumpcionem, in sacramento eucaristie, illius carnis quam assumpsit de virgine ... Ex

[19] Pelster, 'Ältester Sentenzenkommentar', pp. 68, 72–3 comes to the same conclusion.

[20] See below, pp. 152–60; also R. C. Dales, 'The Influence of Grosseteste's Hexaëmeron on the Sentences Commentaries of Richard Fishacre O.P. and Richard Rufus of Cornwall O.F.M.', *Viator*, ii (1971), 271–300. J. Catto, 'Theology and Theologians 1220–1320', in id. (ed.), *The Early Oxford Schools* (The History of the University of Oxford, i, 1984), p. 489, describes Rufus's commentary as a revised and corrected version of Fishacre's, which gives Rufus less than his due. The structure of Rufus's commentary and the issues he tackles are often so different from Fishacre's that in my opinion this is an independent commentary, in which Fishacre is used as one of the adversaries.

[21] For an extensive comparison see below, pp. 234–9.

quibus tribus unionibus videtur aggregari unum quo dicitur Christus integer unus.

. . .

Aliter adhuc alii dicunt quod hoc subiectum est illud unum de quo in Evangelio Joh. 17: *sicut et tu Pater in me et ego in te, ut et ipsi in nobis unum sint* (John xvii. 21). Et dicunt quod istud unum super tres unitates predictas addit duas: unitatem scilicet in substantia Patris et Filii et Spiritus sancti quam notat et cum dicitur: *tu Pater in me et ego in te*. Et cum dicitur: *et ipsi in nobis unum sint*, secundam scilicet unitatem conformitatis, qua scilicet conformatur voluntas creature rationalis cum summa Trinitate.

Videtur quoque illud unum de quo dicit: *ut et ipsi in nobis unum sint*, adicere predictis, quod Filius Verbum sit unum in substancia cum Patre, et per consequens cum Spiritu Sancto. Quam unitatem substancialem expressit Filius cum dixit: *Sicut et tu Pater in me et ego in te*. Adicit quoque et unitatem conformitatis nostre in suprema facie racionis nostre cum summa Trinitate, ad quam conformitatem et deiformitatem inducimur per mediatorem Deum et hominem Christum, cum quo sumus unus Christus. Hoc igitur unum, quo sumus unum in Patre et Filio et Spiritu Sancto—ait enim: *ut et ipsi in nobis unum sint*—conglutinare videtur in se unum substancie Patris et Filii et Spiritus Sancti, unum unionis duarum naturarum in persona Christi, et unum quo sumus omnes unum vel unus in Christo, et unum renovacionis in spiritu mentis nostre cum summa Trinitate. Unde et ab hoc uno sic aggregato et unito, tamquam a subiecto, potest esse descensus ordinabilis in trinitatem, et trinitatis unitatem, et verbum incarnatum, et corpus eius quod est ecclesia, et in deiforme nostrum cum Trinitate.[22]

Dicunt ergo quod unum quod complectitur istas quinque unitates est subiectum huius scientie.

Richard Fishacre, *Commentary on the Sentences*, Prologue

De quo autem sit haec tamquam de subiecto vel materia divisione investigandum. Tria quidem sunt simplicia: scilicet natura suprema, quae est Deus; et natura infima, quae est corpus; et natura media, scilicet rationalis creatura. Tria sunt insuper ex his composita: scilicet compositum ex infima et media natura, homo scilicet; et compositum ex media et suprema, ex quibus fit illud unum de quo Apostolus

Alii dividunt ea que sunt universaliter in sex: summa natura et infima, scilicet corpus, et media, creatura scilicet rationalis. Tria simplicia et tria ex hiis composita: ex infima et media natura homo; ex suprema et media illud unum de quo apostolus 1 Cor. 6: *qui adheret Domino unus spiritus est* (1 Cor. vi. 17). Et hoc unum est ecclesia, caput et membra.

---

[22] Gross. *Hex.* I. i. 1–2, pp. 49–50.

Cor. 6: 'Qui adhaeret Deo, unus spiritus est'—et hoc est unum, quod est ecclesia, scilicet caput et membra; et tertium est quod ex omnibus his componitur naturis, scilicet Christus. . . .

Dicunt ergo quod cum de quolibet istorum sit hec scientia, tamen de uno eorum ut de subiecto, scilicet de illo uno quod est ex natura suprema et media.

Mihi autem videtur quod de quolibet horum trium potest dici hanc scientiam esse sed tamen de unico eorum ut de subiecto. In aliis quidem scientiis videmus quidem aliquid esse minimum et aliquid subiectum et tertium summe compositum in illo genere. Sic dicitur geometria esse de puncto ut de minimo suo; de magnitudine immobili ut de subiecto; de corpore ut de summe composito in illo genere. . . . Similiter

De Deo est ut de minimo in hac scientia, sicut geometria de puncto.

De Christo integro sicut geometria de corpore, maxime scilicet composito quod in se omnia alia complectitur. De predicto uno sicut geometria de magnitudine. (f. 6D)

aestimo hanc scientiam esse de Deo tamquam de minimo et indivisibili, a quo fluit quicquid est in subiecto huius scientiae. De Christo vero est ut de maxime composito habens in se quasi partes componentes quaecumque sunt in subiecto huius scientiae. Sed de illo uno, quod est ex natura media et suprema, est haec scientia tamquam de vero subiecto.[23]

In the discussion of a theological problem the custom in the thirteenth century was to introduce the argument by quoting from the recognized Fathers, the *auctoritates*; our author conforms to this tradition by starting off with a quotation from Hugh of Saint-Victor. Then the author would clarify his own position by conducting a running battle with his immediate predecessors, the *alii*.[24] It may be inferred that a commentary in which Grosseteste and Fishacre are the main adversaries must have originated in Oxford just after these two theologians had finished their teaching; in fact around 1250.

Commentaries on the *Sentences* were typical products of academic theology; they represented one-half of the course for the degree of doctor of divinity. Paris and Oxford were the only two places in Europe, where this highly formalized form of theological teaching flourished in the middle of the thirteenth century. Now it is clear from

---

[23] R. J. Long, 'The Science of Theology According to Richard Fishacre', *MS* xxxiv (1972), 91–2.

[24] O. Lottin, 'L'influence littéraire du chancelier Philippe sur les théologiens préthomistes', *RThAM* ii (1930), 325.

several small hints in the text that this commentary was not produced in Paris: although the author must have been familiar with what happened there, he refers to the city in such a way that it is obvious that he was somewhere else at the time of writing:

Firmiter igitur teneamus quod creatio passio non nihil est et creatura est et non Creator. Et est iste unus articulus qui de novo Parisius damnatus est. (f. 105B).[25]

The author was not only familiar with events in Paris, he had also studied there:

Et nescio si possint isti hanc opinionem firmare per Hugonem de Sancto Victore, in cuius scripto vidi Parisius ipsum de hac materia sic loqui. (f. 145C–D)

This reminiscing about studies in Paris implies that at the time of writing his commentary the author was not in Paris: Oxford is the only alternative.

(iii) *The Question of Its Author*

Having located the commentary in Oxford in the years between 1245 and 1250, we must next ask who the author can be. In the prologue he calls himself the least not only of the modern theologians but also of the Minors.[26] So the author must have been a Friar Minor, in other words a Franciscan.[27]

Now there were not so many Franciscans who taught theology at Oxford in the years around 1250. The only possible candidates are Adam Marsh, Ralph of Colebruge, Eustace of Normanville, or

---

[25] The author mentions this condemnation also on f. 112C. Another example on f. 113A: 'Hic dicunt magistri Parisius cum magistro quod habuerunt angeli unde possent stare, sed non unde proficere, et errorem reputant oppositum huius opinionis et sententialiter prohibent.'

[26] 'Liceat in primis, prout mee infirmitati est possibile, in famosorum predecessorum numerum et in me modernorum, immo minorum, minimum hanc historiam [sc. vidue pauperis] transfigurare' (f. 6A).

[27] Pelster comes to the same conclusion in 'Ältester Sentenzenkommentar', p. 71. Two further arguments to corroborate that conclusion must be rejected. The author's praise of poverty and humility in the prologue does not necessarily turn him into a Franciscan. Poverty was widely considered to be a necessary condition for the acquisition of true learning, so e.g. Bernard of Chartres, quoted by John of Salisbury in D. Knowles, *The Evolution of Medieval Thought* (London, 1962), p. 132. Pelster, op. cit., p. 75 also mentions that the author often quotes Alexander of Hales. This in itself tells us very little, since Alexander was one of the most celebrated theologians of his day. Anyone studying in Paris some time during that period must have been familiar with his work, not just Franciscans.

Richard Rufus of Cornwall.[28] Thomas of York is an unlikely candidate, since, as we have seen, he was hurried through his inception in 1253 without having fulfilled the necessary requirements.[29] Ralph of Colebruge and Eustace of Normanville are not known to tradition as authors of theological works; they are neither mentioned in Eccleston's chronicle as such nor in the works of later learned authors. Adam Marsh was lecturer to the Franciscan convent at Oxford from 1247 till 1250.[30] By that time, however, he must have been quite a mature scholar and it seems unlikely, therefore, that he would have embarked on a course of lectures more typical of a young theologian working for his doctorate.

The most likely candidate is Richard Rufus of Cornwall, who, as we saw, was well known as an author. Both Bacon and Eccleston mention that he lectured on theological topics, and his name continues to be linked with a commentary on the *Sentences*—or even two commentaries—in the later tradition.[31] Two problems seem to stand in the way of a quick identification. The first is that Roger Bacon seems to say that Richard lectured on the *Sentences* at Oxford from the year 1250 onwards: '. . . reprobatus Parisius propter errores quos invenerat, et promulgauerat quando solempniter legebat sentencias ibidem postquam legerat sententias Oxonie ab anno Domini 1250'.[32] At least that is how Little and Pelster interpret this passage.[33] But if Richard is the author of the commentary preserved in Balliol College, he must have finished his lectures by 1250. A closer look at Bacon, however, reveals that the date he mentions does not have to refer to the clause 'postquam . . . Oxonie'; it can just as well refer to Richard's lectures at Paris mentioned earlier in the same sentence. If that is the case, the chronological problem vanishes; he lectured at Oxford until 1250 and at Paris from 1250 onwards. The second problem does not have such an easy solution: no learned author mentions any work of Richard Rufus that has the incipits of Balliol MS 62. So even if all the other evidence proves positive, a small margin of doubt will always remain.

The best argument for identifying this commentary as a work of

---

[28] For biographical details of these friars see Little, 'Franciscan School', pp. 831–9.

[29] See above, p. 8.

[30] Little, 'Franciscan School', p. 835.

[31] See above, pp. 10–13.

[32] Bacon, *Compendium*, iv (ed. Rashdall, pp. 52–3). My translation of the passage on p. 1 tries to do justice to the interpretation defended here.

[33] Little, 'Franciscan School', p. 842; Pelster, 'Ältester Sentenzenkommentar', pp. 65, 79.

Richard Rufus lies, according to Pelster, in the severe denunciation of Rufus by Roger Bacon in the *Compendium studii theologie*.[34] The *Compendium* is a catalogue of logical fallacies that mar theological discourse. The original plan must have been to divide it in three, a first part on univocal, a second on equivocal, and a third on analogical terms. In fact, Bacon never got any further than the beginning of the second part; the rest of the work remained unfinished.[35]

Bacon accused Richard Rufus of two serious logical errors, the first being that Richard maintained that a term can refer to something univocally, no matter whether it is actually there or not; in other words that in using a term we refer to the thing, signified by that term, making abstraction from time. In the eyes of Bacon's adversaries the term *Caesar* refers to the same thing, quite apart from Caesar's actually being alive or not.[36] The second error he denounced was that a term can never lose its significance, even if there is nothing concrete to which it refers: 'Quod homo est animal nullo homine existente'.[37] This is the problem of empty classes. Bacon considered Richard Rufus to be the worst sinner in this respect.[38]

It is not so difficult to find the two logical propositions condemned by Bacon in the commentary, although he never once quotes the work. Discussing the question whether Christ can be called a man in the days between his death and Resurrection the author compares the words *vivere*, *vivens*, *vivus* with their counterparts *mori*, *moriens*, *mortuus*. He maintains that the word *vivus* is a substantive and that the passing of time makes no difference to its significance.[39] In the same connection he also maintains that the significance of the word 'man'

---

[34] F. Pelster, 'Roger Bacon's *Compendium studii theologiae* und der Sentenzenkommentar des Richardus Rufus', *Scholastik*, iv (1929), 410–16.

[35] J. Pinborg, 'Magister abstractionum', *Cahiers de l'Institut du Moyen Âge Grec et Latin*, xviii (1976), 4, identifies Oxford, Bodleian Library, MS Digby 55, ff. 228A–244A (P. says erroneously f. 229) as 'an earlier and more comprehensive draft of this polemical treatise'. In this draft all references to Richard Rufus are absent. The logical errors of which Richard Rufus is accused in the *Compendium* get a few lines only in this draft (f. 231C) under the heading of errors in the use of univocal terms. The draft also covers the equivocal and analogical terms whose treatment remained unfinished in the *Compendium*.

[36] Bacon, *Compendium*, iv (ed. Rashdall, pp. 53–4).

[37] Op. cit. v (ed. Rashdall, p. 63).

[38] Op. cit. iv (ed. Rashdall, p. 52), quoted above pp. 1–2.

[39] 'Ergo nomen est vivus et significat ut in habitu et simpliciter et abstracte ab omni differentia temporis et nullam differentiam temporis definit in eius significato nec aliquod nomen omnino' (f. 222C). For a transcription of the whole passage see Pelster, '*Compendium*', pp. 415–16. This quotation on p. 416.

does not depend on the actual existence of any man.[40] It would be too rash, however, to conclude that the commentary must therefore be the work of Richard Rufus of Cornwall. This would be true if, first, it could be established that Roger Bacon directs his attacks only against Richard Rufus and, secondly, that the author of the commentary invented these logical theories.

Pelster assumes that Richard Rufus was Bacon's only target, but Bacon's own words in the *Compendium* do not bear out that statement.[41] He does say that Richard was the worst, but also that he was one among many and that these errors had a long tradition and were held by most people.[42] This points to a widespread opinion and not to the eccentricities of one man. And furthermore, if the theories that annoyed Bacon so much were widely held, then the author of the commentary cannot have invented them. To take but one example: when the author searchingly explains why a noun refers univocally to being and non-being, one of the possibilities he explores is that a word probably refers to habitual being, not to actual being.[43] Pelster thought this a particularly original contribution to the debate, but William of Shyreswood uses the same distinction in his *Introductiones*, written probably somewhat before 1250.[44] Modern historians have pointed out that, generally, the logical opinions defended in this commentary represent the *communis opinio* and that it is Bacon who is the exception.[45] Bacon is not quite alone in his opinion that the

[40] 'Nequaquam ergo sequitur: non est anima coniuncta carni, ergo non est homo. Nam nomen "homo", ut dixi, non ponit significatum suum in esse actuali' (f. 223D). For a transcription of most of the question see F. Pelster, 'Der Oxforder Theologe Richardus Rufus O.F.M. über die Frage: "Utrum Christus in triduo mortis fuerit homo"', *RThAM* xvi (1949), 275–9. This quotation on p. 279.

[41] For the following I am indebted to S. Ebbesen, 'Roger Bacon and the Fools of His Times', *Cahiers de l'Institut du Moyen Âge Grec et Latin*, iii (1970), 40–4 (90–4).

[42] 'Nam in hiis erroribus maxime vigent autoritas fragilis et indigna et consuetudo longa et sensus dampnabilis multitudinis stulte', Bacon, *Compendium*, iv (ed. Rashdall, p. 52).

[43] 'Nonne sic est de nomine et de modo eius in significando, in habitu et non in tempore?' (f. 222D).

[44] William of Shyreswood, *Introductiones in logicam*, ed. M. Grabmann (*Sitzungsberichte der Bayerischen Akademie der Wissenschaften, philosophisch-historische Abteilung*, 1937), p. 83, where William tries to prove the invalidity of the syllogism 'omnis animal est, omnis homo est animal, ergo omnis homo est' by distinguishing between the *esse actuale* of the predicate of the first premiss and the *esse habituale* of the predicate of the second premiss. See also Ebbesen, 'Roger Bacon', p. 44.

[45] J. Pinborg, 'Bezeichnung in der Logik des XIII. Jahrhunderts', in A. Zimmermann (ed.), *Der Begriff der Repraesentatio im Mittelalter* (Miscellanea mediaevalia, viii, 1971), 247–9. See also Pinborg, *Logik und Semantik im Mittelalter* (Stuttgart, 1972), pp. 92–100.

meaning of a word changes with a change in its denotation. It is shared
by Siger of Brabant, Boethius of Dacia, and Radulphus Brito. But
Bacon is unique among his contemporaries in his views on the
problem of empty classes.[46] The conclusion must be that merely
because this commentary contains the logical propositions denounced
by Bacon, it cannot be inferred that Richard Rufus is the author of the
work. Such an inference would leave two problems unresolved: why
Bacon maintained that these errors began at Oxford and that others
took over what Rufus had taught first.[47] The facts, as Bacon states
them, are as we have seen untrue. The logical opinions Bacon attacks
were neither confined to Oxford scholars, nor invented by Richard
Rufus. The extreme viciousness of Bacon's attack on Rufus also
remains unexplained; he is the only one of Bacon's many adveraries to
be mentioned by name and Bacon does not mince his words:
pessimum, *stultissimum*, *insanus*, altogether too much for a mere
intellectual difference of opinion. It could be that a more personal
grievance lies behind it, but that hypothesis, although forwarded by
two eminent scholars, depends on Bacon's highly doubtful stay at
Oxford.[48]

Another slender indication of the work of Richard Rufus can be
found in Roger of Nottingham's *Introitus ad Sententias*, a public lecture
he gave on entering the course of Bachelor of the *Sentences* (Baccalaureus *Sententiarum*) in about 1350.[49] The subject he chose on that
occasion was the number of principles needed for the creation of the
universe. In the course of his exposition he notes that Rufus agrees with
an intermediate conclusion that given the present order of the world no
higher or better species of being can be created: 'Item, pro con-
clusione videtur esse Rufus, I *Sententiarum*, d. 44, q. 2'.[50] Unfortunately he does not quote Rufus, which makes it very difficult to draw
any conclusions, because i. 44 was the usual place to discuss the
problem of the possible worlds and of the possible perfections of this
world. Roger's reference only confirms that Richard Rufus did,
indeed, write a commentary on the *Sentences*.

[46] Ebbesen, 'Roger Bacon', pp. 42–4; Pinborg, 'Bezeichnung', pp. 247–9.

[47] '... remansit multitudo in huius magistri erroribus ... et maxime invalescit
Oxonie, sicut ibidem incepit hec demencia infinita' Bacon, *Compendium*, iv
(ed. Rashdall, p. 53).

[48] Easton, *Roger Bacon*, pp. 94–5; Little, 'Franciscan School', p. 842. See also above,
p. 5.

[49] Synan, '*Introitus*', pp. 259–60.

[50] Ibid., p. 274.

The only remaining possibility of determining the author is to try to make sense of a number of marginal notes in the prologue of the commentary which refer to a certain Brother Richard. The prologue contains in addition to the usual introductory questions on the nature of theology a quite extraordinary set of questions on topics of epistemological interest: on the nature of truth, the knowledge of truth, the relation of truth and being, and at the end a question on the relation between the object and the subject of knowledge: 'Numquid ergo restat de scientia et scito, de intellectu et intellecto, et de eorum convenientia et unitate aliqua disserere' (f. 11D). The problem is whether in the act of knowing the intellect becomes as it were the known thing. Aristotle took this for granted; he defended the pure potentiality of the mind. In his view the mind is moulded by any form by which it is actualized; it has no independent activity and life of its own; its knowing is its life; therefore, it does not deform our perception. In traditional epistemology there was no such strong link between the mind and outside reality, the mind was considered to have a life of its own which was only partially influenced by sense perception.

The question has also been transmitted in a slightly different version in As, f. 292A–D. Here in the Oxford commentary it has something very curious. More than half of the answer has been erased by a *va—cat* that stretches over two columns from f. 12A to 12C. The author sets out to test the statement that the knowing mind and the known object become one in the act of knowing; Anselm seems to oppose this point of view; Augustine, Aristotle, and Averroes seem to confirm it. The author is in doubt: 'Quo ibo, quid tenebo?' (f. 11D).

The next section is introduced with the words: 'Legi etiam in quibusdam litteris consimilem sententiam, ut videtur, sed satis obscuram: Intellectus in actu est ipsa forma abstracta . . .' (B, f. 11D). This section is marked by a note in the margin in the same script as the main text and with the same colour of ink: 'Dubitationes sunt ab hoc loco usque ad Le. vacat et nulla responsio sufficiens nec que mihi, Ricardo, videtur vera.' (B, f. 11D).[51] The author quotes two passages from Maimonides in support of the Aristotelian position and then

---

[51] Pelster, 'Ältester Sentenzenkommentar', p. 76 and Mynors, *Catalogue*, p. 43 read: 'Dubitationes que sunt . . .'. In the text 'que' has been deleted by a dot. I disagree with Pelster's interpretation that the note says that Richard here wants to delete part of the text; Richard only wants to emphasize that from here till the *va—cat* all is said in the form of doubts and questions.

points to some absurdities that position leads to. Nevertheless he seems to feel himself forced to the conclusion that Aristotle is right:

Quid ergo? Numquid dicemus quod res intellecta est res intelligens aut operatio rei intelligentis? Istud videtur inopinabile, cum tamen ex precedentibus, si concedantur, necessario videatur concedendum.   (B, f. 11D)

Reason seems to force him to accept Aristotle's view, but the author is not convinced, he thinks it is 'inopinabile'. He continues his argument, and once again he seems forced against his will to accept the view of Aristotle:

Opinio cui non consentio 2° de anima	... ergo res intellecta et res intelligens sunt idem. Num video quod actio et passio una res est secundum subiectum et substantiam, definitione tamen et preducatione formali differunt? Sicut ait philosophus: 'Sensibilis actus et sensus idem quidem est et unus, esse ipsorum non idem. Dico autem ut est sonus secundum actum et auditus secundum actum.'
3° Phisicorum	Et alibi: 'Quare similiter unus utrorumque actus, scilicet motivi et mobilis, sicut eadem distantia unius ad duo et duorum ad unum. Hec quidem enim una est, ratio tamen non una.'
Solutionem ratione confirmat sed nihil est hic assertum	Et nonne agens intendit assimilare sibi patiens, et ubi non est contrarietas, statim similia sunt? Et nihil dat quod non habet, nec aliud quam quod habet, igitur eadem res est actionis et passionis: amare enim et amari, quid est nisi amor in amante et amato.[52]
/. sc. cognitio actio .. / sc. cognitio passio	Hec responsio mihi non placet, nec puto verum esse quod cognitio actio et cognitio passio sint res una et vita una, sed illa /. vita est rei cognoscentis, ista .. / autem relatio quedam rei cognite ad rem cognoscentem. (B, f. 12A)

The last sentence of this quotation is crucial, it proves beyond doubt that the author rejects the Aristotelian solution and adheres to a more traditional view of the problem of the acquisition of knowledge. The last part of the question is a defence of the author's choice that the knowing mind has a life of its own.

The curious thing is that after this satisfactory conclusion, another long argument follows in favour of the solution of Aristotle, just

[52] Aristotle, *De anima*, 425ᵇ26–8; id., *Physica*, 202ª15–20.

rejected. This argument is erased by a *va—cat* stretching from beginning till end (B f. 12A–C). In the other redaction of this question in
Assisi MS 138, no trace of this second part can be discovered, only a
more extensive form of the first part. The relation between the two
redactions is probably that the Assisi redaction represents the first
effort of the author to solve the problem, The Oxford redaction is the
summary of that effort. Meanwhile it seems that the author has
become better acquainted with Aristotle's solution: there is a note of
doubt in the Oxford version which is almost absent in the first version.
We have seen how the author keeps asking himself desperate
questions in the second version, and furthermore the number of
quotations from Aristotle and his interpreter Averroes has grown
(B ff. 11D–12A).

If this is true then a possible explanation of the curious *va—cat*
presents itself. It could be that the author, having read Aristotle and
Averroes on the relation between object and subject of knowledge, was
so impressed that he started having doubts about his earlier solution
and tried to formulate in his own way an answer corresponding with
modern, Aristotelian thought. Then, after further thought and more
doubts he probably returned to his earlier answer, but wanted to keep
his new attempt on record. Thus both the doubts in the first part and
the curious fact that three columns are devoted to a rejected answer
would be explained. The second part starts off as follows:

VA	Igitur cognitio actio et cognitio passio eadem res est et vita est, ergo vita eadem est. Igitur sicut prius conclusum est: cognoscens et cognitum, quia utrumque cognitione tale est, utrumque in quantum huius eadem res et eadem vita vivens est ...
Summa solutionis. Nihil tamen est hic dictum per certitudinem nec aliquid cui consentit fr. Ricardus	In capitulo ergo forte dici potest ad dubitata quod species abstracta cognita unde talis et ipsa res cognoscens unde talis ex eadem re et natura sunt huius et ex eadem vita vivunt et sunt unum vivens. (B f. 12A)

The question now is what connection Brother Richard, mentioned
twice in the course of this argument, can possibly have with the author
of the text. The best point to start from seems to be the note: 'Opinio
cui non consentio' (B f. 12A). I agree with Pelster that this is a remark

by the author of the work.[53] The note refers to the sentence beginning
with: 'Num video . . .'. This is the Aristotelian position and although
the author is in doubt and has advanced many reasons to accept it and
will give even more in the *va—cat*, in the end he rejects it. This might
seem rather surprising to some readers; therefore, the author wishes to
stress his rejection by writing in the margin, 'This is not my opinion'.
It would make no sense to suppose that someone else had made a note
like that. Why should a reader voice his disagreement with an opinion
the author himself disagrees with?

The following marginal note has not been added by the author
(because of 'confirmat'), but probably by the scribe, who wished to
guide later readers through the complicated thought processes and
doubts of the master: although he does try to justify the Aristotelian
position here, he does not believe it to be the truth: '. . . ratione confirmat, sed nihil est hic assertum' (B f. 12A). We have seen before that
the scribe did some redactional work; he corrected obvious mistakes
and checked references.[54] The note in the *va—cat* has the same function. Once again the master apparently defends Aristotle, so the scribe
puts up another warning sign that this is not the master's final opinion.
So far the function of the notes is clear; they serve to keep the reader
on the track and to guide him through the doubts of the author.

But is it possible, too, to infer from the last note that the author and
'fr. Ricardus' are the same person? The last note could be seen as a
summary of the previous two, taking over 'consentit' from the first and
'assertum' from the second: 'Nothing of what is said here is certain,
and Brother Richard does not agree with any of it'. Then Richard
would be the author. On the other hand the disjunction between the
two parts of the sentence, stressed by the change of mode and subject,
could also point to a different translation as follows: 'Nothing has
been said here with certainty (by the author), nor anything with which
Brother Richard agrees'. In this case Richard would not be the author.
Against the second possibility, it could be asked why Brother Richard
wants it known that he disagrees with a solution the author does not
advocate anyway. The very first marginal note, where 'Ricardus' is
mentioned as well, merely tells us that a Richard has read the work. It
is quite possible to assume that Richard, being the author, wants to
stress that he has doubts and that the answer is somewhat shaky. On
the other hand Richard could also be a later theologian who, going

---

[53] Pelster, 'Ältester Sentenzenkommentar', p. 77.
[54] See above, p. 23.

through the work, wished to emphasize that the author was not too sure of himself.

To me, the first of these solutions, namely to make 'Brother Richard' the author, appears the more acceptable. A serious objection against the second is that it would make the history of the manuscript rather too complicated. All the marginal notes we have discussed are in the same script and in the same colour of ink as the main text; they must have been copied with the text. To make the second solution work we have to postulate an author who wrote in the margin: 'Opinio cui non consentio', a Brother Richard who went through the author's work, and a scribe who expanded the notes of both the author and Brother Richard. The relation between the author and the actual manuscript seems too close to postulate three stages. It is also incongruous that Brother Richard should wish to censure an opinion the author does not advocate; it is much simpler to assume that Richard himself was the author, anxious to stress that he did not support Aristotle's position. Other circumstantial evidence is also in support of the first solution. Richard Rufus is the only available candidate among the Franciscans, and the author must have been a Franciscan. The commentary was finished in the year 1250, and we have seen that Roger Bacon mentioned that Richard Rufus after having lectured at Oxford went to Paris, where he lectured 'ab anno Domini 1250'.[55] All the evidence, though it is not conclusive, converges on one point, that Richard Rufus is the author of this commentary on the *Sentences*. Corroborative proof, however, would be most welcome, and it exists in the form of an early summary of Bonaventure's commentary on the *Sentences*, the work to be considered next.

---

[55] Bacon, *Compendium*, iv (ed. Rashdall, p. 53); see also above, p. 31.

CHAPTER 3

The Abbreviation of Bonaventure's Commentary on the *Sentences*

ANOTHER work attributed to Richard Rufus is an early abbreviation of Bonaventure's commentary on the *Sentences*. The work is considerably more interesting than the title suggests, since the author does not confine himself to summarizing Bonaventure's questions, but adds his own comments and arguments in many places. The work is wholly or partly preserved in four manuscripts.

(i) *Manuscript tradition*

(*a*) Vatican City, Bibliotheca Apostolica Vaticana, MS lat. 12993 (=V) and Assisi, Biblioteca comunale, MS 176 (=A)

These two manuscripts are complementary. V contains the abbreviation of the commentary on the first and second books of the *Sentences*, A the commentary on the third and fourth books. One look at the two manuscripts is sufficient to see that they are two parts of the same work. The binding, the script, the indications of the contents are the same. The structure of the distinctions and the literary style are similar in both manuscripts. In both, a later hand has indicated several passages, which he marks as 'calumniosum', giving under that exclamation mark the reason why he thinks the particular paragraph a danger to Christian doctrine.[1] Both are ascribed to Richard Rufus of England in a sixteenth-century or probably even later hand. I shall, therefore, treat them as two parts of the same work.

V, i + 320 ff. + i, a single Italian hand of the thirteenth century.

Inc.:   Proemium: Altissimus creavit de terra medicinam. Verbum istud scribitur Ecclesiasticus xxxviii. Quod etsi contineat verborum paucitatem, habet tamen in se non modicam sententie profunditatem ... (f. 1A)

---

[1] G. Gal, 'Opiniones Richardi Rufi Cornubiensis a censore reprobatae', *FS*xxxv (1975), 136–93 has collected and printed all the censored passages.

Prologus: *Cupientes aliquid de penuria etc*. Totali libro premittit magister prologum in quo tangit causas suscepti operis ... (f. 3A)

i: *Veteris ac nove legis etc*. Hic incipit tractatus libri qui dividitur secundum magistrum in duas partes ... (f. 5B)

ii: *Creationem rerum etc*. In hoc secundo libro principaliter intendit de homine ... (f. 131A)

Exp.:   ... in malo obstinatus a quo sumpsit exordium omne malum. (f. 320B)

A, ii + 218 ff. + ii, several Italian hands of the thirteenth century.

Inc. iii: *Deus autem qui dives est in misericordia propter nimiam caritatem suam qua dilexit nos cum essemus mortui peccatis convivificavit nos Christo cuius gratia estis sanctificati*. Verbum istud scribitur ad Ephesios ... (f. 4A)

iv: Sacramenta sunt quedam medicamenta spiritualia et habet eorum medicina duplicem cause efficaciam ... (f. 51A)

Exp.:   ... quod potest per pecuniam, [catchword of the next *pecia*] dari ergo et illa (f. 222D)

V contains the abbreviated commentary on the entire first and second books of the *Sentences*. A contains the commentary on the first nineteen distinctions of book iii, finishing in the twentieth distinction on f. 50A. The next three columns are left blank, which suggests that the abbreviator never got round to the rest of book iii. The commentary on book iv breaks off in the middle of distinction 25 on f. 222D. Here it is obvious that, although the text of the commentary continues, the manuscript is incomplete, since the catchword for the next *pecia* is given at the bottom of the page. At the end of both manuscripts the number of *pecie* is mentioned:

Omnes isti quaterni sunt lxxxi et quatuor folia. (V f. 320b)

In isto libro omnes quaterni sunt lv et duo folia in principio et tria in fine libri. (A f. 222b)

Both manuscripts still retain their original binding, consisting of two wooden covers wrapped in red leather. On the back of the cover a small note is attached to the books giving the title:

Primus et secundus super Sententias magistri Bonaventure de Balneoregio ordinis minorum. Reponatur versus occidentem in solario ij°. (=V)

Tertius et iiij^{us} super Sententias magistri Bonaventure ordinis minorum. Reponatur versus occidentem in solario secundo.   (=A)

Further indications of the author on the inside of the manuscripts are few. In V there is a note on f. 1A: 'Primus Bonaventure', in A the same sort of note on f. 4A: 'iiius Bonaventure'. Both are written in the same hand that wrote the text. A much later hand has added: 'Compilatio Magistri Ricardi Rufi Angli' (V f. 1a), 'Compilatio quatuor librorum sententiarum S. Bonaventurae facta per magistrum Ricardum Rufum de Anglia' (V f. 3a), 'Compilatio Magistri Ricardi Rufi de Anglia' (A f. 4a). A very important contemporary ascription, but unfortunately erased, can be found at the end of the proem (V f. 2A). Koch tries to make sense of it in his edition of Eckhart's Latin works. He reads:

Explicit introitus (?) in libros sententiarum secundum ffra ... (?) R///rdum ///nubiensem.[2]

The two manuscripts must have been written somewhere in the second half of the thirteenth century; a further approximation is impossible. They were copied for and preserved in the Sacro Convento in Assisi. Numerous indications prove that beyond doubt.[3] The first is that Assisi manuscripts often have notes indicating their ownership, although quite often these notes have disappeared in the process of rebinding, or because the manuscripts changed hands. In both V and A such notes can be found:

Volumen istud super primum [et secundum Sen]tentiarum deputatum est ad usum fratris Gerardi Parmen... (?)   (V f. 1a)[4]

Typical of all Assisi manuscripts is the characteristic way of numbering the *pecie*, usually quaternions. They are numbered in roman characters, except for the first, which is marked in letters: 'primus quaternus' (V f. 1a, A f. 4a), at the beginning and at the end of the *pecia*. The number is written in black and is enclosed in four curved lines in the form of a cross. Between the pairs of curved lines there are

---

[2] Meister Eckhart, *Collatio in Libros Sententiarum*, ed. J. Koch (*Die lateinschen Werke*, v, 1936), p. 11. When I had an opportunity to study the MS myself in Rome and read the passage under an ultra-violet lamp, I could only identify the words 'sententiarum', 'R', and 'nubiensem'. The script may well have deteriorated over the last forty years.

[3] The following is drawn from G. Mercati, 'Codici del convento di S. Francesco in Assisi nella Biblioteca Vaticana', in *Miscellanea Ehrle*, v (Studi e testi, xli, 1924), pp. 83–8 and from E. Menestò, 'Codici del sacro convento di Assisi nella biblioteca comunale di Poppi', *Studi medievali*, 3rd ser. xx (1979), 358–61.

[4] Cenci, *Bibliotheca manuscripta*, i. 292, 298.

three points, twelve in total. The point in the middle is always in black ink, whereas the others are in red ink. Together they form a circle between the branches of the cross. This peculiar system of numbering the *pecie*, which we find in both manuscripts under consideration, is also described in the catalogue of 1381.[5] The number of *pecie* is usually mentioned at the end of the manuscript, as is indeed the case here.

Assisi manuscripts survive either in the original binding or in a new binding of 1836, the year that the whole library and its contents were subjected to a thorough overhaul. If they survive in the original binding, as V and A do, then a note is pasted on the back giving title and shelfmark ('versus occidentem in solario ij°'). All the manuscripts were marked again in the eighteenth century, this time by pasting small pieces of paper on one of the first folios, bearing the title: 'Ex libris Bibliothecae Sacri Conventus Assisien'. This new shelfmark is absent in V, but is to be found in A on f. 4a. This could mean that V had disappeared from the library by that time, although Sbaralea still reports it as present in the beginning of the nineteenth century.[6] The final check is whether a manuscript is mentioned in the catalogue of 1381. This, of course, does not prove that it originated in Assisi. It is merely a confirmation of the previous points. The two parts of the abbreviations are in the catalogue under two headings:

Primus. et secundus. super sententias. fratris magistri bonaventure. ordinis minorum. Cum postibus bullatis. Cuius principium est. Altissimus creavit de terra medicinam. Finis vero. A quo sunpsit exordium omne malum. In quo libro: omnes quaterni sunt. lxxxi. F.   (=V)

Tertius et iiij[us]. liber super sententias. fratris bonaventure. Cum postibus bullatis. Cuius principium est. Deus autem. qui dives est in misericordia. Finis vero. Et quod potest per pecuniam. In quo libro: omnes quaterni sunt. lv. K.   (=A)[7]

There can, therefore, be no doubt that the two manuscripts were copied for the library of the Sacro Convento in Assisi, and were preserved there for hundreds of years. V must have disappeared either at the end of the eighteenth century or, more likely perhaps, at the time of secularization in 1866–7. It went through the hands of various private owners, until it was donated to the Vatican Library in the early 1920s. The second manuscript remained in Assisi, and after the

[5] Op. cit. i. 77; see also the picture in Mercati, 'Codici', p. 86.

[6] Sbaralea, 'Supplementum', p. 635.

[7] Cenci, *Bibliotheca manuscripta*, i. 292, 298.

secularization was moved only from the Sacro Convento to a building in the town. Since 1981 it has been back where it belongs; in that year the manuscript collection of the communal library was moved back to the precincts of the Sacro Convento.[8]

(*b*) Vatican City, Bibliotheca Apostolica Vaticana, MS Borghese 362 (=Bo)

104 ff. written in a thirteenth- or fourteenth-century hand. Contains the commentary on the first book of the *Sentences* by Thomas Aquinas (ff. 1–2a, 4a–14a, 15a–95b), interspersed with a question by the same author: 'De potentia articuli varii' (ff. 2a–3b, 14a–b, 95b–96b, 97a, and 98a foot). On ff. 97a–104b a fragment of the abbreviation of Bonaventure's commentary on the *Sentences*, the proem, the prologue, i. 1–3, breaking off in i. 4.

Inc.	Proemium:	[A]ltissimus creavit medicinam. Verbum istud scribitur eccli. xxxviii. Quod etsi contineat verb[or]um paucitatem habet tamen . . . (f. 97a)
	Prologus:	[C]upientes aliquid de penuria. Totali libro premittit magister prologum . . . (f. 97b)
Exp.:		. . . alii dicunt quod proprie supponit (f. 104b= V f. 17A)[9]

The manuscript is in a very bad state indeed. Several pages are completely illegible, because of water damage or exposure to humidity. This is very much the case for ff. 96–104. There is no reference to the author of the fragment, nor is it possible to define the time or place of origin very precisely. The work must have been finished before 1314, as in that year the manuscript, according to a note on f. 104b, was bought by Pierre Roger, monk of the Benedictine abbey of La Chaise-Dieu, later Pope Clement VI (1342–52):

---

[8] When L. Bethmann visited Assisi in 1854 all the libraries were still housed in their original institutions, see 'Dr. Ludwig Bethmann's Nachrichten über die . . . Sammlungen von Handschriften und Urkunden Italiens, aus dem Jahre 1854', *Archiv der Gesellschaft für ältere deutsche Geschichtskunde*, xii (1874), 538–41. Ehrle reports the change that took place after secularization; the friars of the Sacro Convento were assigned a small wing of their former house, the rest was used to house a school, F. Ehrle, 'Zu Bethmanns Notizen über die Handschriften von St. Francesco in Assisi', *Archiv für Litteratur- und Kirchengeschichte des Mittelalters*, i (1885), 470–1. The recent changes were reported to me by the present keeper of the MSS, Father Gino Zanotti OFM Conv.

[9] For a full description of the MS see A. Maier, *Codices Burghesiani Bibliothecae Vaticanae* (Studi e testi, clxx, 1952), pp. 417–18.

Istud scriptum fratris Thome de Aquino super primum sententiarum completum et verax est P[etri] Rogerii de Malomonte, monachi case dei. Quod emit anno domini M°CCC°XIIII die dominica in octavis beate marie (18 August 1314?) precio lv (?) sol. turonensium a quodam fratre . . .

(c) Berlin (West), Staatsbibliothek Preussischer Kulturbesitz, MS Cod. theol. qu. 48 (=Be)

180 ff., written on paper in the early fifteenth century, probably in 1433, if a note on f. 180 is to be believed. 'Scriptum in Magd[eburg] Anno 1433'. Contains the commentary on the first book of the *Sentences* by Peter of Aquila (ff. 2–80b), and a register of this work (ff. 84a–86b), interspersed with random notes (ff. 81a–83a and 179a–180b). F. 83b is empty.

On ff. 87C–178D a part of what seems to be the abbreviation of Bonaventure's commentary on the *Sentences*:

Inc. Prologus: Altissimus creavit de terra medicinam. Ecl. 38. Quod etsi verbum istud contineat verborum paucitatem, tamen habet in se non modicam sententie profunditatem. . . (f. 87C)

[i:]   *Veteris ac nove legis continentiam. Distinctio prima in qua convenit.* Utrum uti sit actus voluntatis. (f. 89B–C)

[ii:]   Creationem rerum. Insinuans scriptura Deum esse Creatorem etc. In hac parte queritur primo an possit esse creatio et an possit scilicet aliquid de nihilo produci . . . (f. 157C)

The work breaks off in dist. 13 of the second book. The owner of the manuscript, who also compiled the register of Aquila's commentary, was the Franciscan Nicholas Lakmann, who was a theologian of some note in fifteenth-century Germany and later became provincial of his own province of Saxony from 1461 till his death in Breslau in 1479.[10] The manuscript probably comes from the Franciscan convent in Brandenburg. It bears no signs that might lead to an identification of the author of the work.[11]

The incipit of the second book does not quite correspond with the incipit of V. And in the incipit of the proem the words 'verbum istud

---

[10] L. Meier, 'De schola Franciscana Erfordiensi saeculi xv', *Antonianum*, v (1930), 157–160. See also id., *Die Barfüsserschule zu Erfurt* (BGPhThMA xxxviii/2, 1958), pp. 26–7, 73.

[11] Although I derive most information from the very full catalogue of V. Rose, *Die Handschriften-Verzeichnisse der königlichen Bibliothek zu Berlin*, XIII: *Verzeichnis der lateinischen Handschriften*, ii/1 (Berlin, 1901), 386–7, I have also used a microfilm of ff. 87C–97D, 157C–162D.

scribitur' have been cut out. Further checks on the manuscript prove
that this fragment is not a straightforward transcription of the text as
found in V and A. The commentary on the text of the *Sentences* has
been left out completely; only the questions are left. This accounts for
the different incipit of the second book. A substantial cut has also been
achieved by reducing the number of questions:

V(i. 1)

Primo queritur quid sit uti. Cum sc.
actus sit cuius potentie anime sit
actus . . . Queritur ergo an sit actus
voluntatis an rationis.   (f. 5B)

Postea queritur de ipso utili vel
utendo, et primo utrum omni creato
sit utendum.   (f. 5D)

Queritur ergo universaliter quo sit
utendum et quo non.   (f. 6A)

Item queritur utrum malum sit utendum.   (f. 6A)

Postea queritur de ipso frui cum sit
unus actus cuius potentie sit.   (f. 6C)

Postea queritur de fruibili, quo sc.
generaliter sit fruendum et quo
non.   (f. 6D)

Be (i. 1)

Utrum uti sit actus voluntatis.
(f. 89C)

Utrum frui sit actus voluntatis.
(f. 90A)

In i. 2 the proof of God's existence has disappeared. In ii. 1 the
number of questions has also been cut down, and within the questions
the number of arguments has been shortened considerably, e.g. the
second question, dealing with the problem of the eternity of the world,
takes up two columns in Be (ff. 157D–158B), whereas it takes up eight
columns of roughly equal length in V (ff. 131D–133D). The fifteenth-
century writer took over two short arguments from Augustine and
Basil and the short reply, cutting out a thoroughgoing discussion on
the nature of time and change in general, which the abbreviator had
taken over from the commentary found in B.

On other points additions have been made, e.g. in the questions on
the prologue. In the first question, whether theology can be called a
science, the first answer comes straight from Aquinas's *Summa*: '. . .
theologia est scientia. Procedit enim ex principiis notificatis in lumine
superioris   scientie   que   est   scientia   Dei   et   beatorum'
(Be f. 88C = *Summa theologiae*, I. 1. 2.). The second answer is supplied

by the abbreviator (Be ff. 88D–89A = V f. 4A–B). In the second question of the prologue, whether God is the formal object of theology, the compiler reverses the order. First he transcribes the answer of the abbreviator (Be f. 89A–B = V f. 4C), adding a few objections of his own, then he gives the answer of Aquinas:

Omnia autem colorantur in sacra doctrina sub ratione Dei, vel quia sunt ipse Deus, vel quia habent ordines [*sic*] ad Deum ut ad principium et finem. Unde sequitur quod Deus vere sit subiectum huius scientie. (Be f. 89B - *Summa theologiae*, I. 1. 7)

Thirdly he summarizes Bonaventure's view (Be f. 89B), left out by the abbreviator, who at this point preferred his own opinion to Bonaventure's.[12]

This manuscript is a summary of the abbreviation of Bonaventure's commentary on the *Sentences*, enriched with the opinions of other eminent theologians on a number of subjects. It is a convenient textbook-cum-anthology for a freshman theological student, eager to come to grips with the positions of his predecessors as quickly as possible. And as such it was used by the owner, Nicholas Lakmann. As a young Franciscan he was sent to Magdeburg, one of the *studia generalia* of the province of Saxony, to begin his studies, which would eventually lead him to a doctorate in theology at Erfurt in 1446. And it was there that he acquired the manuscript in 1433.[13]

(ii) *The Abbreviator and His Work*

The work itself is on the whole a faithful abbreviation of Bonaventure's commentary on the *Sentences*. It follows the divisions made by Bonaventure; the notes on the text of Peter Lombard are taken over without change, most of the *dubia ad litteram* are left out. In the questions proper the abbreviator takes his pick from the arguments *pro* and *contra*, arguments both from authority and from reason, summarizes the answers, and selects the *ad obiecta* corresponding to the arguments opposed to the solution.

The more interesting feature of this abbreviation is, however, that the author does not limit himself to making summaries, but also brings in his own opinions. Sometimes he does so in the form of an addition to the question of Bonaventure, proposing an alternative point of view

---

[12] Bonaventure, *Commentaria in quatuor libros Sententiarum*, proem, 1 (*Opera omnia*, i–iv, 1882–9), i. 7.

[13] Meier, 'Schola Franciscana', pp. 158–9, 165–6.

or expressing his personal dissatisfaction. For instance, in the question whether the Trinity is reflected in the soul of man through memory, intelligence, and will, he adds after summarizing Bonaventure's solution: 'Potest etiam hic responderi . . .' (V f. 13B), or in the question on the mode of procession of the Holy Ghost he says: 'Item iste modus communis est . . .' (V f. 32A); in the question whether love can dwindle: 'Ego in hiis questionibus non video sanctos expresse aliquid definire . . .' (V f. 50B).

Sometimes the abbreviator adds completely different questions. In i. 2 Bonaventure omits the question whether there is a God, starting off with the question whether there is only one God. Here the abbreviator refuses to do the same, he inserts a paragraph on the proof of God's existence (V ff. 7C–8B). In other distinctions he goes even further and substitutes his own questions for Bonaventure's, as e.g. in i. 8:

V	Bonaventure
Hic queritur in principio utrum hec verba: 'fuit, erit' vere dicantur de Deo. (f. 25B)	Utrum veritas sit proprietas divini esse.
De veritate queritur quid sit et an sit una sola veritas. (f. 25D)	Utrum divinum esse sit adeo verum quod non possit cogitari non esse.
Postea queritur an possit interire veritas, hec est non esse. (f. 26B)	
Postea queritur de falso quid sit. (f. 27A)	

Postea queritur de incommutabilitate Dei, utrum scilicet Deus sit omnino immutabilis.   (f. 27B)[14]

The abbreviation, although it is a very good and clever summary of Bonaventure's commentary, is very much the work of a man with a mind of his own, which he uses in a modest but firm manner, when he is convinced of the inadequacy of Bonaventure's solutions or when he misses an essential question. In this respect the work is unique among the many abbreviations of his commentary made throughout the Middle Ages.[15]

There is no immediate evidence to suggest when and where the

[14] Bonaventure, *Commentaria*, i. 8. I. i. 1–ii. 1 (*Opera omnia*, i. 150–8).
[15] Alszeghy, 'Abbreviationes', p. 502.

abbreviation was compiled. Bonaventure finished his lectures on the *Sentences* either in 1252 or in 1253 and, with certain exceptions, wrote them up soon afterwards.[16] Pelster suggests that it was composed almost at the same time, considering the theological opinions defended in it.[17] More light, however, can be shed on these two problems, once we have been able to settle the question of authorship.

There are two fixed points from which the quest for the author of the abbreviations can begin. First of all there is a striking similarity between the added or changed parts of the abbreviation and the Oxford commentary on the *Sentences*, as preserved in B and almost certainly the work of Richard Rufus. And, secondly, there is the ascription to Richard Rufus of England.

The similarity between the abbreviation and the Oxford commentary shows itself first of all in the literary style. In both works the authors intersperse their remarks with personal exclamations and observations, rare in a work of scholastic theology. There are also repeated expressions which show a certain diffidence on the part of the author: 'Nescio . . . In hiis non diffinio . . . De hiis non curo . . .', or other similar expressions. A few examples:

V/A	B
Quid ergo in hiis dicam nisi quod nondum inveni apud sanctos distinctionem ... Quod si invenero, gaudebo. (A f. 217B)	Sed hanc distinctionem non memini me legisse in hiis verbis [sc. Augustini]. (f. 10C)
Ego in hiis questionibus non video sanctos expresse aliquid definire. Puto autem sine preiudicio ... (V f. 50B)	De ipsa essentia non memini me legisse aliquem sanctum damnare seu negare ipsum generare. (f. 69A)
Ego hanc distinctionem apud aliquem sanctum non inveni. (V f. 101D)	Nec video sanctos istam negare, sed vel eam supponere, vel in ea vim non constituere. (f. 78B)
Ego in hiis non intelligo quid ipsa [sc. Virgo] fecit omnino in illa conceptione. (A f. 15D)	Nescio ergo quid intelligunt cum dicunt: una et eadem intellectione. (f. 78A)
Istam reductionem non satis intelligo. (V f. 234D)	Quod non satis intelligo. (f. 77D)

---

[16] Distelbrink, *Bonaventurae scripta*, p. 5.

[17] F. Pelster, 'Literargeschichtliche Probleme im Anschluss an die Bonaventuraausgabe von Quaracchi', *Zeitschrift für katholische Theologie*, xlviii (1924), 515.

Sed ego non definio que pars huius problematis sit ponenda.   (V f.89B)

Ecce quomodocumque sit de sub-iecto [sc. theologie] non curo, nec aliquid unum definio.   (f. 7A)

Nescio. Nihil assero in hiis. (V f. 135C)

Confiteor quod in hac materia sermo mihi deficit, nec scio loqui. (f. 29B–C)

Quo [?] istorum modorum istud pos-uerit Aristoteles ignoro. Magis tamen puto quod secundo. (V f. 131D)

Ego non sic puto, nec puto quod habeat enuntiabile propriam ideam in Deo. (f. 78D)

But apart from this striking similarity in style there is a far closer link between the Oxford commentary and the abbreviation. Many of the additions and alterations— though by no means all—in V and A can be traced back to B. Often they are practically the same, such as in the first question of i. 2, the proof of God's existence. The abbreviator takes from B the chief argument from human reason to prove that there is a God (V ff. 7C–8A) = B f. 20C–D). He omits all the discus-sions of previous theologians' views, which precede this argument in B, and also a discussion of the finitude of causality (B ff. 21B–22C) fol-lowing the main arguments. He picks B up, where he starts discussing 'sophismata ad oppositum' (B f. 22C), selecting one such *sophisma* for discussion (V f. 8A–B).[18]

In i. 28 we find the same procedure. The question is how many notions ('qua cognoscitur persona', B f. 6A) there are in the Trinity. Bonaventure defended the common position that there are five such notions: innascibility, paternity, filiation, active procession or spira-tion, and passive procession. The abbreviator transcribes Bonaven-ture's arguments *pro* and *contra*, but instead of giving the master's solution he finds in B (f. 68B) another possibility, that there is a sixth notion: 'Deus a quo non est Deus', which is characteristic of the person of the Holy Ghost (V f. 71D). This can also be found in Anselm's *De Processione Spiritus Sancti*, but the abbreviator and B add cautiously that Anselm does not employ the term *notio*.[19] The texts in B and V are exactly the same:

[18] G. Gal, 'Viae ad existentiam Dei probandam in doctrina Richardi Rufi OFM', *FnSn* xxxviii (1956), 187–202 has the full argument in its three successive redactions: As ff. 278B–279D, B ff. 19B–21B, V ff. 7C–8B. F. Pelster, 'Die älteste Abkürzung und Kritik vom Sentenzenkommentar des hl. Bonaventura', *Gregorianum*, xvii (1936), 204–5 notes the close parallels between V and B in i. 8 of V, corresponding to the prologue of B.

[19] Anselm, *De processione Spiritus Sancti*, xvi, ed. F. S. Schmitt (*Opera omnia*, ii, 1946), 216–17.

V

... ergo sunt quinque. Quod autem sint sex ostenditur sic: Persona est Deus, aut ergo Deus non de Deo, aut Deus de Deo. (V f. 71D)

Et est prima ypostasis distincta notione ad dignitatem pertinente. Anselmus tamen de Processione Spiritus Sancti in fine, sex ponit proprietates, sed non nominat eas notiones. (V f. 72A)

B

Dividam ergo sic: Persona est Deus, aut ergo Deus non de Deo, aut Deus de Deo. (B f. 68B)

Et est persona ypostasis distincta notione ad dignitatem pertinente ... Nam et sic nuncupat eas Anselmus De Processione Spiritus Sancti in fine, et sex ponit eas esse proprietates, sed notiones non nominat eas. (B f. 68B)

In i. 36 the abbreviator can be seen at work in a different way. He summarizes Bonaventure and uses B, but rearranges it substantially. The problem of the distinction is how all things can be said to be in God. In the first question, after giving Bonaventure's solution, he states his own point of view, by making a distinction between things as they are in God's essence and as they are in God's knowledge. Then he proceeds:

V

Sed hic bene queritur cum scientia Dei sit ipsa essentia Dei quare non sunt in eius essentia ex quo sunt in eius scientia. Et videtur quod sunt in eius essentia quia dicit Anselmus Monologion cap. xxxiv: 'Ista omnia que facta sunt semper in Deo sunt, non quod sunt in seipsis sed quod est idem ipse. In seipsis sunt essentia mutabilis, in ipso vero sunt ipsa prima essentia.' Ecce hic dicitur quod ista sunt non solum in essentia Dei, sed ibi sunt ipsa essentia. Quod videtur contra Augustinum et magistrum hic in littera, qui ait: 'quos habet apud ipsum non in natura sua, sed in presentia sua.' Responsio: scientia aliquomodo respective dicitur essentia vero non. Et casuale cui adiungitur hec propisitio: in, conti-

B

Forte quia scientia aliquo modo dici videtur ad aliquid et respective, essentia vero non et casuale cui adiungitur hec propositio: in, continentiam et rationem continentie denotare oportet, absolute autem intelligitur essentia. Et ideo falsum est dicere: ista sunt in essentia Dei, nam hic parit transitio. Unde et intransitive intelligitur et est ac si diceretur: sunt ipsa Dei essentia. Exemplum quale quale videtur si dicatur: aurum est in archa et archa est ferrea. Sit ita: ergo aurum est in ferro. Ita in proposito: ista sunt in scientia Dei. Hic notatur et transitio et ratio continentie. Nam hoc est dictum: ista subiecta sunt scientie Dei. Sed modo queritur, nam videtur quod sint in essentia Dei. Nam ait

nentiam et rationem continentie denotare oportet quod non facit nomen essentie. Et ideo falso dicitur: ista sunt in essentia Dei, nam hic parit transitio. Unde et intransitive intelligitur et est ac si diceretur: ista sunt Dei essentia. Et exemplum quale quale videtur si dicatur: aurum est in archa, et archa est ferrea. Sit ita: ergo aurum est in ferro. Ita in proposito: ista sunt in scientia Dei, hic notatur transitio et ratio continentie. Nam hoc est dictum: ista sunt subiecta scientie Dei. Ad illud Anselmi et consimilia dicendum: (f. 90C) quod intelligenda sunt et exponenda, sicut illud quod factum est in ipso vita erat et de hoc tangetur prima.   (V f. 90B–C)

Anselmus Monologion cap. 34: 'Ista omnia que facta sunt et antequam fierent et cum iam facta sunt et cum corrumpuntur seu aliquo modo variantur, semper in ipso sunt, non quod sunt in seipsis, sed quod est idem ipse; etenim in seipsis sunt essentia mutabilis. In ipso sunt ipsa prima essentia' et non aliud quam quod est ars ipsa. Et cap. 35: 'Quicquid factum est quocumque modo sit in se, in ipso ipsa est vita et veritas.' Dicam ergo quod quando ista in ipso sunt quod est idem ipse et ipsa essentia prima, necessario vel sunt in ipsa essentia, immo et ibi sunt et ibidem sunt ipsa essentia. Quod videtur contra Augustinum et magistrum hoc in littera qui ait: 'quos habet apud ipsum non in natura sua, sed in presentia sua.'   (B f. 79D)[20]

The next four questions are summaries of Bonaventure, but in the last five, which are his own, he once more takes much of the material from B, reorganizing and editing it substantially.

A perfect example of the way in which the abbreviator conflates Bonaventure with the material from the Oxford commentary can be found in ii. 1, the discussion of the creation of the world. Both he and Bonaventure ask the question whether the world existed from all eternity, or whether it came into being at a certain moment. The question proceeds along the lines of any scholastic argument: arguments for the eternity of the world, arguments against, solution, and refutation of the arguments brought forward to support the rejected position.

Arguments in favour:
from authority

    (i) Augustine, *De civitate Dei* (V f. 131D)
         = B f. 103C:
         'Primum modum recitat Augustinus . . .'.

   (ii) Basil, *Hexaemeron* (V f. 131D)
         = B f. 103C–D:
         'Alius modus recitat Basilius . . .'.

[20] Anselm, *Monologion*, xxxiv–xxxv, ed. F. S. Schmitt (*Opera omnia*, i, 1946), pp. 53–4.

from reason	(1)	Aristotle's argument from the nature of change as quoted by Bonaventure (V ff. 131D –132A)

from reason (1) Aristotle's argument from the nature of
change as quoted by Bonaventure (V ff. 131D
–132A)
= Bonaventure, *Commentaria*, ii. 1. I. i. 2
(Opera omnia, ii. 19)
'Rationes ergo Aristotelis ad hanc partem
quidam formant sic . . .'
+ refutation (V f. 132A):
'Sed iste modus non videtur difficilis ad
solvendum.'

(2) Aristotle's argument from the nature of time
as quoted by Bonaventure (V f. 132A)
= Bonaventure, *Commentaria*, ii. 1. I. i. 2
(Opera omnia, ii. 20):
'Aliam rationem dant ex parte temporis . . .'
+ refutation (V f. 132A):
'Hec enim ratio, sic intellecta, non cogit.'

(3) Reformulation of Aristotle's argument from
time (V f. 132A–B)
= B f. 140C (= Va f. 95A):
'Aliter ergo formemus rationes Aristotelis.'

(4) Reformulation of Aristotle's argument from
the principle of change in general (V f. 132B)
= B f. 104C (= Va ff. 94D–95A):
'Et universaliter sic moveatur dubitatio . . .'.

(5) Reformulation of Aristotle's argument from
motion (V f. 132B–C)
= B ff. 104D–105A:[21]
'Potest ad hoc et aliter formari ratio Aristotelis.'

(6) Another argument from the nature of time
(V f. 132C)
= B f. 104A rearranged:
'Item ad hanc partem obicitur sic.'

Arguments against: (*a*) Aristotle's argument from the finitude of
causality and Averroës' comment
(V f. 132C–D)
= B f. 21C–D (i. 2):
'Ad oppositum sic arguit Aristoteles . . . Et
Avicenna [sic] ibidem . . .'.

---

[21] This formulation comes from Robert Grosseteste, *De finitate motus et temporis*, ed. R. C. Dales, *Traditio*, xix (1963), 257–8.

(b) An argument from the nature of time
(V f. 132D)
=B f. 105B:
'Item totum tempus usque nunc preteritum est.'

(c)–(g) Arguments quoted from Bonaventure
(V ff. 132D–133A)
=Bonaventure, *Commentaria*, ii. 1. I. i. 2
(Opera omnia, ii. 20–2).

Solution:

'Mundus eternus non est, nec motus vel tempus, nec aliqua creatura. Et causa erroris multorum circa hoc fuit quod non poterant intelligere eternitatem sine extensione. Hoc autem non est intelligere eternitatem sed falso imaginari.'
(V f. 133A)

Refutations:
ad 3 and 4

V f. 133A
=B f. 104C (following immediately upon the arguments):
'Ad primum ergo et secundum quia idem sunt dicendum.'

ad 5

V f. 133A–B
=B f. 105A (following immediately upon the argument):
'Ad tertium dicendum quod illa propositio est falsa.'[22]

ad 6

V f. 133B–C
=B f. 104A (paragraph in the middle of the argument)
+f. 105A + f. 105D + addition:
'Ad quartum dicendum quod cum dicitur . . .'.

Refutation of the
first reason against:
ad *a*

Solution of the apparent contradiction in Aristotle's position   (V f. 133C–D)
=B f. 21D:
'Sed ad primum contra etiam responderi oportet quia numquam sibi contrarius fuit Aristoteles.'   (V f. 133C)

---

[22] Op. cit., pp. 259–61.

'Quid igitur sibi vult ille philosophus?
Numquid sibi contrarius est in diversis locis
sue scripture?' (B f. 21D)

The analysis of the sources of the question shows that the abbreviator
had a thorough knowledge both of Bonaventure's commentary and of
the Oxford commentary. The first needs no further explanation; after
all, it was the task he had set himself, to make Bonaventure more easily
accessible to a wider public. The only thing that deserves to be high-
lighted in this connection is that he had certainly digested what he had
read and that he felt free to correct Bonaventure, where he felt that his
arguments had not been formulated rigorously enough, as we saw in
arguments (1) and (2).

On the other hand his knowledge of the Oxford commentary is
stunning. He has completely rearranged and straightened out the
confusing wealth of arguments he found in the treatise on creation
in B. For instance, in the Oxford commentary we find on f. 104C first
the argument for the eternity of the world from the principle of
change, then that from the principle of motion—including time—and
then the refutation of both. Both arguments are borrowed from an
English commentary on Aristotle's *Metaphysics* to be discussed in
Ch. 5. In the abbreviation the two arguments are rearranged in such a
way that there is a descent from the more specific (motion and time) to
the more general (change). The refutation is relegated to its proper
place after the solution. The Oxford commentary then continues with
a rather pointless diatribe against the defenders of Aristotle
(B f. 104C–D), and a short excursion into the creation theories of
Maimonides, who is denounced as 'Quidam multa verba faciens et de
seipso et de aliorum opinionibus' (B f. 104D) and later as 'miser'
(ibid.). And only then follows, completely unconnected, the second
argument for the eternity of the world from the principle of motion
(B ff. 104D–105A), which became argument 5 in V. Another example
of the abbreviator's intimate acquaintance with the Oxford commentary is the refutation of the sixth argument in favour of eternity, where
he strings together his answer with the words from three quite
different and apparently unconnected parts of the commentary (V
f. 133B–c = B ff. 104A + 105A + 105D). Even more surprising is that
he knew where to find useful points in unlikely places, like the argument against the eternity of the world based on the finitude of
causality, which in the Oxford work is more or less an appendix of the
question on God's existence.

So far we have found that in those passages where the abbreviator is clearly at work himself, there is a remarkable similarity of style between his utterances and the Oxford commentary. Both use a rather personal approach, often resorting to the first person singular, or confessing their ignorance or unwillingness to define a certain point. This modesty is quite unusual in scholastic discourse. Typical also is the frequent reference to the *Sancti* as the ultimate authority. Furthermore, it is clear that in many additions and changes the abbreviator either copies or relies heavily on the said commentary, and he shows himself completely at home in this often rather confusing and unsystematic work. Therefore, given the fact that the Oxford commentary was not one of the standard sources everyone used, and also that the abbreviator does not use this work as a convenient source for opposing opinions to outline his own position more clearly, but makes its solutions his own, the conclusion that both works were compiled by the same man now lies within reach. But there is more.

In the question on the eternity of the world the abbreviator introduces his reformulation of Aristotle's arguments in the following way:

V	B
Aliter ergo formemus rationes Aristotelis: detur primus motus et dicatur b. Mobile primum quod movetur illo motu dicatur a. Dico sic: mobile est prius eo quo movetur, combustibile prius eo quo comburitur. Est ergo a. prius mobile quam moveatur a. (V f. 132A)	Hec videtur esse vis propositionis ipsius Aristotelis qua nititur ad eternitatem motus: detur enim motus primus et dicatur b. Mobile primum quod movetur illo motu dicatur a. Mobile est prius eo quod movetur, combustibile enim prius est eo quod comburitur, Est igitur a. prius mobile quam moveatur a. (B f. 104C)

The abbreviator speaks in the first person, involving himself by saying 'Aliter formemus' and 'Dico sic', and then proceeds to copy an argument from another source. The same occurs a little later on when he is discussing Aristotle and Averroes on the finitude of causality:

V	B
	Simili modo quo et ipse [sc. Aristoteles] removet infinitatem secundum rectum in transmutationibus, videtur quod et nos contra ipsum possimus ratiocinari ad destruendum

Sic arguunt sic dicunt isti philosophi. Sic et nos contra eos arguamus:
si infinite revolutiones precessissent
istam revolutionem hodiernam numquam fieret ista revolutio presens, et
ita numquam esset iste dies hodiernus.   (V f. 132D)

infinitatem in transmutationibus
secundum circulum . . . per consimilem rationem cuidam supernis posite:
si infinite revolutiones precessissent
istam revolutionem circularem pre-
sentem numquam fieret ista revolutio
presens, et ita numquam esset iste
dies hodiernus.   (B f. 21D)

Here again the abbreviator appropriates as his own an argument
which was also given as a refutation of the same objection in B. This is
all the more significant, since the abbreviator never prefaces his
summaries of Bonaventure with a first person singular, but always says
something like 'Hic respondetur', or 'Responsio', or 'alii obiciunt'.
The way in which he introduces Bonaventure's summaries of Aristotle's arguments in favour of the eternity of the world illustrates the
point: 'Rationes ergo Aristotelis ad hanc partem quidam formant sic'
(V f. 131D), and 'Aliam rationem dant ex parte temporis' (V f. 132A).

In the third example the arrangement of the argument is different in
A and B, but the solution is the same, although not in exact words: the
question is in what way Mary co-operated in the conception of Christ:

A

Deinde queritur utrum sancta virgo
fuerit in aliquo cooperata Spiritu
Sancto mediante aliqua potentia in
conceptione Filii Dei. Et videtur
quod sic.   (f. 15C)

. . .

Responsio: secundum aliquos credidit Maria angelo promittenti et consensit. Hoc autem non nihil est
agere. Unde cum Christus mulierem
credentem sanasset Mattheus ix
dixit: 'Fides tua te salvam fecit'
(Matt. ix. 22). Et Lucas i: 'Beata que
credidisti (f. 15D) quoniam perfici-
entur in te que dicta sunt tibi a

B

Sed modo restat ulterior questio. An
ipsa generavit omnino Christum
hominem. Et hec questio potuit melius queri in precedenti distinctione.
Et videtur quod sic per predictas
auctoritates; illam scilicet Damas-
ceni ca. 46 simul autem generativam
potentiam tribuens.

. . .

Respondetur quod credidit Maria
angelo promittenti et consensit. Hoc
autem non nihil est agere. Unde cum
Christus mulierem credentem sanasset dixit Matteus 9: 'Fides tua te
salvam fecit' (Matt. ix. 22). Et Lucas
1°: 'Beata que credidisti quoniam
perficiuntur in te ea que dicta sunt
tibi a Domino' (Luke i. 45). Hec

Domino' (Luke i. 45). Sed istud parum videtur ad hoc quod ipsa sit vera mater. Et ideo dicunt alii . . . [follows summary of Bonaventure's solution]. (f. 15C–D)

. . .

Ego in hiis non intelligo quid ipsa fecit omnino in illa conceptione, opere corporali dico, nec etiam quomodo ipsa ministravit dictam materiam. Absit enim quod cogitetur quod ipsa umquam seminaverit. Unde Damascenus 46: 'Non spermaticos, id est non seminaliter, sed conditive per Spiritum Sanctum'.[23] Nec video etiam quod ipsa separavit illam guttam a corpore suo nisi voluntate consentiente, sed Spiritus Sanctus conditive, ut dicit Damascenus. Et aperte dicitur in III distinctione quod opere Spiritus Sancti fuit illa portio a reliqua carne separata, et ita parva erat ut humano visui vix posset subici. Nec video et de aliis membris quid faciant in generatione prolis et quam potentiam activam teneant. Deus enim format in ventre. Jer. i: 'Priusquam te formarer in utero etc' (Jer. i. 5). Et Macc. ii. 'Singulorum membra non ego ipse compegi sed creator qui formavit etc.' (2 Macc. vii. 22).

. . .

Ita hic dici potest: nec qui concubuit nec qui seminavit est aliquid, sed qui format Deus. Nec mater que conceptum portat et partum nutrit est aliquid, sed qui incrementum dat Deus. Ipse enim operatione qua usque nunc operatur facit ut numeros suos explicent semina, et a quibus-

fides Marie secundum Bernardum fuit fermentum quod abscondit mulier in tribus satis farine, id est: in triplici natura in Christo, donec fermentaretur totum.

Aut forte ipsa virgo voluntarie ministravit de suo corpore dictas guttas sanguinis ad constructionem corporis Christi. Et hoc fuit ei forte in principio generare. Demum vero usque ad terminum partus nutrimentum et materiam augmenti de corpore suo prestitit illi homini. Et hoc etiam potest dici generare in Maria. Aut aliquo alio modo mihi ignoto.

Vere tamen et simpliciter mater et genitrix illius hominis fuit et etiam Dei. Semen autem, hoc est sperma, numquam de corpore suo decisum est. Nec tamen propter hoc non est ipsa univoce mater aliis matribus, quia vere de natura et substantia sui corporis constructum est corpus illius hominis et hoc in utero et ibi nutritum et augmentatum.

Nec hoc facit equivocationem quod corpus istius de sanguine, aliorum vero corpora de spermate. Sed unum requirit patrem et matrem, alterum matrem tantum et divinam operationem. Nam et ipse Deus utrobique principalis agens et auctor est. Quippe Deus format in ventre. Jer. 1: 'Priusquam te formavi in utero etc.' (Jer. i. 5). Et 2 Macchab. 7: 'Singulorum membra non ego ipse compegi sed mundi creator qui formavit etc.' (2 Macc. vii. 22). Pater carnalis seminat tantum, sed Deus

---

[23] John Damascene, *De fide orthodoxa. Versions of Burgundio and Cerbanus*, xlvi/2, ed. E. Buytaert (Franciscan Institute Publications, Text Series, viii, 1955), p. 171.

dam latentibus et invisibilibus in formas visibiles huius quod aspicimus decoris evolvant. Et contra iii li. v dist.: seminare ad virum pertinet accipere ad feminam. Hucusque coniuges opere suo possunt. Ut autem concipiatur fetus atque nascatur divini est operis non humani. (A f. 16A)

qui est principalis auctor et artifex, et cum illo semine et sine, potest corpus prolis edificare et indifferenter de spermate mulieris, aut de alia parte sui corporis.

Idem ergo est artifex, ut dixi, et principalis auctor et idem modus operandi. Nam uno et eodem modo format Deus corpus prolis et edificat sive de hac materia sive de illa. Ergo materia alia et alia est, sed auctor principalis idem, et modus operandi idem, quare non equivocum. (B f. 202D)

The last example is interesting, first because of the rather piqued tone in which the abbreviator ventilates his disagreement with Bonaventure, and secondly because it is not a simple transcription from the Oxford commentary, but rather an elaboration, although the basic ideas are the same in both: the conception of any human being is to all intents and purposes a work of God, in particular the woman is always the receptacle, with no active part to play. Seen from that point of view the conception of Christ is not different from any other human conception. Mary remained passive like all other women. What she did contribute, however, was willing acceptance, and therefore she is truly the mother of Jesus Christ.[24]

[24] A. Emmen, 'Einführung in die Mariologie der Oxforder Franziskanerschule', *FnSn* xxxix (1957), 131. Other examples of V's appropriation of arguments of B are to be found, e.g. in the question on God's existence (parallels in B in italics):'Hanc questionem: an sit Deus, omittit hic magister, hanc ergo nos in principio disputemus. Dico ergo: *si est aliquod ens seu verum simpliciter* . . . *Unde verbum primo propositum demonstrat Deum esse, demonstrat enim modos oppositos habendi esse. Et hoc est quod a principio hucusque intendo*' (V f. 7C–8A = B f. 20C–D). In the treatise on the notions in the Trinity, where V transcribes B completely, he does not alter the first persons singular, whereas in other portions of the text he often makes changes, even quite small ones, if that seems better: 'Dico et hoc quia non est idem modus quo Filius est Deus de Deo et quo Spiritus Sanctus est Deus de Deo . . . Sumam et aliam divisionem et dicam: si est Deus, aut est Deus a quo Deus, aut est Deus a quo non est Deus' (V f. 71D = B f. 68B). Compare also the beginning of the solution in the question whether the 'creatio passio' is an intermediate between Creator and creature:

V

Responsio: hic multa dicuntur. Sed mihi videtur quod omnino idem est secundum rem, sed differt solum in modo intelligendi (V f. 134D).

B

Hic puto quod creatio passio creata sit Patre et quod non aliud est creatio passio quam ipsum creatum, sed differens in modo intelligendi (B f. 105B).

Thus, given the fact that the abbreviator always introduces his summaries of Bonaventure in a neutral way and only makes arguments his own when they are borrowed from the Oxford commentary, and also given the fact that many additions in the abbreviation can be traced back to this work and that there is a remarkable similarity in style, the conclusion must be that the author of the abbreviation and the author of the commentary on the *Sentences* written in Oxford about 1250 are one and the same man.

A further step has to be taken. As seen before, the abbreviation has been ascribed to Richard Rufus of England in a much later hand.[25] This ascription is not as weak as it seems at first sight. For one thing it is remarkably specific: Christian name, surname, and country of origin. Moreover, on the cover of both manuscripts is written in large letters that it is a work of 'magister Bonaventura', and it is as such that they are mentioned in the catalogue of 1381. The works in that catalogue that were attributed to Richard Rufus had completely different incipits: 'Cupientes. Totali libro premictit magister prologum', and 'Secundum Hugonem de Sancto Victore in libro de sacramentis'.[26] Thus the later librarian could not have had the idea by looking it up in the catalogue. Koch's conjecture is that he found his clue in the contemporary rubricated ascription at the end of the proem (V f. 2A).[27] The only letters of the name still more or less visible in this ascription are the 'R' at the beginning and '... nubiensem' at the end. The later hand, however, speaks of 'Ricardus Rufus de Anglia' or 'Anglus' and never uses a name in which the fragment 'nubiensem' appears. Assuming for a moment that 'nubiensem' stood for 'Cornubiensem' the later librarian could, of course, have decided to substitute the well-known England for the—to him—unknown Cornwall. Yet the fact that a librarian hundreds of years later, when Richard Rufus's name was completely forgotten, ascribes a major work in two volumes with the name of Bonaventure written all over it to Richard Rufus is remarkable. And whether the erased ascription gave him a clue or not, the beginning 'R' and the

---

[25] Pelster, 'Älteste Abkürzung', p. 197 and Koch in Eckhart, *Collatio*, p. 11 think it is a 16th- or 17th-c. hand. As far as I can see it could well be as late as the 18th c. It could not however, be Sbaralea's; he made some corrections when he visited the library (*Inventario*, p. 103), but he thought the ascription to Richard Rufus mistaken. His idea was that Richard Ruis was the author of the abbreviation. See Sbaralea, 'Supplementum', p. 635 and also above p. 12.

[26] Cenci, *Bibliotheca manuscripta*, i. 292, 303 and also above p. 10.

[27] Eckhart, Collatio, p. 11.

end 'nubiensem' are still two strong indications that the work was written by Richard Rufus of Cornwall. There is one other source, a library catalogue of the Franciscan convent at Siena of 1481, which has an entry that might refer to an abbreviation of Bonaventure made by Richard Rufus.[28]

Quartus Riccardi abreviatus et Doctori Bonaventurae in pergameno bona littera cursiva copertis de corio per totum. Literis BD.

On the other hand, it is a difficulty that the shelfmark of the Sacro Convento only mentions Bonaventure and does not refer to Richard Rufus at all. The testimony of the Assisi catalogue of 1381 has no independent value. Mercati has pointed out that the compiler of that document went about his work in a rather superficial way; for example, when the number of *pecie* was mentioned at the end of the manuscript, he mentioned it in the catalogue entry; if not, then he did not bother to count for himself but simply wrote down: 'In quo libro omnes quaterni sunt'.[29] In the same way he must have taken down the titles he found on the cover of the books without making any attempt at independent research.

Thus we can say that there is a strong tradition that attributes the abbreviation to Richard Rufus of Cornwall, and it is also very likely that it is this name which appears in the erased contemporary ascription. It has also been established beyond doubt that the author of the abbreviation and the author of the Oxford commentary on the *Sentences* are one and the same man. In the previous chapter it has been shown that there are strong reasons to assume that the latter was written by Richard Rufus of Cornwall as well. Thus we have two works, written by the same author, for each of which there is an independent tradition that the author was Richard Rufus. That points in one direction only, that the Franciscan Richard Rufus of Cornwall was the author of both, that he commented on the *Sentences* first on his own account at Oxford about 1250, and a few years later in the form of a summary of Bonaventure's commentary.

The Oxford commentary must have been Richard's first work, since it had been finished by 1250, the abbreviation his second, since he cannot have started on the latter before 1252/3. From a first comparison between the two works, in particular from the detailed

[28] K. W. Humphreys, *The Library of the Franciscans of Siena in the Late 15th Century* (Studies in the History of Libraries and Librarianship, iv, 1978), p. 101, on the date of the catalogue, ibid., p. 11.
[29] Mercati, 'Codici', pp. 86–7.

analysis of the question on the eternity of the world in both works, it
is clear that the Oxford work is a first design; it is somewhat dis-
organized, arguments being strewn around without any clear connection or framework to hold them together. The abbreviation is
much tidier. Richard has clearly profited from his acquaintance with
Bonaventure's rigorous procedures in questioning the truths of the
faith, although the characteristic outbursts are still there, as can be
seen in the question on Mary's co-operation in the conception of
Christ. Despite this more subdued tone the abbreviation is quite
important for obtaining an insight into the workings of Richard
Rufus's mind, because he had to wrestle with one of the most acute
minds of the thirteenth century in this work. It may be assumed that,
where he nevertheless deviates from or adds to Bonaventure, we
shall find his strongest personal opinions and commitments.

Two questions remain to be considered: the time and the place of
origin of the abbreviation. According to Eccleston Richard lectured
on the *Sentences* only once, at Paris *cursorie*. Bacon reports that he
gave two courses of lectures on the *Sentences*, first at Oxford and
from 1250 *solemniter* at Paris. This suits more or less with the information we can glean from Adam Marsh's letters that Richard left
Oxford in 1253. By 1256 he was back to become lector to his Oxford
brethren.[30] Since B is obviously the reflection of Richard's lectures
at Oxford, it is very tempting to assume that the abbreviation is the
fruit of his years at Paris.[31]

There is nothing really against that solution except that Richard
made a few significant changes in Bonaventure's words. In ii. 8
Richard summarizes a question about the bodily functions of angels
appearing as men (V ff. 167C–168A).[32] The last remark is that even if
angels, taking a human form, can sleep with women, it does not
necessarily follow that they can make them pregnant. Bonaventure
leaves it at that, but Richard continues: 'Et sic legitur de generatione
Merlini, scilicet quod generatus fuit a demone incubo' (V f. 168A) and
he reflects for a moment on the curious birth of Merlin, a figure who
played a part in Celtic folklore although also well-known on the Con-
tinent. Yet it may be inferred that Richard added his note because he
wrote for a public familiar with Celtic lore rather than for French

[30] Eccleston, *De adventu*, xi (ed. Little, p. 51); Bacon, *Compendium*, iv (ed. Rashdall,
pp. 52–3); Little, 'Franciscan School', pp. 842, 845; see also above pp. 5–9.
[31] Pelster, 'Älteste Abkürzung', pp. 212–15, taken over by all subsequent writers on
the subject.
[32] Bonaventure, *Commentaria*, ii. 8. I. iii. 1 (*Opera omnia*, ii. 220).

students. Far more indicative is an omission to be found in the question how baptism should be administered, by aspersion or immersion. Richard copies Bonaventure in the first part of the answer; both say that the practice of the apostles was to sprinkle water over the person to be baptized, then they continue:

A	Bonaventure
... et mos ille adhuc servatur in pluribus ecclesiis. Et potest servari eo quod ibi est integra ratio sacramenti. (A f. 67D)	... et mos ille servatur adhuc in pluribus Ecclesiis et maxime in Ecclesia Gallicana. Servari autem potest propter hoc quod est ibi integra ratio Sacramenti.[33]

These slight changes seem to me to be clear signs that the abbreviation is not a work of Richard's period of study in Paris, but a result of his second period at Oxford. My reconstruction is that he spent his years in exile getting acquainted with Bonaventure and with his work. When he returned to Oxford triumphantly to take the place vacated by Thomas of York in 1256, he brought back with him the master's commentary on the *Sentences* and tried to adapt it to an English audience. The adaptation took the form of an abbreviation, because as such it would be more digestible for a less sophisticated public and more suited to the still rather primitive academic circumstances at Oxford in the 1250s.[34]

If this reconstruction is right, then Richard was the first to introduce Bonaventure's thought to Oxford only a few years after the master himself had finished the first survey of his theology. It shows how careful we must be when speaking of an Oxford tradition of theology; the exchange between the two academic centres must have been lively, but if Richard's behaviour is representative, then Oxford was at that stage rather the recipient.

[33] Ibid., iv. 3. II. ii. 2 (*Opera omnia*, iv. 82).
[34] L. Hödl, 'Die sakramentale Busse und ihre kirchliche Ordnung im beginnenden mittelalterlichen Streit um die Bussvollmacht der Ordenspriester', *FnSn* lv (1973), 340, 357, argues that Bonaventure did not prepare the final edition of his commentary before 1256, since allegedly he used a papal decree of that year in iv. 17 and iv. 19. Unfortunately Richard goes his own way in these two distinctions and leaves out the two questions referred to by Hödl.

CHAPTER 4

Disputed Questions

BY the middle of the thirteenth century theological learning had progressed so far that masters were now able and willing to discuss the problems of the faith without relying on standard textbooks like the Bible or the *Sentences*. This progress—if progress it was— led to the compiling of collections of *quaestiones disputatae*. A distinguishable group among these collections is the one reflecting the teaching in the Franciscan school of Paris in the second quarter of the thirteenth century. Most questions in this group are somehow connected with the comprehensive Franciscan encyclopedia of theology known as the *Summa 'Alexandri'*. These collections of questions have complicated relations with each other and with the *Summa*; it would require a separate study to unravel the intricacies. Much of this work has already been done by Doucet in his introduction to the fourth volume of the *Summa*.

Since most of the *quaestiones* are anonymous, scholars in the earlier part of this century were very anxious to identify the authors; they were often too eager to fill in the gaps. In this connection the name of Richard Rufus was mentioned frequently, though not always convincingly. The purpose of this chapter is not to uncover yet more questions in new manuscripts, but to sift the evidence for the attributions made in the past. The best collection to start from once again is As, since one of the questions there is explicitly attributed to 'Ruffus Cornubiensis'.

(i) *Assisi, Biblioteca comunale, MS 138 (=As)*

ii + 292 ff. + i, five hands from the middle of the thirteenth century. The manuscript is described in the catalogue of 1381 as being in the secret library:

Questiones multe disputate. Cum postibus. Cuius principium est. Post hec. est questio de patientia.et primo de formata. Finis vero. Idem dico de lectore.

et maxime magistro theologie. et cet. In quo libro. omnes quaterni sunt. xxxvi.F.[1]

This incipit is not the one found on f. 1, which has a table of contents, but it is the beginning of f. 2, the first question. The ending given in this catalogue is not the end of the very last question (f. 292A–D) but the end of the question before, which ends on f. 291C. On the same page the number of *pecie* is recorded:

In isto libro: omnes quaterni. sunt xxxvi. Unum folium in principio. et unum in fine: sine scriptura.[2]

The collection contains some disputed questions by such masters as Guerric of Saint-Quentin, Guiard of Laon, Robert Grosseteste, and Walter of Château-Thierry, which are marked; most questions, however, are anonymous. Later scholars ascribed them to Alexander of Hales, John of La Rochelle, Eudes Rigaud, William of Melitona, and the authors mentioned above.[3] Many questions are in the form of *reportationes*. A most interesting feature of the manuscript is that it was used by Bonaventure. In the margins copious pencilled notes have been scribbled in the saint's handwriting, either corrections of the text (e.g. ff. 278B, 279C), or ascriptions, or schemes of questions and their internal order (e.g. ff. 263C, 266B, 278B). Henquinet also sought to demonstrate that the collection was compiled under Bonaventure's personal directions and for his use. This seems likely, but is not as certain as the fact that he used the collection.[4] In any case it does establish the date of the collection, about 1250, and the place of origin, Paris, since Bonaventure taught theology only at Paris, and only in the years from about 1251 till 1257, when he was elected General. How the collection eventually ended up in Assisi is a difficult question, since little has been written on the history of the Sacro Convento and its library. Perhaps he took the books set aside for him with him to Italy

---

[1] Cenci, *Bibliotheca manuscripta*, i. 313.

[2] Op cit. i. 314.

[3] An exhaustive list of authors and questions in [V. Doucet], 'Prolegomena', *Summa theologica 'Alexandri'*, iv (1948), pp. cxxxviii–cxli.

[4] F. M. Henquinet, 'Un recueil de questions annoté par S. Bonaventure', *AFH* xxv (1932), 553–4. Also id., 'Eudes de Rosny, O.F.M., Eudes Rigaud et la Somme d'Alexandre de Halès', *AFH* xxxiii (1940), 28. W. Conlan, 'The Definition of Faith According to a Question of MS. Assisi 138', in J. R. O'Donnell (ed.), *Essays. . . A. C. Pegis* (Toronto, 1974), p. 56, expressed doubts about Henquinet's latter claim. Since most of Bonaventure's notes are in pencil, they are not visible on microfilm, so I have to rely on Henquinet.

when he became General, so that after his death they were brought to Assisi, which might have functioned as sort of central library. Certainly the library of the Sacro Convento also possesses an autograph of Bonaventure (Assisi, Biblioteca comunale, MS 186).[5]

One question in As is, as already mentioned, explicitly attributed to Richard Rufus; it is one first broached by Aristotle in the *Metaphysics*, whether God can understand anything except himself, a problem that troubled many theologians at the time (ff. 262C–263A):

Inc.:   Supponendo quod primum principium nobile intelligit, queritur an intelligat aliud a se aut non aliud. Et quod non intelligat aliud a se manifestum est pluribus rationibus. Prima talis ut dicit Commentator super illum locum *Sententia autem patrum* in X° libro Metaphisice . . .

Exp.:   . . . ergo si intelligentie sciunt altera, alteram erit prima scita, sed non equaliter. Ergo per primam, ergo una intelligit alteram in prima. Et hoc mihi manifestum verum.

At the bottom of f. 262C the indication: 'Questio de intellectu divino secundum magistrum ruffum cornubiensem'. The question is an explanation, or rather a summary of Averroes' commentary on Aristotle's *Metaphysics*, book xii (Λ) $1074^{b}1$–$1075^{a}10$. There is not very much, therefore, which is characteristic of Richard Rufus. The passage consists of whole passages from Averroes pasted together by linking sentences. There seems to be no direct relation to the same sort of question in the Oxford commentary or in the abbreviation. We can only guess that Richard's keen appetite for speculations on the divine mind and its workings may have been whetted by these preliminary exercises on Averroes. The question here would then represent a very early stage in his reflections on the subject, more an attempt to come to grips with the thought of the Commentator than an independent effort to determine his own position.

The next question on ff. 263A–264C tackles another popular topic, the problem whether angels are composed of matter and form, in Bonaventure's note: 'De compositione in angelis' (f. 263C):

---

[5] F. M. Henquinet, 'Un brouillon autographe de S. Bonaventure sur le commentaire des Sentences', *Études franciscaines*, xliv (1932), 635, 640. An alternative explanation might be that Bonaventure explicitly beqeathed his library to the Sacro Convento, as one of his sucessors, Cardinal Matthew of Aquasparta († 1302), was to do with many of his personal books. See G. Mazzatinti and L. Alessandri, 'Assisi. Biblioteca del convento di S. Francesco', in G. Mazzatinti (ed.), *Inventari dei manoscritti delle bibliotheche d'Italia*, iv (1894), pp. 22–3.

Inc.: Ad ostendendum spiritus sublimes, quos ratione officii: angelus vocamus, simplices et non ex materia et forma compositos, duplici via proceditur . . .'.

Exp.: . . . Nihil tamen ad hoc asserimus, sed totum studiosis discutiendum relinquimus'.

The last line of the question in itself would almost be enough to attribute it to Richard Rufus. There he displays that characteristic diffidence, or unwillingness to choose, that can be seen in so much of Richard's work. But there is much more. The whole treatment is, in fact, the same as in the Oxford commentary (B ff. 108C–110A), although the arrangement of the arguments is slightly different. In both versions Richard first gives the reasons in favour of the simplicity of the angels, from three points of view: God, the angels themselves, and the character of matter. In As this is indicated in the text:

Rationes autem ad hoc tripliciter accipi possunt: ex parte scilicet agentis primi, scilicet Creatoris illorum nobilissimi, aut ex parte ipsorum, aut ex parte materie. (As f. 263A)

In the Oxford commentary three notes in the margin mark the beginning of each section (B f. 108C–D).

In As this first part is followed by a blank of more than half a column (As f. 263B–C), upon which follow the arguments in favour of the composition of angels of matter and form, first from reason (ff. 263C–264B), then from authority (f. 264B–C). In the Oxford commentary the order is reversed: first the arguments are given from authority (f. 109A–B), then from reason (ff. 109B–110A). The reason for the blank in As must have been to keep an open space to fill in the appropriate authorities supporting the simplicity of angels; in the Oxford commentary the author quotes one or two Fathers who do so (B f. 109A). This blank, and also the fact that the Assisi version is somewhat more elaborate—although in some places the Oxford version is better supplied with quotations from Augustine—seem to indicate that the Assisi version represents the first design. Later on Richard uses his earlier reflections without bothering too much about the missing arguments from the Fathers, he supplied a few and left it at that. The ending of the two versions is different in wording, although the same in content. Richard, as so often, refuses to choose between the alternatives. In the Assisi version he defends this stance by pointing out the inadequacy of our language. The word 'matter', he says, is used in two different ways: properly used it stands for sheer potency, but commonly used it stands for that which remains the same in every change, the 'stuff'. He introduces this conclusion in very characteristic phrases:

Quid dicemus ad hoc? Quam partem asseremus? Fateor ignorantiam meam, nescio. Sed hoc veraciter scio quod illorum beatorum spirituum species et essentia sensum nostrum et rationem ineffabiliter excedunt.   (As f. 264B)

The third question in As which is from the hand of Richard Rufus beyond any doubt is a small treatise on ff. 277C–285A:

Inc.:   Miserabilis est humana condicio, nihil perfecte ad implendum in hoc statu cognoscimus. Et quando ita est fatuum et presumptio est in ambiguis occultis in terris asserere, sed dubitare de singulis non est inutile.[6] Iunior fui, etenim iam senui, et aliquando qualitercumque in philosophia naturali necnon et moralis studui . . .

Exp.:   . . . et potentia causa est operationis, si efficiens ut aqua egreditur operatio et e contrario: operatio causa est finalis potentie sive virtutis ut cuius gracia sunt.

The treatise is handed down in an extremely bad state: the text is corrupt in many places and the writing is sometimes almost illegible. There is no doubt, however, that it is a piece of Richard Rufus. The opening sentences immediately display that sense of personal commitment which pervades all the writings of Richard. Besides, much of the treatise can also be found literally, although slightly abridged, in the Oxford commentary: the proof of God's existence (As ff. 278B–280C = B ff. 20C–22A), a discourse on God's perfect unity (As ff. 280C–281A = B f.23A–23C), and on God's eternity (As f. 281A–281C), of which there is only a summary in B (f. 23C).

To illustrate the similarity and difference between the two versions, I quote the beginning of the paragraph where Richard, starting from the notion of truth, tries to prove the necessity of God's existence:

As

Item numquid de vero et veritate tacebo? Non possum. Sed dico quod si est minimum verum sive quodcumque, est Deus. Quod ostendo, omnibus rationibus et modis beati

B

Item, si est minimum verum sive quodcumque verum, est Deus.

---

[6] Cf. Aristotle, *Categoriae*, 8ᵇ21–4, quoted by Peter Abelard, *Sic et non*, ed. B. Boyer and R. McKeon (Chicago, 1977), Prologus, p. 103.

Anselmi omissis. Si est verum, est   Nam si est verum, est veritas; et si est
veritas; si est veritas mutabilis con-   veritas mutabilis si contingens, est et
tigens, sic est aliqua veritas immuta-   veritas aliqua immutabilis, nam illa
bilis, nam illa respectu talis dicitur.   respectu talis dicitur.   (B f. 21A)
(As f. 279A)[7]

The Assisi version confines itself to giving arguments from reason for
the necessity of God's existence, no doubt because it was clearly conceived as a philosophical treatise. In the Oxford commentary on the
Sentences, Richard deals extensively with Augustine and even more so
with Anselm before embarking on the rational arguments. This
second part is more elaborate in the Assisi version—as is clear from
the quotation and it no doubt represents the first attempt.[8] In this first
design Richard's style is even more florid than later on; that is perhaps
the reason why he decided to abridge. A good example:

Vir Dei, an dormis, an suspenso animo expectas? Sed ora pro me, quia ego
laboro pro te. Accipe hoc corollarium in portionem tuam, quod autem ante
univocationem necessario est equivocatio et equivocum. Quod si scirent
pueri, qui legunt Categorie [*sic*] Aristotelis, o quam bene dicerent Aristotelem
preposuisse capitulum de equivocis capitulo de univocis . . .   (As f. 279B)

The second part of the treatise (ff. 281C–285A) consists of questions
about the soul, none of which I have been able to trace back to
Richard's other works so far.

I have started off with these three questions to clarify the criteria with
which the other disputed questions can now be tackled. Three characteristic features emerge which mark all writings of Richard Rufus.
First the very personal style, florid, overloaded with exclamations,
rhetorical questions, irritable outbursts of temper, such as are also
observed in the two major works. We may recall the beginning of the
treatise 'Miserabilis est humana condicio', the digressions at the end
left out in the Oxford commentary and the abbreviation: 'Vir Dei an
dormis . . .? Dic mihi, pes musce, numquid tu demonstras Deum
esse?' (As f. 279B and C). Or from the question on the composition of
angels: 'Quid dicemus ad hoc?'
   The second feature is Richard's striking diffidence or, perhaps,
inability to choose between two alternatives. At the beginning of the
treatise 'Miserabilis est humana condicio' he explains this diffidence

[7] Gal, 'Viae', p. 197.
[8] Ibid., p. 182.

as inherent to the present human condition. Any claim to certainty would be presumptuous 'in ambiguis occultis in terris' (As f. 277C). In addition to that he also seems to say—but it is difficult here to reconstruct the meaning from the corrupted text—that self-confidence is for young men, and is really rather *puerile*. Instead of relying on his own wit Richard prefers the authority of the *Sancti*; he is always looking for confirmation in the writings of the Fathers, as he says in his commentary on the *Sentences*:

> Ecce, non definio in re tanta et tam authentica, sed acutioribus iudicandus relinquo. Quod si sanctos viderim expresse aliquid de hoc dicere, securius tunc potero de hoc asserere.   (B f. 78B)

The third characteristic is a negative one, but is a great help in discarding passages allegedly by Richard Rufus. It is the lack of organization which is obvious in all his works. The careful layout and annotation of the fair copy of the Oxford commentary on the *Sentences* has been admired by many. But it is not for nothing that this work is so richly annotated and provided with marginal notes, references to other passages, and summaries of questions. Without these props it would have been impossible to follow the course of the argument without getting caught in one of the many digressions, sometimes on the most unexpected and loosely connected subjects. In the abbreviation this chaos is less, because Bonaventure offers the framework in which to proceed. So, whenever a disputed question is neatly stated, the different sides of the problem covered by corresponding questions, every question divided into arguments for, arguments against, solution, and *ad obiecta*, whenever arguments are counted, or otherwise put into order, serious doubts as to Richard's authorship arise. This last criterion can serve to make a first selection .

Most of the questions between the disputation on the composition of angels and the end of the manuscript have been attributed to Richard Rufus by Pelster.[9] The first question, immediately following that on angels and in the same handwriting, is called by Bonaventure 'De poenis' (f. 266C);[10] it extends from f. 264C till f. 267D.

Inc.:   Circa penam 8 sunt investiganda; quorum primum est de eius quadruplici definitione, 2^m de ortu pene et numero penarum, $3u^m$ de causa

---

[9] F. Pelster, 'Neue Schriften des englischen Franziskaners Richardus Rufus von Cornwall (um 1250)', *Scholastik*, viii (1933), 564–8.

[10] Henquinet, 'Recueil', p. 555.

efficiente pene, 4ᵐ quid sit primum et per se subiectum pene, 5ᵐ utrum
aspectus naturaliter prius puniatur quam affectus, 7ᵐ [*sic*] qualiter
omnis culpa sit pena, 8ᵐ an in anima secundum idem id est secundum
eandem partem possit esse culpa et pena. Circa primum sic
procedamus ...

Exp.: ... Item Augustinus in 6° Musice: 'Diligenter considerandum est
utrum nihil sit aliud quod dicitur audire, nisi aliquid corpore in anima
fieri'. Sensus est susceptum sensibilium specierum sine materia
spiritus per aliquid.

Although only seven questions are mentioned in the first summary,
the author has, in fact, nine questions to ask about punishment and
guilt. The second and third questions are introduced with a 'Sequitur
de ortu pene' (As f. 264D), and 'Sequitur quid sit per se causa pene
efficiens' (As f. 265C); the next six are introduced with numbers:
'Quarto queritur quid sit primum et per se subiectum pene scilicet
debite pro peccato' (f. 266A), and so on till the ninth question. The
question missing in the summary is: 'Sexto queritur an ignorantia et
concupiscentia sint una pena' (f. 267A).

The initial summary is, as said before, a device most uncharacteristic of Richard Rufus, who seems to discover the questions on the
way; the same is true of the numbering of the questions. On the other
hand the use of the concept *aspectus-affectus* makes English provenance
of this question an overwhelming possibility; it points to the influence
of Robert Grosseteste. But if we have to put a name to it, then Richard
Fishacre is the man to think of. He loves neat summaries before
embarking on the work, summaries which often amount to an analysis
of the different aspects of the problems at hand. There are many good
examples of this method, I quote one:

Hic de Dei visione in patria queratur. Gratia cuius primo queratur an Deus sit
infinitus, secundo quot modis ipse possit dici infinitus, tertio quomodo se
compatiantur infinitas vel numerositas et simplicitas summa, quarto quomodo
creatura rationalis, cum sit virtutis finite, possit ad illud infinitum (Ba f. 10B,
O f. 11D)

The formal similarity is striking enough to justify the conjecture. But
even if this question is not Fishacre's, it is still impossible to attribute
it to Richard Rufus. It displays nothing of the rhetorical outbursts and
tormented doubting habitually found in his works.

The next question, still in the same handwriting, is also attributed
to Richard Rufus by Pelster. It is a reflection on man's glorified state

in heaven, in Bonaventure's words: 'De statu in patria' (ff. 268A–270B):[11]

Inc.:   De statu in patria queritur primo de radicali essentia, deinde de scientia in apprehensiva, deinde de potentia in motiva. De essentia queritur utrum mensuretur esse, scilicet actus essentie, tempore an eternitate. Ante terminationem autem huius problematis precedit inquirere de eternitate. De eternitate queritur an sit, quid sit, quorum sit . . .

Exp.:   . . . ergo non habuerunt unde possent stare, multo magis forma naturalis et materia et compositio.

Although the summing-up of the several aspects of the question at the beginning does not lead the reader to suspect so, Pelster is quite right in attributing it to Richard Rufus. The phrase 'De eternitate queritur an sit, quid sit, quorum sit' recurs in the Oxford commentary in another connection: 'De predestinatione queritur an sit, quid sit, quorum sit' (B f. 90A). And further on some prime examples of Richard's style appear:

. . . de eternitate numerorum fateor numerus numeratus non est Deo coeternus.   (f. 268D)

Ergo concedo quod ibi [sc. in limbo parvulorum] erit tempus etiam stante primo mobili. Sed quo modo dico quod mihi videtur non asserens ibi esse et nihil repugnans verbis sanctorum sequitur. Intelligo, ut patet ex doctrina sanctorum in multis locis, infernum esse locum corporalem.   (f. 269B–C)

Hoc non assero, sed tamen hoc vel aliquo consimili stabant sermones sanctorum.   (f. 269C)

Fateor, non video, quin possit de potentia . . .   (f. 280B)

All these formulations are very typical of Richard, of his doubts, of his refusal to commit himself, and of his constant appeal to the authority of the Fathers instead. Another indication is that the summing-up of questions at the beginning hardly corresponds to the actual problems he deals with in the course of the treatise. After a while the reader is completely at sea wondering what aspect the author is tackling now. Unfortunately it is impossible to find literal parallels in either of Richard's two main works, since the problem of man's state in heaven is treated at the end of the last book of the *Sentences*, which is lacking in both the Oxford commentary and the abbreviation. The formal

[11] Ibid.

similarities, however, are striking enough to assign this question to Richard Rufus with confidence.

After the treatise on man's state in heaven, the rest of f. 270B is blank. The next series of questions begins at the top of f. 270C in a different and often illegible hand, which continues up to the end of the treatise 'Miserabilis est humana condicio' on f. 285A. The first two questions make a pair and consider some psychological puzzles (f. 270C–D):

Inc.:　*Quoniam autem sentimus* etc. Dubitatio utrum potentia sensitiva possit reflectere se supra suum actum sicut potentia intellectiva potest convertere se ad se et ad suum actum . . .

Exp.:　. . . in somno et vigilia est quod potentia communis que ipsum videt et videt actu iudicat omnes.

Even Pelster, who gives Richard the benefit of every possible doubt, is unable to discover any positive traces of his style in these two questions. He can only say that there are no indications to the contrary. He sees one faint possibility: the author quotes from Alghazel: 'Unde dicit Algazel in sua Metaphisica', a work also quoted by Richard in another connection.[12] Alghazel's work, however, was too well known to take this quotation as an indication of Richard's authorship. Many others used Alghazel in the middle of the thirteenth century. Moreover, I have discoverd nothing in the text which either betrays Richard's style or his preoccupations. It is, therefore, most unlikely that this question is his work.

The question immediately following in the same column (ff. 270D–276A) considers God's knowledge, in the words of Bonaventure, *scientia Dei*.[13] Bonaventure must have been interested in this problem

---

[12] F. Pelster, 'Quästionen des Franziskaners Richardus Rufus de Cornubia (um 1250) in Cod. VII C. 19 der Nationalbibliothek Neapel und Cod. 138 der Stadtbibliothek Assisi', *Scholastik*, xiv (1939), 224. Pelster is less sanguine in 'Neue Schriften', p. 566, where he merely states that he can find no decisive evidence to attribute these two questions to Richard Rufus; some formulae rather remind him of Eudes Rigaud. F. M. Henquinet, 'Autour des écrits d'Alexandre de Halès et de Richard Rufus', *Antonianum*, xi (1936), 203, picks up this suggestion and wonders whether perhaps they are fragments of Eudes Rigaud's treatise on the soul, preserved in Trier, Stadtbibliothek, MS 62, f. 105b, which is impossible, since this treatise is in fact a copy of John of La Rochelle's treatise on the soul, see John of La Rochelle, *Tractatus de divisione multiplici potentiarum animae*, ed. P. Michaud-Quantin (Textes philosophiques du Moyen Âge, xi, 1964), pp. 43, 53.

[13] Henquinet, 'Recueil', p. 555.

since the margin is littered with notes in his hand.[14] It falls apart into two sections:

Inc.: Cum duplex sit cognitio Dei, activa scilicet qua cognoscit, et passiva qua cognoscitur; de prima habetur Jo. x: 'Cognosco oves meas', de secunda habetur I Cor. xiii: 'Cognoscam sicut et cognitus sum' . . . De hac autem cognitione Dei possint queri xx^{ti} in summa que postea sunt exquirenda. (f. 271A) Primo utrum Deus intelligat aliquid vel non. Secundo, dato quod intelligat, utrum intelligat se solum vel se et aliud a se . . .   (As ff. 270D–271A)

Exp.: . . .dicendum quod mala abscondita sunt cognitioni approbationis, non necessitate simplicis.   (As f. 275A)

Inc.: Supra quesitum est de cognitione Dei activa in quantum est Deus. Hic secundo queritur de cognitione Dei in quantum homo seu de scientia Christi in quantum homo. De qua quesita sunt xx^{ti} in numero sic. Primo utrum Christus secundum quod homo habeat scientiam increatam. Secundo, si non, utrum in eo simul aliqua scientia creata alia ab increata vel non . . .   (As f. 275A)

Exp.: . . . et scientia intellectualis, sed scientia sensus que recipit augmentum in eo.   (As f. 276A)

The first part of this question can also be found in N, which will be discussed later. As ff. 270D–274B equal N ff. 5D–7B. This treatise on *scientia Dei* became a bone of contention between Pelster and Henquinet, the first claiming it for Richard Rufus, the second for Alexander of Hales. Pelster attributed the question to Richard originally mainly on the strength of such turns of phrase as 'ad oppositum', 'ad secundum problema', 'ad contra obiectum', 'Item ad idem'.[15] Henquinet observed that such feeble arguments would not do. This question is a *reportatio*, and formulae like the ones mentioned are often used in this sort of writing; they betray very little about the original author.[16] Henquinet's main objection against Richard's authorship is that each part of the question is introduced with a summing-up of an extraordinary number of sub-questions, twenty for the first part, twenty for the second, making forty in all.[17] It is not so much the

[14] For a transcription of these notes see F. M. Henquinet, 'Trois petits écrits théologiques de saint Bonaventure à la lumière d'un quatrième, inédit', *Mélanges Auguste Pelzer* (Louvain, 1947), pp. 210–12.   [15] Pelster, 'Neue Schriften', pp. 566–7.
[16] Henquinet, 'Autour des écrits', p. 204. At p. 198 n. 2 H. notes—rather maliciously—some examples of Pelster's mistaken belief that this sort of formula can lead us to the discovery of the author.
[17] For the sub-questions of the first part see Pelster, 'Neapel, pp. 217–18 for a full survey and Pelster, 'Neue Schriften', p. 563 for a summary.

summing-up as such, but the extraordinary number of sub-questions, which according to Henquinet is most uncharacteristic of Richard Rufus.[18] He also points out that in these two questions Richard's taste for digressions never appears.[19]

Pelster defended himself by pointing out that the author knows Averroes' commentary on the *Metaphysics*. This is not proof one way or the other, since the history of the reception of Averroes in Paris and Oxford is not well known. Neither can the use of the distinction *potentia passiva* and *activa* suffice to identify the author as Richard Rufus. Pelster tried to meet Henquinet's main objection by referring to two other questions which he had already declared to be Richard's, and which are indeed, preceded by a summing-up of the sub-questions, although by no means as many. The first of these is the question on punishment (As ff. 264C–268A). It is most unlikely, however, as explained before, that Richard Rufus is the author of this treatise; Richard Fishacre is a much more probable candidate. The second question Pelster refers to is called 'De aureola' and can be found in London, BL MS Royal 8 C. iv. Although Pelster discovered all the peculiarities of Richard Rufus in the literary style of the question, it is, in fact, a transcription from Richard Fishacre's commentary on the *Sentences*, as will be shown later.[20] Thus, in fact, he has no reply to Henquinet's main objection. Moreover, in the questions no trace can be discovered of Rufus's involved and tortuous style, nor of his marked diffidence and distrust of human constructs. Whether the question is the work of Alexander of Hales instead, I leave for others to judge; all I can say is that Henquinet's arguments seem convincing. It certainly belongs to the circle around the *Summa 'Alexandri'*, since several passages of the second part, on the knowledge of Christ, can be found in the *Summa* as well.[21]

The next question on the wise men's star follows immediately in the same script (ff. 276B–277B):

---

[18] Henquinet, 'Autour des écrits', p. 203. See also id., 'Les questions inédites d'Alexandre de Halès sur les fins dernières', *RThAM* x (1938) 162 n. 65.

[19] Ibid.; there he also gives all the arguments to attribute this question to Alexander of Hales, e.g. that in N the question 'De Dei cognitione activa' is part of a coherent series of Halesian questions (ff. 1A–7B), an argument refuted quite convincingly by Pelster, 'Neapel', pp. 222–4. The discussion need not detain us any longer, since it does not affect the problem of Richard Rufus's authorship.

[20] Pelster, 'Neapel', pp. 225–8; see also below, pp. 92–3.

[21] Henquinet, 'Autor des écrits', pp. 197–8, where he manages to reconstruct an unclear passage in the *Summa* by comparing it with As and N. Both used the same source, probably an earlier question by Alexander of Hales.

Inc.:   Queritur utrum magi potuerunt venire in notitiam ortus Christi per stellam, et in quam notitiam Christi per illam venire potuerunt et qualiter. Quod autem per illam stellam in notitiam Christi venire potuerunt videtur primo per hoc quod dicit Glossa . . .

Exp.:   . . . quare si illa stella fuisset aliqua aliarum cum esse desineret Deus aliquod factum ad per [. . .] in suo esse non conservaret; quod est inconveniens.

This question can also be found in Padua, Biblioteca Antoniana MS 152, f. 49a–b. Pelster first attributed it to Walter of Château-Thierry, later to Richard Rufus.[22] Several points speak against an attribution to Richard Rufus, such as the clarity of the structure: first all the arguments for, then the arguments against, the solution, and then the refutation of the arguments favouring the rejected position. Neither is there any trace of Rufus's peculiar style. And more positively, the author introduces sub-questions very often with the phrase 'huius gratia', e.g.:

Huius gratia queritur si stella aliquid potuit significare universaliter super ortum Christi vel mortem.   (f. 276B)

Huius gratia queritur que [*sic*] stella significet super mortem regis et non super ortum et quare super ortum regni et non regis.   (f. 276C)

Contrary to Pelster I have not found this introductory phrase in Richard's two main works, at least not as a regular feature. Pelster also argues that the fact that this question is written in the same hand as the following treatise 'Miserabilis est humana condicio', which is authentically Ricardian, is a point in Richard's favour. This amounts to special pleading, since in this collection the script offers no clue as to the author; questions by many different authors are written in the same hand. Moreover, there is a clear break between this question and the treatise 'Miserabilis' in the form of a blank of half a column on f. 277B. If this means anything, it would rather tell against Richard as the author of this question, since it seems to indicate that the scribe wished to separate it very clearly from the following contribution, perhaps because they were by different authors.

After the treatise 'Miserabilis', which we have discussed before, two more questions follow, the first probably by Alexander of Hales (f. 286A–D), the second ascribed in the manuscript itself to Walter of

---

[22] F. Pelster, 'Cod. 152 der Bibliothek von S. Antonio in Padua und seine Quästionen', *RThAM* ix (1937), 36; id., 'Neapel', p. 224.

Château-Thierry (ff. 286D–291C).[23] The manuscript finishes with the
added question on the relation between the subject and object of
knowledge, with which I have dealt in an earlier chapter (f. 292A–C).[24]

So far we have checked on Pelster's attributions. But As also contains a series of questions on philosophical topics whose author is not
mentioned in the manuscript (ff. 249A–261D). The first question is a
fragment of a commentary on the *Posterior Analytics*; the next four deal
with such varied subjects as the eternity of the world, the nature of
predication, the principle of individuation, and universals; the last
part is formed by a treatise on the soul. Doucet established that all this
must be the work of one author. He denied that it was John of La
Rochelle, who was Pelster's final choice, and thinks of Richard Rufus
instead, although he does not press his claim.[25] The beginnings and
endings are as follows:

Inc.:   *Est autem quorundam quedam altera causa* etc.[26] Hoc capitulum quod est
de definitione divisum est in duas partes in quarum prima opponit de
definitione dupliciter.   (f. 249A)

Exp.:   ... et rationes predicte hoc idem sufficienter arguunt si subtiliter
considerentur.   (f. 249D)

Inc.:   Si consequentia aliqua fuerit necessaria et antecedens fuerit necessarium, consequens eadem necessitate erit necessarium ...   (f. 249D)

Exp.:   ... licet ergo non ens solum prius est natura ente tali et non tempore
vel nunc.   (f. 250A)

Inc.:   Ens predicatur de substantia et de aliis predicamentis, aut ergo
univoce aut non univoce. Non univoce constat ...   (f. 250A)

Exp.:   ... ergo nullum eorum de inferiori determinantur. Quod concedi-
mus.   (f. 250B)

Inc.:   Questio de individuatione. Et supponimus quod nihil individuetur a
seipso, sed quod individuetur per aliquod eius.   (f. 250B)

Exp.:   ... nec est in eo ponere materiam et formam, ipsa nec erit universale
nec particulare.   (f. 250D)

Inc.:   Ostenso autem quod materia non sit individuum, sed principium
individuationis, de universalibus ...   (f. 250D)

---

[23] [Doucet], 'Prolegomena', p. cxli; the first question has been edited in Alexander of
Hales, *Quaestiones disputatae 'antequam esset frater'* (Bibliotheca Franciscana Scholastica
Medii Aevi, xxi, 1960), pp. 1578–87. In the introduction it is described as 'incerte
halesiana' (Bibliotheca, xix, 1960), p. 8*.   [24] See above, pp. 35–7.

[25] [Doucet], 'Prolegomena', p. ccxxv.

[26] Aristotle, *Analytica posteriora. Translatio Jacobi*, 93b21, ed. L. Minio-Paluello and
B. G. Dod (Aristoteles Latinus, iv/1–4, 1968), p. 83.

Exp.: ... vel figuratis; qua autem in hiis necesse sit hec esse in aliis relinquamus. (f. 251C)

Inc.: Postquam dictum est de forma substantiali, quoniam substantia est, et de accidentali, quoniam hoc est esse solum et non ens, revertens ad formam substantialem dicemus de quadam specie eius scilicet de anima ... (f. 251C)

Exp.: ... ergo post mortem natus est homo ad regenerationem ut sic consequatur summum bonum humanum, quod est simpliciter summum bonum. (f. 261D)

The treatise on the soul offers the best opportunities for this enquiry, since it is in some ways comparable with genuine works of Richard Rufus.

The first thing that stands out is the extremely lucid structure of the treatise. The author deals first with the substance of the soul, then with its divisions (vegetative, sensitive, intellective), then with the powers or *virtutes* of each part of the soul: the powers of the vegetative soul (nutrition, growth and generation), the sensitive soul (the five senses, the common sense, movement, and imagination), the intellective soul (the active and passive intellect). The last part is devoted to the major distinction within the soul between knowing and willing. And it is the latter which draws the soul to its origin and end: 'Summum bonum humanum, quod est simpliciter summum bonum' (f. 261D). This lucidity is maintained in the treatment of the single problems. That is unlike Richard Rufus.

Neither is there any similarity in the treatment of the questions whether the soul is fully present in each single part of the body (As f. 252A = Richard in B f. 40B) and whether in the soul there is a plurality of forms or one single soul. Our philosopher only knows about two possible positions in this dispute, either one soul with three potentialities or three souls (As f. 252D), whereas Richard distinguishes three positions, the third being an effort to reconcile the other two by maintaining that the vegetative and sensitive principles of the soul are both a power and a substance (B f. 145A–D).[27]

The most important difference between Richard and the anonymous author arises at the end of the treatise, where the fundamental distinction between intellect and will, between knowledge and movement, comes to the fore:

[27] D. Callus, 'Two Early Oxford Masters on the Problem of Plurality of Forms, Adam of Buckfield, Richard Rufus of Cornwall', *Revue néo-scolastique de philosophie*, xlii (1940), 439–45 gives a transcription of the passage.

Omnes philosophantes de anima eam determinaverunt in duobus, scilicet in cognitione et motu. Solum enim hec duo perducunt nos ad cognitionem anime. Non est cognitio nisi in substantia incorporea apprehendente, nec motus alicuius corporis a seipso, nisi in ipso fuerit substantia incorporea a corpore moto separata secundum substantiam ... cognitio per apprehensionem, motus vero per affectum seu appetitum. (f. 260A)

Two concepts of *apprehensio* and *appetitus* as the formal descriptions of the two foremost acts of the soul are from here on essential to the argument, e.g.:

Consequenter querendum quid addit appetitus supra apprehensionem. Et primo utrum sit ibi additio virtutis supra virtutem, ut alia sit virtus appetitiva et apprehensiva, sicut actus differentes. (f. 260C)

Richard conceives of a similar distinction, but couches it in different terms; he calls the grasping of knowledge *aspectus* and the movement of the will *affectus*. Both terms derive from Robert Grosseteste:

Sufficienter dividitur anima in aspectum et affectum. Et affectus est voluntas et aspectus ratio. (B f. 160C)

Hec iam in vita contemplativa constituta 2 minuta mittit etc. Que sunt apex intelligentie et principalis affectio seu unitio que communiter appellantur aspectus et affectus. Hee 2 pariter sursum feruntur mutuo se promoventes et pariter in divina spectacula ascendentes, illa speculando, ista desiderando, precurrente intelligentia, nec tamen ingrediente profunda Dei, quia videns per speculum non pervenit in substantiam. Unitio autem que speculum nescit immittitur in totum desiderabile et non totum intelligibile. (B f. 6B)

Although the distinction both authors make within the soul seems quite the same, the terminology in which they describe these two functions of the soul is so different that they must be two different men. Therefore, I cannot confirm Doucet's conjecture and claim these questions for Richard Rufus; his treatment of the soul is very different, and, unfortunately, far less lucid.

So, all in all, we have been able to identify three *quaestiones disputatae* on the divine intellect, the composition of angels, and man's blessed state in heaven and a sizeable treatise on the human condition as works of Richard Rufus. The result fits in very well with the external divisions of the manuscript, as indicated by the changes of scribe and the blanks. Till f. 270B the text is without interruption and written by the same hand. This covers Rufus's commentary on Averroes, his reflections on the angels, Fishacre's (?) question on punishment, and Rufus's questioning of man's state in heaven. Thus, at the end of this part of the manuscript, there appears a whole cluster of questions of English provenance, because not only these, but also the two questions preceding Rufus's comment on Averroes are of English origin; Robert Grosseteste is probably their author. The first is a 'Questio de fluxu et refluxu maris a magistro R. Oxon. [*some have* R. Exon.] in scolis suis determinata' (ff. 261D–262B), the second a question 'De modis subsistendi' ascribed in the margin to 'magister R. Grosseteste' (f. 262B–C).[28]

The next part is formed by the two epistemological questions, the disputation on God's knowledge, and the question on the significance of the star of Bethlehem. This part is marked by a change of writer at the beginning and a substantial blank at the end. This group seems to have originated in a more Parisian background, since one belongs to the circle around Alexander of Hales, and another is probably the work of Walter of Château-Thierry.

The next part, in the same script as the previous one, but clearly marked at the beginning by the blank on f. 277B, consists of the treatise 'Miserabilis est humana condicio'. The last part, indicated both by a blank (f. 285B–D) and a change of hand, consists of pieces by Alexander of Hales (?) and Walter of Château-Thierry. Finally, on the last folio the question on the relation between the subject and the object of knowledge, which we have studied earlier, has been added. Thus there seems to be a certain amount of organization. Richard's questions appear in a series of English origin; his treatise on God and the soul stands on its own. This series of English questions is perhaps one of the most remarkable features of this manuscript, because it proves that relations existed between Oxford and Paris in the 1240s and that the intellectual contact was not completely one-way, but that there was an exchange. The compiler of this manuscript, whether Bonaventure or some lesser-known Parisian Franciscan scholar, was apparently so interested in the results of English

---

[28] The first question has been edited by R. C. Dales, 'The Text of Robert Grosseteste's *Questio de fluxu et refluxu maris* with an English Translation', *Isis*, lvii (1966), 459–68. Grosseteste's authorship is still a matter of debate: J. McEvoy, *The Philosophy of Robert Grosseteste* (Oxford, 1982), pp. 483–4 comes down on the side of Grosseteste; R. W. Southern, *Robert Grosseteste: The Growth of an English Mind in Medieval Europe* (Oxford, 1986), pp. 122–3 declares against authenticity. O. Lewry, 'Robert Grosseteste's Question on Subsistence: An Echo of the Adamites', *MS* xlv (1983), 19–21 has edited the second question.

theological and philosophical reflection that he included this series in his selection[29]

(ii) *Toulouse, Bibliothèque municipale, MS 737 (=T)*

294 ff., several hands, a compilation of *quaestiones disputatae* by masters like William of Melitona, John of La Rochelle, Walter of Château-Thierry, Eudes Rigaud, and Alexander of Hales, giving an excellent survey of the problems that concerned theologians in the second quarter of the thirteenth century, especially in the years 1240–50. The manuscript was provided with a list of contents and marginal notes by Gerardinus of San Giovanni in Persiceto, who used it for his courses in one of the *studia generalia* of the Franciscan province of Bologna, probably Parma, in the period before 1269.[30] In 1436 it was bought from a Jew by the Austin friars of Toulouse.[31]

Two questions in this manuscript, one on the moment of change and the other on seminal principles, have been attributed to Richard Rufus by Henquinet, who discovered some striking similarities between these questions and some philosophical digressions in Richard's Oxford commentary.[32] They are the following:

Inc.: Mutetur Socrates de sanitate in egritudinem. Ponatur ergo quod fuerit Socrates sanus toto tempore A, eger toto tempore B . . . (f. 158A)

Exp.: . . . nec quod C nunc primo non est, nec quod C nunc ultimo non est et istud generaliter tendunt. Et hec ad presens de hiis. (f. 158C)

Inc.: De rationibus seminalibus queritur quid sint. Accidentia non sunt, cum sint substantiarum principia et cause, sicut vult Augustinus in multis locis . . . (f. 158C)

Exp.: . . . et ita semper proceditur ut numquam aliquid idem numero inveniatur in prole et parente excepta materia prima. (f. 160B)

Henquinet, it can be shown, was quite right, but the evidence he gives is not enough in itself to justify the ascription. A comparison of the treatise on seminal principles with a question on the same subject in

[29] For the problem of the *reportationes* in As ff. 77C–84D, for which some claim Richard Rufus as the reporter, see below, pp. 85–6.

[30] A full description of the MS in [Doucet], 'Prolegomena', pp. cxlii–cxliii. F. M. Henquinet, 'Frère Gérardin de San Giovanni in Persiceto, O.F.M., usager du manuscrit Toulouse 737', *AFH* xxxi (1938), 523–4 thought that the MS was compiled by Gerardin. This is denied by J. Barbet, 'Notes sur le manuscrit 737 de la bibliothèque municipale de Toulouse', *Bulletin d'information de l'Institut de Recherche et d'Histoire des Textes*, v (1956), 8–9.

[31] Henquinet, 'Frère Gérardin', p. 523.

[32] Henquinet, 'Autour des écrits', pp. 211–12, 215–16.

Richard's abbreviation of Bonaventure's commentary on the *Sentences* proves the point completely. Bonaventure deals with the problem in ii. 18, and it is there that Richard concentrates on the same issue (V ff. 208D–212A). Richard's treatment, however, is completely different from Bonaventure's. He is mainly interested in the question whether seminal principles have exhausted all their potentialities once they have caused the thing whose seedling they are:

Deinde queritur: quid sit ratio seminalis secundum essentiam. Et cum sint forme et cause alique rerum, ut vult Augustinus, queritur, utrum sint forme universales, aut singulares. Et queritur in primis: ratio seminalis, cum ex illa producitur aliqua forma specialis, aut manet et salvatur illa producta, aut non. Probatio quod manet. Quia dicit Augustinus ubi supra; 'Neque tunc in huiusmodi fetus . . .'   (V f. 208D)

In the Toulouse manuscript the author first defines seminal principles as 'forma substantialis universalis' or 'communis' (f. 158C–D), then he proceeds:

Hiis ergo positis queritur, cum sint forme substantie, aut sunt universales aut singulares. Et omnino quomodo se habeant ad istas. Constat enim quod producunt istas ad esse actu. Quero ergo aut manent in ipsis formis productis et salvantur in illis aut non. Probatio quod manent. Ait Augustinus, De Trinitate, ubi supra: 'Nec tunc in huiusmodi fetus . . .'   (T f. 158D)

From here the arguments in V and T run parallel till V f. 210B (=T f. 159B). After this point V summarizes the more extensive arguments of T. To establish this parallel does not exclude the possibility that Richard simply makes use of T to make his point; nothing is more normal in the Middle Ages than this kind of plagiarism. However, given that Richard in the abbreviation also transcribed all the sentences in which the first person singular appears, this possibility seems to fade:

Ex hiis concludo quod si ratio seminalis est forma substantia possibilis . . .   (V f. 208D = T f. 158D)

Dico ergo adhuc: est C D, quod essentialis erat predicatio . . .   (V f. 209B = T f. 159A)

Procedo: aut singularis eiusdem speciei specialissime . . .   (V f. 209C = T f. 159A)

Arguo ergo sic: sicut se habet E ad F, sic se habet C ad D.   (V f. 210A = T f. 159B)

It was also established earlier that in those cases where Richard deviates from Bonaventure, it is to vent his personal opinions. It should also be taken into consideration that, when quoting the opinion of others, he usually prefaces these quotations—like other scholars—with expressions like 'Alii dicunt . . .'. He does so even when summarizing an opinion of Bonaventure's with which he disagrees afterwards. In the introduction to the question on seminal principles in V, on the other hand, there is nothing that would indicate that Richard is now relying on someone else.

There are two more parallels between T and the authentic works of Richard. In the Oxford commentary he has a passage on the nature of change: 'De modo transmutationis entis in ens' (B f. 144C–D), which closely resembles in treatment an argument in the Toulouse question on seminal principles, although in the latter the author is more concerned with the problem of generation in the process of change, whereas Richard stresses the problem of corruption in that process.[33]

In the question 'Mutetur Socrates' the author wrestles with the problem of the exact moment of change; so does Richard in his Oxford commentary in connection with the question whether angels move from place to place instantaneously or whether they need some time. He quotes several solutions, then rejects them.

Nihil est istud. Et proveniunt, ut mihi videtur, tales errores ex defectu cuiusdam philosophici. Querit igitur philosophus: si fuerit Socrates albus toto tempore A, non albus vero seu niger toto tempore B . . .   (B f. 85D)

Instead of opposing Socrates' illness and health, Richard opposes his whiteness and blackness, but the ensuing argument is exactly the same in line, though not in wording. Even more striking is that at the end of the Toulouse question the author points out that proper thinking on the moment of change is particularly helpful in problems like the movement of angels and the spreading of corporeal light. It is exactly to clarify these two points that Richard uses these philosophical reflections in his Oxford commentary, first here and later on in the second book, to explain the way in which light spreads (B ff. 112D and 131A). And in both this question and the Oxford commentary the readers are cautioned not to confuse the movement of angels with the

---

[33] In B the discussion is introduced as follows: 'Et quia de transmutatione aliquantulum tactum est, nescio si liceat propter iuniores aliquantulum digredi et de modo quo sit transmutatio entis in ens disserere. Generetur igitur ex B aere A ignis . . .' (B f. 144C). Compare with T ff. 158D–159B, especially from 'Et ut manifestius arguamus, ponamus quod ex B aere generetur A ignis . . .' (f. 158D).

spreading of light (T f. 158B, B ff. 112D and 131A). This is convincing enough to ascribe the question on the moment of change to Richard Rufus as well.

Richard must therefore have been interested in philosophy. Indeed, he seems to have felt more at home in philosophy than in theology, for in these two questions he expresses very few doubts, there are no anxious exclamations about man's inability and weakness; on the contrary he proceeds with effortless superiority.

There remains the problem of trying to determine in what years these two questions could have seen the light. Both seem to be prior to the two main works, that is to say before 1250. They could form part of the written version of his lectures at Paris as a regent master of arts, before he entered the Franciscan order in 1238. Two things seem to speak against that solution: the technicality of the discussion on change, elicited by a study of Aristotle's *Physics*, but carried far beyond that, seems to point to a slightly later period and, secondly, the fact that the questions are incorporated in a clearly Franciscan collection.

The second possibility would be that Richard studied some philosophy, while teaching at Oxford before 1250, although the Franciscans officially did not take courses in philosophy but launched into theology at once.[34] Richard, however, points out that philosophical speculation sometimes contributes to the solution of major theological problems: the movement of angels, the doctrines of transubstantiation and justification cannot be fully understood, he says, without preliminary philosophical discussion (T f. 158A). Probably he introduced these philosophical problems in the course of his theological expositions, as in the example mentioned before: while talking about the creation of man (B ii. 17) he feels compelled to say something about change in general and 'propter iuniores aliquantulum digredi et de modo quo sit transmutatio entis in ens disserere' (B f. 144C). These 'iuniores' could well be the young Franciscans, to whom Richard, within the framework of theology, taught some philosophy to cope with theological problems. If this is true, then these two questions reflect in more detail Richard's first teaching period at Oxford in the years just before 1250, and they are further proof that the intellectual exchange between Oxford and Paris was no mere one-way process.

---

[34] Felder, *Geschichte*, p. 459; see also pp. 94–6 for Francis's dislike of philosophy.

(iii) *Naples, Biblioteca nazionale, MS VII. C. 19 (= N)*

iii + 147 ff. + i, thirteenth century, several hands. The manuscript contains the commentary of Albertus Magnus on the third book of the *Sentences* (ff. 8A–85A), and of Richard Fishacre on the fourth book (ff. 86A–147D). The two fragments are preceded by four disputed questions: 'Questio est de providentia divina' (ff. 1A–3C; cf. Vatican City, Bibl. Ap. Vat., MS lat. 782 ff. 182–184D and Assisi, Bibl. com., MS 186 ff. 7A–8D), 'Questio est de statu anime separate reprobe' (ff. 3D–4B; cf. As ff. 81C–82D), 'Questio est de ipsa anima separata electa' (ff. 4B–5A; cf. As ff. 82D–83C), and the question on God's knowledge (ff. 5B–7B), the same as in As ff. 270D–274B. The manuscript came to the Biblioteca nazionale from the Augustinian convent of San Giovanni a Carbonara, and it must have been there for a long time, because the decorations on the medieval binding are typical of this convent. It could be, however, that its origins must be sought in the main Dominican convent of Naples, San Domenico Maggiore.[35]

The last question before the beginning of Albert's commentary is identical with As ff. 270D–276A, but breaks off in the middle.

Inc.: Cum duplex sit cognitio Dei: activa, scilicet qua cognoscit, et passiva qua cognoscitur; de prima habetur Jo. x.: 'Cognosco oves meas', de secunda habetur I Cor. xiii: 'Cognoscam sicut et cognitus sum' ... (N f. 5B = As f. 270D)

Exp.: ... unde etiam in personis divinis est ordo nature, sicut dicit Augustinus, ergo in ideis est ordo. Item ideata in esse producta. (N f. 7B = As f. 274B l. 14)

The text of N is in much better condition than that of As; it is both more legible and more reliable. The problems about the author of this question have been discussed already and need no further clarification.

There is a minor point, however, about two of the previous questions on the reprobate and elect souls (ff. 3D–5A). They are part of a larger collection of questions on the fate of man after death to be found in As ff. 77C–84D: 'De ultimo iudicio' (ff. 77C–80B), 'De igne conflagrationis' (ff. 80B–81C), 'De statu anime reprobe' (ff. 81C–82D), 'De statu anime electe' (ff. 82D–83C), 'De statu anime in purgatorio' (ff. 83C–84D). The first, second, and fifth questions can also be found

---

[35] A full description of the MS in Pelster, 'Neapel', p. 216 and in C. Cenci, *Manoscritti francescani della Biblioteca nazionale di Napoli* (Spicilegium Bonaventurianum, vii–viii, 1971), i. 402 n. 1; see also [Doucet], 'Prolegomena' p. cxlviii.

in Troyes, Bibliothèque municipale, MS 1245ff. 193B–210D. They are *reportationes*.[36] A dispute has arisen whether Richard Rufus could be the *reportator* of these anonymous questions. To me it seems a very hazardous enterprise to make guesses when there are two unknown factors, author and reporter. This uncertainty is reflected in the dispute. The question is even more complicated by the fact that the three *reportationes* may well be the work of three different reporters, As representing the eldest tradition. Pelster first maintained that the reporter must remain unknown, then he mentioned Richard Rufus, and finally he tried to show that the N version is either the work of Richard Rufus or, less likely, of John of La Rochelle. At some point he also mentioned Eudes Rigaud.[37] Henquinet noticed that the Troyes version is ascribed to Alexander, but in the end he remained undecided as did Conlan. I concur entirely with their suspension of judgement; there are too many possibilities and too many unknown factors.[38]

(iv) *Paris, Bibliothèque nationale, MS lat. 16406 (= P)*

230 ff., several hands, was owned by Master Gérard of Abbeville (+ 1272), who bequeathed the book to the Sorbonne at his death:

Iste liber est collegii pauperum magistrorum in theologica facultate Parisius studentium. Pretii L solidorum ex legato magistri Gyraudi de Abbatisvilla.   (f. 230b; cf. f. 1b)

It is a collection of disputed questions of masters like Alexander of Hales, John of La Rochelle, and Eudes of Châteauroux.[39] It also contains anonymously Alexander's commentary on the fourth book of the *Sentences* (ff. 153A–217D).[40]

---

[36] [Doucet], 'Prolegomena', p. cxxxix.

[37] To follow Pelster's vacillating opinions see F. Pelster, 'Zwei ehemalige Turiner Handschriften aus dem Kreise um Alexander von Hales', *Scholastik*, xii (1937), 536 n. 24; id., 'Cod. 152', p. 45 n. 45; id., 'Neapel', pp. 232–3; id., 'Beiträge zur Erforschung des schriftlichen Nachlasses Odo Rigaldis', *Scholastik*, xi (1936), 525.

[38] Henquinet, 'Questions inédites', pp. 169 n. 70, 172; Conlan, 'The Definition of Faith', p. 57.

[39] For a description of the MS see Ch. Samaran and R. Marichal, *Catalogue des manuscrits en écriture latine portant des indications de date, de lieu ou de copiste*, iii: *Bibliothèque nationale, fonds latin (no. 8001 à 18613)* (Paris, 1974), p. 705. For a survey of the contents see [Doucet], 'Prolegomena', pp. cxxxvii–cxxxvi.

[40] F. M. Henquinet, 'Le commentaire d'Alexandre de Halès sur les Sentences enfin retrouvé', in *Miscellanea Giovanni Mercati*, ii (Studi e Testi, cxxii, 1946), p. 367.

In this manuscript Pelster considered that he had discovered two questions of Richard Rufus.[41] The first question is on the involuntary movements of the senses (ff. 75C–79D):

Inc: Circa sensualitatem queruntur quinque. Primo queritur utrum sensualitas contineatur sub anima sensibili aut sub rationali, quod est querere utrum sensualitas humana et brutalis congruant vel differant. Et questionem hanc ordinat [?] incipiendo inferius a tali signo ...

Exp.: ... ad illud Iob quod xii° obicitur dicendum quod consensus ad delectandum potest esse mulieris respectu sensualitas, sic est veniale, vel viri respectu mulieris, sic potest esse mortalis, maxime post deliberationem.

The two most important sub-questions must be mentioned since they figure in the index on f. 1A–B:

Quarto queritur de compage sensualitatis humane ...   (f. 76D)

Habito per questionem utrum fomes possit movere sensualitatem ad motum vitiosum, queritur consequenter, utrum primus motus sit in sensualitate et ut unius [?] vocabuli intelligatur quid scilicet primus motus ...   (f. 77D)

The question does not belong to the first gathering, it was written in later at the end of a *pecia* (quaternion) whose last twelve folios had been left blank. This is obvious, not only from the slightly different colour of the ink, but also from the fact that this question was entered into the list of contents later on in the following manner. On f. 1A we' see two entries: 'Questiones quator de manifestatione Christi post resurrectionem', corresponding to ff. 72D–75C, 'Questio est de apparitione sive manifestatione Christi post resurrectionem eius ...', and 'Questiones octo de divinatione', corresponding to ff. 81A–83D, 'Questio est de divinatione ...'. Between the two entries in the index is a sign in the form of a cross, which is repeated at the bottom of f. 1B. Next to the second sign is written: 'Questio de sensualitate anime humane. Questio de fomite in qua vi sit ut in subiecto. Questio de primis motibus. Questio de vita angeli.' The first three entries correspond to the questions mentioned above, the fourth can be found on f. 80A–C and has no connection with the previous one; it is merely a scribbled note in a different hand. This implies that the question on human senses is not part of a series and that the identity of the author cannot be inferred from the fact that it is right in the middle of a long series of questions by Alexander of Hales (ff. 54A–75C, 81A–110A).[42]

---

[41] Pelster, 'Neue Schriften', *Scholastik*, ix (1934), 258–64.

[42] [Doucet], 'Prolegomena', pp. cxxxvii–cxxxviii; cf. Pelster, 'Neue Schriften', p. 259.

Pelster has two reasons to justify his attribution. The first is that in the text Averroes is always called 'Alvarus', which, according to Pelster, is a typically English custom. Be that as it may, it is no indication that Richard Rufus is the author, rather the contrary, since Richard refers to Averroes as 'Avenroes' or 'Averroes' (e.g. B f. 21C, 21D). Pelster also discovers Richard's literary style in this question.[43] Lottin has already expressed grave doubts about the latter argument, and I share his hesitations.[44] The personal touch, the explanations, the rhetorical questions, the nagging doubts, the reluctance to choose, are all lacking in this question.

More positively, the author has a marked preference for the Gloss to support his arguments, e.g. on f. 78C, where he draws upon the Gloss six times to prove that the first motion of the senses is always sinful. Richard Rufus uses the Gloss, as scholastic theologians do, but not to an extraordinary extent; his two main authorities are Augustine and Anselm. A second point is that the author never fails to solve all the arguments opposing his solution, which again is most uncharacteristic of Richard Rufus, who often leaves loose ends. But the most striking point about the author's style is his almost obsessive use of the verb *notare*, e.g.:

Item nota quod omnes potentie anime sensibilis vires sunt . . .   (F. 76A)

Item nota quod a potentia et sensuali anime rationalis fluunt . . .   (f. 76A)

Nota etiam quod hec vis in hoc communicat cum sensualitate . . .   (f. 76A)

Notandum quod primus motus est passivus vel passio, non actio . . .   (f. 77A)

Ut videtur ex definitione: primus motus est in sensualitate, sed nota quod per hoc quod dicitur sensualitatis tangitur causa materialis seu subiectum. Sensualitas est enim primus motus in quo est motus. Notandum tamen quod sensualitas mota non est inordinatum, sed mota secundum impulsum fomitis . . .   (f. 77D)

This is not characteristic of Richard Rufus, whose use of the verb *notare* is not above the average. Of course, if the question were a *reportatio*, then the repetitive use of *notare* might be blamed on the reporter. But that is not the case, as can be seen from phrases like:

Et breviter omnes auctoritates vel rationes probantes primum motum esse in sensualitate . . . concedo.   (f. 78B)

---

[43] Ibid., pp. 262-3.
[44] O. Lottin, *Psychologie et morale aux XIIᵉ et XIIIᵉ siècles*, ii: *Problèmes de morale* (Louvain etc., 1948), p. 556 n. 1: on pp. 556-7 an edition of part of the question 'De sensualitate' (ff. 78C-79A).

Ex hiis auctoritatibus et rationibus et visis aliis que imponit Augustinus dicimus. (f. 78D)

Sicut de ira prius dixi . . . (f. 79D)

Sic iam, ut dixi, ex definitione primi motus habemus quod est in sensualitate . . . (f. 78A)

This is sufficient to disprove Pelster's claim that Richard must be the author of this question. Unfortunately it is impossible to compare the contents, since Richard does not touch upon these issues in his Oxford commentary and does no more than summarize Bonaventure in the abbreviation (V ff. 239D–240A). However, it shows that the problem was of little concern to him, which makes it all the more unlikely that he devoted a special question to it.

The second question alleged to be by Richard Rufus concerns the problem of the nature of the body after the resurrection of the flesh (ff. 110C–112D), commonly called 'De veritate humane nature':

Inc.: Cum certum sit quod nihil aliud resurget nisi veritas humane nature, necessario queritur, quid sic sit veritas humane nature. Et circa hanc questionem notandum quod duplex est opinio, quarum quedam dicit quod caro nutrimentalis sit veritas humane nature, alia quod seminalis, et illa tantum resurget.

Exp.: . . . per quas posset multiplicari ab augmentativa anime rationalis in omnes posteros sine additamento quanti exterioris.

This question, too, was added later, the scribe using a blank at the end of a *pecia*. A corresponding addition was made in the list of contents:

Questio de veritate humane nature Laurentii, secundo. (f. 1B)

Note that in this case the author is named: 'Laurentius'. Pelster explains this away by assuming that the compiler of the index must have made a mistake: the manuscript contains three questions 'De veritate humane nature', one in the original draft (ff. 144B–146D), and two added later, namely that with which we are concerned, attributed to one Lawrence, and a short note on f. 152C–D. But if one takes a good look at the index, it is obvious that the scribe, far from being careless, took great care to separate and distinguish the three questions when he corrected the index to accommodate the two later additions. In the original index he found the entry: 'Questiones tres de veritate humane nature' (f.1B) which referred to the question on ff. 144B–146D. To distinguish this entry from the two he was going to make he added: 'Alexandri'. Then he proceeded to make his own additions: 'Questio de veritate humane nature Laurentii, secundo', stressing the fact that this was a completely different question by giving the name of the author, Lawrence, and also by mentioning that this was a second question on the same subject; and 'Item de veritate humane nature, tertio', referring to the note on f. 152C–D; again he emphasized that the collection contained yet a third question on the same issue. It seems to me unlikely that a scribe who took so much care to amend the index would have been so negligent as to attribute the wrong question to 'Laurentius', the more so since the ascription of the first question to Alexander is absolutely correct.[45]

The internal structure of the question is another counter-indication. It is a crystal-clear argument. First the author gives twenty-eight arguments, all except the first introduced by 'Item', in favour of the first position, then sixteen arguments favouring the second opinion. He chooses the latter position with Bede and the Master of the *Sentences*, and then proceeds to refute all arguments to the contrary one by one, numbering them punctiliously:

Ad illud Eph. iiij[to] . . . (f. 111D)

Ad obiecta commentatoris 4.5.5. (sic) loco . . . (f. 112A)

Similiter potest solvi ad VII. (f. 112A)

Ad XI dicendum dupliciter . . . (f. 112A)

Ad XX dicendum quod ad notitiam philosophorum non perveniat veritas humane nature. (f. 112C)

Such a closely reasoned argument speaks against Richard Rufus. Nor is it likely that we have a *reportatio* of Richard's lectures because of expressions like: 'Ne autem meum estimes quod dixi' (f. 112B). The organizing hand is that of the author, not the reporter.

Finally a word about the relation between the two questions must be added. They cannot have been compiled by the same author. The abundant use of 'nota' and 'notandum' which punctuated the first question is completely absent from this treatise on the glorified body; and the second is far more tightly organized than the first. The conclusion is that in this collection of questions by Alexander of Hales, John of La Rochelle, and Eudes of Châteauroux four questions have been added subsequently on the blank pages, three from the hand of unknown authors ('De sensualitate', 'De vita angelica', 'De veritate humane nature tertio'), one from the hand of Lawrence, a theologian otherwise unknown to us.

[45] The question has been edited in Alexander of Hales, *Quaestiones*, iii. 1284–303.

(v) *London, British Library, MS Royal 8 C. iv (=L)*

210 ff., several hands, thirteenth to fourteenth centuries, a collection of miscellaneous treatises (ff. 2A–156D), bound with a medical collection since the fifteenth century (ff. 157A–209D). Both parts of the manuscript belonged to the Abbey of Bury St Edmunds, as is visible from the pressmarks and from the beginning of the index on f. 1b: 'Liber Sancti Edmundi Regis in quo continentur ...'. They were bound together during the reorganization of the library carried out in the middle of the fifteenth century, probably by John Boston in connection with the construction of a new library building. Lumley bought the manuscript from the abbey, and King James I purchased it from him for the royal collection.[46]

The first part is a haphazard mixture of tracts like Grosseteste's *Templum Domini*, the *Stella Maris* of John of Garland, and three disputed questions of Alexander of Hales, the last of which is the question 'De veritate humane nature' (ff. 100B–103B) also encountered in P ff. 144B–146D.[47] The collection contains two items which are of interest here. The first is a fragment of Richard Rufus's Oxford commentary on the *Sentences* from the beginning of the second book till ii. 8 (ff. 88A–96C):

Inc.:   *Creationem rerum*. A principio dictum est a magistro quod primo tractat de rebus scilicet in primis tribus libris, in quarto de signis ...   (= B f. 103C)

Exp.:   ... Ita enim confortatur eis quodammodo non id existendo sed putando, non quo se imaginem putet, sed omnino illud ipsum. [*Different hand continues*] cuius imaginem secum [?] habet cum ita se aliquod putat tale corpus se esse putat. Et c. 8: 'Hec sensibilia etc'. Idem De Spiritu et Anima cap. 28: 'Anime que in corporibus viventes etc'. Ergo si talis pena iuste a Deo anime peccatrici et diabolo inflicta ut se putent corpora esse erga que prave et illicite afficiebantur, non videtur mirum si penam accipiant ab igne corporali eius presente. (= B f. 120D) propter hoc compoti ... videtur ... Augustinus De ...

The text of this fragment corresponds with the text of B, but there are a few curious points. Most of the original marginal notes have been left out, e.g.

---

[46] For a description of the MS see G. Warner and J. Gilson, *Catalogue of Western Manuscripts in the Old Royal and King's Collections* (4 vols., London, 1921), i. 229–32. Its history was described in E. F. Wilson, *The* Stella Maris *of John Garland* (Cambridge, 1946), pp. 81–2.

[47] All three questions were edited in Alexander of Hales, *Quaestiones*, iii. 1246–316. Garland's *Stella Maris* was edited by Wilson, op. cit., pp. 87–154.

Ante Incarnationem transierunt quinque cyclades. [*marg.*] i.e. 5 circulationes, et dicitur a cyclos quod est circulus.   (B f.107D = L f. 81C)

L leaves out the explanation of the word 'cyclades'. The passages which in B were marked for erasure by a *va—cat* have also been left out, except for one, which in B runs as follows:

Ecce quod [angeli mali] aliquam beatitudinem habuerunt, sed minorem quam boni qui steterunt. Et si queris quantum et quid habuerunt de beatitudine VA respondeo secundum illud supra: nescio, sed in tantum beati, quantum acceperunt de cognitione et amore Dei CAT.
[*marg.*] Responsio huius habetur plane libro de correptione et gratia.   (B f. 113C = L f. 88A)

L leaves out the marginal note, but not the text within the *va—cat*. A third point is that L has some quite substantial additions to the text in the form of marginal notes, some in the hand of the scribe who wrote the main text, some in a different hand.[48] This suggests either that the scribe of the London manuscript had access to a fuller text or that they are comments of a later reader. It is difficult to decide, but the first solution seems the more convincing, although it leaves some other questions unanswered. But the notes seem in the same style and continue the process of thought that was developing in the main text. So, a more complete text of Richard's commentary seems to have circulated, perhaps his original notes, which he had amended for the official edition as it now appears in B but which were used by the two scribes who made these additional notes. This solution becomes even more attractive as we see that some marginal notes in both hands can be found in B. Apparently the two scribes did not want to make remarks, but wanted to provide as good a text as possible.

After the fragment of Richard's commentary the same scribe con-

[48] To take one example, in the main text we find the following argument: 'Item, satis mirum videtur quod dicunt non-esse, quod est pura negatio, et esse de eodem subiecto simul esse vera, cum affirmatio et negatio de nullo eodem simul sint vere, nec [*L* ut] hoc capit intellectus aliquis omnino, scilicet quod de eodem simul affirmatio et negatio' (B f. 104B = L f. 77D). In a marginal note in the same hand as the main text L continues: 'Sed dicet aliquis, simul, quare bene capit intellectus hoc, sed non simul natura. In eodem vero nunc temporis sunt multa prius et posterius secundum naturam. Sed in definitione secunde dictionis cadit tempus, cum dicit simul in eodem tempore et non simul natura et prius natura. Item, si ita iudicanda sunt 2ª dictio per simul natura et prius natura, nequaquam essent aliqua talia 2ª dicta, etiam: homo non est animal rationale, quia hec est prior natura: non est animal, quam ista: est homo. Et hec similiter: non est animal rationale, prior natura quam: est homo. Et tamen hoc falsum est, ergo prioritas nature non est hic consideranda.'

tinues and transcribes the three questions of Alexander of Hales, mentioned before (ff. 96C–103B), and a fourth question, called 'De aureola' (ff. 103C–111C):

Inc.:   Cum aureola debeatur, ut dicitur communiter virginibus, martyribus, doctoribus, primo inquiratur de ea que est virginum, 2° martyrum, 3° doctorum. Et cum aureola sit quedam preeminencia queritur primo an sit, 2° quid sit, 3° in quibus sit. Et videtur primo quod non sit talis preeminentia alia virginum in celo . . .

Exp.:   . . . et hoc posset ecclesie constare, posset eius celebrare meritum. De aureola doctorum alias dicam cum Deus voluerit.

Pelster would ascribe this question to Richard Rufus, he discovers Richard's phraseology throughout.[49] In fact, the question is an excerpt from Richard Fishacre's commentary on the *Sentences* iv. 33, where he introduces several questions on virginity:

Hic de virginitate aliqua dicenda sunt, et primo de habitu, secundo de fructu . . . Sequitur de fructu. Sed cum fructus virginitatis dicatur fructus centesimus, qui dicitur aureola, aureola vero, ut dicitur communiter, debetur virginibus, martyribus et doctoribus, primo hic inquiratur de ea que est virginum, secundo de ea que est martirium [*sic*], 3° de ea que est doctorum. Et cum aureola sit quedam preeminencia primo queritur an sit, secundo quid sit, 3° in quibus sit. Et videtur primo quod non sit aliqua preeminentia virginum in celo . . .   (O f. 447D; Ba f. 316D, text corrupt)

From there the London manuscript follows the text of Fishacre's commentary literally till the end of distinction 33:

. . . et hoc posset ecclesie constare, posset enim celebrare martyrium. De aureola doctorum alias, cum Deus voluerit.   (O f. 456C; Ba f. 324A)

Apparently Fishacre's questions were in demand, it is interesting to see that this question is connected with three questions of Alexander of Hales. This strengthens the claim that As as well might contain a question of Fishacre, although it is a largely Franciscan collection.[50]

[49] Pelster, 'Neue Schriften', p. 258.

[50] In Padua, Biblioteca Antoniana, MS 152 (i + 180 + i ff., several hands of the middle of the 13th c., a collection of disputed questions) there is a question 'De ieiunio' (ff. 175B–180D, 167A–C) which Pelster, 'Cod. 152', pp. 54–5 wants to attribute to Richard Rufus, because he discovers a certain similarity with the question on God's knowledge in As ff. 270C, 276A, ascribed by him to Richard Rufus. I have not been able to see this MS, but if there is a resemblance between the two questions, Richard cannot be the author, because, as we have seen, he is not the author of the question in As. A description of the MS is given in G. Abate and G. Luisetto, *Codici e manoscritti della Biblioteca Antoniana* (Fonti et studi per la storia del Santo a Padova, i–ii, 1975), i. 187–8. See also [Doucet], 'Prolegomena', pp. cxliii–cxliv.

CHAPTER 5

Other Works Ascribed to
Richard Rufus

VARIOUS other writings have been ascribed to Richard Rufus but none of them with plausibility.

(i) *A Commentary on Aristotle's* Metaphysics

An important work often ascribed to Richard Rufus is a commentary on the *Metaphysics*, preserved in four manuscripts scattered all over Europe: Oxford, Rome, Erfurt, and Prague. It is certain, as we shall see in more detail later, that this commentary was extensively used by the author of the Oxford commentary.[1] Its interest is even greater, as it is ascribed to 'magister Ricardus' in the Vatican manuscript. If it were possible to prove that this commentary on the *Metaphysics* was written by the same author as the commentary on the *Sentences*, preserved at Balliol, the ascription of both works to Richard Rufus of Cornwall would be a certainty. But before tackling this question, I shall discuss the manuscripts very briefly.

Vatican City, Bibliotheca Apostolica Vaticana, MS lat. 4538 (= Va)

102 ff., written in several tiny hands of the thirteenth century.

Inc.: Placet nobis etc. [?] parumper disserere de quadam propositione quam dicit Aristoteles in veteri philosophia. Dicit enim quod omnes homines natura scire desiderant. (f. 1A).

Exp.: . . . ad philosophiam non spectat, sed divine scientie que est divina simpliciter. (f. 102C).

This manuscript contains the full commentary and nothing else but the commentary. The only peculiarity to note is that f. 100 is out of place. The reading order is: f. 97–100–98–99–101, as is indicated in the

---

[1] The fundamental article is G. Gal, 'Commentarius in *Metaphysicam* Aristotelis, Cod. Vat. lat. 4538, fons doctrinae Richardi Rufi', *AFH* xliii (1950), 209–42.

margin of f. 100: 'Istud folium debet antecedere duo folia immediate istud folium antecedentia'.

The commentary is ascribed to master Richard three times, twice on f. 1a: 'Super ... scriptum magistri ricardi super ...' now erased and damaged by dampness, and the second: 'Scriptum super metaphysicam magistri ricardi d. ...'. This second ascription is in the same hand as that which adds directions in the margin of the text, such as chapter headings and titles and remarks like the one quoted above. At the end of the text a different hand writes on f. 102C: 'Explicit ... metaphysica magistri ricardi'. This could be the same as the first damaged hand on f. 1. It is impossible to see whether any of these hands corresponds with those in the text, but the rubricator is apparently a contemporary.

Oxford, New College, MS 285 (= Ne)

ii + 251 ff. + ii, a collection of commentaries and questions on several works of Aristotle, written and bound together at the end of the thirteenth or beginning of the fourteenth century.[2]

The questions in this manuscript on *De generatione et corruptione* (ff. 38A–57D), on the *Physics* (ff. 114A–115D), on *De sensu et sensato* (ff. 164A–189B), and on *De memoria et intelligentia* (ff. 189B–193B) have been identified as being Geoffrey of Aspall's.[3]

Aspall was a fellow student of Peckham in Paris or Oxford, he took his MA in 1264, and became Archdeacon of Dublin in 1278. Peckham reproached him for holding too many benefices. He died in 1278.[4] On ff. 14A–27D (damaged) there are abbreviations of several works of Aristotle. These summaries represent the first stage of assimilation of Aristotle's philosophy at Oxford.[5] The Oxford origin of the manuscript is attested by Callus, who calls it a valuable witness to the development of Aristotelianism and the different stages of assimilation of the great philosopher's thought at Oxford.[6]

---

[2] H. Coxe, *Catalogus codicum MSS. Collegii Novi* (Oxford, 1852), p. 99; A. Zimmermann, *Verzeichnis ungedruckter Kommentare zur Metaphysik und Physik des Aristoteles aus der Zeit von etwa 1250–1350* (Studien und Texte zur Geistesgeschichte des Mittelalters, ix, 1971), p. 33.

[3] E. Macrae, 'Geoffrey of Aspall's Commentaries on Aristotle', *Mediaeval and Renaissance Studies*, vi (1968), 102.

[4] Ch. Lohr, 'Medieval Latin Aristotle Commentaries', *Traditio*, xxiv (1968), 150.

[5] D. Callus, 'Introduction of Aristotelian Learning to Oxford', *Proceedings of the British Academy*, xxix (1943), 275–6

[6] Ibid., pp.278–9.

The commentary on the *Metaphysics* is the last work in this manuscript. It is to be found on ff. 194A–251D, written in two different hands (ff. 194A–205D, 206A–251D), both probably English. The incipit is slightly different from Va: '[. . .] liceat parumper disserere de quadam propositione'. There are no indications of the author. The commentary is defective:

ff. 234A–238B   The same text as the Vatican manuscript on books i–iv (α, A–E) of the *Metaphysics* (=Va ff. 1A–44B).

ff. 234–238B   The latter part of the commentary on book xii (Λ), from 'Non sunt nisi substantie separate a materia' (=Va f. 100A) till the end of the book: . . . sed ad theologiam que est divina simpliciter' (=Va f. 102C).

f. 238B–238C   Part of the commentary on book xii, to be inserted just above the end of the whole commentary on f. 238B, indicated by a sign.

ff. 238C–251D   The commentary on book vii (Z) and the beginning of book viii (H). The full text is given till f. 241A (=Va ff. 44B–46C). From there the questions are dropped, and only the exposition of Aristotle's text is given. The text breaks off in the middle of a sentence on f. 251D: '. . . forma autem ultima non dat genus, cum sit imperfectum, sed dat perfectionem et est convertibilis cum re. Per ipsam autem . . . (=Va ff. 46D–69A).

Erfurt, Bibliotheca Amploniana, MS qu. 290

122 ff., a collection of questions on the *Metaphysics* of Aristotle, on his natural philosophy, and several works of Proclus in the Latin translation by William of Moerbeke.[7] The first 45 ff. of the manuscript are in a distinctly English hand, dating from the middle and the latter half of the fourteenth century.

The commentary on the *Metaphysics* is the first work in the collection (ff. 1A–40B): 'Inc. quest. metaphisice. Liceat nobis parumper disserere de quadam propositione quam dicit Aristoteles in veteri philosophia'. The ending is: '. . . expresse significat oppositionem. Epl. quest. super libr. prime philos', is to be found on f. 101D in Va, so that it seems as if the Amplonian text contains almost the whole commentary. The script is, according to the catalogue, very small and pointed, undoubtedly of English origin. In the catalogue of the

---

[7] As I could not lay hands on a microfilm of this MS I had to rely on W. Schum, *Beschreibendes Verzeichnis der Amplonianischen Handschriften-Sammlung zu Erfurt* (Berlin, 1887), p. 530.

Amplonian collection of the year 1412 the commentary is ascribed to Walter Burleigh:

Primo commenta et questiones Burley super metaphisicam Aristotelis et sequitur antiquam translacionem.[8]

This ascription is spurious. Walter Burleigh worked in the first half of the fourteenth century and died in 1343, whereas this commentary must have been finished by 1250, since it was extensively used by Richard Rufus of Cornwall. Besides, in the manuscript itself this mistake has not been made. Where the author is known he is mentioned in the incipit, e.g. on f. 83B: 'Inc. elem. phil. Proc. Concinna sunt quorum', or f. 99B: 'Inc. liber Proc. de f. et pr. ad Theodorum Mechanicum. Conceptus quidem tue anime'.[9] The incipit of the *Metaphysics* commentary is, as we have seen, anonymous.

Prague, Library of the Metropolitan Chapter, MS M. lxxx (=Pr)

162 ff., a collection of disputed questions on several works of Aristotle, some of them probably of English origin. Probably first half of the fourteenth century.[10]

On ff. 42A–89A(?) a collection of questions on Aristotle's *De anima*, beginning with the second book, gathered from the works of several masters. Some of them are ascribed to Adam of Whitby (ff. 43D, 44A, 44C, 46B, 56B), an unknown master, to whom a commentary on *De sensu et sensato* is ascribed.[11] There are also series of questions on the *Meteorologica* (ff. 90A–108C), on *De somno et vigilia* (ff. 109A–131C), *De sensu et sensato* (ff. 131D–137B), and on the *Physics* (ff. 138A–146C), which, according to a note at the end, are by 'Antissiodorensis'.[12] Further unconnected questions on ff. 147A–162B and on f. 32C–D. The questions on ff. 33A–41B could be on the first book of *De anima*. It is extremely difficult to identify the authors of these works, since the manuscript is obviously something like a working copy, and therefore

[8] Ibid., pp. 530, 818.

[9] Ibid., p. 531.

[10] A full description of the MS in A. Podlaha, *Soupis rukopisů knihovny metropolitní kapitoly pražské* (2 vols., Prague, 1910–22), ii. 314.

[11] According to Lohr, 'Commentaries', *Traditio*, xxiii (1967), 324, Adam of Whitby's commentary is preserved in Paris, Bibliothèque nationale, MS Lat. 16149, ff. 62a–67a: 'Quoniam autem de anima—In parte precedente continente librum De anima . . .'.

[12] Neither William of Auxerre, nor the abbreviator of his *Summa Aurea* Herbert of Auxerre, nor the logician Lambert of Auxerre (on whom see Lohr, 'Commentaries', *Traditio*, xxvii (1971), 307) is known to have composed a commentary on Aristotle's *Physics*.

has only the chapter headings of the Latin Aristotle text, and the disputed questions, leaving out all commentary, introductions, and explanations. To trace the authors through a list of incipits is, therefore, hazardous.

The commentary on the *Metaphysics* is on ff. 1A–32B. It is defective: the summaries and explanations of Aristotle's text are omitted; the questions follow immediately after the chapter headings. Besides, the latter half of book v (*Δ*) is omitted, it breaks off with the words: '. . . utrumque autem esset necessarium, si propositio esset indefinita. Sed hec propositio' (Pr f. 13D = Va f. 40D; Ne f. 230B). Book vi (*E*) is wanting completely. Book xii (*Λ*) breaks off almost at the beginning on f. 32B: '. . . sit illud mobile A et ille motus B mobile per (?) prius eo quod movetur combustibile' (= Va f. 95A, wanting in Ne). There is no indication of the author.

The commentary itself is based on the text of Aristotle's *Metaphysics*, as established by Averroes, and translated into Latin, together with Averroes' *Magnus commentarius*, probably by Michael Scotus in the years 1220–30. This is clear from both the incipits of the books and chapters, and from the order of the books, which is the same as in Averroes. The commentary begins with book ii (*α*), followed by the latter half of book i (*A*) from i. 5 (978^{a}9), then books iii (*B*) to x (*I*), followed by book xii (*Λ*), 1–10 (till 1075^{b}11). Books xi (*K*), xiii (*M*), and xiv (*N*) are omitted altogether.[13] The author also used Averroes' commentary to throw light on the many obscure passages in Aristotle's text. It is remarkable that he already regards him as *the* Commentator, e.g. in the treatise on the extent of God's knowledge:

Consequenter querit commentator istam questionem utrum Deus sciat ista causata aut non.   (Va f. 101B, Ne f. 237B)

This also gives us a first rough indication as to the time at which this work was written. Modern scholars now generally agree that Averroes' works were not generally known and used until 1230, and that it took the decade 1230–40 for Averroes to acquire the authority that made him known as the Commentator.[14] Therefore, this commentary cannot have been composed long before 1240. The work must have

---

[13] Aristotle, *Metaphysica. Translatio anonyma sive media*, ed. G. Vuillemin-Diem (Aristoteles Latinus, xxv/2, 1976), p. xii.

[14] F. Van Steenberghen, *Die Philosophie im XIII. Jahrhundert* (Munich etc., 1977), p. 111.

been finished at the very latest by 1250, when it was used by Richard Rufus in his commentary on the *Sentences*. Another indicator of the *terminus a quo* is the fact that the author makes use of Robert Grosseteste's *De libero arbitrio*. He refers to Grosseteste, before quoting him at length as 'vir excellentissimus in scientiis'.[15] Grosseteste probably wrote this work during his years as a lector to the Franciscans from 1229 to 1235.[16]

The author's pious reference to the Bishop of Lincoln also makes it quite clear that the commentary originated in Oxford. If on the one hand the author uses Grosseteste's works, and on the other he is used by an Oxford Franciscan in the year 1250, one may safely assume that Oxford is the place to seek the author.

It must be one of the earliest commentaries on the *Metaphysics*, and as such it is quite an original enterprise, since it is well organized, very elaborate, and by no means completely dependent on Averroes' work. The author follows the same procedure throughout. First he clarifies some words or terms, then he gives a summary and explanation of Aristotle's argument, and finally discusses his own questions. For the time this work was written this must be considered a highly modern procedure. The older tradition, copied from Avicenna, was to follow Aristotle rather loosely, and to compose in fact more or less a treatise of one's own, as e.g. John Blund's treatise *De anima*, written at the beginning of the century.[17] In the 1230s more modern philosophers began to follow the example of Averroes, and follow the text of Aristotle very closely, glossing it. And it was even later that they began to add their own questions to it, which implied a departure from Averroes' method as well as from Aristotle's. Averroes' commentaries never take the form of disputed questions.[18] If this is true, then the present work represents a very early example of a mature commentary on one of Aristotle's most difficult and puzzling books. The question who the author can be becomes all the more pressing.

The first thing to ask in this connection is whether the author of this commentary and the author of the commentary on the *Sentences*

---

[15] Gal, 'Commentarius', p. 228; D. Callus, 'The Subject-Matter of Metaphysics According to Some Thirteenth-Century Oxford Masters', in P. Wilpert (ed.), *Die Metaphysik im Mittelalter* (Miscellanea mediaevalia, ii, 1963), p. 393.

[16] D. Callus, 'Robert Grosseteste as Scholar', in id. (ed.) *Robert Grosseteste, Scholar and Bishop* (Oxford, 1955), pp. 28–9.

[17] John Blund, *Tractatus de anima*, ed. D. Callus and R. W. Hunt (Auctores Britannici Medii Aevi, ii, 1970), p. xi.

[18] Callus, 'Introduction', pp. 264–5.

preserved in Balliol can be the same. The latter uses the former extensively and, moreover, there is a fair chance that both are called Richard. As we saw, Richard Rufus of Cornwall is the author of the commentary on the *Sentences*, and there is no reason to assume in advance that the ascription of the *Metaphysics* commentary in Va is spurious, since it is contemporary. Gal has discussed the whole problem extensively. He shows that the author of the Balliol commentary uses the *Metaphysics* commentary on various questions, such as the nature of truth and its relation to being, the soul, the eternity of the world, and *scientia Dei*. He comes to the conclusion that the authors are different, and argues that the *Metaphysics* commentary was written by a master Robert, since the author uses this particular name as an example to illustrate a point on the nature of definitions. He does not explain why he considers the ascription to Richard to be spurious. Finally, he rejects the possibility of Robert Kilwardby as the author, because of the differences in doctrine and form.[19] In two later articles he has partly withdrawn from these firm conclusions, and he now allows for the possibility that they are the same after all, although he gives no reasons for his doubts.[20] Another enquiry is necessary.

A very clear example of the relation between the two works is the question on God's knowledge, and more in particular the question, elicited by Aristotle's remarks in book xii of the *Metaphysics*, whether God knows anything outside himself. It is generally agreed that, although there remain difficulties of interpretation, Aristotle answered the question in the negative.[21] This was unacceptable in a Christian concept of God. The God emerging from Scripture is someone who knows man more intimately than man knows himself. So, from the moment the *Metaphysics* became part of general knowledge, any theologian had to handle the challenge somehow.

The commentator on the *Metaphysics* first tackles the question, whether God really understands anything but himself, and he comes to the conclusion that he does. This leaves him with the problem of proving that, despite the fact that God knows other things beside himself, this does not imply multiplicity in God. Much of the ensuing argument copied is by Richard Rufus in his struggle to come to grips with the same questions:

---

[19] Gal, 'Commentarius', pp. 230–1.
[20] Gal, 'Viae', p. 177 n. 5: id., 'Opiniones', p. 137 n. 5.
[21] D. Ross, *Aristotle* (5th edn., London, 1956), pp. 183–4.

B

Metaphysics Commentary

Postea queritur illud quod ponunt philosophi, scilicet an Deus intelligat aliud a se aut non.

. . .

Ad oppositum. Dicunt isti philosophi quod in separatis a materia idem est intellectus et quod intelligitur. Ergo Deus non intelligit aliud a se. Et iterum in Deo intelligere est sua substantia etc. Item si intelligit aliud a se, ergo quodcumque aliud a se, ergo intellectus Dei perficitur per quodcumque intellectum ab ipso. Intellectus enim qui aliud a se intelligit sua substantia transmutatur in aliud, ut dicunt, hoc est: recipit aliud in se, et illud aliud est forma seu perfectio eius recipientis. Multi nituntur philosophi in hac sententia et opponunt, ut videtur, subtilius, si hic cum Deus intelligit hominem et lapidem etc.

. . .

Si intelligit aliud a se per se qua ratione unum aliud et quelibet intelligit, ergo quecumque aliud a se, eius igitur intellectus perficitur per quecumque: ergo eius intellectus transmutatur in aliud . . . Intellectus enim qui intelligit aliud a sua substantia transmutatur in aliud, hoc est: recipit aliud et illud aliud est forma et perfectio eius. Quod falsum est de suo intellectu.   (Ne f. 236B; Va f. 99B)

Istud, ut dixi, multis modis conantur astruere et defendere, dicentes quod sit fallacia accidentis cum sic arguitur: Deus intelligit album in quantum album et nigrum in quantum nigrum una et indivisa intellectione.

. . .

Ad argumentum oppositum: Dicendum quod quamvis intelligat album in quantum album et nigrum in quantum nigrum, et album et nigrum sint diversa inter se et ab ipso, quia tamen una et eadem intellectione ista intelligit, non sequitur quod intelligit aliud a se sive diversa. Sed fallacia accidentis sic: album in quantum album intelligit et nigrum in quantum nigrum et ista una et indivisa intellectione. Sed ista sunt diversa inter se et ab ipso. Ergo ista in quantum diversa inter se et ab ipso, una intellectione intelligit.

Et ista sunt diversa inter se et etiam a Deo. Ergo ista, in quantum diversa sunt inter se et ab ipso, una et eadem intellectione intelligit.

   Et est simile argumentum: una et eadem intellectione intelligit Deus hominem et asinum. Sed homo et asinus est aliud et aliud. Ergo una et

   Et est simile argumentum [*Only in Va* quartum]: una et eadem intellectione intelligit hominem et asinum. Sed homo et asinus sunt aliud et

eadem intellectione intelligit aliud et aliud. Et dicunt quod hec propositio est impossibilis: una intellectione intelligit aliud et aliud. Hec tamen vera: una intellectione intelligit hominem et asinum.

Quod non satis intelligo. Nam alia est ratio hominis et alia asini in mente divina. Unde et alia idea, sicut ait Augustinus 83 questione 46: 'Restat ut omnia ratione sint condita nec eadem ratione homo quam equus. Hoc enim est absurdum estimare'.[22] Dicam ergo, ut videtur contra philosophos, quod cum Deus ratione alia et alia, idea alia et alia hominem condidit et asinum, et alia et alia ratione et idea hominem intelligit et asinum et tunc si alia specie et alia intelligit hoc et illud, aliud et aliud intelligit. Nam secundum hoc habetur et alietas obiectorum et suo modo alietas eorum per que intelliguntur. (f. 78A) Nescio ergo quid intelligunt, cum dicunt una et eadem intellectione. Nam ratio sive idea alia et alia est, et obiecta alia et alia sunt inter se et ab ipso intelligente. Nescio ergo quomodo non aliud a se intelligat et alia inter se.   (ff. 77D–78A)

aliud, ergo una et eadem intellectione intelligit aliud et aliud. Hec enim propositio est impossibilis: una intellectione intelligit aliud et aliud. Hec autem vera: una intellectione in(Va f. 101B)telligit hominem et asinum. Ista enim in ratione in qua sunt intelligibilia ab ipso, non sunt aliud et aliud. (Ne f. 237A; Va f. 101A–B)

From the quotations it is clear that Richard Rufus wishes to create as much distance as possible between the *philosophi* and his own opinions: 'Dicunt isti philosophi ..., Multi nituntur philosophi in hac sententia ..., Istud, ut dixi, multis modis conantur astruere et defendere.' Such are the introductions to extensive quotations from the *Metaphysics* commentary. The opposition becomes particularly clear where he says: 'Et dicunt quod hec propositio est impossibilis ... Quod non satis intelligo', and further on: 'Nescio ergo quid intelligunt, cum dicunt una et eadem intellectione.' Even if we allow for development of thought, it is impossible that the same man who wrote

---

[22] Augustine, *De diversis quaestionibus lxxxiii*, xlvi. 2, ed. A. Mutzenbecher (CC xlivA, 1975), p. 72.

the commentary on the *Metaphysics* should have to admit a few years later that he does not understand his own thoughts any more. They must be two different authors. In fact, Richard Rufus distances himself as far as possible from the philosophers, refutes the solutions proposed in the *Metaphysics* commentary point by point, and asserts traditional Christian doctrine in quite forceful terms against Aristotelian novelties: 'Videtur mihi quod sane possit concedi quod Deus intelligit aliud a se; nec video sanctos istam negare, sed vel eam supponere, vel in ea vim constituere' (f. 78B); the saints do not argue the point, they believe, and Richard follows them.

The same opposition between the two authors can be seen in the question on creation. The commentary on the *Metaphysics* is quoted repeatedly, but always introduced with the same sort of formulae: '. . . alia difficultas que hic solet induci talis' (f. 104C). Quoting from an answer of the Commentator on the *Metaphysics* on the eternity of the world our friar says: 'Hic respondetur . . . Isti responsioni hucusque consentio. Sed isti idem addunt aliquid de subtili quod non verum esse intelligo' (f. 104A) and in the margin here is written: 'Cavillo'.

In three other important questions on the nature of truth and its relation to being, on the infinity of causality, and on seminal principles, there is no similarity in treatment whatsoever, although certainly the first two questions are problems only for someone who has been confronted with Aristotelian philosophy.

Moreover, if Richard Rufus is the author of the Balliol commentary, then the dates do not fit. Richard Rufus studied arts in Paris till 1238, and then entered the Franciscan order. Therefore, if he is the writer of the *Metaphysics* commentary as well, he must have written it as a Franciscan, which seems unlikely in view of the position of the early Franciscans on studying philosophy for its own sake. However, the decisive argument against identification of the two writers is the impossibility of envisaging a man saying in one of his later works that he no longer understands the arguments that he put forward in an earlier work.

Is it possible to say something more positive about the author? Most probably he was a Master of Arts of the university of Oxford, or at least spent much time there, both because of his acquaintance with the treatise of Grosseteste and the later quotations from his work in an Oxford commentary on the *Sentences*. Early Oxford scholars known to have written commentaries on the *Metaphysics* are Geoffrey of Aspall, Adam of Bocfeld, and Roger Bacon. Their works have survived and are very different from this commentary. So, unless they went over the same text twice, they must be discounted.[23] Robert Kilwardby studied arts in Paris till 1245 and, while at Oxford, studied only theology.[24] Could he be the elusive Adam of Whitby, whose name appears in Pr, as the author of questions on *De anima*? We cannot tell.

Another obvious candidate is Richard Fishacre, certainly if the ascription in Va is anything to go by. This, too, is highly unlikely, first of all, because the sort of questions Fishacre deals with in his commentary on the *Sentences* are very much in the traditional mould, and do not betray any very extensive reflection on Aristotle's thought in general, nor on the *Metaphysics* in particular. For instance in the problem of God's knowledge he only deals with the usual questions of direct theological significance, about predestination and reprobation, how God knows good and evil, how God knows created things through their existence in him as ideas.[25] The new problem, raised by Aristotle, whether God knows anything at all outside himself, is not discussed. Secondly, Fishacre's mode of proceeding, as seen in his commentary on the *Sentences*, is very different from the method followed in this philosophical treatise. Before starting out, Fishacre gives a short survey of the questions he is going to treat, and what their order and mutual dependance is.

A beautiful example of Fishacre's neatness is the treatise on ideas:

Queritur de existentia omnium in Deo. Et quia omnia sunt aut complexa aut incomplexa, primo queritur de incomplexis, secundo de complexis. Et quia omnia incomplexa sunt aut bona aut mala, primo queritur de existentia bonorum in Deo, secundo malorum. Et quia omnis creatura Dei bona, creatura autem communiter sumpta dividitur in substantiam et accidens, primo queritur de existentia substantiarum in Deo, demum accidentium. Et quia substantia dividitur in materiam et formam et compositum, queritur primo de materia, secundo de forma, tertio de composito, 4° de accidentibus, 5° de malo, 6° de complexis.   (Ba f. 62B; f. 93A)

The commentary on the *Metaphysics* is far less methodical and much

---

[23] On Aspall's commentary on the *Metaphysics* see Macrae, 'Geoffrey of Aspall', p. 112; on Adam of Bocfeld's see Lohr, 'Commentaries', *Traditio*, xxii (1967), 318; on Roger Bacon's questions on the *Metaphysics* see Lohr, 'Commentaries', *Traditio*, xxix (1973), 117–19.

[24] The commentary on the *Metaphysics* assigned to Robert by Gal, 'Robert Kilwardby's Questions on the *Metaphysics* and *Physics* of Aristotle', *FS* xiii (1953), 9–16, is probably Aspall's, according to Macrae, 'Geoffrey of Aspall', pp. 109–11.

[25] In particular the treatise on predestination and reprobation is extraordinarily long: Ba ff. 67C–70A, 70D–71C; O ff. 101A–104D, 106B–107B.

more rambling. Most sequences of questions do not seem to follow a coherent pattern. Therefore, provisionally the commentary can only be assigned to an Oxford Master of Arts, probably named Richard.

(ii) *A Paris University Sermon*

University sermons were important acts of corporate worship in medieval universities. Many of them have been preserved in manuscript form, like the collection of sermons preached for the University of Paris in the academic year 1230/1. One sermon in that collection has been attributed to Richard Rufus.

Paris, Bibliothèque nationale, MS Nouv. acq. lat. 338

260 ff., one hand of the first half of the thirteenth century, a collection of 84 sermons preached for the members of the University of Paris in the academic year 1230/1 by several masters like Eudes of Châteauroux, Guiard of Laon, William of Auvergne, Bishop of Paris, Philip the Chancellor, John of Saint-Gilles OP, and Gregory of Naples OFM.[26] The first sermon in the collection was preached at the feast of Mary's Nativity (8 September 1230) by Master Eudes of Châteauroux, the last at the feast of the Decollation of John the Baptist (29 August 1231) by Master Guiard of Laon. The MS is not the original but a later copy. A few folios are missing at the end; the last sermon is incomplete. It used to belong to the abbey of Cluny. The author must have been a clerk, commissioned by the university to keep notes of all the sermons, as all the sermons are summaries, *reportationes*.[27]

Several sermons of this cycle were preached by friars, such as the one for the feast of St Nicholas (6 December 1230), 'fratris Ricardi de ordine fratrum minorum' (f. 51B). Davy assumes that this Richard must have been Richard Rufus, without giving any reasons for this attribution. The only problem she sees is that according to the best biographical data available to her, Richard did not enter the order before 1238. This crucial date is taken from Eccleston, who writes that Richard entered 'eo tempore quo frater Helias totum turbavit ordinem'. This is an ambiguous statement which could refer to the

---

[26] For a description of the MS see Davy, *Sermons universitaires*, p. 10; Samaran–Marichal, *Catalogue*, iv. 1: *Bibliothèque nationale, fonds latin (supplément), nouvelles acquisitions latines, petits fonds divers* (Paris, 1981), p. 71. A list of the sermons with author, occasion, and place in Davy, pp. 3–6, a list of incipits, pp. 7–10.

[27] Davy, *Sermons universitaires*, p. 21.

year 1230 as well as to 1238, as we saw in the first chapter.[28] If, for a moment, we assume that Richard entered in 1230, he must have preached his university sermon as a novice.[29]

Although in itself there is nothing against novices preaching, in this case it is clear that the university had chosen more experienced men. Most of the other clerics, who had been selected, were men well advanced in years and, even more important, well advanced in their careers. One sermon was preached by the Bishop of Paris himself, another by Philip, chancellor of the university of Paris; then there were masters of theology like Eudes of Châteauroux and Guiard of Laon, both canons in the early 1230s; Guiard was elected Bishop of Cambrai in 1238, and in 1244 Eudes was created Cardinal-Bishop of Tusculum. The Dominican John of Saint-Gilles was a doctor of medicine of some standing and had incepted in theology a few years before; Gregory of Naples was Provincial of France at the time and one of the top men of the Franciscan order.

There is a gap between the Richard Rufus who takes his place among the ecclesiastical dignitaries of Paris in 1230 and the Richard Rufus who lectures on the *Sentences* at Oxford in 1250. Either he was of their age and weight, a master of theology at the very least, and then it is hardly possible that a man who had held such a pre-eminent position in Paris in 1230, kept silent for twenty years, while his contemporaries were mounting the steps of the hierarchical ladder, only to reappear on the stage as a lecturer on the *Sentences*, a task for beginners. Or he was a very young Franciscan in 1230, and then he does not belong in the company of the Bishop and the chancellor at all. I simply cannot imagine that university preachers were selected from among the young novices of a comparatively new and contested order, anxious to establish its reputation, the more so, since all the others, as far as their names are known, were typical establishment men. Therefore, Friar Richard, the university preacher of Paris in 1230, and Richard Rufus, lecturer on the *Sentences* at Oxford in 1250, cannot be the same man.[30]

[28] Eccleston, *De adventu*, xi (ed. Little, p. 51). See also above, p. 3.

[29] Davy, *Sermons universitaires*, p. 142 argues that Richard must have entered long before 1238, because in 1239 he became a member of a commission of four, charged by the General, Haymo of Faversham, to prepare a document on the binding interpretation of the rule. In fact, Richard was never on that commission; it was 'Rigaldus' not 'Ricardus', see Little, 'Franciscan School', p. 841 n. 11.

[30] J. B. Schneyer, *Repertorium der lateinischen Sermones des Mittelalters für die Zeit von 1150—1350, (Autoren R—Schluss)* (BGPhThMA xliii/5, 1973), 150, attributes another

(iii) *A Collection of Logical* Abstractiones

Recent research on the achievements of medieval logicians has unearthed many new texts and treatises. Many of them are anonymous, and strenous efforts have been made to attach names to them. Such a text is the collection of 282 propositions called in some manuscripts 'Abstractiones magistri Ricardi Sophiste'. De Rijk, who first drew attention to this text, was inclined to attribute it to Richard Fishacre.[31] More recently Pinborg has wondered whether this unknown sophist could be Richard Rufus. The logical tenets defended in the *Abstractiones* are very much like the errors of which Roger Bacon in his *Compendium* accuses Richard Rufus.[32] The *Abstractiones* have been handed down to us in six manuscripts, of which two have the complete text.

Oxford, Bodleian Library, MS Digby 24 (=D)

ii + 105 ff. + ii, consisting of two parts of unequal size, which, as in so many manuscripts of the Digby collection, originally did not belong together. The first part consists of ff. 1–16 in 16mo, and has to be inserted into Di before f. 80. It contains the greatest part of William of Montoriel's *Summa predicamentorum*, the rest of which can be found in Di.[33] The second part consists of ff. 17–105 in small quarto, written in

sermon, preserved in Cambridge, Pembroke College, MS 87 ff. 217b–220b, to Richard Rufus, probably on the strength of the ascription of the sermon at the end on f. 220b: 'Frater Ricardus permissione divina abbas de Sancto Eadmundo dilectis sibi'. (M. R. James, *A Descriptive Catalogue of the Manuscripts in the Library of Pembroke College, Cambridge* (Cambridge, 1905), p. 80, has mistakenly: '... dilectis situ'.) The ascription of the sermon to Abbot Richard, however, need not be in doubt. The sermon is clearly aimed at monks: 'In isto labore estis vos constituti ieiuniis, vigiliis et orationibus peccata preterita expiantes' (f. 217b). The preacher seems to be a member of the community: 'Nos igitur, quia vincimus animal nostri generis, id est mundum, pro tanta victoria cum omni diligentia laudare Deum debemus' (f. 218a). There were two abbots called Richard at Bury St Edmunds: the twelfth abbot (formerly abbot of Barton), 1229–34, and Richard of Draughton, 1312–35. As paleographical evidence suggests that this copy of the sermon was written in the late thirteenth century, the first Richard is the more likely candidate for the authorship.

[31] L. de Rijk, *Logica modernorum* (Assen, 1962–7), ii/1. 71–2.

[32] Pinborg, 'Magister abstractionum', pp. 3–4. Tending to the same conclusion: O. Lewry, 'Grammar, Logic and Rhetoric 1220–1320', in J. Catto (ed.), *Early Oxford Schools*, pp. 417, 422, and A. de Libera, 'La littérature des *abstractiones* et la tradition logique d'Oxford', in O. Lewry (ed.), *The Rise of British Logic* (Papers in Mediaeval Studies, vii, 1985), pp. 97–9. The team of editors now working on a critical edition of the *Abstractiones*, under the direction of P. A. Streveler and S. Ebbesen, is convinced that it is a work of Richard Rufus. I shall explain my doubts after discussing the MSS.

[33] De Rijk, *Logica*, ii/1. 59–60.

different hands of the thirteenth and fourteenth centuries. It contains several writings of a logical nature.[34]

The list of propositions, called *Abstractiones*, is to be found on ff. 61A–90B, written in a later thirteenth century English hand.[35]

Inc.: Nulla est affirmatio in qua universale universaliter sumptum predicatur, ut dicit Aristoteles. Et hoc potest esse dupliciter: aut quod non predicatur universale sumptum universaliter, aut quod falsa sit affirmatio in qua universale sic se habens predicatur . . .

Exp.: . . . in prima enim sumitur esse ut nunc, in secunda esse habitudinis sive consequentie et ita equivocatur esse.

> Expliciunt ista que tu, Ricarde sophista,
> fecisti, morum flos et doctor logicorum.
> Dirige scribentis, Spiritus alme, manum.
> Expliciunt Abstractiones.

Bruges, Bibliothèque publique de la ville, MS 497

i + 95 ff., several hands of the thirteenth and fourteenth centuries, a collection of logical works, containing among other works the *Summa logice* of William of Ockham (ff. 1A–40B). The *Abstractiones* can be found on ff. 74A–95C, written in a thirteenth-century hand. The incipit is the same as in D, the ending is slightly different:

Exp.: . . . habitudinis sive consequentie et ita equivocatur esse. Expliciunt abstractiones magistri Ricardi sophiste.

> Expliciunt ista que tu, Ricarde sophista,
> fecisti, morum vir doctus, flos logicorum.[36]

Spade attributes the treatise, despite the last lines, to William Heytesbury, the fourteenth-century logician.[37] Paleographical evidence, however, shows that this cannot be maintained. Heytesbury lived from about 1313 till 1372/3, whereas most of the manuscripts of our treatise

---

[34] For a fuller description and a summary of all works see ibid. ii/1. 59–62, 73–6.

[35] Compare with S. H. Thomson, *Latin Bookhands of the Later Middle Ages, 1100–1500* (Cambridge, 1969), no. 95. The looped S at the end of a word and the extravagantly split R are typical.

[36] A. De Poorter, *Catalogue des manuscrits de la bibliothèque publique de la ville de Bruges* (Catalogue général des manuscrits des bibliothèques de Belgique, ii, 1934), pp. 578–80.

[37] P. Spade, 'Robertus Fland's *Consequentiae*: An Edition', *MS* xxxviii (1976), 54 n. 4. His opinion is founded on a reference in C. Wilson, *William Heytesbury: Medieval Logic and the Rise of Mathematical Physics* (Publications in Medieval Science, iii, 1956), p. 207, where it is called a doubtful work of Heytesbury.

are late thirteenth century.[38] The treatise apparently was printed in 1495 in Bologna by Benedictus Hectoris.[39]

Oxford, Bodleian Library, MS Digby 2 (= Di)

ii + 152 ff. + ii, written in different hands all dating from the second half of the thirteenth century. It contains several works on a wide variety of subjects, theological, philosophical, grammatical, and astronomical.[40] The collection can be dated to the early 1280s, and is probably of Franciscan origin, since the *natalis* of Francis has been included in the calendar. According to Dr O. Lewry the miscellany reflects the interests of the Greyfriars' *studium* and the largely anonymous world of mid-thirteenth-century Oxford.[41] The *Abstractiones* can be found on ff. 123A–140B, preceded by a drawing of the tree of Porphyry on f. 122A. The script is late-thirteenth-century English. The incipit is the same as in D; the text breaks off in f. 140B in the middle of the sophism: 'Omnis homo est et quilibet videns illum est asinus':[42]

Exp.: ... et sensus omnis homo est et quilibet videns illum sit.   (= D f. 63D; C f. 208C (338C))

This ending cannot be found in exactly the same words in D and C; the textual traditions apparently vary slightly.

Paris, Bibliothèque nationale, MS. lat. 14069

204 ff., written in different hands, dating from the thirteenth or fourteenth centuries. It contains a very mixed collection of texts such as the *Compotus* of John of Garland and a calendar for the year 1407. The manuscript comes from the abbey of Saint-Germain-des-Prés.[43] The *Abstractiones* are on ff. 26A–33A under the title *De dialectici tricis*, a title added by a seventeenth-century hand. The work is incomplete.[44]

[38] The data for Heytesbury's life in J. Weisheipl, 'Repertorium Mertonense', *MS* xxxi (1969), 212.

[39] Spade, *Consequentiae*, p. 54 n. 4.

[40] A fuller description in de Rijk, *Logica*, ii/1. 55–9.

[41] O. Lewry, 'The Miscellaneous and the Anonymous: William of Montoriel, Roger Bourth and the Bodleian MS. Digby 2', *Manuscripta*, xxiv (1980), 75. See also A. de la Mare and B. Barker-Benfield (eds.), *Manuscripts at Oxford* (Oxford, 1980), p. 119.

[42] De Rijk, *Logica*, ii/1. 63, sophism 28.

[43] A fuller description of the MS in de Rijk, *Logica*, ii/1. 84–5; Samaran and Marichal, *Catalogue*, iii. 355.

[44] De Rijk, *Logica*, ii/1. 71.

Oxford, Corpus Christi College, MS 293B (= C)

227 ff., written in several hands of the thirteenth and fourteenth centuries. It contains a miscellaneous collection of works on philosophical and logical, scientific and theological topics. After the publication of Coxe's catalogue CCC MS 293 was divided into two in 1910, and now consists of two volumes,[45] of which this is the second, it has been refoliated, though references are still made to the former foliation. Some parts of the MS come from Dr. John Dee's library, and are described in the 1583 catalogue as separate items. They must have been bound together later on.[46] The *Abstractiones* can be found on ff. 207A–215D (= ff. 337A–345D). It is an incomplete copy, breaking off in the sophism: 'Sortes decipitur nisi decipiatur'.[47] The *incipit* is the same as in all other copies; the ending is as follows:

Exp.: ... Item credat Sortes decipi et proponatur sic: Sortes decipitur nisi decipiatur. Et probatur sic: Sortes credit se decipi et illud est falsum, nisi decipiatur, ergo credit [*catchword*:] falsum nisi decipiatur et qui credit. (= D f. 74B)

The script is English, second half of the thirteenth century, most probably before 1280.[48] There is no indication of the author. The whole text has been corrected and added to from another and apparently better copy.

The text of C seems fuller than the one found in D. One example may show this (the words between brackets are only to be found in C):

Omnis homo est totum in quantitate. (Probatio et improbatio que prius). Et solvendum est distinguendo. Est enim multiplex secundum equivocationem, quia omnis est equivocatio ad ista duo: scilicet ad quodlibet singulare huius termini 'homo' et ad totum respectu singularium (huius termini 'homo'). Cuius multiplicitas est in hoc quod dicitur 'totum' quia secundum unam significationem (significat idem quod quelibet pars et secundum alteram) idem quod completum ex partibus secundum quod 'omnis' significat illud totum respectu singularium huius termini 'homo'. (C f. 207A; D f. 61A)

Of the three Oxford manuscripts, this one is by far the most legible, and perhaps the most reliable.

---

[45] In the copy of H. Coxe, *Catalogus codicum MSS. Collegii Corporis Christi* (Oxford, 1852), p. 128, kept in Duke Humfrey's Library, the rebinding has been duly recorded.

[46] M. R. James, *Lists of Manuscripts Formerly Owned by Dr. John Dee* (Transactions of the Bibliographical Society, Supplements, i, 1921), 20, 28.

[47] De Rijk, *Logica*, ii.1. 66, sophism 131.

[48] Richard Rouse helped me in fixing the date.

London, British Library, MS Royal 12 F. xix

187 ff., written in different hands from the second half of the thirteenth century. The manuscript belonged to Reading abbey and contains treatises on logic by Walter Burleigh, arithmetical works, a eulogy on Aristotle, a compendium of Aristotle's *Organon*, and other similar works. The *Abstractiones* are to be found on ff. 112C–115B. The text is incomplete and slightly different from D, Di, and C. On the one hand it is a summary of the first 54 propositions,[49] but it seems also slightly more extensive than either of the other versions. Thus the introduction is much longer.

Nulla est affirmatio in qua universale universaliter predicatur, ut habetur ab Aristotele in primo peri Hermeneias. Hec auctoritas communiter glossatur sic: Nulla est propositio affirmativa vera in qua universale etc. . . .

After the last sophism, which is also discussed in other versions: 'Isti sciunt septem artes' (Cf. 210D; D f. 67A), the text continues with a discussion of a sophism not to be found in the other variants: 'Omnis anima est in te', which ends thus:

. . . Sequitur enim 'Omnis anima est in te', ergo anima vegetativa est in te et anima sensitiva et anima intellectiva. Omne quod est verum est verum in hoc oppositi (?).

The work itself is a collection of propositions, each of which represent a logical trap. Several propositions are grouped together under one heading, e.g. sophisma 71–8 are all concerned with the use of *totus* as a logical sign:[50]

'Totus' differt a signis precedentibus eo quod distribuit inter partes integrales et ita inter partes subiectivas. 'Totum' enim idem est quam quelibet pars; est enim equivocum ad illa duo: quelibet pars et perfectum ex partibus, et per distinctionem unius solvitur hoc sophisma: Totus Sortes est minor Sorte. (C f. 212A; D f. 68D)

So far Richard Fishacre and Richard Rufus have been mentioned as possible authors. I agree with Pinborg that it is very unlikely that Richard Fishacre is the author of this piece of logical nitpicking. Fishacre is basically an old-fashioned theologian, not much given to extensive discussions on the nature and the possibilities of language. The authorship of Richard Rufus cannot be so easily dismissed.

[49] Ibid., ii/1. 62–4.
[50] Ibid., ii/1. 64.

The argument of Pinborg and Libera that the treatise shows the same logical presuppositions as the errors denounced by Roger Bacon is inconclusive. I have shown in the second chapter that the denounced logical positions were very common, not at all peculiar to Richard Rufus, and that Bacon was aware of the fact, in the *Compendium* he is attacking a whole number of scholars, not just Richard Rufus, although he singles him out for special treatment. The fact remains, however, that this is a logical treatise of English origin, written before the middle of the thirteenth century by a man called Richard.[51]

Whether it is Richard Rufus is not easy to decide. The first problem is that treatises on logic carry their own style, moulded by the rather severe subject they are dealing with. The reader is introduced into a field where cool reasoning and sharp argumentation reign supreme, where objectivity is the ultimate aim. Medieval authors would strive after that aim by assuming a style as strictly neutral as possible, for lack of convenient logical symbols. And they succeeded. There is a curiously unhistorical air about these works; they seem timeless. They neither bear rhetorical exclamations, nor emotional appeals to the reader, nor tormented hesitations. And these are exactly the things whereby we can recognize Richard Rufus in his other writings very easily. But in a logical treatise one would expect him to strike a rather different note.

Therefore, the only way to see whether he is the author is to look for parallels or for a marked preference for logical arguments in his commentaries. On the whole he seems to be well aware of the great value of logic in theological propositions and of the confusion which can arise from logical fallacies. In one of the introductory questions of the Oxford commentary he tries to find his way out of a sticky problem by pointing out that one of the terms under discussion can have two *supposita*, that it can refer to two different things (B f. 12A). In both commentaries a long discussion on the nature of propositions is attached to the question whether God knows not only things (*incomplexa*), but also states of affairs (*enuntiabilia*); here Richard shows himself familiar with terms like *significatio*, *suppositio*, and *appellatio* (B f. 78C–D; V ff. 110C–112C). And in the question whether Christ can be called a man between his death and the Resurrection, Richard shows himself well aware of the logical problem this question involves, as we have seen before, even though Bacon does not like his

---

[51] Pinborg, 'Magister abstractionum', p. 1.

answer. But all this does not point to this collection of sophisma, but rather to a treatise *De modis significandi*. Neither can I find exact parallels between the *Abstractiones* and Richard's commentaries.

My further impression is that the subject that really excites Richard is not logic, but natural philosophy: the theory of change, of motion, the nature of time, are problems that he enjoys and picks up wherever he can (e.g. B ff. 85C–86B; 103D–106B; 144A–D). My guess is that Aristotle's *libri naturales* have far more appeal for him than his methodological works. Although Richard shows himself aware of logical problems, he is not a logician.

Moreover, the supply of Richards at Oxford before the middle of the thirteenth century is not exhausted with Richard Fishacre and Richard Rufus. We have seen before that there exists a commentary on the *Metaphysics* of English origin, most probably written by a Master Richard. It could be that this Richard is the same person as 'Ricardus sophista', the author of the *Abstractiones*. Because of all of these positive and negative reasons, I am unwilling to attribute the *Abstractiones* to Richard Rufus, at least for the time being.

(iv) *Conclusion*

At the end of this critical survey of all the writings attributed to Richard Rufus by various scholars, it is perhaps useful to recapitulate all those works which are without doubt authentic and the manuscripts in which they can be found.

Oxford commentary on the Sentences (before 1251)

i–iii	Oxford, Balliol College, MS 62	
ii. 1–8	London, BL MS Royal 8 C. iv	ff. 88A–96C

Abbreviation of Bonaventure's commentary on the Sentences (after 1256)

i–ii	Vat. City, Bibl. Ap. Vat., MS Vat lat. 12293	
i. 1–4	Vat. City, Bibl. Ap. Vat., MS Borghese 362	ff. 97a–104b
i, ii. 1–13	Berlin (W), Staatsbibl. Pr. K., MS th. qu. 48	ff. 87C–178D
iii. 1–20, iv. 1–25	Assisi, Bibl. com., MS 176	

Disputed Questions (before 1250)

On the divine intellect	Assisi, Bibl. com., MS 138	ff. 262C–263A
On the composition of angels		ff. 263A–264C
On man's state in heaven		ff. 268A–270B
On the acquisition of knowledge		ff. 292A–D
On the moment of change	Toulouse, Bibl. mun., MS 737	ff. 158A–C

On seminal principles   ff. 158C–160B

Treatise on the existence of God and the properties of the human soul (before 1250)
                    Assisi, bibl. com., MS 138   ff. 277C–285A

Even a summary like this tells us a lot about Richard's interests. Commentaries on the Bible are conspicuously absent. The philosophical bias is strong, which may have something to do with the fact that he taught young Franciscans who had little knowledge of philosophy, but it also reflected his own interest, if the enthusiasm with which he embarks on the solving of philosophical problems is anything to go by.

That philosophy loomed large in Richard's mind becomes even clearer when we consider those of his works that must be lost. In the treatise 'Miserabilis est humana condicio' (As ff. 277C–285A) Richard himself refers to a commentary on the *Metaphysics* of Aristotle which might well be his own: 'De oppositione relationis et relatione alibi tractatum est, scilicet super quintum Metaphysice' (As f. 278A).[52] In any case, it cannot be the commentary discussed before.

Richard may also have written a commentary on the *Meteorologica* of Aristotle. There are several references to such a work in the encyclopaedia *De proprietatibus rerum* of Bartholomaeus Anglicus, e.g.: 'Haec omnia dicuntur in libro Meteorum expresse et quae a Ricardo sic exponuntur'. From an earlier part it is clear that the expositor is Richard Rufus.[53]

Another reference to a lost work seems to occur in the ancient catalogue of St Augustine's library in Canterbury: it lists as one of the items: 'Sincathegorematica Ricardi Cornubiensis'.[54] If, after all, the *Abstractiones* should turn out to be a work of Richard Rufus, this entry might well refer to that work. As evidence, however, that Richard composed the *Abstractiones* it is of no use.

But even without the lost works, the list of Richard Rufus's genuine writings is extensive enough to venture a survey of his theological opinions, the more so because one may safely assume that most of his thought returns in one way or another in the two main works, the commentary and the abbreviation. These two will form the basis for Part II.

[52] Gal, 'Viae', p. 178 n. 5.
[53] More quotations in W. Lampen, 'De fr. Richardo Rufo, Cornubiensi, O.F.M.', *AFH* xxi (1928),405–6.
[54] J. C. Russell, *Dictionary of Writers of Thirteenth Century England* (Bulletin of the Institute of Historical Research, Supplements, iii, 1936), p. 120. Little, 'Franciscan School', p. 845 n. 2 thinks that this work must be of a Richard of later date.

Richard Rufus of Cornwall and Robert Grosseteste: A Study in Theological Outlook and Tradition

The Extent of Richard's Indebtedness

As Richard Rufus probably did not join the Franciscan order before 1238, three years after Grosseteste had left Oxford to be Bishop of Lincoln, he cannot strictly be called a pupil of Grosseteste. Nevertheless, any study of a Franciscan theologian, teaching at Oxford a few years after Grosseteste's departure, has to begin by tracing his relationship to the great Bishop of Lincoln.

Robert Grosseteste had stood at the cradle of the university, especially of its faculty of theology. And even more important for our present purpose, in the year 1229/30, he had accepted an invitation from the Franciscans to become the *lector* to their Oxford convent. He continued to fill this post till his elevation to the see of Lincoln in 1235. The latter event changed but did not weaken his relations to the Franciscans, they remained very close until his death in 1253, the year of Richard Rufus's departure to Paris. Matthew Paris, when reflecting on the Bishop's career, called him: 'Praedicatorum et Minorum pater et consolator'.[1] The intimacy of their relationship is well described in the words Grosseteste himself once addressed to Agnellus of Pisa, the first English Provincial, when consoling him on the death of a friar:

... in ad invicem amantibus, utriusque sit amans et utriusque amatum, et quasi mutuo visu uterque in alterum totus eat, et mutuo amplexu sese indissolubiliter astringant.[2]

And in a letter to Elias of Cortona, the then General of the Franciscans, he writes that the Friars Minor have embraced him with the arms of love and that the affection of the sons cannot be separated from the affection of the father.[3]

They both shared a passion for a reformed and purified Church, based on poverty, unsullied by worldly pursuits, and wholly devoted to the cure of souls. The Franciscan order had grown out of a widespread reform movement in the Church; and Grosseteste had shown his deep commitment to the cause of reform in 1231, when he resigned

---

[1] Matthew Paris, *Chronica majora*, ed. H. Luard (RS, 1872–83), v. 408.
[2] Robert Grosseteste, *Epistolae*, ii, ed. H. Luard (RS, 1861), p. 18.
[3] *Epistolae*, xli (ed. Luard, p. 133).

from all his benefices but one.[4] The loss of income that resulted from this move must have brought him even closer in spirit to his Franciscan students. After his elevation to Lincoln the co-operation took a more practical turn. In many visitations the Bishop put his theory into practice. In a statement, made to the Pope and cardinals in 1250, Grosseteste describes the pattern of such a visitation: while he addressed the clergy, a Franciscan or Dominican preached to the people. Subsequently the friars heard confessions and gave penances.[5]

Grosseteste also took extreme care in making appointments to vacant benefices: much of his correspondence with Adam Marsh consists of vetting the prospective candidates. Adam Marsh clearly served as his Oxford contact in this respect.[6]

Still with an eye on the reform of the Church, he also exerted gentle pressure on the Franciscans to educate themselves properly. He was convinced that they would not be able to take up the challenges of the times unless they devoted themselves wholeheartedly to the study of theology. He once told Peter of Tewkesbury, later Provincial, that, if the Franciscans did not apply themselves to the study of theology more seriously and did not spend more time in reflecting on the divine law, they would end up like all the other religious orders, in the darkness of ignorance.[7] It can be expected, therefore, that the shadow of Grosseteste loomed large over the first generation of Franciscan theologians at Oxford; many scholars call him the founder of the Franciscan school at Oxford, a conclusion which, so far, has not been warranted by evidence.[8]

There is a conspicuous absence of a continuous tradition of Grosse-

---

[4] L. Boyle, 'Robert Grosseteste and the Pastoral Care', *Mediaeval and Renaissance Studies*, viii (1979), 4–7.

[5] 'Unde episcopatum meum cepi circuire per singulos decanatus rurales, faciens clerum cuiuscunque decanatus per ordinem certis die et loco convocari, et populum premuniri ut eisdem die et loco adessent cum parvulis confirmandis, ad audiendum verbum dei et confitendum. Congregatis autem clero et populo, egomet ut pluries proponebam verbum dei clero, et aliquis frater predicator aut minor populo. Et iiiiᵒʳ fratres consequenter audiebant confessiones et iniungebant penitentias', *Councils and Synods with Other Documents Relating to the English Church*, II: *A.D. 1205–1313*, ed. F. M. Powicke and C. R. Cheney (Oxford, 1964), i. 265.

[6] Marsh, *Letters*, ix, x, xii, xiv, xxiii, xxvii, lxii, lxvi, lxix (ed. Brewer, pp. 92, 93, 94–6, 97–8, 108–9, 116–19, 171, 173–4, 176).

[7] Eccleston, *De adventu*, xv (ed. Little, p. 91).

[8] See e.g. R. Seeberg, *Die Theologie des Johannes Duns Scotus* (Studien zur Geschichte der Theologie und der Kirche, v, 1900), pp. 12–16; Felder, *Geschichte*, pp. 262–8; Little, 'Franciscan School', p. 808; D. Sharp, *Franciscan Philosophy at Oxford in the Thirteenth Century* (Oxford, 1930), pp. 9–12; J. Beumer, 'Robert Grosseteste von Lincoln, der angebliche Begründer der Franziskanerschule', *FnSn* lvii (1975), *passim*.

teste manuscripts. Dr Smalley has pointed out that the bulk of existing manuscripts date from the late fourteenth and fifteenth centuries, which would indicate that his work had been neglected and that there was a revival of interest by that date. She also notes that quotations from Grosseteste's work are very rare before the middle of the fourteenth century; Wyclif seems to have been the first theologian who has any great use for Grosseteste in his writings.[9] It is true that diligent scholars have come up with a few quotations from earlier periods— Scotus quotes Grosseteste's opinion on the object of theology, and also his effort to reconcile the Greek and Latin view on the procession of the Holy Ghost; Robert Cowton (fl. *c*.1310) quotes him on a Trinitarian problem—but these are all insignificant.[10] Grosseteste did not influence the generation of great Oxford theologians around and just after 1300.

It may be different in the thirteenth century. Our knowledge of that period is still rather patchy; the works of very few thirteenth-century Oxford theologians have been studied sufficiently to draw any conclusions. But it has been discovered that both Richard Rufus and his Dominican predecessor, Richard Fishacre, use Grosseteste's commentary on the first two chapters of Genesis, the *Hexaemeron*, extensively in their commentaries on the *Sentences*.[11] That discovery poses a second problem: the fact that Richard Rufus used Grosseteste's works is not sufficient proof that he was influenced by him, or that Grosseteste may after all, be called the founder of the Franciscan school of thought at Oxford or of the Oxford tradition of theology. To reach that conclusion a continuity of thought would have to be established. It would be necessary to show that Grosseteste and Rufus have at least the same opinion on important subjects, or even better, share the same outlook or have a common approach to theological problems. It is this question that I propose to deal with in the second part of this work. The answer to it will also yield a further result, a first outline of Richard Rufus's own

---

[9] B. Smalley, 'The Biblical Scholar', in D. Callus (ed.), *Robert Grosseteste*, pp. 83, 95.

[10] A. Michel, 'Trinité, ii: la théologie latine du viᵉ au xxᵉ siècle', *Dictionnaire de théologie catholique*, xv (1950), pp. 1731–2; for the quotations in Scotus see John Duns Scotus, *Ordinatio*, Prologus, iii. 3 (*Opera omnia*, i, 1950), pp. 119–20 and i. 11. 1 (*Opera omnia*, v, 1959), pp. 2–3; other early quotations in the work of Henry of Harclay, see Dales, 'Influence', p. 272, and in the works of William of Alnwick and Robert Holcot, see Smalley, 'Biblical Scholar', pp. 80, 83.

[11] Dales, 'Influence', was the first to discover the extensive use both friars make of the *Hexaemeron*; he speaks of 'plundering', p. 272. Richard Rufus also used other works of Grosseteste, as will be seen.

theological outlook on those points where he develops or opposes Grosseteste's solutions.

The practical difficulties of this part are considerable. Both Grosseteste and Richard Rufus left a considerable *œuvre*. This in itself would not be so daunting if their work could easily be compared, for instance, because its structure was very similar. This, however, is not the case, a significant fact in itself, since the forms of theological teaching and writing were one of the most lively debated issues in the thirteenth century. Grosseteste never wrote a systematic work, neither as a philosopher, nor as a theologian. His method was jotting down notes, writing short treatises, commenting on a Bible text. Dr McEvoy distinguishes between Grosseteste's accuracy and methodology in his working habits and in his analysis of problems, and his inability to gather all the strands of his thought into one systematic exposition.[12] Rufus left his thoughts mainly in the form of two commentaries on the *Sentences* and a few disputed questions.

This difference in method is so striking that the enquiry must start from there. Chapter 6 will consist of a discussion of the formal aspects of Grosseteste's theological thought. And though data are probably scattered over many of his theological writings, they can easily be grasped, because in the *Hexaemeron* he both defends his method of theology and executes it in a model commentary on the first two chapters of Genesis.[13] I shall go on to compare Grosseteste's views with those of Richard Rufus. In the introduction to his Oxford commentary on the *Sentences* Richard justifies his departing from Grosseteste's theological method, and formulates his own theory of theology and more rationalistic way of approaching his subject.

Since in the thirteenth century the practice of theology was far ahead of the theory, I will consider Richard's answer to Grosseteste in practice in Chapter 7. Richard uses the *Hexaemeron* extensively in his discussion of the works of creation, and it will be interesting to see how he adapts Grosseteste's effusive prose to his own more systematic needs in practice.

Chapters 8 and 9 will be concerned with more particular aspects of their thought. Richard drew upon Grosseteste in his discussion of

---

[12] McEvoy, *Philosophy*, p. 447.

[13] I have not taken into consideration the five theological questions attributed to Grosseteste and edited by D. Callus, 'The *Summa theologiae* of Robert Grosseteste', in R. W. Hunt et al. (eds), *Studies in Medieval History Presented to Frederick Maurice Powicke* (Oxford, 1948), pp. 194–208. Southern, *Grosseteste*, pp. 29–31 proves convincingly that the questions are spurious.

free will in man and also subjected Grosseteste's discussion of the reasons for the Incarnation to a close scrutiny, which merits our attention since Grosseteste was the first in the thirteenth century to suggest the possibility of Christ's absolute predestination.

Finally, a word of caution. Not consulting all Grosseteste's theological work causes two problems: on the one hand the picture of his theology may be one-sided, and on the other hand there may be many more passages in Rufus's commentaries borrowed from Grosseteste which I did not recognize. Therefore, the conclusions of my work must be considered rather as a stimulant for further research than as an effort to say the last word on the matter.

CHAPTER 6

The Dispute on Method in Theology

(i) *Robert Grosseteste and the Tradition of the Fathers*

AN important key to Grosseteste's theological thought can be found in
a strongly worded letter he wrote to the regent masters of theology at
Oxford in the middle of the 1240s.[1] In this letter he severely criticizes
their teaching methods and he advises them most urgently to use
nothing else but the books of the Bible for their main lectures
('lectiones ordinariae'), and to give these lectures in the morning, the
time most suited for it:

Lapides igitur fundamentales aedificii, cujus estis architectonici, praeter quos
nemo potest alios invenire aut in fundamento ponere, libri sunt Prophetarum;
inter quos et legislator Moyses non immerito est annumerandus; libri quoque
Apostolorum et Evangelium: quos lapides fundamentales vos in fundamento
ponitis et . . . secundem mentem editorum auditoribus exponitis. Omni igitur
circumspectione vobis cavendum est, ne inter fundamentales lapides, vel pro
fundamentalibus, non fundamentales ponantur.[2]

The Bible had to remain the root of the study of theology. Even the
books of the Holy Fathers would not do as textbooks for young
students, since they were mere superstructures erected on the one
foundation.[3]

The ghost that Grosseteste was trying to exorcize was the call for a
thorough reform of the theology course at Oxford to bring it in line
with the new custom at Paris. The time-honoured tradition had been
to use the Bible as a textbook for theology. The lecturer chose a book
of the Bible and went through it passage by passage, first commenting
on the text, then bringing out its deeper significance, and finally
singling out questions which arose from the text, but went far beyond
it in scope, for special, more systematic treatment. Over the years,

---

[1] Most of my thoughts on Grosseteste's theology have taken shape in conversations
with Sir Richard Southern. For a further exposition of his views I refer my readers to his
new book on the subject.
[2] Grosseteste, *Epistolae*, cxxiii (ed. Luard, pp. 346–7).
[3] Ibid.

however, the amount of speculative questions grew so great and the method of treating them had become so different that the need was felt to separate commentary from questioning.[4]

But the urge for a more systematic treatment of the sacred doctrine went beyond the isolated question. In the twelfth century several theologians had composed *Summae*, anthologies of texts (*Sententiae*) from the Bible and the Fathers, which were arranged not in the order in which they occurred in Scripture but from a rational point of view.[5] Thus a whole new framework was created into which questions could be fitted far better than in the traditional lectures on the Bible.

The final push for a drastic revision of the theology course came in the beginning of the thirteenth century when Aristotle's philosophy of science began to make its impact felt, although the sources had been known for some time.[6] Quite soon the Aristotelian concept of science became the norm for all disciplines and led to an even more rigorous systematization in all branches of knowledge. Although most theologians hesitated as to whether Aristotle's rigorous demands could be applied to theology, which, after all, was based on faith and not on knowledge, in the end they were unable to resist the spirit of the age and had to ask themselves how far theology could be or rather become a science.[7] Aristotle required three things: all sciences must have a clearly stated subject, and that subject must be one;[8] scientific knowledge can only result from a demonstration that has a syllogistic, i.e. deductive form.[9] Thirdly, for the conclusions to be certain and necessary the demonstration must start from premises which are true, indemonstrable—at least in that particular branch of knowledge—and immediately obvious: *principia per se nota*.[10] The *Summae* of the twelfth

---

[4] B. Smalley, *The Study of the Bible in the Middle Ages* (2nd edn., Notre Dame, 1970), pp. 66–77, 209–13.

[5] A. Lang, *Die theologische Prinzipienlehre der mittelalterlichen Scholastik* (Freiburg i. B., 1964), pp. 58–62; U. Köpf, *Die Anfänge der theologischen Wissenschaftstheorie im 13. Jahrhundert* (Beiträge zur historischen Theologie, xlix, 1974), pp. 35–6.

[6] The main sources were the *Prior* and *Posterior Analytics*. Boethius' translation of the former had been discovered in the 1120s; a translation of the *Posterior Analytics* by James of Venice became available somewhat later, but before 1150, see B. G. Dod, 'Aristoteles Latinus', in N. Kretzmann *et al.* (eds.), *The Cambridge History of Later Medieval Philosophy* (Cambridge, 1982), pp. 46, 75.

[7] M.-D. Chenu, *Introduction à l'étude de S. Thomas d'Aquin* (3rd edn., Publications de l'Institut d'Études Médiévales, xi, 1974), pp. 232–3.

[8] Aristotle, *Metaphysica*, 1074^{b}34–107^{a}5; *Ethica Eudemia*, 1216^{b}11–15; on the unity of subject: *Analytica Posteriora*, 87^{a}38–^{b}4.

[9] Aristotle, *Analytica Posteriora*, 73^{a}21–4; the valid forms of inference are the subject of the *Prior Analytics*.

[10] *Analytica Posteriora*, 71^{b}19–23, 72^{a}5–8, 76^{a}31–3.

century, although they might be eminently suitable as textbooks, were not sufficiently condensed to fit that last definition; in them the contents of Scripture had not been reduced to a few maxims which could serve as a point of departure for a theological science rooted in the Catholic faith. And before long theologians began to agree that the articles of faith, as found in the Apostles' Creed, constituted exactly that body of premises which at the same time fulfilled the requirements of Aristotle and safeguarded the priority of faith. William of Auxerre was the first to come to this conclusion.[11]

Around the second decade of the thirteenth century we can speak of two entirely different approaches within the one field of reflection on Christian doctrine: exposition of the Bible and systematic questioning of its contents in the light of new philosophical insights. Since the two methods were so different, they could not possibly be contained within the framework of one set of lectures. The old system had to be adapted to meet new developments; speculative theology had to be given its own separate lecture course. And as lecturing without a textbook was inconceivable for medieval scholars, the best choice seemed to be one of the collections of *Sententiae* inherited from the twelfth century. According to Roger Bacon the first to make that connection was Alexander of Hales when he taught at Paris in the early 1220s.[12] He chose the *Sentences* of Peter Lombard as his textbook, no doubt because Peter Lombard was in the unique position of having received the highest possible seal of approval, that of the Fathers of the Fourth Lateran Council (1215), who vindicated his Trinitarian doctrine in one of their decrees.[13] Alexander's choice proved to be crucial for centuries to come. By 1240 the custom of giving lectures on the *Sentences* was firmly established at Paris. Richard Fishacre was the first theologian at Oxford to lecture on the *Sentences* in the first half of the 1240s, and it is highly probable that these lectures were the immediate cause of Grosseteste's stern letter to the faculty to adhere to the old custom.[14]

Grosseteste's effort to stem the tide flowed from a deeply felt conviction that theology could well do without too much method. He preferred biblical commentary to the reasoned and systematic exposi-

[11] Lang, *Prinzipienlehre*, pp. 110–14.

[12] Little, 'Franciscan School', p. 809.

[13] 'Nos autem, sacro et universali concilio approbante, credimus et confitebimur cum Petro ...', *Conciliorum oecumenicorum decreta*, ed. J. Alberigo *et al.* (3rd edn., Bologna, 1973), p. 232.

[14] Smalley, *Study*, pp. 276–80; Long, 'Science of Theology', pp. 71–4.

tion of Christian doctrine. His own theological works bear testimony to that belief; they are all Scripture commentaries in one form or another, except for the treatise *De cessatione legalium* on the relation between the Old and the New Testament and on the validity of the Law in the New Covenant. But even this treatise has a strong scriptural flavour and, indeed, one of the most beautiful and perspicacious passages in it is the analysis of messianic prophecies in the Old Testament.[15]

His style reflects his disdain for any system as well. There is rarely any method in his treatment of a problem; if a word through some association recalls an interesting problem, he will follow it at sometimes considerable length, before returning to the main argument. In his commentaries he always seems to have in mind the particular passage or word he is commenting on, nor does he make an effort to grasp the whole. All this makes for a rambling style, and a disconnected series of arguments about the most diverse subjects, very obvious in the *Hexaemeron*.[16]

He is also very slow to use dialectical methods to solve contradictions, e.g. between the Fathers. There are several examples of this.[17] One occurs in the *Hexaemeron*. There was a substantial difference of opinion between the fathers on the interpretation of the first creation narrative (Gen. i. 1–ii. 4): was the story of the six-day creation to be considered an accurate historical account, or an allegorical account on the literal level of the text? The Greek Fathers in the tradition of the school of Antioch had preferred the former point of view, and had been followed in the West by such authorities as Ambrose and the Venerable Bede. The support for the allegorical interpretation came from Origen and the school of Alexandria, and was upheld in the West by Augustine. Grosseteste makes no effort to

---

[15] The best text of *De cessatione legalium* is Oxford, Bodleian Library, MS Lat. theol. c. 17, ff. 158A–189A (= Ox), with corrections in Grosseteste's own hand; see R. W. Hunt, 'Notable Accessions. Manuscripts', *Bodleian Library Record*, ii (1941–9), 226–7. A very good example is the treatment of the prophetical passage predicting 'the days . . . that I will raise unto David a righteous branch' (Jer. xxiii. 5–6), where Grosseteste shows convincingly that Jeremiah here could not have possibly referred to any earthly king, but that the prophecy, in its original intention, must be understood as referring to the Messiah (f. 171A–B). It is characteristic of the whole work that Grosseteste wants to meet his adversaries on the literal level of the text.

[16] McEvoy, *Philosophy*, p. 27 calls Grosseteste an 'inveterate scribbler'.

[17] See e.g. Smalley, 'Biblical Scholar', pp. 90–4 on the difference of opinion between Augustine and Jerome on the controversy among the apostles concerning the observation of the Law. Grosseteste solves the problem by historical rather than dialectical methods.

gloss over the difference, and offers two possible explanations. First he remarks that Augustine does not seem to be too sure of himself, because in some of his writings he seems to advocate the historical interpretation.[18] Later on he suggests that Augustine might have come to his theory of instantaneous creation because of the text he used, that some Greek texts, however, have quite a different wording.[19]

Another example of Grosseteste's aversion to dialectics is his treatment of the question whether there is a difference between heaven (Gen. i. 1) and firmament (Gen. i. 6). He quotes several authorities who do not wish to identify the two, then Josephus and Gregory of Nyssa, who are in favour of such an identification, and concludes, rather lamely, that he does not feel called upon to solve the controversy, that, however, if there is a difference, then heaven is immobile.[20] This shows how far removed Grosseteste is from scholastic method, where contradictions between the ancient authorities were the driving force of theological progress: only where a problem presented itself did theological development take place.

In his introduction to the *Hexaemeron* Grosseteste justifies this way of proceeding. In Scripture, he says, every statement is equally trustworthy, since every single sentence has been written under divine inspiration. Therefore, we should pay no attention to what is said first, and what is said later, nor should we try to deduce one thing from another through syllogisms:

Nam que in hac sapiencia proprie credibilia sunt, a dicentis auctoritate sunt credibilia. Unde, cum in hac scriptura indifferens sit dicentis auctoritas, Dei videlicet loquentis *per os sanctorum, qui a seculo sunt prophetarum eius*, indifferens est et credendorum in hac scriptura credibilitas, ... De eque autem credibilibus, unde sunt eque credibilia, non est curandum quid prius, quidve posterius dicatur, nec alterum ex altero sillogizandum, quia ex hac parte unde sic credibilia sunt, nullum altero est notius.[21]

In these words Grosseteste rejects the application of Aristotle's philosophy of science to theology, which for him equals the exposition of the Bible. On the basis of the equal trustworthiness of every word or sentence he opposes the tendency to draw from the body of Scripture

---

[18] Gross. *Hex.* I. x. 1, pp. 64–5; II. iv. 3–v. 2, pp. 88–90; II. v. 5, p. 92.

[19] Ibid. x. iii. 1, pp. 293–4.

[20] 'Horum autem auctorum controversiam non est meum determinare, sed si celum istud primum sit aliud a firmamento secundo die creato, videtur quod illud sit immobile', ibid. I. xvii. 1, p. 75.

[21] Ibid. I. ii. 2, p. 51; the biblical quotation is Luke i. 70.

a number of axioms ('nullum altero est notius'), and the demonstrative method ('nec alterum ex altero sillogizandum'). There is no hierarchy of truths to be believed, therefore the demonstrative method is superfluous. The Bible cannot be structured from a human principle of organization without distortion; the God-given order must be respected.

But the order of the books of Scripture should not only be respected because it is God-given, but also because it is rational. In order to prove this, Grosseteste continues his introduction by drawing a distinction between those things which can be easily imagined and those things which cannot. Now the easiest things to imagine are the forms and species of this world: heaven, earth, the sea, and all that is living in or on them. All these visible things can be considered not only as objects of scientific enquiry but also from the point of view of faith ('venientes sub fidem'). And as such they are for simple people the best starting-point on the road to God.[22] For that reason the Bible begins with the story of the creation of heaven and earth; the divine pedagogy starts with simple things we can see around us, not with abstract principles:

Quapropter hec scriptura que proponitur simpliciter toti humano generi, a sensibilibus huius mundi secundum quod sub fidem veniunt debet inchoari. Omnis namque doctrine primordia hiis quibus proponitur eadem doctrina, debent esse magis capabilia ... Mundi igitur sensibilis creacio, per modum quo mundus ymaginabilis est et per corporis exteriores sensus apprehensibilis, in primordio huius scripture debuit enarrari, ut quivis eciam rudis huiusmodi narracionem facillime possit per ymaginacionem et rerum corporalium ymagines apprehendere, et per dicentis auctoritatem in fide firmare.[23]

This refusal to reduce the contents of Scripture to a few abstract premisses, from which further conclusions can be drawn by syllogistic reasoning, is most characteristic of Grosseteste's theology. He still belongs to, or rather reverts to, the school of theologians whose imagination was not fired by problems and questions but by long and lingering reading which savoured the words of Scripture, where every word, every sentence, was equally worth while contemplating, equally

[22] 'Tamen de sic eque credibilibus quedam sunt facilius imaginabilia et quedam difficilius. Facillime vero ymaginabilia sunt species et forme huius mundi sensibilis, utpote celum, terra, mare et que in eis sunt species sensibiles. Iste igitur sensibiles mundi species, inquantum sunt extra certitudinem sensus et scientie et venientes sub fidem, sunt simpliciter fidei magis et facilius capabiles', Gross. *Hex.* I. ii. 2, p. 51.

[23] Ibid. I. ii. 2–3, pp. 51–2.

suitable for comment. The theologian is the servant of the text, the hearer of the Word; God speaks to him in every word of the Bible and in every creature he sees around him, in Augustine's words: 'Your book be the divine page that you may hear it, your book be the whole world that you may see it.'[24]

For theologians like Grosseteste the book of nature and the book of Scripture do not constitute a value in themselves but only as a preparation for the book of life; they are essentially seen as symbols, entrance doors to the hidden, but intelligible world of ideas in the divine mind, and thus to God himself. In such a vision the syllogistic method is out of place; it is too clear and does not convey the sense of mystery which is at the heart of all visible things. Theological discourse must respect that mystery and be as open-ended as the reality it describes. But such a language existed: the allegory. The allegorical method had been designed as a means of showing the hidden depth of visible reality, of transcending the letter, and disclosing that reality of which all visible things are only a weak reflection. As such it is particularly suited to theology. Grosseteste calls the allegorical method 'fidei congruens'.[25] Only through allegory can we penetrate into the intelligible reality:

. . . licet nonnulli, ut Augustinus commemorat, paradisum ad sola intelligibilia referant, et solummodo allegorice et spiritualiter hunc locum exponendum putant.[26]

In the *Hexaemeron* Grosseteste pays attention to many problems but again and again he expresses his impatience to move on to higher and more important things:

Et quia legislator non tam intendebat docere nos aquatilium naturas quam ordinacionem ecclesie et morum informacionem, aliqua in hiis allegorica et moralia breviter sunt annotanda.[27]

He also provides his readers with a theoretical foundation for his allegorizing, using a famous remark of Boethius, that everything here on earth is formed after the celestial order:

[24] Augustine, *Enarrationes in psalmos, i-l*, xlv. 7, ed. E. Dekkers and I. Fraipont (CC, xxxviii, 1956), p. 522.
[25] Gross. *Hex.* VIII. xxx. 1, p. 253.
[26] Ibid. XI. v. 1, p. 310.
[27] Ibid. VI. xii. 1, p. 193.

Considerandus est autem nobis in hiis aliquis intellectus spiritalis, et aliquis fructus spiritalis carpendus. Sicut enim ait Boetius: 'Mores nostri et tocius vite ratio ad celestis ordinis exemplar formantur.'[28]

From the remark that we must both understand and pick some spiritual fruit, it can be gathered that for Grosseteste, as for all other theologians, spiritual understanding has different levels. The lowest is moral understanding, which grows on the earth of the historical level and is the food of the simple, just as the grass growing on the earth is the food of animals.[29] From there we move on to allegory in the stricter sense and then to the highest possible level, the anagogical, where man contemplates the first glimpse of his future glory. Grosseteste describes this spiritual ascent in his commentary on Pseudo-Dionysius' *Mystical Theology*:

Post hanc spiritalem purgacionem fit homo interior aptus ad audiendam et intelligendam scripturam, cuius tube multivoce sunt symbolice dicta multipliciter multa significantia; lumina vero multa sunt spiritalia significata per symbola a materialibus sumpta, que puros et multimode fusos radios mittunt in humanas intelligentias clarificandas. In hiis autem communicant multi: intellectum enim scripture hystoricum et allegoricum et moralem habent multi, sed interior homo, querens videre Deum incircumvelate et vere, hiis non est contentus, sed ab hiis se segregans et hos transcendens, ascendit cum electis et sacris contemplativis et doctoribus ad summitatem anagogicorum intellectuum, in quibus . . . contemplatur locum ubi stetit Deus.[30]

There could be no clearer statement of the difference between Grosseteste and his contemporaries. Whereas a dialectic theologian would want to state his terms as clearly as possible and try to reach the ideal of clear concepts, Grosseteste seems to revel in equivocations when speaking about the words of Scripture as many-voiced trumpets, signifying many things in many ways; for most of his contemporaries this would be mere cacophony.[31]

There is one passage that seems to contradict the importance of allegory in Grosseteste's theological method. It occurs in the *De Cessatione Legalium*, where at some point he seems to say that allegory

[28] Ibid. v. xix. 1, p. 177.

[29] Ibid. iv. xxix. 6, p. 153.

[30] Robert Grosseteste, *Commentarius in mysticam theologiam*, i. 4, ed. U. Gamba (Milan, 1942), p. 35.

[31] M. D. Chenu, *La Théologie au douzième siècle* (3rd edn., Études de philosophie médiévale, xlv, 1976), pp. 184–5.

obscures the truth, and that it is better to keep to the historical level where everything is plain and clear:

Oportuit etiam ut authentica scriptura signaret verbis manifestis et nullam allegorie obscuritatem habentibus dispensationem nostre salutis, ut ipsa salutis nostre dispensatio testimonium haberet ab authentica scriptura manifestissima verbis nudis et manifestis illam denuntiantibus. (Oxf. 164C)

These words undoubtedly imply that allegory can obscure the truth. But reading them in a wider context it soon becomes obvious that Grosseteste in this passage does not reject the allegorical method as such, but that he merely wants to say that the truths concerning our salvation must be brought out so clearly that no misunderstanding is possible, even for the simplest minds, since it is at the same time the most difficult thing to believe and yet should be believed with utmost certainty.[32] This concern for the simple and uneducated, shown here, fits in with what he says in the introduction to the *Hexaemeron* that for the sake of the uneducated the Bible begins with the story of creation, although there the implication is that even simple people are capable of moving on from created reality to higher things by way of allegory. However that may be, it does not change the picture that Grosseteste in his riper years rejected modern theological methods and clung to the Bible, going back to what Dr Smalley calls the 'pre-logical ethos of the Benedictines or the Victorines'.[33]

This, however, is not a complete picture. Grosseteste is not simply a theologian of the old school who, in the seclusion of the cloister, did not notice that he had been overtaken. If he is old-fashioned, then it must be added immediately that his return to older ways was a conscious reaction to what even in his days had become common practice. There is no simple, unbroken continuity between the canons of Saint-Victor and Grosseteste. Grosseteste was well-versed in works of Aristotle which had hardly influenced the Victorines. He commented on two of them: the *Physics* and the *Posterior Analytics*, the last being a sophisticated discussion of that scientific method of which he

---

[32] 'Veritas dispensationis nostre salutis, que est omnium veritatum in se considerata a fide longissima, et quam tamen oportet apud fidem esse certissimam, testimonium haberet omnium maximum et evidentissimum' (Ox f. 164C).

[33] Smalley, 'Biblical Scholar', p. 94; further discussions of Grosseteste's theological traditionalism in McEvoy, *Philosophy*, pp. 358–63 and also in S. Gieben, 'Traces of God in Nature According to Robert Grosseteste', *FS* xxiv (1964), 145–8.

disapproved so much when applied to theology. That he has absorbed the teachings of Aristotle, even though he does not agree with many of Aristotle's basic positions, is shown mainly in the philosophical works, but also in the introduction to the *Hexaemeron*, where he discusses the three points Aristotle raises about scientific method.

First he raises the question of the formal object and answers wholly in keeping with an influential school of thought in his days that the subject-matter of theology is Christ, who combines in his person a fivefold union. He unites in himself God and man, he is one with the Church, his mystical body, and the faithful are united with him in the Eucharist; he is also one God with the Father and the Holy Ghost, and through Christ man is drawn into that divine unity.[34] Thus all creatures are dealt with in this wisdom, in so far as they flow from the One and return to him:

Creature eciam omnes, in quantum habent essentialem ordinem ad dictum unum huius sapiencie subiectum, hoc est in quantum ab hoc uno fluunt et in hoc unum recurrunt, ad istam pertinent sapienciam.[35]

Grosseteste's answer to Aristotle's other points, about the premisses and the method of proceeding, has already been dealt with: he emphasizes that the principles of this wisdom are not known by themselves, nor deduced, but accepted in faith on the authority of him who speaks. They have been laid down in the Bible in the order God wishes and no new conclusions can be drawn from them by syllogistic reasoning.[36] So, Grosseteste was aware of the new methods and the efforts to turn theology into a scientific discipline, but he rejected this development.

This was not because he was opposed to reform. But his idea of reform was a very different one, similar to some extent to the ideas of Hugh of Saint-Victor.[37] He did not want to reject the old methods of

[34] Gross. *Hex.* I. i. 1–2, pp. 49–50; Scotus, when quoting Grosseteste on this point, slightly misrepresents his solution: 'Aliter tamen ponitur Christum esse primum subiectum secundum Lincolniensem in Hexaemeron, et hoc secundum quod Christus est unum triplici unitate, quarum prima est ad Patrem et Spiritum Sanctum, secunda Verbi ad naturam assumptam, tertia Christi capitis ad membra', *Ordinatio*, Prologus, iii. 3 (*Opera omnia*, i. 119–20).
[35] Gross. *Hex.* I. i. 3, p. 50 (*recensio secunda*); a more extensive treatment of Grosseteste's thought on the subject of theology in E. Mersch, 'L'objet de la théologie et le "Christus totus"', *Recherches de science religieuse*, xxvi (1936), 138–42.
[36] Gross. *Hex.* I. ii. 2, pp. 50–1. See also above, pp. 126–7.
[37] For Hugh of Saint-Victor's emphasis on the importance of the letter as a firm basis for allegory, see Smalley, *Study*, pp. 89–90.

reflecting on the mystery of faith, but to strengthen the basis of them. The foundations of theology were creation and Scripture. Or perhaps that is too neat a distinction: the Bible itself contains everything, including creation. Although creation speaks of God, it was the Bible which offered the key to the right interpretation of natural phenomena.[38] Therefore, according to Grosseteste, here echoing Augustine, all the resources of human knowledge could be and had to be applied to serve the right understanding of Scripture, historical and allegorical.[39] And finally, on the foundation of the properties and peculiarities of created things, guided by Scripture, allegories could be discovered and a deeper understanding be gained.

Grosseteste's programme was to strengthen the foundations of this ancient method by supplying new information on created reality. He saw very well that allegory derives its strength from the firmness of the sign. The symbol must be taken seriously, since, even though it is a weak reflection, it does participate in the higher reality and is our only way of access to it. In the early Middle Ages much allegorical thinking had been rather arbitrary; the standards of the natural sciences and of linguistics had been abysmally low, so that little could be known about created reality in itself. The leap to higher things came too soon, emptying created reality of its value in itself, and thereby also weakening its value as a symbol. But in Grosseteste's days that situation had changed and he was not slow to recognize it; Aristotle's natural philosophy had revolutionized the knowledge of creation and he grasped the possibilities it offered immediately.

Using Aristotle could help him to come to a better understanding of Scripture and to give new momentum to the allegorical method. The more we know of the properties of the icon, the better we shall be able to grasp the reality to which the icon refers. Grosseteste's many treatises on the comets, on light, on the heavenly bodies in general

---

[38] McEvoy, *Philosophy*, p. 359; Grosseteste also states it explicitly: 'Continet igitur in se hec scriptura totum quod continet natura, quia post mundi creacionem non est nove speciei seu nature adiectio', Gross. *Hex*. I. iv. I, p. 54. In the *De cessatione legalium* he formulates rules for the interpretation of the things of creation: 'Hanc itaque regulam debet habere penes se fixam discipulus huius scripture, ut ubi verba huius scripture significant res creationis aut res conversationis populi israelitici prophetalis, ibi querat ex alio scripture loco quid quelibet res singillatim significat, et postea significationem connexam ex multis rebus signantibus investigat in verbis veritatem fidei vel caritatis nude signantibus' (Ox f. 164D).

[39] Gross. *Hex*. I. iv. I, p. 54, where he quotes the relevant passage from *De doctrina christiana*: 'Unde putet quam veraciter dicit Augustinus quod "quicquid homo extra hanc scripturam didicit, si noxium est in ista dampnatur, si utile est in ista invenitur" '.

must be understood in this way; they came to serve a religious purpose. And the same is true for the word of Scripture. Unremittingly, Grosseteste tried to establish the most accurate text, comparing the Vulgate with the Septuagint and the Vetus Latina and sometimes even with Aquila, to reinforce the foundations of spiritual understanding. Aristotle's philosophy of science cannot be applied to theology, because theology is based on faith—therefore not on reason but on authority—but his natural philosophy offers a golden opportunity to broaden the scope of the allegorical method, 'fidei congruens'.[40]

This reform programme is carried out in the *Hexaemeron*. In most respects this commentary is of a well-known structure: the whole of the first and part of the second chapter of the book of Genesis is chopped up in small passages of which first the literal interpretation is given, followed by the allegorical and moral application, and in a few cases the anagogical. The highly original feature of this commentary is, however, that after every act of creation Grosseteste adds a long treatise on the natural properties of the things just created. And he does so, he says, not from idle curiosity but to improve allegorical understanding:

Tamen non ab re est, si celi proprietates, quasdam nobis certas quasdam vero minus certas, ab expositoribus tamen suppositas et in misticas significationes assumptas, pro modulo nostro hic interserere curemus, ut habeat lector parvulus in promptu—non enim sapientibus et perfectis ista scribimus—ex quibus proprietatibus et similitudinibus possit faciliter aptare celum supradictis significatis et alibi dicendis.[41]

Here the connection is made: the study of natural science, of the natural properties of things, stands in the perspective of allegorical understanding; it is especially important for beginners, for those who need in their ascent to God the species and forms of the world of the senses, as he put it in the introduction.[42]

Grosseteste also sees the danger of moving on to higher things too quickly. In one passage he apologizes for not going into too many details about the property of things but he warns his readers that it

---

[40] See also McEvoy, *Philosophy*, pp. 363–8.

[41] Gross. *Hex.* III. xvi. 1, p. 117.

[42] The importance of the study of the property of things for symbolical theology was generally recognized, see H. Brinkman, *Mittelalterliche Hermeneutik* (Tübingen, 1980), pp. 45–6, 261. 273–4. Grosseteste wanted a reform not of the method, but of the content.

134 *Richard Rufus and Robert Grosseteste*

should really be done, because not knowing about them is like looking at a finely chiselled sculpture from a long distance:

Ista et superiora sub brevitate perstringimus ad vitandum fastidium prolixitatis. Exigeret enim istorum plana exposicio ut manifestaretur per quas proprietates speciales unumquodque dictorum nominum, vacui et tenebrosi, signaret singula suorum signatorum ... Unde noverit lector huis sciencie quod, donec sic possit exponere tam predicta quam ea que sequuntur, speculatur velud a longe distans qui subtilem sculpturam magno interiecto loci spacio contuetur, nec signatas apprehendit sculpture protracciones, nec distinguit sculpture varietate formatum a ligno rudi et informi.[43]

Here Grosseteste also indicates that this commentary is preliminary; it merely provides a first draft of what ought to be done. The motivation for his interest in natural philosophy is also described in the introduction to the description of the natural properties of plants, the creatures of the third day:

Hanc itaque spiritalem germinacionem de terra spiritali vidit Deus aspectu beneplaciti quod esset bona. Vidit quoque et ipsam naturalem germinacionem vegetabilium de terra naturali quod esset bona, significans germinacionem spiritalem per suas proprietates et utilitates naturales.[44]

Another point he makes is that some creatures bring man closer to God than others. In the discussion of the sun and the moon, which are in the words of Gen. i. 14 'for signs', Grosseteste stresses that the spiritual significance of the lights of heaven is greater and more obvious, probably because in their splendour they participate in the highest symbol of all, light, the first form of all that is:

Ut enim ipse Augustinus testatur, ex omni creatura est per aliquam similitudinem significacio mistica trahenda. Sed forte istud quadam speciali prerogativa inter corporalia assignatur celi luminaribus, quia in hiis est signacio spiritalium maior et evidentior et in scriptura celebrior quam in ceteris corporalibus.[45]

The many treatises on heavenly bodies in Grosseteste's scientific works testify to the special importance he attached to them as higher

[43] Gross. *Hex.* I. xix. 2, p. 79.
[44] Ibid. IV. xxix. 6, p. 153.
[45] Ibid. V. vii. 1, p. 163. The importance of light as the first and highest symbol is expressed by Grosseteste in a commentary on some verses of Ecclesiasticus: 'Inter cetera corpora deducentia nos in intellectum et visionem invisibilium, propinquissime potest deducere cognoscentem ipsam in visionem gloriae maiestatis', J. McEvoy, 'The Sun as *res* and *signum*: Grosseteste's Commentary on Ecclesiasticus ch. 43, vv. 1–5', *RThAM* xli (1974), 65; see also 73–4.

symbols, which because of their nobility are better images than anything else, man excluded.

Although all nature speaks of higher things, Grosseteste is very careful in not making too quick a leap into the world of ideas. This much is clear from many passages in the *Hexaemeron* which seem, at first sight, to contradict all he says about the value of the allegorical method. In several passages he remarks that the study of created things and their properties is worthwhile in itself because creation is good and all things are useful in themselves, they are not just stepping-stones:

Et quia bonum, quod vidit Deus in aquarum congregacione et apparicione aride, aque, maris et terre comprehendit utilitates, de naturalibus eorum proprietatibus, per quas suas exercent utilitates, pauca dicemus.[46]

Hec ad presens breviter perstricta sint de utilitatibus aque, maris, et terre; ... Secundum Basilium enim 'bonum' de quo dicitur: *Vidit Deus quia bonum*, rei facte comprehendit utilitatem. Et in huius verbi explanacionem ipse et Ambrosius singulorum factorum naturales usus enarrare conati sunt.[47]

With the help of Basil, Grosseteste here defines the meaning of the word 'good' in this context. The goodness of things is connected with their utility, which they exercise through their natural properties. It should be noted immediately that the goodness of things is not exhausted in their utility, hence the use of *comprehendit*. If goodness equalled utility, it would be difficult to understand how he would connect his praise of the lights of heaven as the most obvious and clearest symbols with the following sentence, which occurs a few paragraphs later:

Et quia bonum quod vidit Deus in factis luminaribus comprehendit eorum in hoc mundo utilitates quas perficiunt per naturales eorum proprietates, de hiis pauca dicemus.[48]

The utility of a thing has much to do with the part every creature has been assigned in the functioning of the whole universe. Speaking about the creation of the animal world he says:

... vidit Deus quia bona, hoc est, in rerum universitate utilia. De eorum [sc. animantium] igitur proprietatibus quibus in universitate servant utilitatis ordinem, aliqua in genere dicenda sunt.[49]

[46] Gross. *Hex.* IV. xii. 4, p. 136.
[47] Ibid. IV. xv. 4, p. 141.
[48] Ibid. V. xxi. 1, p. 179.
[49] Ibid. VII. xii. 4, p. 207.

Grosseteste recommends the study of the natural properties of things not only because of their symbolical significance but also because of their usefulness, which they exercise through their natural properties. Everything is useful, because it plays a part in the maintenance of the whole, every creature according to its own nature, which is visible from its properties; and it is because of this contribution, among others, that all things can be called good in God's sight. That does not mean, however, that Grosseteste, despite his symbolism, conceives of the universe as a self-sufficient mechanism. He makes it quite clear that the universe itself is good only because it is a reflection of the highest good:

Quelibet igitur creatura, quamdiu servat sue creacionis bonum, simpliciter in se bona est. In ordine autem suo ad universitatem melior est. Ipsa autem universitas valde bona est. Ipse autem Creator universitatis summe bonus est.[50]

The last remark shows that Grosseteste did not see any contradiction between the fact that all created things have a value in themselves and a value as signs; the two go together, as is also obvious from an earlier remark, where he said about the growing of plants 'quod esset bona, significans germinacionem spiritalem per suas proprietates et utilitates naturales'.[51] Their usefulness in themselves is exercised through their natural properties, the same properties on which their value as a sign is based. The natural consistency of a thing and its symbolic value do not clash, or even if they do, it is from that confrontation that symbolism draws its strength, the likeness of the unlike. The consistency of the symbol guarantees the truth of the reality in which the symbol participates and gives an objective basis to allegorizing. The arbitrariness of symbolical theology is checked, at least in Grosseteste's eyes, by the great care taken to ensure the objective basis of the allegorical ascent.[52] In his treatment of visible light, Grosseteste brings the two functions of all created things together, and the absence of any suggestion that they could contradict each other is striking:

Et quia in bonitate lucis quam vidit Deus intelligitur utilitas ipsius et usus bonus, que agit in universo suis naturalibus proprietatibus, de lucis corporalis

---

[50] Ibid. VIII. xxvii. 1, p. 252.
[51] See above p. 134.
[52] McEvoy, *Philosophy*, pp. 363–4; Brinkman, *Hermeneutik*, pp. 46, 261, 273; H. Dunbar, *Symbolism in Medieval Thought* (New Haven, 1929), p. 281.

proprietatibus pauca dicamus, ex quibus intelligi valeant eciam proprietates rerum per lucem corporalem mistice signatarum.[53]

Augustine had outlined the programme when he said that all human resources had to be used to gain a thorough understanding of Scripture; the biblical scholar, using pagan disciplines, could be compared with the Israelites plundering the wealth of Egypt.[54] But even in Augustine's days the spoils had been small and it had become worse in subsequent centuries. Grosseteste felt that in his days, when so much new, reliable scientific material, till then hidden in the unknown works of Aristotle's natural philosophy, had become available, theologians would be able to carry out the task set by Augustine and to deepen their understanding of the invisible by a profounder knowledge of the visible. Grosseteste also thinks that the renewal of this classical approach is worth while because it offers an easy way for simple and uneducated people to gain access to the mysteries of faith. They can start off with the things that can be easily imagined and ascend from there to the mysteries of the Christian faith. It is a conjecture, but could it be that in this tenacious struggle to keep theological speculation tied to its source and to its traditional methods, Grosseteste is motivated by his concern for the reform and renewal of the Church, which pervades so much of his policy as Bishop of Lincoln? The statutes he issued for his diocese seem to point in that direction. In them all priests on parish duty, many of whom had only a scanty education, were encouraged to be steeped in Scripture as the poles in the rings of the ark of the Covenant.[55] It was this intimacy with the Bible which Grosseteste sought to promote in all his writings.

(ii) *Richard Rufus and the Demands of the New Age*

Grosseteste's efforts to keep the floodgates closed met with some very partial success at Oxford in the beginning, but in the end he failed to get his way. His letter to the Oxford theologians was very probably intended to admonish Richard Fishacre for his lectures on the *Sentences* and to warn that there should be an early end to this new

---

[53] Gross. *Hex.* II. x. 1, p. 97.

[54] Augustine, *De doctrina Christiana*, ii. 40, ed. J. Martin (CC xxxii, 1962), pp. 75–6.

[55] 'Omnes quoque pastores animarum et sacerdotes parochiales, finitis in ecclesia divinis officiis, orationi et lectioni sacre scripture diligenter intendant ... sintque semper inserti in doctrina et operatione scripture tamquam vectes in anulis arche, ut assidua lectione, veluti cotidiano cibo, alatur et pinguescat oratio', *Councils and Synods*, II. i. 269.

custom. Simon of Hinton, Fishacre's successor as *lector* to the Dominicans, did not as far as we know comment on the *Sentences*.[56] The Franciscan John of Wales, who succeeded Richard Rufus as *lector*, is another example of a theologian who stuck to the more old-fashioned methods, as is, of course, Adam Marsh, Grosseteste's greatest friend among the Franciscans.[57] But the beginning of Grosseteste's defeat became visible as early as 1253, when a statute was passed which decreed that bachelors should either lecture on a book of the Bible, or on the *Sentences*, or on the *Histories* of Peter Comestor.[58] This statute seems an effort to compromise. A decade later Roger Bacon in his complaint about the evils of modern theology remarked that, if anything, the *Histories* seemed more suitable as a text-book than the *Sentences* because it had at least the advantage of remaining much closer to the text of the Bible.[59] It could be that the legislators of 1253 thought along the same lines, and included Comestor's book in an effort to find some middle ground between the advocates of the Bible and those who used the *Sentences*. By 1267, however, Oxford had completely conformed to the new custom. It was in that year that Bacon made his bitter complaint about modern theologians who forgot the living source of theology and used the *Sentences* instead—and these to such an extent that knowledge of the Bible had become a rare thing.[60] And this complaint applied to Oxford as well as Paris.

Richard Rufus started his lectures on the *Sentences* in the middle of this debate, just before 1250. His position, indeed, must have been awkward after Grosseteste's letter, for Grosseteste remained, even after his elevation to the see of Lincoln, the most influential friend and protector of the Franciscans, as we have seen. And to go against his express wishes on such an important point as the education of future priests might easily lead to a break, or at least a more than passing coolness in that long-standing and fruitful relationship.

The awkwardness of the position is obvious in Richard's intro-

[56] Smalley, *Study*, pp. 277–8.

[57] Roger Bacon testifies to Adam Marh's 'soundness', Little, 'Franciscan School', p. 809; for John of Wales, op. cit., p. 846; Thomas Docking on the other hand, although he is mainly known for his extensive Bible commentaries, did lecture on the *Sentences* as well, see: J. Catto, 'New Light on Thomas Docking O.F.M.', *Mediaeval and Renaissance Studies*, vi (1968), 136 n. 4.

[58] *Statuta* (ed. Gibson, p. 49). For the text of the statute see above, p. 26.

[59] Little 'Franciscan School', pp. 808–9.

[60] A comprehensive survey of Bacon's philippic against the theologians in J. Beumer, 'Biblische Grundlage und dialektische Methode im Widerstreit innerhalb der mittelalterlichen Scholastik', *FnSn* xlviii (1966), 230–6.

duction to his commentary on the *Sentences*. He is always on his guard, he takes Grosseteste's words very seriously, and he is on the defensive. He is well aware throughout that he is breaking new ground, at least in Oxford; as far as we know he was, after Fishacre, the first theologian at Oxford to give a course of lectures on the *Sentences*, and he treads, therefore, very warily. Grosseteste's defence of symbolical theology, as given in the *Hexaemeron*, is constantly before his eyes.

He begins the prologue in a conventional way with a detailed explanation of a quotation from the Bible, in this case from the story of the poor widow's mite (Mark xii. 42), and then proceeds to discuss the status of theology. The three main questions he deals with at some length are: the object of theology, the author or subject of theology, and the status of theology as a science. Richard admits his reluctance to embark on these questions: it is the custom to do so, he says, and to have doubts about the nature of theology, but to him it all seems superfluous, because what follows is not theology, nor even a part of it; divine Scripture is perfect in itself without any appendix:

> Quisbusdam placet hic quedam generalia de ipsa theologia dubitare et hoc gratia huius summe magistri. Quod non videtur mihi necessarium, cum hec summa non sit ipsa theologia, nec aliqua pars eius. Est enim divina scriptura in se integra perfecta absque hac et omni alia summa.   (B f. 6C)

The problem of the relation between the *Sentences* and Scripture appears here immediately and it is at the background of all the introductory questions. In the second question, on the authorship of theology, it comes to the fore.[61] And whereas in the two other questions he is very hesitant, even diffident, as is normal for him, here he asserts his position with the force of someone crossing swords in a battle:

> Ipse [Deus] et auctor, ipse de se scribens sui tradens cognitionem, sui precipiens dilectionem ... Ecce quomodo sit de subiecto non curo, nec aliquid unum definio. Est autem Deus auctor, ut dixi, et nulla creatura. (B f. 7A)

Man in all his ingenuity, he argues, can never transcend the bonds of nature and can never, therefore, reach out to that which is pure grace, the faith and the Incarnation of the Word. These mysteries can only be revealed to man by God, and the human authors, who bore witness to

---

[61] The formula 'God, the author of theology/Scripture' goes back to late antiquity and was coined in the struggle against Manichaeism; see A. Bea, 'Deus auctor Sacrae Scripturae. Herkunft und Bedeutung der Formel', *Angelicum*, xx (1943), 27–8.

them, are mere instruments. Philosophers who maintain that through human wisdom they can investigate the Trinity have become fools, although they are convinced of their own wisdom. Augustine was quite right when he said that, although there was much in the books of the Platonists that reminded him of John's gospel, he had never been able to discover in them that the Word had become flesh. (B f. 7A)[62]

The result is then confirmed by a syllogism: what is said in this science is either true or not true. If it is not true, then it is not knowledge. But if it is true, then, both because of its truth and of the fact that to this science nothing can be added nor can anything be subtracted from it, this science must come from God, since mere human science is always incomplete and can be perfected. The premiss that theology gives us an insight into the truth is assumed. The second premiss is justified with quotations from the Bible, which looks like begging the question.[63]

After giving his own reasons he demolishes Richard Fishacre's answer to the problem. Fishacre comes to the same conclusion as Rufus but gives as his main reason that the truth, expressed in this doctrine, is infinite, whereas man has only finite powers.[64] Rufus objects that this argument is not cogent, since the infinite truth is expressed in Scripture in finite language (B f. 7A). Finally he meets the opposition of a quibbler ('cavillator') who, like the Manichees, maintains that God may be the author of some parts of Scripture but not of others by quoting at great length from Augustine's *Contra Faustum*.[65] The quoted passage does not quite meet the problem, since Augustine tries here to defend the authenticity of the human authors, not that of the divine author.

Richard's strong emphasis on God as the author of this doctrine clarifies his position on the relation between Scripture and theology:

[62] Augustine, *Confessiones*, vii 9, ed. P. Knöll (CSEL xxxiii, 1896), pp. 154–5.

[63] 'Item aut verum est, quicquid in hac scientia dicitur, aut non. Si non, scientia non est. Si sic, ergo, cum in hac dicitur quod huic nihil possit addi nihil minui et hoc verum erit, sed omni inventioni naturali creature est possibilis additio, ergo nulla creatura est auctor huius. Dicitur autem Deuteronomio 4.a. . . .' [follow quotes: Deut. iv. 2 and Rev. xxii. 18–19] (B f. 7A). In the margin the remark: 'Nota hanc rationem' in the same hand as the main text.

[64] 'Veritates enim infinitae sunt, quia numeri et figurae infiniti sunt, de quorum quolibet multa sunt vera. Sed omnis veritas in ea [Scriptura] est. Ergo infinitae veritates in ea sunt. Sed si linguis hominum loquar et angelorum non sufficiam dicere infinita, quia sum finitae potentiae. Ergo nec homo nec angelus, immo nec homo et angelus, nisi virtute alicuius qui est virtutis infinitae—quod convenit soli Deo—huius auctor esse potest. Ergo Deus huius est auctor', Long, 'Science of Theology', pp. 87–8.

[65] Augustine, *Contra Faustum*, xxxiii. 6, ed. J. Zycha (CSEL xxv, 1891), pp. 792–3.

he identifies Scripture with theology. Nowhere but in Scripture can we hear about the Incarnation of the Word, and it was in Scripture that Augustine had found what he could not find in the books of the Platonists. Therefore, real theology is nothing but exposition of the Bible. This implies that lecturing on the *Sentences*, whatever else it may be, is not theology in the proper sense. Richard himself comes to the same conclusion, a commentary on the *Sentences* cannot be called theology, nor even part of it; Scripture is perfect in itself. The only scope Richard sees for a work like his is that it can help the theologian in his difficult task, because it contains clarifications and explains obscure passages, useful for us, but not necessary:

Sed sunt tales summe elucidationes alique aliquorum que in illa obscure dicta sunt, propter nos utiles et adhibite.   (B f. 6C)

He had already made the same sharp distinction before in the commentary on Mark xii. 42. There he calls the Bible 'theologice facultatis volumen sacrum' (B f. 6A); and in explaining the work of a theologian he explains that it consists of four different tasks: the praise of God in the divine office, the exposition of the Bible, the teaching of morals, and:

4° nodosa enodamus, difficilia explanamus, ambigua certificamus, obscura prout possibile est, elucidamus. De hoc ultimo quadrante solo intenditur in presenti negotio.   (B f. 6B)

A commentary like this is what the notes are to an edition of a classic masterpiece, a help for the reader, but ultimately unnecessary, and certainly without any binding authority. At the end of the introductory questions he stresses it once more: these notes do not constitute a part of Scripture and, therefore, not of theology:

Dividere autem sacram scripturam propter officium assumptum ad presens non curo. Non est enim presens summa aliqua pars sacre scripture ut estimo.   (B f. 7C)

The terms in which he couches the rejection of his own work as part of theology are very strong indeed; his position is unique among theologians in the middle thirteenth century. None of them downgraded the *Sentences* so much as Richard does here, mere clarifications, footnotes.[66] It seems to me that the tense situation in which Richard embarked upon his work accounts for his extraordinary

[66] Köpf, *Wissenschaftstheorie*, pp. 32–3, 266.

position. An important clue is the sentence in which he sums up his reflections on the status of theology, that for the present he does not care to divide Scripture according to the task laid upon him. This rather mysterious phrase can be explained, if it is taken as a reference to Fishacre's views on the relation between lectures on the Bible and on the *Sentences*.

Fishacre had maintained in the introduction to his commentary on the *Sentences* that there are two sides to theology, coinciding with the division in man between reason and will, between *virtus apprehensiva* and *virtus motiva*. Theology seeks to effect the unity between the mind and the highest Truth, and also the unity between the heart and the highest Good; the first is effected by systematic questioning, the second by moral exposition.[67] In Scripture these two are intertwined. The modern masters, however, treat them separately, attaching moral instruction to their lectures on the Bible and speculative questions to their lectures on the *Sentences*. Lecturing on the *Sentences* is, in Fishacre's eyes, part of the explanation of the Bible and, therefore, part of theology.[68] And far from being less important, it is the more difficult part. To justify this view he claims that Peter Lombard's *Sentences* are, in fact, an excerpt from the Bible:

Haec autem pars difficilior de canone sacrarum Scripturarum excerpta in isto libro qui Sententiarum dicitur ponitur.[69]

By drawing the *Sentences* into the orbit of the Bible, he can maintain that both lectures are really part of the same course, the explanation of Scripture. Where Richard Rufus is exclusive, Richard Fishacre is inclusive, in trying to find a single theoretical framework for a division which had been made for purely practical reasons. It is the one Bible which is divided over two different sets of lectures and taught according to two very different methods. This view is turned down by Richard Rufus, when he says that he does not care to divide Scripture according to the task laid upon him and that Lombard's *Sentences* are not a part of the Bible. Grosseteste's protest is now more under-

---

[67] Long, 'Science of Theology', p. 96; Fishacre uses the terms *aspectus* and *affectus*, which have strong Grossetestian overtones.

[68] Fishacre assumes, just like Rufus and, indeed, like all theologians before the middle of the 13th-c., that theology equals Biblical exposition. See Long, 'Science of Theology', pp. 87–9, where Fishacre deals with the authorship—or as he calls it, the efficient cause—of theology. He only sets the boundaries wider to include speculative questions.

[69] Op. cit., p. 97.

standable: Fishacre made room for the use of the new syllogistic method in the heart of theology, the reflection on Scripture.

The intention of Richard Rufus's strong remarks on the subject now becomes clearer too; his analysis serves a double purpose. It was directed against Fishacre in the first place, as is clear from his constant emphasis on the fact that the *Sentences* have nothing to do with the Bible, but they were also intended to pacify the anger of Robert Grosseteste. That would account for Richard's very odd position. On the one hand he takes an extremely low view of the *Sentences*, relegating them to the status of explanatory notes; on the other hand he bothers to lecture on them at length, and later on took great pains to make a careful summary of yet another commentary, that of Bonaventure. And it is also interesting to see that in the abbreviation the whole problem of the relation between Scripture and the *Sentences* has disappeared completely; only the two questions about object and method are left (V f. 4A–D). But by then Grosseteste was dead, and Richard was no longer obliged to strike a balance between the demands of modern education and the wishes of a conservative Bishop.

In 1250, however, he had to defend himself for engaging in a practice condemned by the Bishop of the diocese in which Oxford lay, and over whose schools the Bishop had jurisdiction. And he did it by putting Scripture and theology firmly on one side and lectures on the *Sentences*, in which dialectics and syllogisms could be used, on the other, assigning to the latter the humble status of elucidation, perfectly legitimate, very useful for us, but not theology. The solution has an artificial, not to say political ring about it; it does not seem to contribute very much to the problem at hand, but it had the practical advantage of enabling Richard to continue his course without offending Robert Grosseteste, the diocesan Bishop, the guardian of the university's orthodoxy, and the protector of his order. In his second work, where he can speak more freely, it becomes clear that he was not really interested in the problem for its own sake, and there it has disappeared.

In the other two questions of the introduction Richard confronts Grosseteste more directly, since they are the same as the Bishop had deemed worthy of consideration in his introduction to the *Hexae-meron*. The first is the question about the subject-matter of theology, in other words: what theology is all about. Richard approaches the question from several sides. He starts off by quoting Hugh of

Saint-Victor: everything can be divided into the works of creation ('opera conditionis'), through which came into being all things which were not, and the works of recreation ('opera restaurationis'), through which things were made better after the fall. The works of creation constitute the object of the secular sciences, the works of recreation of theology (B f. 6C–D).[70] To quote Hugh at the outset of this question is common and requires no special explanation.

He then mentions Grosseteste's opinion that the subject-matter of theology is Christ, since in him we find that fivefold union which embraces Creator and creature (B f. 6D).[71] No comment is given. The next opinion he quotes is Fishacre's, who deals with the question under the heading of material cause. Fishacre reduces all reality for the present purpose to three simple natures, of which the highest is God, the lowest the body, and the middle the rational creature. Three further natures can be distinguished, which consist of certain combinations of the three simple natures: mankind (lower and middle), the Church (higher and middle), and Christ (all three). Since the subject-matter of theology cannot be of lower or middle nature only, we are left with three choices: God, Christ, and the Church. By comparing theology with geometry he comes to the conclusion that the Church is the real subject-matter of theology, but that it also deals with God as its minimal point, and with Christ as embracing everything.[72] Rufus rejects this opinion in no uncertain terms: such words are false and cannot be accepted, first of all because the division is inadequate, secondly because nothing is composed of God and something else, and thirdly because Christ is not composed of three elements; in him there are three elements, but they are in no way mixed.

Rufus's own opinion is vague; he does not really decide the matter, but proposes several solutions, and ends by saying that he does not really care (B f. 7A, quoted above). In his reply two problems are dealt with at the same time: he speaks both about the subject-matter itself and about its unity. The main solution he proposes is that Christ is the subject of theological thought. In all creation there is a natural unity of all corporeal things with each other, in man there is a personal unity of corporeal nature with rational creature, in Christ of both with the divine nature. And there is also a unity which consists in the conformity of the wills of all rational creatures with each other and with

---

[70] Hugh of Saint-Victor, *De sacramentis*, Prologus, ii–iv (PL clxxvi, cols. 183–5).

[71] Gross. *Hex.* I. i. 1–3, pp. 49–50. See also above, pp. 130–1.

[72] Long, 'Science of Theology', pp. 91–3; Köpf, *Wissenschaftstheorie*, pp. 96, 101–2.

God; a unity that is particularly strong because it is the bond of love, of which Paul says that nothing 'shall be able to separate us from the love of God, which is in Christ Jesus our Lord' (Rom. viii. 39). Only in Christ are all these really united; he, therefore, is the subject of this doctrine (B f. 6D).[73]

At this point he stresses, as at the beginning, that he only speaks about these matters to satisfy the philosophers. He proceeds by remarking that the unity of theology is safe, despite the fact that Creator and creature have nothing in common and that, therefore, what is predicated of the one cannot, unqualified, be predicated of the other. Richard answers that, though this is true, there is a certain likeness between Creator and creature, which allows us to maintain the unity of subject.[74] And as an afterthought he finally mentions the other solution given to this question in the thirteenth century that the subject of theology is God himself without explaining why or how (B f. 7A).

On the whole the answer is disappointing, a combination of Fishacre and Grosseteste. From Fishacre he takes the distinction of the three elements which are all in Christ, and from Grosseteste the idea of the bond of love which unites God and man in a common purpose. The most striking feature of his treatment is that he mentions both Grosseteste and Fishacre but takes issue only with the latter, almost accusing him of heresy. Grosseteste's opinion stands as it is and Richard does not enter into a debate with him.[75]

Finally Richard comes to the question whether theology can be called a science. He puts the arguments for the negative first, mainly

---

[73] Richard even speaks of a fourth union: 'Omnes iste 3. unitates sunt in Christo . . . Potest igitur dici probabiliter quod unitas 4ª resultet ex hiis tribus: unitas scilicet aggregationis illarum unitatum et quod est hac unitate unum, est subiectum huius doctrine' (B f. 6D).

[74] See also Köpf, *Wissenschaftstheorie*, pp. 120–1.

[75] In the abbreviation Richard leaves to his readers the choice between three solutions: Hugh of Saint-Victor's and Grosseteste's, and a third to be found in the *Summa 'Alexandri'*: first we must distinguish between material and formal subject ('circa quod' and 'de quo'); in the formal subject a distinction must be made between essence, potency 'and operation: 'Si subiectum accipiatur quantum ad essentiam, sic est divina essentia, si quantum ad virtutem, sic est Dei virtus, scilicet Christus, si quantum ad operationem, sic sunt opera recreationis principaliter et per consequens opera conditionis. Subiectum vero circa quod sunt res et signa. Omnes isti modi convenientes mihi videntur, nec sibi contrariantur' (V f. 4C). Cf. *Summa theologica 'Alexandri'*, Introductio, i. 3 (i, 1924), p. 6; the author of this particular question in the *Summa* is either Alexander of Hales or, less likely, John of La Rochelle; in any case it is earlier than 1250, so that Richard must have taken it over from them. [Doucet], 'Prolegomena', p. ccxlvii.

by quoting a long passage from the introduction to Grosseteste's *Hexaemeron*. He focuses on two main points. The first is that Christ can be neither premiss to nor conclusion from a scientific argument. This requires some explanation. The premisses or *principia per se nota* are axioms; they must be immediately obvious to the mind. Everyone agrees, however, that there is nothing obvious about Christ's person or about his coming, which is a contingent historical event. Nor could his coming and the work of redemption possibly be regarded as the outcome of a rational and necessary process and, therefore, form the conclusion of a scientific argument. Christ's appearance is a work of love and grace and, therefore, not predictable nor deducible a posteriori. The second is Grosseteste's main point that, since in the Bible all things are equally known and equally believable, we cannot proceed by the way of syllogisms.[76] He also mentions Fishacre's opinion that the authority of the Bible is such that it guarantees a degree of certainty which can never be reached by sheer human reasoning. This sceptical view of the powers of human reason in general is as characteristic for Fishacre as it is exceptional in the thirteenth century.[77]

Rufus does not agree with this negative point of view. He argues that demonstration and proof can have a legitimate place in theology. The argument itself is rather confused, the more so as near the end the sentences become almost elliptical, as if they were jotted down in shorthand. The solution Richard tries to formulate is based on a distinction of four different kinds of history, each governed by its own laws: the natural order, the history of mankind, the history of the divine miracles, and the history of our redemption. In the history of the natural order, human reason can proceed by way of demonstration, because everything in nature is subjected to unchanging laws of causality: '... est secundum causalem decursum in sempiterna uniformitate perseverantem' (B f. 7B). The same is true for the history of the divine miracles, as far as their natural components are concerned: 'Potest esse demonstratio quoad investigationem rationum naturalium ministrantium Dei verbo' (B f. 7B). In the history of mankind scientific demonstration is impossible, since it consists of the accumulated free decisions of man 'cuius vagus est effectus exiens de

[76] He first quotes from Gross. *Hex.* I. ii. 1–2, pp. 50–1—not recognized as such by Köpf, *Wissenschaftstheorie*, p. 165—and then adds a sentence from Fishacre: 'Demonstratio autem procedit ex magis notis ad minus nota, ergo hec non erit demonstrativa' (B f. 7B=Long, 'Science of Theology', p. 90).

[77] Köpf, *Wissenschaftstheorie*, pp. 164, 214.

persona per potestatem valentem opposita' (B f. 7B). And the same holds true for the history of man's salvation:

Omnino non potest esse demonstratio propter inscrutabile arcanum quod secundum liberum divine voluntatis electionem ex qua sola processerunt salutares reparandi regni Dei dispensationes.   (B f. 7B)

The source of this ingenious distinction may well have been Anselm, who in *De Conceptu Virginali* draws a similar, though less elaborate, distinction on the basis of how all things came into being: either through God's will, or through their own God-given nature, or through the will of man. Therefore, there are three courses of events: miraculous, natural, and voluntary. The history of man's redemption is a mixture of these three: it has natural, voluntary, and miraculous components.[78] Although Richard draws the borders between reason and faith slightly differently, the two conceptions are very much the same. Richard knew Anselm's work very well, and uses it a great deal in both commentaries.[79] Their concern is the same: both are trying to find the areas of theological thought to which rational concepts can be applied.[80]

But after this, Richard makes a strategic retreat in the second part of his solution. First he asserts that human reason is not autonomous, but can only penetrate into unknown areas if it is aided by divine illumination.[81] But that is not all: man is now even more helpless and in a greater state of confusion, because in the fall from grace he has turned away from the light without darkness. But God in his mercy has provided a cure, namely that man can come to true knowledge even now by surrendering to divine authority, so that through the merit of faith he will learn the gift of beatitude. Therefore, no one can now safely use reason unless he is grounded in the Catholic faith. Without faith there can be no knowledge in our present state.[82]

---

[78] Anselm, *De conceptu virginali et de originali peccato*, ix, ed. F. S. Schmitt (*Opera omnia*, ii, 1946), p. 154.

[79] See e.g. B ff. 9D, 10B, 10C, 15C, 19C–20C, 67A, 68A–C.

[80] G. Evans, *Old Arts and New Theology* (Oxford, 1980), p. 130.

[81] Gal, 'Viae', p. 179 proves that Rufus held the theory of divine illumination in his epistemology.

[82] 'Et quamvis in his que dicta sunt possit ex influentia divini luminis humana ratio in ignotorum notitiam decurrere secundum seriem sillogisticam, tamen volens Deus omnium clementer confuse ... contractis per aversionem a lumine in quo non est tenebra ulla [cf. John i. 15] prospexit omnibus ut in hiis tantummodo credatur divine auctoritati, ut meritum credulitatis premiet munere beatitudinis et declinentur perniciose occasiones erronee seductionis. Nulli tamen possibile est sine lapsu erroris in hiis que predicta sunt ratiocinari, nisi ei qui super fundamentum catholice fidei

On the basis of this conclusion Richard then tries, in a third part, to find out whether he can go any further from there. He seems to be back at the point from which he started. For if there is no knowledge without faith, then in theology, i.e. the Bible, there is no room for demonstration and argumentative language. He is aware of the impasse as is clear from the fact that, at this point, he muses again on Grosseteste's words that in the Bible everything is equally believable. But then he tries to escape by making an important distinction. Could it not be that only from our point of view all things in the Bible are equally true and equally believable, because we have lost the power to penetrate into the depth of reality? We must accept every single word of Scripture on trust and are not allowed to argue about what is more and what is less important. But in true fact there is a hierarchy of being, because some things are nearer to their source (*principium*) than others. This hierarchy cannot be discovered by us but it is, of course, known to God, who reveals it to us in Scripture. And the way he does it, according to Richard, is by showing how the existence of the things further removed from their source can be proved from the existence of the things close to their source. Richard wonders why this cannot be called a scientific argument or a demonstration, not ours, but God's. So how can anyone say that the language of science, the argumentative language is not used in the Bible?[83]

The meaning of the last rhetorical question is further clarified in the next part. Once more Richard repeats that there is an order in all things, known to God but not to us, at least not without divine illumination. It is the order of causality: God is the first cause of things and they in their turn the cause of other things and so on; God can explain that order to us:

Licet Ipse [sc. Deus] non indigeat aliqua certificatione, potest tamen Ipse ipsum ordinem causalitatis, que in rebus, et earundem appropinquationem et remotionem ad se vel a se declarare.   (B f. 7B)

---

sustentatus aciem oculi intellectualis in divine virtutis splendores valet sublimare, iuxta illud prophete: "Nisi credideritis, non intelligetis" [Isa. vii. 9 Vet. Lat.]' (B f. 7B).

[83] 'Sed licet ad nos, qui fide hec accepimus—prout hic dictum est—forte non sit demonstratio, quare non quoad ipsum Auctorem scribentem? Quamvis enim credibilia unde talia in hac doctrina eiusdem et equalis credibilitatis sint quoad nos, qui hac via accepimus, sunt tamen aliqua eorum secundum suum ordinem propinquiora principio et quedam remotiora. Si ergo concludat ipse Scriptor, qui et principium, que remotiora sunt per ea que propinquiora ordine nature, quare non erit demonstratio?' (B f. 7B). An important underlying assumption of this argument is that the hierarchy of concepts in the mind corresponds with the hierarchy of being outside.

His question is: is it not the case that God in the Bible explains to us, who are blinded by sin, the order of nature and the relation of all things to each other and to their Creator? Richard answers in the affirmative. If there is an order of nature, a hierarchy of being, there is a corresponding hierarchy of knowledge. The proper language to express this hierarchy is the language of premisses and conclusions, in other words the language of scientific argument; the premisses containing what is ontologically prior, or in Richard's words closer to the source, and the conclusions what is ontologically posterior, further removed from the source. So if the Bible explains that order to us, it must be full of demonstrations: 'Forte plena est hec doctrina de demonstrationibus efficacissimis' (B f. 7C). Richard gives two examples of such demonstrations, which show clearly in his opinion that some things in Scripture are inferred from others:

'Igitur perfecta sunt celi et terra et omnis ornatus eorum', Genesis 2 (Gen. ii. 1). Quasi conclusionem infert ex premissis, celi et terre, et totius mundi perfectionem. Sequitur enim istorum perfectio ex perfectione numeri senarii, ut enim ait Augustinus: 'Senarius numerus non ideo perfectus est, quia 6 diebus opera Deus perfecit, sed ideo 6 diebus opera Deus perfecit, quia senarius est perfectus'. Quare ergo non erit predicta demonstratio? (Bf. 7B–C).[84]

'Thus the heavens and the earth were finished, and all the host of them' (Gen. ii. 1). As if it were a conclusion he infers the perfection of the whole world from the premisses: 'the heavens and the earth'. For their perfection follows from the perfection of the number six; for as Augustine says: 'The number six is not perfect, because God perfected his works in six days, but God perfected his works in six days, because the number six is perfect'. Now why should the foregoing argument not be a demonstration?

In this example Grosseteste's theory, which Richard has just tried to refute, is challenged directly. The example is taken from the *Hexaemeron*; thus Richard shows that Grosseteste here gives a practical example that does not fit the description of biblical language he had given in the introduction. Here Grosseteste admits that demonstration is used in the Bible. There is no need for Richard to seek a dispute with the Bishop, the blatant contradiction speaks for itself.[85]

[84] Gross. *Hex.* IX. i.1, p. 263. Roughly the same argument on the possibility of demonstrative language in the Bible is given by Thomas Aquinas: 'Haec doctrina . . . ex eis [articulis fidei] procedit ad aliquid ostendendum; sicut Apostolus I ad Cor. [xv. 12] ex resurrectione Christi argumentatur ad resurrectionem communem probandam.' (*Summa theologiae*, I. i. 8).

[85] In the abbreviation Richard answers the question in a very different way by distinguishing three uses of the word *scientia*. In a very general way it is used in the same

(iii) *Conclusion*

The whole introduction as such leaves an unsatisfactory feeling. The most striking feature of it is that Richard tried very hard to keep Scripture and theology together in theory, not, as Fishacre had done, by accommodating speculative questioning within the texture of the Bible, but by eliminating it completely from theology, reducing it to the status of footnotes and reserving the name 'theology' for the old-fashioned Scripture commentary. Of all his contemporaries he was the one who took the lowest view of lecturing on the *Sentences* and of using speculation within theology.

That move had probably been politically inspired. Richard had to take note of the Bishop of Lincoln's letter to the Oxford theologians, which took the form of a spirited defence of the identity of theology and Bible commentary, at least in theory.

But what he gave away with one hand, he took back with the other when he tried hard to prove that demonstration is used even in the Bible. This shows clearly that his heart was elsewhere, that he had no feeling for Grosseteste's very real concern that theological reflection was moving too far away from its only source, the Bible. Grosseteste, however, was a provincial, who had never visited the great centres of learning during his education, and was largely self-taught; Richard had been trained as a dialectician in the great schools of Paris, where he had been taught many skills, but perhaps not to have an eye for the richness of Scripture, for its imaginative language, its use of metaphors, and its way of speaking in general. The only thing his eye can focus on, when skimming through the contents of the Bible, is the passage where the author speaks like a dialectician. With such a lack of understanding of the peculiar nature of a narrative text he could never become a convinced defender of Grosseteste's theological method, the allegory.

Richard was, of course, in the overwhelming majority. Almost all the theologians of the thirteenth century tried to some extent to reshape theology into a rational branch of knowledge which fulfilled

---

sense as *sapientia* (V f. 4A), and if understood that way, theology is a science (V f. 4B). A more proper definition of science is 'cognitio rerum humanarum', (V f. 4A); if understood thus, theology is only partly a science: 'Ubi enim instruuntur humana, sicut sacramenta, virtutes et peccata, scientia dici potest; ubi mysterium Trinitatis et gloria futura sapientia' (V f. 4B). An even more restricted definition is: 'nuda cognitio creaturarum' (V f. 4B), which is probably the same as natural science. If science is defined thus, it does not apply to theology at all (V f. 4B).

the requirements laid down by Aristotle. By 1250 the practice was firmly established, and although theoretical reflection upon that practice lagged behind, its importance was realized to improve the new method, and perhaps even more to become aware of its limitations. But here Grosseteste's influence on Richard worked in the negative. As long as theology and Scripture were simply identified in theory, the point of departure was wrong;[86] the conclusion that, therefore, speculation as practised in the lectures on the *Sentences* was nothing more than an unimportant appendix was equally unenlightening, and it certainly failed to clarify the complicated relationship between the two different ways of approaching the one mystery.

This false start also accounts for the muddle Richard finds himself in when he wishes to discuss the question of method explicitly. He has tied himself to the defence of Grosseteste's position that commenting on the Bible constitutes the only real form of theology, and that implies that he has tied himself to a narrative, descriptive, and symbolical way of speaking. On the other hand, he is starting a course of lectures in which a very different mode of proceeding prevails. Perhaps the only thing he could do to bridge the gap was to try to see whether perhaps even in the Bible the demonstrative way of speaking is not sometimes used. This attempt must fail, even if some isolated examples of syllogisms can be traced, and even if he can catch his order's mentor in a contradiction.

Richard was not the only one who failed to clarify the relations between exposition of the Bible and systematic questioning. In fact none of his contemporaries came up with a really satisfactory, theoretical distinction.[87] But Richard was in a particularly bad position to advance thought on this point, caught as he was by the influence of a theologian whose concerns he could not share, but whose authority was such as to restrain him from making a really adventurous effort.

[86] Köpf, *Wissenschaftstheorie*, p. 262.
[87] Ibid. p. 262–7.

CHAPTER 7

The Work of the Six Days

(i) *Creation: Biblical Study or Natural Philosophy?*

HAVING considered the positions of Robert Grosseteste and Richard Rufus as regards the methods of theology, we must now examine whether in practice they differ as much as in theory. Grosseteste has left us in the commentary on the *Hexaemeron*, the work of the six days, an example of how in his view theology ought to progress. The originality of this work lay on the one hand in the tenacity with which Grosseteste clung to the time-honoured method of allegory, on the other hand in the ample attention he paid to the natural properties of all the works of creation in order to improve the basis of allegorical understanding.

Richard Rufus made much use of Grosseteste's *Hexaemeron* in his own treatise on creation, as has been shown by Dales.[1] It would be highly premature, however, to infer from this that he was influenced by Grosseteste's treatment of the subject. Richard Rufus deals with creation in the normal place, the beginning of the second book of the *Sentences*. In the first distinction he discusses the problem of creation in general and tries to establish the Christian position on the beginning of the world by contrasting it with the opinion of the philosophers. The next ten distinctions are devoted to the angels, and in the twelfth distinction he returns to the rest of the work of creation to deal with each single day of creation in more detail in distinctions 12–17. It is in these seven distinctions on creation that Richard has Grosseteste as one of his two main sources, the other being Richard Fishacre's commentary on the *Sentences*.

He mentions the name of Grosseteste only twice in the course of his treatise, the first time in ii. 12, when dealing with the question whether the heaven, created on the first day, and the firmament, created on the second day, are one and the same or different. Before giving Basil's solution he says:

---

[1] Dales, 'Influence', *passim*.

Nam ut de aliis omittam ad presens, quia hoc alias habetur. [*marg.*] In scripto
episcopi Lincolniensis super opera 6 dierum. Distinctio 1a. (B f 127A)

The second time Rufus mentions Grosseteste is in the course of ii. 15,
where he touches very briefly upon the question why the week has
seven days. His answer is that some pagan philosophers attribute this
to the number of the planets, but another explanation would be the
mystery of the number seven. This last possibility is merely mentioned, the reason is: 'Et habetur de hoc ab episcopo Lincolniensi
super hunc locum' (B f. 139C).[2]

There are two manuscript traditions extant of Grosseteste's
Hexaemeron. The first family is represented by Ox ff. 190A–243A, a
direct copy of Grosseteste's autograph with corrections in his own
hand, and two other manuscripts. The second family is represented by
four later manuscripts.[3] Rufus must have used a manuscript of the first
family, although it cannot be established whether, in fact, he used
Grosseteste's own copy. In the prologue to his commentary on the
Sentences he quotes from the longer version of Grosseteste's introduction, as preserved in the Bodleian manuscript. In other places, too,
he follows the reading of that manuscript where it diverts from the
other tradition, e.g. 'concreata' (B f. 127D = Gross. *Hex.* I. xi. 1, p. 67)
for 'creata'; 'Et tropologice per fidem et mores anime informacio'
(B f. 127A = Gross. *Hex.*, I. iii. 2, p. 52) for 'anime conveniens informacio'; and somewhat longer: 'Unde spiritus, hoc est bona voluntas,
Domini super aquas' (B f. 127B = Gross. *Hex.* I. vii. 1, p. 57) for 'et
spiritus Domini ferebatur super aquas'. Richard even takes over a
spelling mistake: 'ut sic habeat parvulus quod suggat' (B f. 126D =
Gross. *Hex.* I. iii. 1, p. 52) as against all other manuscripts: 'sugat'.

As his second main source Richard used Richard Fishacre's commentary on the *Sentences*. Both works must have been on his desk as he
wrote; most of the ordinary short elucidations of words in the
Sentences, and a great many longer explanations, are taken over
completely. In fact, far more than half of the present text of the Oxford
commentary can be traced back either to Grosseteste or to Fishacre.
This in itself is not so curious since originality was not highly
acclaimed, although it poses a question as to how far the commentary
we have before us actually reflects Richard's teaching in the class-
room. It could well be that he only lectured on the disputed questions,

[2] See Gross. *Hex.* IX. x. 1, p. 280.
[3] Ibid., Introduction, pp. xv–xvi. Ox also contains the main text of the *De cessatione legalium*; see above p. 125 n. 15.

some of which we shall consider later, and that he used Grosseteste and Fishacre only later in the process of writing up, to fill in the gaps and to achieve a fully developed commentary. It is more curious that he often quotes Grosseteste through Fishacre. An example of this occurs in the discussion of the light of the heavenly bodies where Fishacre borrows from Grosseteste two heavily abbreviated quotations from Basil and John Damascene. Since Rufus abbreviates Grosseteste here in exactly the same way, he must have borrowed that passage from Fishacre.[4] In other places, however, Richard Rufus uses the *Hexaemeron* far more extensively than Fishacre.

The question is whether he only used Grosseteste as a convenient source or whether he continued and extended Grosseteste's ideas. Borrowing as such from the *Hexaemeron* was very easy; the beginning of the second book of the *Sentences* follows the outline of the first two chapters of the book of Genesis quite closely, always with the exception of the ten distinctions on angels. Rufus, therefore, did not have to plunge too deeply into the rather confusing mass of the bishop's theological works, it was all there in one work. The following table shows the pattern of borrowing:

Rufus	Grosseteste	
ii. 1 ii. 12	part I	first day
ii. 13	part. II	
ii. 14	part. III part. IV part V part. VI	second, third, fourth, fifth day
ii. 15	part. VII part. IX part. VII	sixth, seventh day
ii. 16	part. VIII	creation of man
ii. 17	part. X part. XI	second creation narrative

The only exception to the parallel is part. IX. Grosseteste keeps the order of Scripture and deals with God's rest on the seventh day after the creation of man, whereas Rufus, following Lombard, first deals

---

[4] Gross. *Hex.* v. v. 1–2, pp. 160–1, taken over by Fishacre (Ba f. 108D, O f. 166A), borrowed by Rufus (B f. 135D).

with the whole of creation and its aftermath before turning to man; it is the order of the *Sentences* and not the order of Scripture which dictates Rufus's use of Grosseteste.

This first sign of disagreement is confirmed by subsequent scrutiny. Richard completely breaks down the carefully planned framework of Grosseteste's commentary. The three-tier system of literal explanation, allegorical application, and description of the natural properties of things has entirely vanished. He has no use for Grosseteste's allegories, his ascent to the contemplation of intelligible reality. Not only does he not touch any of the long passages in which Grosseteste gives an allegorical exegesis,[5] but even in those literal passages in which Grosseteste slips in an occasional allegorical comment, he cuts it out.

Rufus's first question in ii. 12 may serve as an example. He asks whether the creation of the angels is mentioned on the literal level of the text (B ff. 126C–127A). He decides that such is not the case, and in support of his position he quotes Grosseteste's explanation of the words 'heaven and earth'. Grosseteste explains them twice, each time beginning with the assertion that on the literal level of the text the words 'heaven and earth' stand for visible creation only, then he continues by unfolding their spiritual meaning. In the first passage he tells us that there are six different possibilities of spiritual exposition in the first sentence of Scripture, each corresponding to one of the days of creation.[6] Richard Rufus takes over the literal part and sums up the six possibilities without taking over the elaborate and ingenious correspondence theory (B ff. 126D–127A). In the second passage Grosseteste explains that spiritually, 'heaven and earth' signify the militant and triumphant Church; morally, active and contemplative virtue, anagogically, the archetypal world in the divine mind.[7] Richard takes over the first part, where Grosseteste had invoked the authority of Bede and Ambrose to ascertain that on the literal level 'heaven and earth' only signify visible creation, and here he does not mention the possible spiritual applications at all (B f. 127A).

Richard's lack of interest in spiritual interpretation is equally obvious and more significant when he comes to interpret the word

---

[5] Ibid. I. xii. 2–4, I. xix–xx, II. ix, III. xiv–xv, IV. xi–xii, xxix, V. xix–xx, VI. xii–xvii, VII. xi–xii, VIII. xxx–xxxv, IX. vii–ix, X. viii–ix, XI. vi–ix, xxii–xxv, xxviii; pp. 68–9, 78–80, 96–7, 112–7, 131–6, 151–3, 177–9, 193–8, 205–7, 253–62, 274–80, 301–5, 312–16, 322–9, 335–7.

[6] Ibid. I. iii. 2–8, pp. 52–3

[7] Ibid. I. xii. 1–4, pp. 68–9.

'beginning'. From Grosseteste he takes over many meanings of the word 'beginning', from the most literal, such as that the world was created in the month of Nisan, to the more remote, such as that God is the efficient cause of all that exists (B f. 127C–D).[8] Grosseteste, however, goes further and maintains that 'beginning' also refers to the Word Incarnate.[9] It is common Christian doctrine, of course, that God had created the world through the Word. Just because this is theologically such a significant point, one might suppose that Richard would use it here despite its doubtful exegetical origin, but he does not. This is not because he doubted that God had created the world through the Word; later on he takes over Grosseteste's discussion of the words 'And God said: Let there be light' (Gen. i. 3), in which it is affirmed that the only help God received in the creation of the world was that of the Word (B f. 129D).[10] But he did not rely on what he considered a doubtful interpretation of a biblical text.

Grosseteste also saw the whole Trinity expressed in the opening sentences of the Bible; the Father and the Son in the words 'And God said' (Gen. i. 3), and the Holy Ghost in the words 'And the Spirit of God moved upon the face of the waters' (Gen. i. 2).[11] Here again there could be no doubt that the creation of the world was the work of the whole Trinity, as Augustine had established once and for all. But Richard did not follow Grosseteste, although he copies both the foregoing and the following part.[12] He must have left it out because he could not see such an arbitrary use of the text as a firm foundation for this doctrine.

It might be argued that the complete abstinence from any of Grosseteste's allegorical elaborations has no deeper significance than this, that Richard, after all, was not composing a commentary on Scripture but a work of speculative theology, in which allegory could have no place by definition. That would certainly be true for a later generation of theologians, for whom the distinction between the two ways of approaching Christian doctrine had become crystal-clear. But in Richard Rufus's generation such clarity had not yet been reached, as can be gathered from the laborious efforts, described above, to make a theoretical distinction between biblical exposition and

[8] Ibid. I. x. 1–10, pp. 65–7.
[9] Ibid. I. xiii. 1, pp. 69–70.
[10] Ibid. II. i. 1, 3, pp. 85–6.
[11] Ibid. II. ii. 1, p. 86.
[12] B f. 129D. 23–36. Gross. *Hex.* II. i. 3, p. 86; B f. 129D. 36–43 = Gross. *Hex.*, II. iii. 2, p. 87.

theology. Even Richard Fishacre, who had managed to make quite a neat separation between Bible and theology in theory, mixed up the two in practice. In theory he had defended the idea that the purpose of lectures on the Bible was moral instruction to achieve the union of the will with the highest Good, and that the purpose of lectures on the *Sentences* was to satisfy the wish for knowledge about God.[13] In fact Richard Fishacre fell back quite frequently in his lectures on the *Sentences* on allegorical and moral interpretation. For instance, in the discussion of God's immutability and simplicity he does not speculate at all, but launches into a diatribe against instability and greed, two vices to which he comes through a moral interpretation of the text (Ba ff. 21C–22A; O ff. 29D–30B). And this is by no means the only example. Richard Rufus never uses allegory in his commentaries; in this he is one step further removed from Grosseteste than Fishacre; he was trained as a dialectician and was, therefore, no longer familiar with the less rigorous method of allegorical understanding advocated by Grosseteste, and still used by Fishacre.

The most original feature of Grosseteste's commentary was his effort to improve the allegorical method and strengthen its foundations by applying all the many new insights in linguistics and natural philosophy. Grosseteste's linguistic points sometimes find their way into Richard's commentary: e.g. he often quotes Grosseteste's remarks on the differences between the several translations of the Bible, such as that the Septuagint speaks about the gathering together of the waters three times, whereas the Vulgate and the Hebrew speak about it only twice (Gen. i. 9–10) (B f. 135C).[14] But where it becomes too complicated Richard simplifies. Grosseteste gives an etymology of the word *celum*: it might have some connection with *cernere* or *celare*, but should also be compared with the Greek and its etymology. Richard is interested in the first two conjectures and leaves out the third (B f. 132C).[15] Neither does he develop the linguistic approach by adding new material; all observations on language are borrowed from the *Hexaemeron*. Richard simply did not have the tools to pursue Grosseteste's line of enquiry; from the commentary it is obvious that he had no knowledge of Greek. Following Grosseteste he often quotes from the *Hexaemeron* of Basil of Caesarea. But whereas Grosseteste usually left out the number of the homily he was quoting,

---

[13] Long, 'Science of Theology', pp. 96–7; see also above, p. 142.
[14] Gross. *Hex.* IV. ix. 1, pp. 129–30.
[15] Ibid. III. v. 1, p. 105.

Richard always supplies the right number (e.g. B f. 128A. 2).[16] And quite a few times he adds quotations from Basil which cannot be found in the *Hexaemeron* at all (e.g. B ff. 127B. 40, 128C. 45).[17] So, Richard must have gone through the *Hexaemeron* of Basil himself, inspired, no doubt, by Grosseteste's use of the homilies. It is striking, however, that his quotations are always from the first nine homilies and that, when Grosseteste quotes from a later homily, Richard is suddenly unable to supply the right number; compare e.g. f. 142B.19 with Gross. *Hex.* VIII. xviii. 4, p. 244. The reason must be that there was a translation in Latin of the first nine homilies, made by Eustathius; the rest would have to be consulted in Greek. Grosseteste could do this, Richard apparently not. Interesting as he must have found Basil's commentary—if use is any indication—it did not challenge him enough to learn Greek himself. The thrust of Richard's thought was directed not to linguistic, but to dialectical precision.[18]

Grosseteste's abiding interest in natural philosophy found its expression in the *Hexaemeron* in the long descriptions of the natural properties of the things just created. An analysis of all the relevant parts of Richard's commentary shows that he ignored these passages almost as completely as the allegorical sections. On only two occasions does he quote a few phrases. The first is when he discusses the nature of light, a subject to which I shall return in more detail. There he uses Grosseteste's treatise on the properties of light as a convenient source for quotations from Augustine and John Damascene (B f. 131B).[19] The second borrowing is more substantial. Coming to the end of the second day of creation, Grosseteste discusses the properties of heaven. One of the points he makes is that on earth the light of heaven is received in its most concentrated form, since the earth is the geometrical centre of the sphere of heaven.[20] This point is taken over by Richard, but in a completely different setting. At the end of ii. 17 he discusses the problem of the site of paradise, which he assumes to be on a high mountain overlooking the earth, and the consequences of that site for the climate and the fertility of the soil. It is in that connection that he takes over Grosseteste's speculations to

---

[16] Ibid. I. xxi. 4, p. 81.

[17] Basil of Caesarea, *Hexaemeron, Eustathius, ancienne version des neuf homélies sur l'Hexaéméron de Basile de Césarée*, I. vii. 9, II. vii. 1–2, 6, ed. E. Amand de Mendieta and S. Rudberg (Texte und Untersuchungen zur Geschichte der altchristlichen Literatur, lxvi, 1958), pp. 12, 26–7.

[18] Dales, 'Influence', pp. 297–8 comes to the same conclusion.

[19] Gross. *Hex.* II. x. 1–2, pp. 98–9.   [20] Ibid. III. xvi. 5–7, pp. 118–20.

prove that paradise is not worse off than the rest of the earth because of its height, since compared with heaven the earth is a mathematical point, and that all parts, therefore, receive the same amount of light (B f. 146D). The fact that this reflection of light from the outer heaven all the way down to the earth is an essential part of Grosseteste's cosmogony seems to escape Richard, who merely seeks to make a meteorological point. It is clear, therefore, that although Richard borrows twice from Grosseteste's treatises on the natural properties of things, the context is so different that it cannot be said that he shared Grosseteste's outlook.

It would be wrong, however, to conclude from these omissions that Richard Rufus was not interested in the workings of nature, or that his only interest was speculative theology. This would be patently untrue; in several places throughout his commentaries he devotes many pages to the nature of change and motion, to the concepts of form and matter, and other important physical theories, to which we must return later. But the focus of his interest seems to have shifted. Two very significant omissions point to the direction in which he wants to go. Grosseteste's interest in astronomy is well-known: comets, planets, and the movements of the stars had his life-long interest. The *Hexaemeron*, too, bears witness to that: having mentioned the standard question of the difference between heaven and the firmament, he says that he does not know the answer, but that, if they differ, then heaven is immobile, and he elaborates this point at length.[21] Rufus borrows the first argument but skips the second (B f. 127A). Later on when Grosseteste comes to speak about the firmament, he argues for some time about the number of heavens. Here again, although Richard Rufus takes over the whole discussion of the firmament, he leaves out this astronomical excursion.[22]

Another of Grosseteste's many interests was mathematics. It has been argued that one of the decisive contributions of Grosseteste to the development of modern science was to take a first step in the direction of quantification instead of giving in to Aristotelian empiricism and a more descriptive natural philosophy.[23] Although this

[21] From Gross. *Hex.* I. xvi. 3, p. 75; omitting I. xvii. 1, pp. 75–7.

[22] In B ff. 132C–134D Richard finds a place for practically everything in Gross. *Hex.* III. i. 1–xi. 2, pp. 102–11, with the single exception of chs. viii–ix, pp. 107–9, where Grosseteste argues about the number of heavens.

[23] McEvoy, *Philosophy*, p. 210; F. Van Steenberghen, 'La philosophie de la nature au XIIIᵉ siècle', *La filosofia della natura nel Medioevo*, Atti del terzo congresso internazionale di filosofia medioevale (Milan, 1966), pp. 126–7.

argument is mainly based on the treatises *De Luce* and *De Lineis*, some of these mathematical preoccupations can be seen in the *Hexaemeron* as well. In discussing the problem of the gathering together of the waters on the third day, Grosseteste tries to prove mathematically that because of the roundness of the earth the waters can, as it were, rise above the level of the land, and that thus there is enough room for all the water of the earth to be gathered in the oceans.[24] Rufus passes over this problem in silence, although his whole treatment of the gathering together of the waters is copied from the *Hexaemeron* (B ff. 134D–135B).

The main function of the celestial bodies was that they were 'for signs' (Gen. i. 14). This biblical hint provided Grosseteste with an opportunity to inveigh against the dangers of astrology.[25] This philippic was copied and slighty summarized by Richard Rufus, who filled it out with bits taken from Fishacre (B f. 136A–C). One glaring omission is the passage where Grosseteste tried to prove that even if the stars had some influence over man's life, this could never be proved by mathematicians, whose instruments and calculations are far too blunt to trace, for example, the differences of influence the stars have on two children born in the same house at the same time.[26]

Richard's lack of interest in astronomy and mathematics are as significant as his neglect of allegorical explanation and linguistic analysis, because these two disciplines had been long-time favourites with all scholars in the tradition of Neoplatonism. They combined both interests in their speculations on the harmony of spheres, thus revealing that the visible world was the shadowy image of heavenly reality. Richard is turning away from that tradition and trying to come to terms with an altogether different view of the world, in which visible reality is no longer valued for its symbolic properties but has acquired a consistency of its own, in which harmony and participation have made room for clear-cut distinctions and a science of causes.

(ii) *The Origin of the Animal Soul*

Grosseteste's purpose in writing the *Hexaemeron* had been to show that the world, as we see it, is a reflection of a higher, intelligible reality, the ideas in the divine mind. It is my contention that Richard Rufus, in accordance with most of his contemporaries, took a quite different view and regarded the visible world not so much as an image

[24] From Gross. *Hex.* IV. i. 1–vii. i, pp. 121–9, omitting chs. v–vi, pp. 127–8.
[25] Ibid. v. vii. 1–xi. 1, pp. 163–71.   [26] Ibid. v. ix. 1–2, pp. 165–6.

of the invisible but as a largely autonomous system, governed by the unchanging laws of nature. Hence the shift of interest from the study of the properties of things to the study of the laws of motion, of substantial change, of generation and corruption, themes which had been studied by Aristotle and were now being rediscovered by Richard and his contemporaries. There is no better way of testing this hypothesis than by looking at some of the passages where Richard Rufus does not just copy Grosseteste, only voicing his disagreement by omitting the parts he does not like, but faces up to Grosseteste's thought, subjects it to a close scrutiny, and draws his own conclusions. These are passages where he really becomes independent from his two sources and develops his own thought.

An important problem he tackles in this manner is the question of the origin of the sensitive soul, the *anima brutorum*. The question of the origin of the soul was not a new one in the thirteenth century. The central problem had always been, and still remained, whether each soul was directly created by God or simply generated in the act of conception. In earlier days the discussion had been limited to the soul of man and the context of the dispute had always been the problem of the transmission of original sin. Augustine's doctrine that original sin was so deeply rooted in man as to be transmitted in conception made it very difficult to admit that God contributed to man's conception by creating the soul of each new human being. That looked as if God, somehow, had a share in the propagation of evil. Augustine himself never came to a decision on the point.[27]

The introduction of Aristotle's reflections on the soul and those of his Arab commentators changed this picture completely. The whole discussion on the origin of the soul became detached from its theological context, and was firmly put on a biological basis.[28] Aristotle was interested in the soul as the principle of life, embracing all living things, not just human life. Hence his division of the soul according to the three different ways in which life manifests itself, vegetative in plants, sensitive in animals, and rational in man. This new perspective in which man was more linked to what was below him than to what was above him, more to animals than to God, gave the debate on the origin of the soul a new urgency. If man's soul was not created, but generated in the act of conception, then man, soul and

---

[27] J. da Cruz Pontes, 'Le problème de l'origine de l'âme de la patristique à la solution thomiste', *RThAM* xxxi (1964), 184–200.

[28] McEvoy, *Philosophy*, p. 227.

body, was totally a part of corruptible nature. The immortality and the spiritual nature of the human soul were in danger of disappearing, and with that the point in which man was most closely linked to God, and the possibility of being united with God in the beatific vision.

To save the unique spiritual nature of the soul, theologians now began to favour more strongly than before the theory that each human soul is created by God. But this caused philosophical problems; Aristotle had never said anything about divine intervention in the generation of souls, but had regarded it as a perfectly natural process. The only way to escape Aristotle's naturalism was to give more than due weight to some rather mysterious sentences in his writings, where he seems to admit that the intellect is not transferred through the natural process of procreation but comes from the outside (*ab extrinseco*).[29] Since the intellect is part of the rational soul, the concept of a direct creation of the rational soul did not seem to be contrary to the principles of the philosopher. The resulting position was that the vegetative and the sensitive soul could be regarded as generated, and the rational soul as created. This satisfied a number of scholars, but most theologians thought that it did not go far enough and they affirmed that in man the whole soul with all its powers was created by God, and not just the rational part.[30] From this difference of opinion the debate on the plurality of forms took its origin, which, however, does not concern us for the present.

Grosseteste's position in the debate is clear: all souls are created by God. Commenting on the words: 'Producat terra animam viventem' (Gen. i. 24) he insists that even the souls of animals are created by God, not only in the beginning, but even now.[31] So far the debate had circled around the origin of the human soul; Grosseteste was the first, and probably the only one, who extended God's direct intervention to the realm of animal life.[32] He explains the Bible text, which seems to suggest that the earth itself brings forth the living soul, by saying that we must understand this as meaning that the animal's body has an inclination to receive its soul from God. Again Grosseteste's singular

[29] Da Cruz Pontes, 'Origine de l'âme', pp. 197–8; Th. Crowley, *Roger Bacon. The Problem of the Soul in His Philosophical Commentaries* (Louvain etc., 1950), p. 125.

[30] Richard discusses this issue in ii. 17; see below pp. 172–3.

[31] 'Deus enim, sicut nos credimus, animas eciam brutorum creat ex nichilo et infundit eas corporibus organicis aptatis earum receptioni. Neque enim ex traduce credimus eas esse, neque eductas de potentia in actum ex aliqua materia corporali' (Gross. *Hex.* VII. i. 2, p. 200).

[32] McEvoy, *Philosophy*, p. 314 n. 77. Fishacre favoured the theory of creation of the animal souls as well (Ba f. 110D, O f. 169A–B), but he is dependent on Grosseteste.

position in the history of thirteenth-century theology comes to the fore: he is perfectly aware of the contemporary debate, and of the problems created by Aristotle's theory of the soul, and takes them into account, but he also tries to ward off any danger of naturalism by emphasizing God's role in the origin of all animal and human life. There is no area where nature operates autonomously, the whole of nature is the theatre of God's creative power and love. It is the same concern which, in the debate about theological method, drove him to defend allegory and to reject dialectics and to protest against the encroachment of autonomous human reason upon the territory of faith.

It is probably because of this extraordinary extension of God's immediate intervention by Grosseteste that Richard Rufus felt compelled to devote such a long treatise to the problem of the origin of the sensitive soul in animals. Especially in his Oxford commentary, he develops his own thoughts on the subject at great length; the echo can be found in the abbreviation, where he corrects and completes Bonaventure on this point.

Richard first quotes Grosseteste's explanation of Gen. i. 24 that the animal's body yearns to receive its soul from God, and he answers rather curtly that in that case the creation of the body of man should also have been described as: 'Producat terra animam rationalem', since man's body has the same yearning (B f. 139C).

Then he takes up some of Fishacre's arguments in favour of the creation of the animal soul and demolishes them one by one. Fishacre argues that the primary division of all being is into corporeal and incorporeal. Since the soul is a spiritual form, it is much closer to spiritual intelligences than to corporeal creatures, therefore more likely to be created than to be generated. Richard retorts that, although this division is correct, animal souls are material and corporeal forms and at the origin of a bodily being, and it is this origin which counts most (B f. 139C–D).[33]

The next objection has a certain interest, because it reveals that Rufus and Fishacre were divided on a hotly debated issue, the question of universal hylomorphism. Fishacre shows himself in favour of hylomorphism when he states that every soul is composed of matter and form.[34] This being so, if a new soul is not created but generated from a body, it receives from that body both matter and form, with the

---

[33] Ba f. 110D, O f. 169B.
[34] Ba f. 110D, O f. 169B; for Fishacre's hylomorphism see R. J. Long, 'Richard Fishacre and the Problem of the Soul', *The Modern Schoolman*, lii (1975), 267.

result that that body, losing matter, shrinks every time it produces a new soul. Rufus answers by distinguishing between human and animal souls: human souls do have matter, because they do not perish like animal souls, but can live on their own without a body, but animals' souls are not composed of matter and form; their only matter is the actual substance of which they are the forms.[35]

Having dealt with Fishacre, Richard gives a series of arguments which can be brought against the creation of the animal soul (B ff. 139D–140B).[36] Most arguments point to the narrow link between the sensitive soul and the body, related as form and matter. A further assumption is that the manner of corruption corresponds to the manner of generation. Thus he argues that, since the essential function of the sensitive soul in animals is to be the form of the body, the soul must dissolve when the body dies. Therefore, the animal soul is not created, but generated, because 'si ergo hee [i.e. anime brutorum] sunt corruptibiles, sunt et generabiles' (B f. 140A); the beginning must correspond to the end.

Another argument, hinging on the same principles, is that the highest Good, who makes nothing but good things, does not destroy any of the good things he made. And since 'being' is undoubtedly 'de genere bonorum', he will never destroy anything existing. Nor can a finite creature reduce something to nothing, since the abyss between something and nothing is infinite. So, unless a change can take place without a cause, no existing thing can ever be reduced to nothing. Therefore, when an animal dies, his soul does not dissolve into nothing, but it subsists in another nature—supposedly in an incomplete or potential manner, since against Fishacre he maintains that 'Hee enim forme esse per se separatum habere non possunt' (B f. 139D)—and since in every change that which disappears returns to where it appeared from, the soul of animals must spring forth from some natural body. He illustrates his conclusion with Aristotle's dictum 'Intellectus tantum intrat ab extrinseco et quod ipse solus habet esse divinum' (B f. 140A = V f. 196C–D).[37]

Richard also argues that no forms which can subsist in separation

---

[35] 'Hee enim forme [sc. animarum brutorum] esse per se separatum habere non possunt, potest autem anima rationalis. Unde hec materiam habet propriam, ille non habent' (B f. 139D). In other respects Richard was a hylomorphist, as in the question of the composition of angels; see Lottin, *Psychologie. . .*, i: *Problèmes de psychologie* (2nd edn; Gembloux, 1957), pp. 454–9.

[36] Some are taken up again in the abbreviation (V f. 196C–D).

[37] Aristotle, *De generatione animalium*, 736^{b}27.

from the body—angels and human souls—share in any changeable principle of the body, nor do they come forth from the body. Just the opposite is true of forms which are inseparable from the body (B f. 139D = V f. 196C). The conclusion is that Richard agrees with the majority of his contemporaries: the souls of animals are not created, but generated naturally.

The next question Richard asks himself is how the souls of animals are produced.[38] Since they are neither created by God nor human artefacts nor come to be accidentally, they must be produced by a natural process: the process of generation. In that process the animal souls are generated from their seminal principles, pre-existent forms, incomplete, hidden in matter, actualized in the act of conception. That matter is not purely passive, but must have an active principle is clear from the words of Scripture: 'Let the earth bring forth' (Gen. i. 24). If all matter were as passive as e.g. bronze, then we could also say: 'Let the bronze bring forth a statue'.[39] Although, however, it is a natural and autonomous process, Richard is very anxious to show that in it God still operates. Not only in the beginning, but even now the souls of animals are produced from their seminal principles through the will of God's word:

Huius Verbi virtute producebantur in principio, ut eiusdem virtute producuntur et nunc ... Voluntate igitur iubente et Verbo eterno producuntur iste, et voluntate etiam bonorum angelorum, quibus obediunt iste inferiores creature; hoc tamen volente et iubente Deo.   (B f. 140C = V f. 197B–C)

Richard distinguishes two different levels in the production of the animal souls, the natural and the supernatural. This does not imply that God, or even the angels, are in any way involved in the natural process; the relation between the process of generation and the action of God or the angels is not one of necessity, but of free will.[40] Thus

---

[38] In what follows I take the order of the reorganized reply as Richard gives it in the abbreviation (V f. 197B–C), because it is better arranged, though I continue to follow the wording of B, because it is more explicit.

[39] Grosseteste uses the same argument to defend the theory of seminal principles (Gross. *Hex.* VII. i. 1, p. 199).

[40] In the discussion on creation Richard distinguishes two forms of efficient causality: '... dupliciter est causa vel principium rei: principium naturale agit sine ratione et agit necessitate et ideo posita tali causa sufficiente statim ponitur effectus. Causa autem voluntaria non agit necessitate sed pure voluntarie et cum potestate rationabili que semper valet ad opposita' (B f. 103D). Equally in the discussion of God's knowledge: 'Sed distinguitur quod duplex est causa efficiens: natura et voluntas, vel sicut dicit philosophus: natura et intellectus. In naturalibus causis efficientibus statim ad existentiam cause coexistit causatum. Talis enim causa est causa que dicitur

Richard tries at the same time to safeguard God's freedom, and to recognize the autonomy of the natural process:

In alterationibus autem que fiunt in materia est movens, scilicet alterans physice, in ipsa materia. Non producit ergo istas corpus celeste, sed per sua lumina movet materiam, et transmutat cum virtutibus elementaribus. Intellectus autem, scilicet Deus vel angelus, voluntate educit has de potentia ad actum ex suis rationibus seminalibus in materia.   (B f. 140C = V f. 197C)

To support this last point he quotes Augustine's remark that everything on earth is subjected to the angels.[41]

This answer leaves unsolved the problem of spontaneous generation, or generation *ex putrefactione*. Animals like cheese-mites and bees often multiply in decaying organic material. As these vermin have a habit of suddenly appearing in a cheese or a corpse, it was generally assumed that they had come to life in a way that looked like creation out of nothing, because no normal act of procreation was seen to have taken place.[42] The main question was the immediate, efficient cause of such generation. In the case of natural generation there is no problem: the parent animals are the efficient cause, through which the new soul is brought forth from potential existence in its seminal principle to actual existence in the new body, although the celestial bodies, moved by God or the angels, have some influence in bringing about the change. But in the case of spontaneous generation there are no parents, and yet the cause of the genesis of these new souls must be some living thing, since the effect cannot be nobler than the cause, and a living being is nobler than anything else.[43] Richard solves this impasse by assuming a more direct influence of the celestial bodies

necessitas. Sed causa voluntaria non subiacet alicui coactioni vel necessitati; unde non est causa que est necessitas sed que est voluntaria benignitas et ideo ad illam non sequitur necessario coexistentia causati' (B f. 86C).

[41] 'Ac per hoc sublimibus angelis deo subdite fruentibus et deo beate seruientibus subdita est omnis natura corporea, omnis inrationalis uita, omnis uoluntas uel infirma uel praua, ut hoc de subditis uel cum subditis agant, quod naturae ordo poscit in omnibus iubente illo, cui subiecta sunt omnia', Augustine, *De Genesi ad litteram*, viii. 24, ed. J. Zycha (CSEL xxviii/1, 1894), p. 263.

[42] The legend that bees spontaneously generated in decaying corpses was part of a common inheritance and can be found in the Bible (Judg. xiv. 8), as well as in Virgil, *Georgica*, iv. 197–202, 284–558; for a medieval report see Peter Comestor, *Historia scholastica*, In Genesim, viii (PL cxcviii), col. 1062, quoted by Richard Rufus (B f. 141A).

[43] 'Istud generans [sc. animam bruti] necessario est res vivens. Huius ratio est quia hee forme sunt res viventes et causa generans dans esse non est minus nobile generato. Est autem res vivens omni non viventi nobilior' (B f. 140B = V f. 197A–B).

than in the process of natural generation. Against this solution it can be objected that it implies that the heavenly bodies are animated, a theory which Richard has previously rejected after some hesitation.[44] Therefore, it must be God or the angels who through the influence of the celestial bodies are more directly responsible for the process of spontaneous generation. This much can be concluded from the rather confused argumentation. The difference in the degree of supernatural co-operation between the two processes seems to be that in the case of natural generation the instrument is nature itself, and in the case of spontaneous generation a celestial force:

Animal etiam ipsum generans generat aliud animal sibi simile in specie, et producit hanc animam de potentia ad actum, sicut natura est instrumentum artificis scilicet intellectus. Sed in putrefactione, ubi non generatur simile ex simili tunc est, ut prius dixi, in materia virtus celestis et elementaris simul quasi instrumentum artificis qui est intellectus separatus. (V f. 197C)[45]

The distinction is specified in a passage where Richard says that in natural generation it is the parents who act *immediate*, and God and the angels only *mediate*, whereas in spontaneous generation the heavenly powers act more immediately.[46] Although the influence of the celestial bodies on the process of procreation was generally recognized—it derived from two texts in Aristotle, *Physics* ii. 2, 194^{b}13, and *De Generatione Animalium* xx. 3, 737^{a}1-4—Richard's

---

[44] He says that, although there are very good arguments to the contrary, he thinks that the heavens and the heavenly bodies have no principle of life in themselves but are moved by the angels (B f. 133D).

[45] This passage cannot be found in B. I am inclined to think that the ommision must be a mistake of the scribe, because the *responsio* on f. 140C only makes sense if this passage is inserted just before the words: 'Et hec eductio proprie creatio non est sed nec generatio'.

[46] 'Iam patet a quo [anime brutorum] scilicet producantur, quia ubi simile in specie generatur a simili in specie, tunc producuntur a generante immediate, mediate vero ab intellectu, scilicet ab artifice. ... Cum autem est generatio equivoca, sicut in putrefactione, tunc producuntur tales ab intellectu increato et creato, ut predictum est. Et hec productio non est dicenda proprie generatio, sed eductio de potentia ad actum ex materia. Communiter tamen dicitur quod celum generat hec animalia ex putrefactione, non quod corpus celi educat has formas sicut agens principalis' (V ff. 197D–198A). A similar distinction between 'Virtus celestis' and 'elementaris' is made by Albert the Great. The 'virtus elementaris' is that force through which the corpse is decaying; once this has happened the heavenly force acts upon it producing the forms of the animals growing in the corpse: 'Dicendum quod ad generationem talium animalium duae virtutes requiruntur, scilicet virtus superior et virtus inferior. Virtus enim inferior disponit materiam ad putrefactionem ... virtus caelestis in materia disposita per virtutem elementarem operatur ad formam animalis imperfecti', *Liber de natura et origine animae*, xvii. 14, ed. B. Geyer (*Opera omnia*, xii, 1955), p. 295.

strong insistence on the role of the will of the angels, and of the will of God, derives from another source. The most likely seems to be Avencebrol, who more than any other commentator of Aristotle had stressed the role of the divine will in the drama of the universe.[47]

A comparison of Richard Rufus's solution with Grosseteste's answer yields some interesting points. The first is that Richard clearly has a different conception of God's relation to the world. He makes a serious attempt to limit the extent of God's creative activity: in the beginning God created the world out of nothing, but now he only creates new human souls. The souls of animals are not created, but produced from their seminal principles. Even in the case of spontaneous generation, which at first sight looks so much like creation, God's action, though more direct, is really not more than the bringing about of a change from potentiality to actuality in an existing thing, hence not an act of creation in the strictest sense. Nevertheless Richard is not an eighteenth-century deist, a man who thought that God had withdrawn from the world after bringing it into being. He makes it quite clear that higher powers are at work and that natural processes can only run their course, if God or an angel, as God's emissary, wants them to do so. What he loses by limiting God's immediate intervention in autonomous natural processes, he wins by putting such strong emphasis on God's will which permits these things to happen.

The second difference is more difficult to define. By now it is obvious that both Grosseteste and Richard Rufus have a strong interest in the workings of nature, and that both are in the end theologically motivated. But Grosseteste's interest was in the property of things and in subjects with a strong mathematical bias, like astronomy and optics. Grosseteste's approach could perhaps be called descriptive; as such it is more suited to mathematical treatment. Richard Rufus's interest seems to be not so much in things as in the fundamental processes of nature; the nature of change, coming to be, and passing away, of which the production of souls is a good example, processes that could not be quantified, for which there was no mathematical language. Grosseteste's universe is more static; he looks at things and their properties to discover how far they participate in

[47] Avencebrol, *Fons vitae*, i. 2 and iii. 46, ed. C. Bäumker (BGPhMA i/2–4, 1895), pp. 4, 184. See also E. Gilson, 'Pourquoi saint Thomas a critiqué saint Augustin', *Archives d'histoire doctrinale et littéraire du Moyen Âge*, i (1926–7), 27–9. William of Auvergne seems to admit an almost direct action of God in the case of spontaneous generation, see *De universo*, II, iii. 19 (*Opera omnia*, i, 1674), pp. 1055–6.

higher forms. And the language of numbers reveals these forms. His concern is formal causality, to teach man how to direct his gaze upwards. Richard is far less interested in that aspect of reality, his universe is more dynamic and more horizontal. He is interested in the question how things come to be and pass away, how they move from A to B; he is fascinated by change in general. Efficient causality is what he is looking for. His conception of nature is far more influenced by Aristotle than Grosseteste's and his main problem is how in a universe, governed by the laws of nature, he can find a new way to define God's place in it.[48] From what we have seen so far it seems as if he tries to make the connection of the natural with the supernatural not through participation, but through a strong emphasis on God's will.

(iii) *The Nature of the Human Soul and the Problem of Substantial Change*

This fundamental change of perspective also marks Richard Rufus's treatment of the human soul. From Richard's point of view Grosseteste has very little to offer him in the *Hexaemeron*. Commenting on the words 'Let us make man in our own image' (Gen. i. 26) Grosseteste celebrates man as the image of God, the supreme symbol, excelling all other vestiges in the clarity of its signification. He argues that man shares in God's creative power, and also that the angels, although they are more perfect and spiritual, are appointed to minister to man.[49] Especially the higher part of man's soul: memory, reason, and will, are the highest possible image of the triune God: 'Et ita secundum hanc supremam virtutem unam et simplicem dicto modo memorantem, intelligentem et diligentem, est homo summa similitudo et per hoc imago unius Dei Trinitatis'.[50] The likeness to the divine exemplar is so close that through it the supreme God can be seen 'sine nubulo fantasmatum'.[51] Grosseteste finds it impossible to stay with the soul only, he has to say something about him in whose image the soul has been made; therefore, he interrupts his reflections on man for a long digression on the mystery of the Trinity and man's access to it.[52]

---

[48] For the difference between the mathematical and the physical approach, see J. Weisheipl, 'The Interpretation of Aristotle's Physics and the Science of Motion', in N. Kretzmann *et al.* (eds.), *Cambridge History*, p. 525, and Van Steenberghen, 'Philosophie de la nature', pp. 122–3, 126–7.

[49] Gross. *Hex.* VIII. xvii. 4, VIII. xv. 2, pp. 242, 240.

[50] Gross. *Hex.* VIII. v. 1, pp. 224–5.

[51] Ibid.

[52] Ibid. VIII. iii–v. 3, pp. 220–5.

Richard Rufus has no use for all these exalted speculations. When he comes to the analysis of the words 'Let us make man' in ii. 16, he uses Grosseteste's exegetical commentaries, but avoids the enthusiastic outbursts about man and his close likeness to God. Only in two other theological points does he follow Grosseteste; with some hesitation he agrees with him that not only the soul but man as a whole has been created in the image of God:

Est ergo ut videtur summa solutionis in hac questione quod principaliter est homo factus ad imaginem Dei in anima, et principalissime in suprema parte anime, ubi illa tria naturaliter signantur: memoria, intelligentia, voluntas. Communiter vero et tamen vere totus homo integer, conformato scilicet exteriore homine interiori qui duo sunt unus homo. Et hec ex sententiis sanctorum predictis collige.   (B f. 142A)[53]

He also takes over Grosseteste's distinction between image and similitude. Scripture tells us that man has been created in God's image and after his likeness (Gen. i. 26). Through his creation man is the image of God, which is part of his nature; likeness he becomes through his elevation, which is bestowed upon him by grace. Grosseteste speaks of a natural image, which man never loses, and a renewed or reformed image, which he loses through sin but regains through the grace of the Holy Ghost. Rufus follows Grosseteste without any comment; he merely rearranges his main observations on the point (B f. 142C).[54] He finishes the sixteenth distinction with some remarks on the creation of the body of Adam and Eve, taken over from Grosseteste, adding a few lines of his own on seminal principles (B f. 142C–D).[55] The overall impression is that the whole question of the soul as God's image does not tempt Richard very much, as it invites no further probing.

Richard waits for the next distinction to give a broad survey of his own views on the soul of man, a choice not without significance. By separating the treatise on the soul from the question of the soul as God's image, where theoretically it would have fitted perfectly, Richard gives away, probably unconsciously, the shifting focus of his interest; it is the soul of man as such and not the soul as symbol of God on which he seeks to concentrate.

[53] For Grosseteste's almost unique position see McEvoy, *Philosophy*, pp. 398–401 and R. C. Dales, 'A Medieval View of Human Dignity', *Journal of the History of Ideas*, xxxviii (1977), 569–71.
[54] Gross. *Hex.* VIII. vi. 1, viii. 1, 3, pp. 227, 230–1.
[55] Ibid. X. vi. 1–2, pp. 299–300.

The very long treatise (B ff. 143B–146C) can be divided into two:
the beginning and the end consist of the conventional questions on the
soul, the middle is more exceptional, it is an enquiry into the process
of substantial change in general. The first question is a comment on
the text of Genesis and is a problem arising from the text, whether
God could have created the soul of Adam in seminal principle first
and have given it perfection later. The problem arose because the
creation of man is mentioned twice in the text (Gen. i. 26 and ii. 7). In
between the author declares 'Thus the heavens and the earth were
finished' (Gen. ii. 1) which was interpreted as meaning that after the
sixth day nothing new had ever been created. A possible solution was
to assume a creation in two stages, first in seminal principle and later
in actuality. It was difficult, however, to imagine a seminal soul.
Therefore Augustine had proposed that only the body of Adam had
been created in seminal principle and that his soul had been created
fully actualized and had remained hidden till its union with the body,
which had taken place when God breathed upon man.[56] Rufus
criticizes Augustine for inventing superfluous problems. The soul of
man and the angels belong to the same nature. So, even if God had
created the soul of Adam after the sixth day, he would not have created
a new nature, and that is all the word of God finishing his work means:

Puto ergo quod beatus Augustinus tunc non vidit probabiliorem modum nec
tolerabiliorem ponendi de prima anima quam modo predicto.   (B f. 143C)

A far more interesting and important point is the question that
comes next, about the origin of the other souls: are they created by
God or simply produced by the first soul, a problem that became very
urgent in the thirteenth century, when theologians had to face the
challenge of Aristotle's naturalism. Moreover, they had no guide to
lead them, for Augustine had never reached clarity on the point.[57]
Richard sees Augustine's hesitant attitude very well and makes no
effort to hide it: Augustine found it difficult to reconcile the concept of
direct creation of the soul with the notion of original sin (B f. 144A).
He himself, however, has no doubts: each new soul is created by God,
all other possibilities can be excluded. Because of its changeability the
soul cannot be produced from the substance of God, and because of
its rational nature it cannot be produced from some material,
irrational form such as the vegetative or the sensitive soul (B f. 143C).

[56] Augustine, *De Genesi ad litteram*, vii. 24 (ed. Zycha, p. 223).
[57] See above pp. 161–2 for a more extensive discussion.

So, if the soul is produced from some other form of life, it must be from a being endowed with rational life: an angel or another human soul. Without explanation Richard maintains that a human soul cannot be produced from an angel: 'Durum est autem dicere angeli aut angelorum filiam esse animam' (B f. 143C). In the end the only serious alternative to direct creation is the possibility that all human souls spring forth from Adam's; this could happen in three possible ways, creation, division, or substantial change. It is obvious that Adam's soul could not have created other souls from nothing, since that ability is God's only. Neither is it possible for a human soul to be divided, since a soul is a simple, indivisible spirit. Nor can a soul go through a process of substantial change, it would be destroyed, whereas the human soul is immortal and incorruptible. The only possibility left is that all human souls are created from nothing by God.[58]

Another debated point was the time of creation, whether all souls had been created at the same time and from then on had been waiting for their union with the body, or whether each soul was created at the appointed hour. Richard flatly rejects the first position; one of the main characteristics of the soul is that it has a natural desire to be united with and to reign over a body; that fundamental desire would remain unfulfilled for too long, if all souls had been created together at the beginning of time (B f. 145A).

The last question Richard discusses in connection with the origin of the soul is the classical problem of the plurality of forms, whether the rational, sensitive, and vegetative powers of the soul had to be regarded as one substance, or whether they were three different substances.[59] As we have seen, Aristotle's position was that all souls, human or not, were generated naturally and that only the intellect came from somewhere outside, an opinion that was in direct conflict with the Christian conviction that the human soul is in no way a part of

---

[58] 'Videtur ergo in principio de ista presente quod non possint omnes anime ex una prima anima esse, quia cum anima sit spiritus simplex, quod anima fieret ex anima et non per creationem—quia anima animam ex nihilo creare non potest—hoc non posset esse nisi aut per divisionem ipsius anime prime in substantia aut per transmutationem eiusdem. Sed ipsa divisibilis secundum substantiam non est in animam et animam, non est sic de ipsa sicut de luce corporali. Nec per transmutationem prime anime sunt alie, quia secundum hoc corrupta esset prima cum producebatur secunda; et sic universaliter ulterius productio unius esset prioris destructio; quod enim transmutatur non manet' (B ff. 143D–144A).

[59] This question has been edited by Callus 'Oxford Masters', pp. 439–45. See also Crowley, *Roger Bacon*, pp. 127–8 and da Cruz Pontes, 'Problème', pp. 210–12.

corruptible nature, but is endowed with unique qualities, such as immortality and spirituality. Two positions resulted. The theologians, who were anxious to safeguard the supernatural origin and the unique qualities of man's soul, bluntly asserted that in the case of man the whole soul was created by God as one substance with three potentialities. The philosophers, as Richard calls them, unwilling to admit that Aristotle could have been wrong, maintained that in man only the rational part of the soul was created—which saved Christian doctrine—and that, as Aristotle had said, the vegetative and the sensitive part were generated from nature. Because of the different origin of the different parts of the soul the philosophers also had to assume a plurality of forms.[60]

Richard describes the two positions in great detail. He himself, however, seems inclined to support an intermediate position, although with his usual modesty he does not make a final choice. He distinguishes in man a double vegetative and sensitive principle: one, which may be called substantial, is generated from nature, and another which is of the same substance as and a potentiality of the created soul:

Tertii sunt qui volunt concordare philosophos cum theologis, et dicunt in homine esse sensitivam et vegetativam dupliciter; sunt enim hee due sicut dicunt theologi potentie tantum et eadem substantia numero cum intellectiva, unde et veniunt ab extrinseco. Sunt iterum nihilominus sensitiva et vegetativa in homine, que proveniunt ex materia, et per illas est homo animal imperfectum, possibile perfici per rationalem cum suis potentiis, ut sit animal perfectum in specie hominis; et sunt iste substantie non potentie tantum. (B f. 145C)[61]

Richard seems to regard the generated vegetative and sensitive substance in man as, somehow, in potentiality and capable of being perfected by the vegetative and sensitive powers of the rational created soul. He gives authority to his opinion by quoting from Hugh of Saint-Victor, whose works he consulted in Paris.

The last three questions on the soul of man all revolve round the subject of the soul's relation to the body, whether they are related through a medium or not. An interesting question, because the answer to it is a measure of any author's adherence to the tenets of

---

[60] See above pp. 161–2; da Cruz Pontes, 'Problème', pp. 197–200.
[61] Callus, 'Oxford Masters', p. 443.

Neoplatonism and to Augustine, its most articulate and influential exponent in the West. Theologians in the Platonic tradition could not possibly admit a direct contact between the soul and the body, any contact there was had to be established through a third substance, either light, or fire, or ether, since of all material things they were the most akin to spirit.[62]

Richard is apparently aware that he is about to make an important choice and therefore avoids the issue in his characteristic way. First he asks the direct question and his answer is that he does not know:

Nescio, si in hac questione dicam quod lux corporalis et calor vitalis fit proprium subiectum vegetative potentie et hec fundamentum sensitive, sicut trigonus se habet ad tetragonum, sensitiva autem cum superioribus virtutibus propria dispositio susceptiva potentie rationalis.   (B f. 146B)

But that is not the end of it; he returns to the same theme by formulating the same problem in a slightly different way: how man, who is composed of body and soul, can be called one. To open the discussion he quotes an opinion he finds in *De fide orthodoxa*, that man is not of one nature but of two, body and soul, and that not man as such but these natures are the proper subjects of predication. The concept 'man' can only be used as a subject for predications about the species (B f. 146B).[63] This opinion is rejected because, as Richard argues, such being the case nothing that is composed of matter and form is of one nature: 'Sed dubitatur in hac ratione, quia secundum hoc nec ignis est una natura, nec aliud compositum ex materia et forma' (B f. 146B). By putting it like this he betrays that apparently he conceives of the relation between body and soul as one of matter and form. But before working out this point, he quotes very prudently from Hugh of Saint-Victor to strengthen the position of those who wished to maintain a sharp distinction between body and soul.[64]

The philosophers have a very different view of the relation between body and soul; they deny any medium between the two for fear of threatening the unity of man. Averroes wonders how a man can be one if he has a body and soul that are both actualized. His answer is that in man the soul is the perfection and the form of the body. Richard objects: what is so diverse as the rational spirit and the dust of the earth? The answer is that, just as a torn-out eye cannot be called an eye

---

[62] McEvoy, *Philosophy*, pp. 278–80.

[63] John Damascene, *De fide orthodoxa*, x. 1–4 (ed. Buytaert, pp. 244–7).

[64] Hugh of Saint-Victor, *De sacramentis*, ii. i. 11 (PL clxxvi, cols. 407–10).

unless equivocally, dead flesh cannot be called flesh. A body without a soul is only a body in the material sense, it is the soul which gives it form. If this is the case, the whole question of a medium is superfluous:

Sic forte intelligunt philosophi quod corpus non existit sine anima, id est: corpus non est corpus simpliciter et secundum speciem, sed solum secundum materiam sine anima. Et ita anima dat corpori suam definitionem et speciem. Unde eadem videtur esse ratio anime et corporis, et ita videtur quod sint una natura in actu et due in potentia. Unde uno nomine significatur tota natura humana, nomine scilicet carnis. Unde proprie dictum est: 'Verbum caro factum est' (John i. 14), id est: homo . . . Et sic universaliter intelligunt philosophi in composito naturali, nec est apud ipsos questio quid sit medium inter animam et corpus.   (B f. 146B–C)

Richard does not say in so many words that he agrees with the philosophers, but he has indicated that he thinks the same way. And even if that might be pushing him too far, it can still be underlined that he is obviously aware that the classical Christian conception of the soul as an entity in itself whose relation with the body is tenuous and problematic is not the only way of looking at it. Richard fully appreciates that in Aristotle's and Averroes' anthropology the unity of man is no longer a problem. That this new definition of the relation between body and soul also raised new questions and did not quite fit the Christian concept of the soul, was a point that Richard did not yet see. He was still too busy digesting the new learning; it had to be left to a later generation to criticize it.

Even more telling than the answers Richard gives to conventional questions on the soul is a curious deviation he permits himself from the main subject of the distinction. After he has come to the conclusion that each new soul is created by God from nothing, he interrupts his treatment of the soul of man for a moment and wonders first whether perhaps God might be able to produce souls from a lower nature. And then he realizes that this question is part of a far wider problem, the question of substantial change. He broaches it by asking whether for God it is possible to change anything into anything (B f. 144A). Such is not the case; certain rules govern the process of substantial change which, apparently, even God cannot modify.

The first rule is that substances cannot be changed into accidents, nor the other way round (B f. 144A). The second is that simple or unmixed things cannot be changed into other simple things; only things which are composed of two or more parts are changeable. This is an important rule for Richard, who gives many proofs to show its validity, such as that the assumption that simple things can undergo substantial change leads to the absurd conclusion that, in fact, no change took place:

Videtur ergo quod simplex in simplex transmutari non possit. Ponatur enim quod A simplex transmutatur et fiat B simplex. Quod fit proprie aliquid erit illud. Ergo A si proprie fit B in fine transmutationis erit A B. Ponitur ergo et dicam A est B et A non est aliud nunc quam ipsum prius fuit. Nam quod transmutatur fuit aliquid prius in actu et est illud idem ipsum modo in potentia. Ergo A fuit prius B, ergo A non fit B.   (B f. 144A)

One of the underlying assumptions of this argument, which Richard is going to work out in the next question, is that in a process of change nothing is gained or lost, that the first thing is, somehow, preserved in the second, as the second was already present in the first. In one of the other arguments Richard formulates another rule for substantial change, which he also works out in the next question, that substantial changes can only take place within the same *genus*, since there must be something in common between the terms of change. The change proper is that in two things of the same sort the specific difference of the one is replaced by the specific difference of the other, which, incidentally, is yet another proof that changeable things are composed of different parts:

Item non est transmutatio de uno genere in aliud genus. Ergo omne quod transmutatur in aliquid, transmutatur de ente unius generis in ens eiusdem generis. Ergo omne id quod transmutatur et id in quod transmutatur communicant idem genus. Et que communicant idem genus communicant et aliquam eandem materiam. Ex quo evidenter sequitur quod tam id quod transmutatur quam id in quod transmutatur est compositum. Nam si idem genus communicant et in aliquibus differunt, necessario sunt composita. (B f. 144A–B)

Having laid down the rules for substantial change, Richard wonders how exactly such a change takes place, a problem that must have fascinated him. One of the disputed questions is devoted to it, and he returns to it again and again, in the abbreviation even more than in the Oxford commentary.[65] He uses the insights he gained also to clarify theological issues, here to show that God could not have produced

---

[65] T ff. 158C–159B; the main exposition in the abbreviation, largely taken over from T (see above pp. 82–3), V ff. 208D–212A; see also V f. 115A–B, ff. 184B–185B.

souls from lower natures. In the abbreviation he explains some difficulties on transubstantiation by referring to his views on substantial change, especially the question whether the species of bread disappears completely after the Consecration.[66] Richard finds the subject so important that he insists that his students, whose knowledge of philosophy may be faulty, must hear about it.[67]

The problem of substantial change for Richard, as for others, was that things appeared and disappeared, but that nothing was created or reduced to nothing, since this is beyond the power of natural agents:

Generetur igitur ex B aere A ignis. De forma substantiali ipsius B queritur an ipse cedat omnino in pure nihil aut non. Si omnino in pure nihil, iam ipsius transmutatio non est corruptio, sed in pure nihil redactio. Esset enim secundum hanc positionem in generabilibus corruptio forme eiusdem in pure nihil redactio et consimilis forme generatio esset eiusdem creatio. Et ita generatio esset eiusdem creatio. Et ita generatio est vel esset omnino creatio, quod non ponitur.   (B f. 144C)[68]

The question then was, if not from or to nothing, where a new thing comes from, and the old one goes to. If the old is preserved in the new and the other way round, there must be something in common between the terms of a change. For Richard prime matter did not meet that requirement. We can already gather as much from the rule he had made that substantial changes can only take place within the same *genus*. But he also makes it explicit in the disputed question:

... necesse est ut non solum post B fiat A, sed ut aliquid ipsius B maneat et illud fiat A. Istud aliquid non potest esse sola materia prima. Si enim sic esset, forma B aeris cederet in pure nihil et forma A ignis crearetur et non esset generatio et corruptio. Unde patet quod sola substantia materie prime non sufficit ut maneat communis in transmutatione, sed necesse est etiam cum materia aliquam formam manere communem.   (T f. 159B = V f. 210A)[69]

---

[66] A ff. 90D–91A, 104A–B.

[67] 'Et quia de transmutatione aliquantulum tactum est, nescio si, liceat propter iuniores, aliquantulum digredi et de modo quo sit transmutatio entis in ens disserere' (B f. 144C).

[68] In the margin of this passage the remark: 'Omnino similiter potest obici, cum panis transmutatur in carnem'. So, the thought of applying the principles of substantial change to the Eucharist was always on Richard's mind; see also T f. 158A.

[69] Also V f. 115A–B: 'Si in hac transmutatione sola nuda substantia materie manet, forma substantialis ipsius A cedit in pure nihil, quia in alia materia salvari non potest ... Si ergo hec forma non cedit in pure nihil, ipsa remanet aliquid in eadem materia in qua ipsa fuit prius et illud in quo resolvitur simul cum materia manet commune in transmutatione.'

In a process of substantial change a common form, the form of the *genus*, is necessary besides prime matter. With this principle Richard finds himself in line with the position that later became typical of the so-called Augustinian school, but was normal in his days. It was extremely realist in the assumption that forms and prime matter were things existing in themselves and not just parts of a thing which could not exist in themselves, as Aquinas and his followers were to maintain later.[70]

If forms can exist in themselves, the question where they are and how they are, if they are not fully actualized, becomes a pressing problem, especially when dealing with generation and corruption. The form of a new thing cannot be present, fully actualized, in the old thing, nor the other way round, because that would imply that an actual existing thing was really two things at the same time, which is absurd. Two theories had been designed to avoid that deadlock. Avicenna had held that in a process of substantial change the new form was created by God, the so-called *dator formarum*-theory. Since Richard, as we saw, made a sharp distinction between generation and creation, acknowledging a creative act of God in the course of nature now only in the case of the soul of man, he had to reject that theory. A second opinion, ascribed to Anaxagoras, was that the forms of all possible things were hidden in matter, fully actualized, waiting to appear, which made a mockery of the whole notion of substantial change.[71]

Richard tried very hard to find a third way to account for the forms of the new things in a change, without postulating that they either were created on the spot or had been there all the time. The key to his answer lies in his assumption that in every existing thing several substantial forms, arranged in a hierarchy, contribute each to the further perfection of that thing. The highest and most perfect form is called the *species specialissima*, and this form produces the individual

---

[70] S. Wlodek, 'La génération des êtres naturels dans l'interprétation de Thomas Sutton', A. Zimmermann (ed.), *Die Auseinandersetzungen an der Pariser Universität im XIII. Jahrhundert* (Miscellanea mediaevalia, x, 1976), pp. 351–2. For Aquinas's inconsistency on the point see A. Kenny, *Aquinas* (Oxford 1980), pp. 38–45.

[71] 'Et hec fuit opinio illorum qui posuerunt datores formarum que reprobata est a philosophos et ab omnibus sapientibus. Ergo ipsa [sc. forma] est aliquid in illa eadem materia antequam producatur in actum. Sed ipsa non est ibi simpliciter hec quod ipsa est, ex. gr. igneitas existens in potentia non est igneitas, quia sic esset ibi simpliciter et in actu, sed nos solum lateret. Et hec erat opinio illorum qui posuerunt latitationem formarum que etiam reprobata est' (T f. 158D = V f. 209A); see also Wlodek, 'Génération', p. 352.

thing upon coming into contact with matter.[72] The lowest form, at the other end of the hierarchical ladder of forms, is a universal form, determining the *genus*.

Now if fire changes into air, the form of fire must be, somehow, preserved in the air, but not as *species specialissima* or as any other singular form, because then it would become individualized again when in contact with matter, with the result that the new air would be fire at the same time. The form of fire, therefore, is not preserved on the level of a singular, but of a universal form; it retires into the form of the *genus*, which, in this particular case, is probably the element. And from the same level the new form of air is generated which, with matter, produces this particular quantity of air. The universal forms, then, are the forms which are common and establish with prime matter the necessary link between the two terms in a process of substantial change. The old singular form is absorbed into the universal form to which it belongs, and from that same universal form the singular form of the new thing is produced. Richard sums it up for his young students at the end and draws up a scheme to illustrate this complicated process:

Modum ergo universaliter transmutationis entis in ens possumus sic imaginari seu intelligere. Transmutetur B in A et sint ambo individua. Retractat forma individualis ipsius B in formam speciei specialissime ipsius B et illa adhuc supra recurrit usque in formam generis proximi quod est commune genus duarum specierum quarum sunt individua B et A, materia sub omnibus istis semper concomitante. Et iste primus cursus 'ascensus' dicitur et 'corruptio' in naturalibus dici potest. Similiter etiam est descensus quidam qui incipit ab eodem genere et in quod terminabatur ascensus precedens et ex illo genere per virtutem agentis extrahitur de potentia ad actum differentia essentialis constitutiva speciei ipsius A. Et ex illa specie specialissima extrahuntur propria individuantia et constituitur hoc individuum, scilicet A, et 'generatio' in naturalibus dici potest. Et iste videtur modus universalis in omni transmutatione substantiali entis in ens. Tum ergo vide si istud potest pertractari et ubi possit. Et in exemplo

[72] 'Cum omnis species specialissima completa sit et perfecta, ipsa numquam inmateria est sine proprio individuo' (B f. 144D).

hic prescripto forte facilius intelliges que dicta sunt.
(B f. 144D)[73]

Two things deserve to be noted: first that the summary here and the short summary in the abbreviation introduce a new element in the discussion, the *forma individualis*. Although Richard has said something else before, here he suddenly seems to say that individuation is not just caused by the contact between the highest singular form and matter, but has its own form. If this is true, we have here the first trace of Duns Scotus' notion of *haecceitas*, the notion that every individual has a form through which it is that individual and not another. The second point is that from the disputed question it may be inferred that the universal substantial forms which, with matter, are the common element in any process of substantial change can also be called seminal principles. As far as I can see, Richard never says so himself, but he starts the discussion of change in the question with a definition of seminal principles: 'forma substantialis universalis' (T f. 158D), and then describes the process of change in similar terms, though even more extensively, as in the Oxford commentary (T ff. 158D–159B). There must be some connection, and it seems to be that the seminal principles are the forms from which new things are generated and into which old things retire.

The most interesting point about Richard's digression from his main subject is not so much the answer he gives, although it has some surprises, as e.g. the notion of a *forma individualis*, but it is the fundamental difference in outlook that, once again, separates Rufus from his predecessor Grosseteste. When reflecting about the soul, Grosseteste succumbs immediately to the temptation to move on to higher things, to the triune God in whose glorious image the soul has been created, for visible things, even man, are but a shadow of the real world, the world of eternal light. Where Grosseteste's gaze goes upward, Richard's stays on one level with the earth. The soul as image of the Trinity is a thought he notes with reverence, but it cannot tempt him; the soul is, of course, created by God, but once that has been said, it can be discussed as an entity in itself. Moreover, Grosseteste has, because of his exalted views of the soul, the usual problem of establishing a link between the soul and the body. Richard does not find the idea of a direct contact between soul and body, i.e. the idea of the soul

[73] A more compact survey of the process of change in V ff. 211D–212A, where Richard speaks about it in connection with the generation of Eve from a rib of Adam.

as the form of the body, in any way repulsive, on the contrary he finds it very acceptable. And where he digresses, it is not to move upwards, but to move downwards, to the fundamental processes of nature. It is very telling that the problem of the origin of the soul leads him on to a study of substantial change, because, without saying so once, he implicitly admits that to a large extent even the soul of man can be treated as a part of nature, part of that intricate pattern of cause and effect that had been so beautifully explained by Aristotle in his natural philosophy. God is there through his creation, but the unity of heaven and earth that Grosseteste still could see, has vanished from Richard's sight. He must explore other possibilities to re-establish the link between God and his creation.

(iv) *Allegorical and Physical Light*

A similar change of focus becomes visible when we compare Richard Rufus's discussion on the nature of light with Grosseteste's philosophy of light. For Grosseteste light was the metaphor that enabled him to express the unity of all being. His concept of light as the unifying force of the universe, first as first corporeal form, giving shape to first matter, and subsequently as natural light, underpinned his Neoplatonic concept of reality, and gave a firm basis to a philosophy of participation and to a theology of symbols.[74] The participation of all creatures in the form of light made it easier to understand that allegory was not just an arbitrary literary device, but an adequate expression of the deepest structure of reality itself; Grosseteste's philosophy of light seemed to make the transparence and unity of reality an almost mathematical certainty.[75]

Although Grosseteste developed most of his thoughts on the central importance of light in his philosophical treatises, some of it found its way into the *Hexaemeron* in the two passages mentioned before. Oddly enough he does not repeat any of his ideas on the origin of the universe in these two passages of the *Hexaemeron*; he does not speak about the first light (*lux*) at all, but only about natural or corporeal light, the light we see. The first, the explanation of the influence of the light of the

[74] 'Et patens est, quoniam omne corpus superius secundum lumen ex se progenitum est species et perfectio corporis sequentis. Et sicut unitas potentia est omnis numerus sequens, sic corpus primum multiplicatione sui luminis est omne corpus sequens' Robert Grosseteste, *De luce*, ed. L. Baur, *Die philosophischen Werke des Robert Grosseteste, Bischofs von Lincoln* (BGPhMA ix, 1912), p. 56.
[75] McEvoy, *Philosophy*, pp. 151–8, 161; D. Lindberg, *Theories of Vision from Al-Kindi to Kepler* (Chicago etc., 1976), p. 96.

first heaven on life on earth, is copied by Richard Rufus in its entirety.[75a]

The second remark on light occurs, as was to be expected, in the description of the properties of the things created on the first day. When talking about the properties of light, he first draws attention to its most striking quality, its ability to spread in a moment:

Est itaque lux sui ipsius naturaliter undique multiplicativa, et, ut ita dicam, generativitas quedam sui ipsius quodammodo de sui substancia. Naturaliter enim lux undique se multiplicat gignendo, et simul cum est generat. Quapropter replet circumstantem locum subito.[76]

Then he turns to the question of the nature of light. According to Augustine light is that which is subtlest in corporeal nature, therefore very close to the soul; nevertheless light is corporeal. Through John Damascene, Grosseteste is acquainted with the Aristotelian view that light is a quality, an accident and not a substance at all. He decides that both Fathers are right and do not contradict each other:

... necesse est lucem dupliciter dici: signat enim substanciam corpoream subtilissimam et incorporalitati proximam, naturaliter sui ipsius generativam; et significat accidentalem qualitatem, de lucis substancie naturali generativa accione procedentem. Ipsa enim generative accionis indeficiens mocio qualitas est substancie indeficienter sese generantis.[77]

In *De Luce* he comes to the same conclusion that light is a spiritual body, or, if preferred, a bodily spirit.[78]

Only this last passage is able to hold Richard Rufus's interest. Nowhere does he give any indication that he shares Grosseteste's views on the fundamental role of light in the origin and in the present structure of the universe. He is not interested in light as the first corporeal form, which unites all being, but only in the light we see: 'lux in medio'. The few paragraphs Grosseteste devotes to this problem are extended by Richard into a treatise of five columns (B ff. 131A– 132B).

But before turning to this treatise we must collect a few remarks Richard makes about the nature of light in other connections, remarks he does not repeat in the treatise. In one of his *quaestiones disputatae*

[75a] See above, pp. 158–9.

[76] Gross. *Hex.* II. x. 1, p. 97.   [77] Ibid. II, x. 2, pp. 98–9.

[78] 'Et sic procedit a corpore primo lumen, quod est corpus spirituale, sive mavis dicere spiritus corporalis', Grosseteste, *De luce* (ed. Baur, p. 55).

Richard grapples with the problem of the exact moment of change. A good example is the sudden change from darkness to light. It is in that connection that he warns his readers that they must not mistakenly assume that the light, when it spreads from east to west, is numerically the same in the west as it was in the east. Light generates itself on the spur of the moment; in one moment there is an infinite number of different lights, each generating the next, which, taken together, fill the sky from east to west.[79] In fact, this is the same theory as Grosseteste's. From these sentences one might conclude that Richard, just like Grosseteste, must have conceived of light as a corporeal substance, and not in Aristotelian terms as an accident, namely the actualization of a body called the *diaphanum*, the transparent, which is present in all lucid bodies like air and water. Aristotle's theory of light was designed to account for the sudden dispersion of light in all directions; because, being a change of state in a body, i.e. the transparent, the suddenness of the change required no further explantion.[80] The fact that Richard sees the instantaneous spread of light as a problem suggests, therefore, that he subscribed to the Augustinian view of light as a corporeal substance.

Yet this conclusion is too quick. In the treatise on the nature of light in ii. 13 he shows himself familiar with all the relevant texts, not only from Augustine, but also from Aristotle and Averroes, and the conclusion he arrives at is very different and far more nuanced than the one suggested here.[81]

The first question he tries to decide is whether light is an accident or a substance. Light cannot be an accident, he says, because every accident must be the accident of some substance *per se*, which means that it is inseparable from that substance. Light could not be an accident of the air, since air is not *per se* luminous, neither of the sun, because in the sun light is that which is noblest. From this last remark

---

[79] 'Similiter de luce corporali que in instanti multiplicat se ab oriente in occidente. Sed hic nota quod non eadem lux numero, sicut erat idem angelus numero, sed alia et alia lux numero, una gignens aliam. Et sunt quasi infinite generationes lucium et omnes sunt simul in uno instanti, in illo scilicet instanti in quo primo est lux genita in occidente (*sic*). Est tamen una generatio natura prior altera et lux gignens luce genita' (T f. 158B). See also B f. 86B and f. 112D, where Richard gives the same explanation in slightly different words and adds: 'Et satis puto quod sit cavendum ab imaginatione falsa in hac materia. Si enim esset una lux numero, esset re vera illa singularis in eodem instanti ubique in medio et in occidente, quod est impossibile.'

[80] Lindberg, *Theories*, p. 8.

[81] Richard also airs his own views on light in the appendices to Bonaventure in the abbreviation (V ff. 187A, 187C–D, 188D–189A).

he takes his cue and decides that, since light is the noblest creature in existence, it cannot be a mere accident.

If light is not an accident, it must be a substance, either corporeal, or incorporeal. This problem is dealt with in two stages. He begins by clearing a misunderstanding about the word 'incorporeal'. Not all incorporeal substances are necessarily spirits, angels or human souls; the substantial forms of non-living things are incorporeal but not spiritual. In defence of the position that light has a bodily nature he quotes Augustine (B f. 131B).[82] For the opposite part he quotes Aristotle's verdict on the theories of Democritus: 'Lux non est corpus, nec defluxus corporis' (B f. 131B).[83] Another argument with Aristotelian overtones is that light has its opposite in the form of darkness. Since a body can never have something which is its opposite, light cannot be a corporeal substance, but must be a *habitus* (B f. 131B).[84] It must also be considered that no two bodies can occupy the same place, unless together they form a mixed body, in which only the form of the mixture is actualized. Since, however, light and air occupy the same place, while both are fully actualized, light cannot be a corporeal substance. Furthermore, if light is corporeal, it consists of matter and form. In that case the sun, shedding light continually, would gradually shrink and very soon be reduced to nothing.

Through these and other arguments Richard comes to a first tentative conclusion, a distinction which will form the basis of the following deliberations. The word 'light' is used equivocally, sometimes to describe the luminosity of the air or the water, sometimes to describe the substance from which that luminosity springs forth. Aristotle and John Damascene use it in the first sense, Augustine in the second. But even granted that distinction, it still is highly unlikely that light, in either case, can be called a corporeal substance (B f. 131C–D). The same conclusion appears in the abbreviation:

Lux ergo, proprie dicta, corporalis dico, triplex esse habet, aut in corpore luminoso, aut in medio diafano, aut in mixtis per incorporationem cum materia. Et nullo istorum modorum est lux corpus. (V f. 187A)

In the second part of the treatise Richard makes another effort to decide whether light is a corporeal or incorporeal substance. (B ff.

[82] A quotation taken from Gross. *Hex.* II. x. 1, p. 98.

[83] Aristotle, *De anima*, 418 [b]14–16.

[84] Richard does not seem to notice that it is impossible that a disposition (*habitus*) is a substance, as he has by now decided light is. A disposition is always the disposition of something, as the word implies, therefore an accident.

131D–132B). He starts off once more with two series of arguments for and against the corporeal nature of light, some the same as before, some new. For instance since light spreads naturally in all directions, it cannot be a body, since a body can only move in one direction at a time. He also uses Aristotle's definition of light: 'Lux est forma, quia ipse est actus lucidi' (B f. 131D).[85] New arguments in favour of the corporeal nature of light are for instance, that a body cannot move something incorporeal; but light can be deflected by a body, therefore it must be corporeal itself. Moreover, a body can only be generated by another body, therefore, since light falling through a concave mirror can generate fire, it must be corporeal.

The final effort to define the true nature of light is introduced with Richard's typical diffidence: 'Quid ergo in hiis et tantis dicam? Nescio.'[86] Building on the distinction he has made earlier, he first affirms that light in the sun and in other luminaries is not a body, but a substantial form. In the abbreviation he goes further and says that in the sun light is the highest and final form which gives the sun its perfection and makes it really what it is (V f. 187D).[87]

Light in a medium has to be distinguished carefully from light in a luminary body. The question is not just what the nature of light is in a medium, but also what relation it bears to the light in its source. It is not corporeal, although it shines forth from a body, neither is it, properly speaking, a substance or an accident. To find a way out he makes a comparison with the relation as it exists between a coloured body and that same colour in a medium:[88]

Quid de specie coloris hic in medio dicam, an color est? Nec color, nec alia natura quam color, non res alterius predicamenti. Hec species albedinis non est res alterius speciei specialissime quam sit hec albedo, a qua gignitur, non est individua sub specie specialissima albedinis, non sunt coindividua eiusdem speciei. Hec species proles, et illa albedo parens. (B f. 132A, V f. 189A)

[85] Aristotle, *De anima*, 418^{b}9–12.
[86] The whole reply in B f. 132A–B; also in V ff. 187C–D, 188D–189B.
[87] On this point Richard agrees with Albert the Great, who maintains:'Differunt luminare, lux et lumen et splendor. Luminare enim est corpus, quod in se ut formam habet lucem, sicut sol et luna et stellae. Lux autem dicitur forma luminis in luminari sive in eo quod est fons luminis primus', *De anima*, II. iii. 8, ed. C. Stroick (*Opera omnia*, vii/1, 1968), p. 110.
[88] Albert the Great draws the same parallel: 'Lumen autem, quod est, sicut dictum est, generatum a luminoso corpore in perspicuo, habet se ad lucem, quae est forma corporis luminosi, sicut se habet intentio coloris generata in perspicuo ad formam coloris, quae est in corpore colorato', *De anima*, II. iii. 12 (ed. Stroick, p. 116).

Because they relate to each other as progenitor and progeny they are far closer to each other than two white things of the same species of whiteness, they are even closer related than two things that only differ in number. And yet they are not quite the same, because whiteness in a medium is more spiritual than the colour itself (B f. 132A–B, V f. 189A).

The same applies to light:

Adapta, vide an tali modo possit dici de lumine proiecto a corpore solari, an ipsa dici possit species illius lucis que substantia et forma est in corpore solis, sed esse alterum habens, et ideo hic supscepta in medio nec proprie nomen substantie nec accidentis retinens.   (B f. 132B)

Richard thinks that this solution—that light in the sun is related to light in a medium as a parent to its child, the only difference being that the latter has a more spiritual existence—agrees with Aristotle's definition that light in a medium is the actual state of the transparent, or rather a disposition of the transparent. Averroes explains this saying that light in a medium is not a body, but the presence of an intention in the transparent.[89] Richard lumps the two together and presents them as an adequate description of the mode of existence of light in a medium; by calling it *habitus* he avoids the label accident, by calling it *intentio* he avoids the label substance:

Ecce secundum philosophum quod lumen habitus est et intentio, sed habitus aeris, intentio corporis luminosi. Et habitus non accidens, intentio non substantia, quia nomen tam substantie quam accidentis amisit propter alterum esse quod suscepit, et est aliquo modo nobilius quam esse lucis in suo fonte.   (V f. 189B)

The comparison of the modes of being of light with the relation between progenitor and progeny may well be borrowed from Trinitarian theology. On the one hand it stresses near-identity, on the other hand it allows for a minimal difference, since in material things progenitor and progeny cannot be fully identical:

[89] '. . . lux non est corpus, sed est presentia intentionis in diaffono cuius privatio dicitur obscuritas apud presentiam corporis luminosi. Et hoc quod dixit manifestum est, quoniam subiectum obscuritatis et lucis est corpus, et est diaffonum; lux autem est forma et habitus istius corporis, et si esset corpus, tunc corpus penetraret corpus', Averroes, *Commentarium magnum in Aristotelis De anima libros*, ii. 70, ed. F. S. Crawford (Corpus commentariorum Averrois in Aristotelem, versionum Latinarum, vi/1, 1953), p. 237.

... est lumen vel essentia luminis proles genita de illa que est forma substantialis, et est illi parenti simillimum in creatura et ei maxime conveniens,
non tamen idem numero cum illa. In materialibus enim non potest omnino
idem esse per essentiam gignens et genitum. Unde philosophus: Generans
non generat aliud nisi propter materiam. (V f. 189B)

The difference of interest between Grosseteste and Rufus is
obvious. Light as the allegorical expression of the unity of being is a
theory that cannot attract Richard Rufus: he never talks about light as
a form pervading all being; nor does he develop the passage in the
Hexaemeron where Grosseteste speaks about the mathematical structure underlying the radiation of light from the first heaven to the
earth.[90] He does develop, however, Grosseteste's short remarks on the
nature of corporeal light beyond all recognition and extends them into
a full treatise on the physics of light.[91] In doing so, he enters a different
tradition. Lindberg distinguishes two traditions in the study of light
and optics in the Middle Ages, the mathematical or perspectivist
tradition with Neoplatonic overtones, and an Aristotelian tradition
with a more ontological and qualitative bias. Both Grosseteste and
Roger Bacon belong to the first group; Bacon picks up where Grosseteste left off.[92] Richard Rufus on the other belongs undeniably to the
Aristotelian tradition, as the similarity of his reflections with those of
Albert the Great show. He may not have understood Aristotle all too
well, his answers may be different from Aristotle's, but it is Aristotle's
work that challenges him and puts questions to his mind, and not
Robert Grosseteste's. The same shift in outlook as in the treatment of
the soul comes to the fore.

(v) *The Eternity of the World*

So far we have mainly considered the points on which Richard
deviates significantly from Grosseteste in his treatment of the six days
of creation. Now we must turn to those passages where he uses
Grosseteste in a more constructive way and builds on the foundations
laid by his predecessor. It is clear by now that from the three sections
of the *Hexaemeron* he uses only one: the literal exposition of the text.
This is the only part that can help Richard in the task he has set
himself: to compose a theological *summa* in the form of a commentary

---

[90] McEvoy, *Philosophy*, pp. 172–5.
[91] Lindberg, *Theories*, p. 144, speaks of an 'ontology of radiation'.
[92] Ibid. pp. 143–4; on Grosseteste, pp. 94–103; on Bacon, pp. 107–16, where he warns
against the mistake of ascribing all Bacon's insights to Grosseteste, though his
influence on Bacon is beyond doubt.

on the *Sentences*. Sometimes the passages he copies are very short, e.g. when trying to elucidate the meaning of a word or a short sentence, sometimes they are very substantial.

Thus he copies almost completely Grosseteste's report of the difference of opinion that had arisen between Augustine and the majority of the Western Fathers on whether the world had been created instantaneously or in six days. Connected with that problem was the question whether the light of the first three days—before the creation of the sun—was a real light or merely stood for the angelic nature. Richard takes up the two points in ii. 13, B f. 130A–D. An analysis of the sources shows, among other things, how deeply indebted Richard is to his two predecessors at Oxford. The passage is structured as follows:

A. Literal position: f. 130A. 16–39 = Gross. *Hex.*, ii. iv. 1–2, p. 88.

B. Allegorical position (Augustine): f. 130A. 39–130B. 33.

   f. 130A. 39–50.
      = Gross. *Hex.* ii. v. 4, pp. 91–2 (paraphrased).

   f. 130A. 50–52
      = Gross. *Hex.* ii. vi. 1, p. 92 + addition:
      '. . . et per celum natura angelica informis'.

   f. 130A. 52–130B. 7.
      = Gross *Hex.* ii. vii. 1, p. 94.

   f. 130B. 7–14
      = Interjection by Richard Rufus:
      'Et nota quod primus dies non habuit mane, sed vesperam, quia non novit angelus se faciendum, sed se factum. Se quidem factum cognovit in Deo prius et post in se. Sed illa cognitio sui in Deo non dicitur mane, quia mane semper dicitur cognitio in Deo rei faciende. Similiter dies qui est cognitio quietis Dei ab opere, vel cessationis eius ab opere novo non habet vesperam, quia quies vel cessatio non tendit ad occasum, cum semper sit, nec cognoscitur, nisi in ipso Deo quiescente.'

   f 130B.15–33
      = Gross. *Hex.* ii. vii. 1–2, pp. 94–5 (vii. 2 paraphrased).

C. Summary of both positions: f. 130B. 33–45

   f. 130B. 33–36
      = Summary of allegorical position by Rufus:
      'Est ergo sententia Augustini quod hec lux natura angelica intelligitur, et quod hii dies temporales non sunt et quod mundi creatio subito fuit et in primo instanti temporis omnes hii sex dies et omnia opera sex dierum.'

f. 130B. 36–45
   Summary of literal position
      = Gross. *Hex.* II. v. 1–2, p. 89.

D. Objections to allegorical position:
   f. 130B. 45–130C. 3
      = Gross. *Hex.* II. viii. 1, pp. 95–6 (= Fishacre, *Sent.* ii. 13, Ba f. 104A, O f. 159C).

E. Objections to literal position: f. 130C. 3–30
      = Gross. *Hex.* II. v. 3, pp. 90–1 (cf. Fishacre, *Sent.* ii. 13, Ba f. 104A, O f. 159C–D, different from Rufus, equally dependent on Grosseteste).

F. No contradiction between the Fathers on essential points:
   f. 130C. 30–130D. 27.
   f. 130C. 30–130D. 24.
      = Fishacre, *Sent.* ii. 13, Ba f. 104A–B, O ff. 159D–160A
   f. 130D. 24–27
      = Gross. *Hex.* II. v. 5, p. 92.

G. Vindication of Augustine: f. 130D. 27–46.
   f. 130D. 27–34.
      = Gross. *Hex.* II. viii. 2, p. 96.
   f. 130D. 34–46
      = Augustine, *De Genesi ad litteram*, iv. 28 (ed. Zycha, pp. 126–7), 'Sed quomodo? Numquid proprie dicitur lux de hac corporali et figurate de aliis? Ita dicet aliquis. Sed audi Augustinum: . . .'

The passage illustrates how Richard, while relying heavily on Grosseteste and Fishacre and contributing almost nothing of his own, nevertheless moves the discussion to a logical conclusion. Grosseteste offered no solution at all. He was quite happy to leave loose ends hanging; he did not feel any urge to reconcile contrary positions by means of dialectics. His only suggestion was that Augustine was not too sure himself—a statement copied by Richard (B f. 130D 24–27)— and that he might have come to his theory of instantaneous creation because he used a text different from the Greek used by Basil, who advocated the literal position.[93] Richard is not satisfied any more with this, he must try to solve the contradiction. To achieve this he borrows Fishacre's reflections on contradictions in the Fathers in general, and so prepares the way for a final choice.[94] As an effort in dialectics it is

[93] Gross. *Hex.* x iii. 1, pp. 293–4.
[94] In the abbreviation he chooses Augustine's position without hesitation: 'Et hec positio Augustini de luce et sex diebus subtilis est et delectabilis. Et tamen communiter doctores aliam eligunt, scilicet quod dierum distinctio erat materialis et prime diei operatio formatio lucis corporalis que tres dies fecit ante productionem solis' (V f. 185D).

not too successful, quite apart from the fact that he merely structures
what he finds elsewhere, but the underlying motive is clear, a desire
for coherence and an aversion to loose ends, which shows the mind
and the will of a dialectical theologian, a mind different from
Grosseteste's.

The same desire to find a coherent solution can be seen in
Richard's treatment of the question whether a difference exists
between heaven, created on the first day, and the firmament, created
on the second day. Richard starts off by summarizing the different
positions mentioned by Grosseteste.[95] While Grosseteste, however,
concludes that it is not his task to solve the controversy,[96] Richard
continues the debate by adducing new material, this time from Hugh
of Saint-Victor.[97] Hugh, he says, thinks that on the first day the earth
was created in its proper form, but heaven and all the other elements
only confusedly, mixed together in a kind of primordial nebula.[98] On
the second day God separated all the components of this nebula,
creating two heavens, the waters above and the waters under the
firmament (B f. 127A–B). Hugh's position was original in so far as he
maintained that, although there were a heaven and a firmament, both
were created on the second day. Richard considers Hugh's answer
carefully but in the end he rejects it, together with the opinion that
heaven and firmament are identical, for the simple reason that if there
had been no heaven before the second day, there would have been no
natural place for the angels to go to on the first day (B f. 127B). Here
we see the same approach as in the previous example: Richard pushes
on to find a solution, where Grosseteste is quite happy to leave the
matter unsolved.

On three points Richard extends the discussion of the work of six
days far beyond his two predecessors. So far we have seen two: the
problem of the soul and the nature of light. The third is the treatise on
the concept of creation in the very first distinction of the second book.
It must be considered here, because on this point Richard found much
to his liking in Grosseteste's works.

---

[95] B f. 127A. 7–9 = Gross. *Hex.* I. vii. 1, p. 56; B f. 127A. 10–25 = Gross. *Hex.* I. xvi. 1,
pp. 72–4; B f. 127A. 25–35 = Gross. *Hex.* I. xvi. 3, p. 75.

[96] Gross. *Hex.* I. xvii. 1, p. 75.

[97] Hugh of Saint-Victor, De *Sacramentis*, I. i. 6 (PL clxxvi, cols. 190–1).

[98] 'Ecce quod vult Hugo quod in isto exordio terra habuit suam naturam elementi
propriam, rudem scilicet et inanem, sed adhuc celum, nullum elementum habuit suam
naturam propriam et speciem, sed erant omnia illa confusa in illa materia suspensa per
modum nebule' (B f. 127A).

The notion of creation is fundamental to Christian doctrine; it is the foundation of the faith that everything in existence is wholly dependent on God for its being and well-being.[99] In the early thirteenth century this doctrine came under attack from two sides: from the Cathars, who maintained that there had been other—evil—principles at work in the world besides God, and from the philosophy of Aristotle. Aristotle did not assume the activity of a supreme creative being, so, since nothing can come from nothing, the world must always have existed and will always exist.[1] One point on which Aristotle had not reflected was the cause of being as such, what in the Middle Ages was called the *causa essendi*. This gap was filled by Plotinus, the first ancient philosopher who, in his theory of emanation, tried to find an answer to the question why there exists anything at all. To which he replied that the goodness of the One was such that it had to overflow and communicate itself, thus causing the existence of a whole hierarchy of beings which participated in the goodness of the One in an ever diminishing degree. Although Plotinus' idea had some similarity with the Christian doctrine of creation, it had two fatal flaws: it did not account sufficiently for the fact that God did not need the world, but created it because he willed it, and it did not offer an alternative for Aristotle's theory of the eternity of the world. The process of emanation was eternal in Plotinus' view, in other words cause and effect were equally eternal. Augustine illustrated this point of view in a famous passage, quoted by both Grosseteste and Rufus, comparing it with the imprint of a foot in the sand. Although the imprint may be there from all eternity, yet anyone can see that it was caused by a foot.[2] Both Avicenna and Averroes had taken up this idea of God as the eternal cause of an eternal world. And since most of the knowledge of Aristotle in the thirteenth century was passed on through their works, many theologians in the West failed to see that Aristotle himself had only spoken about the eternity of the world without bothering about the cause of its being, and that the idea of a creator-god was purely Neoplatonic.[3]

---

[99] A survey of the development of the doctrine of creation in L. Scheffczyk, *Creation and Providence* (London etc., 1970), esp. pp. 132–53; Z. Hayes, *The General Doctrine of Creation in the Thirteenth Century* (Munich, 1964), esp. pp. 97–117.

[1] F. Van Steenberghen, 'La controverse sur l'éternité du monde au XIIIe siècle', in id. *Introduction à l'étude de la philosophie médiévale*(Philosophes médiévaux, xviii, 1974), pp. 512–13.

[2] Augustine, *De civitate Dei*, x. 31, ed. B. Dombart and A. Kalb (CC xlvii–viii, 1955), i. 309.

[3] Van Steenberghen, 'Controverse', p. 513; J. Rohls, *Wilhelm von Auvergne und der mittelalterliche Aristotelismus* (Münchener Universitätsschriften, v, 1980), p. 150.

Grosseteste tackled the problem of creation in the first section of the *Hexaemeron*, while commenting on the words 'In the beginning'. First he turns to the question of the eternity of the world. He emphasizes very strongly that Aristotle had undeniably taught that the world was eternal and that all efforts of modern philosophers to turn him into a Catholic are vain and dangerous.[4] The misunderstanding of the ancients is caused, according to Grosseteste, by false fancy; they could not but imagine before all time yet more time, and beyond all space yet another space. If they had purged the mind's affections, they would have realised the difference between time and simple eternity which has no extension in time.[5]

In the next chapter he attacks the idea that the world is eternal but created.[6] The philosophers, according to Grosseteste, rely too much on the argument that cause and effect must exist simultaneously. This is true when both come under the same measure, such as when both are eternal or both are temporal. Since this is clearly not the case here, the rule does not apply, and he concludes:

Deus ... eternus causa est mundi temporalis et temporis, nec precedit ista tempore sed simplici eternitate.[7]

Finally he devotes some lines to the error that there was more than one principle involved in the production of the world. Plato had assumed that matter and ideas had always existed independently of God, and that God had made the world after the model of ideas. Aristotle thought that prime matter had always existed independently of God. Against these and others we must hold firmly that everything has been created out of nothing, as Moses indicates in the words: 'In principio'.[8]

Richard Rufus uses these chapters of the *Hexaemeron* extensively in his treatise on creation; their philosophical flavour must have appealed to him. As an introduction he gives a survey of the errors of the philosophers, drawn completely from Grosseteste (B f. 103C–D).[9]

---

[4] Gross. *Hex.* I. viii. 1–2 and 4, pp. 58–61; in viii. 4, p. 61 the famous passage in which Grosseteste inveighs against '... quosdam modernos, qui nituntur contra ipsum Aristotilem et suos expositores de Aristotile heretico facere catholicum, mira cecitate et presumptione putantes se limpidius intelligere et verius interpretari Aristotilem ex litera latina corrupta quam philosophos, tam gentiles quam catholicos, qui eius literam incorruptam originalem grecam plenissime noverunt.'

[5] Smalley, 'Biblical Scholar', p. 87.   [6] Gross. *Hex.* I. viii. 3, 5, pp. 59–61.

[7] Ibid. I. viii. 6, p. 62.   [8] Ibid. I. ix. 1–4, pp. 62–4.

[9] Title in the margin of f. 103C: 'A. Opiniones philosophorum de eternitate mundi contra quas disputatur'.

Then he turns to his own discussion of the notion of creation; it is in the form of seventeen objections against the concept of creation, immediately followed by the answer. Richard pays little attention to the philosophers who maintained that several principles had been at work in the production of the world, against which Christians hold that the world was created from nothing. He analyses the proposition 'ex nihilo nihil fieri'.[10] This proposition is only true when applied to the efficient cause, not when applied to the material cause, since not every new thing comes forth from matter. Moreover in the expression *ex nihilo* the preposition does not refer to the material out of which the world is made, but it is used in the sense of 'after': 'sicut: ex nocte fit dies'.[11]

Then he moves on to the main issue: the challenge of Aristotle, the problem of the eternity of the world, a problem that clearly fascinated him, if the amount of space he devotes to it is any indication. In the abbreviation, too, he is not satisfied with summarizing Bonaventure, but gives once more his own ideas on the subject, ideas which he had developed in the Oxford commentary.[12]

He did not come to full clarity on the matter: thus unlike Grosseteste he did not detect the difference between Aristotle and the Neoplatonists. That much is clear from the abbreviation, where, before questioning, he mentions two theories about the beginning of the world: according to Augustine some maintain that the world was created by God's will, but coeternal with God; others maintain, according to Basil, that the world from all eternity has come forth from God, as light spreads its shining or a body casts a shadow. Although he is in doubt as to which theory Aristotle subscribed to, he suspects it must be the second.[13] Here he betrays that he must have read Aristotle through his Arab commentators and did not see that the emanation theory was a later accretion.

I shall first discuss some of the more important objections which are to be found only in the Oxford commentary, and then go on to those which he deemed worthy to be repeated in the abbreviation. In the

[10] Aristotle, *Physica*, 187^{a}29.

[11] In the abbreviation Richard pays more attention to the question 'an possit esse creatio et an possit scilicet aliquid de nihilo produci' (V f. 131A–D); question and answer are both independent of Bonaventure.

[12] See the survey of the pattern of borrowing in ch. 3, pp. 52–5.

[13] 'Quo istorum modorum istud posuerit Aristoteles ignoro. Magis tamen puto quod secundo secundum illud exemplum de vestigio pedis in pulvere' (V f. 131D). Both Augustine's and Basil's opinions also in B f. 103C–D and in Gross. *Hex.* I. viii. 3, pp. 59–60.

first category is Grosseteste's argument, based on the rule that cause and effect must coexist, that, therefore, the world must be eternal. He repeats Grosseteste's reply and then adds another reply of his own; distinguishing between two forms of causation, natural causes and voluntary causes. In nature cause and effect coexist, but where something is caused by someone's will, there can be no necessity, and there is always the possibility of doing the opposite. Since creation is a purely voluntary act, the aforesaid rule does not apply (B f. 103D).

The same emphasis on God's will is visible in the next objection: there is no good reason why God should not have created the world before he actually did (B ff. 103D–104A). This argument comes from another source Richard uses frequently here and in other contexts, the anonymous commentary on the *Metaphysics* of English origin.[14] This question is not really an issue, according to Richard; it can be reduced to the more fundamental question, why God did not create the world from all eternity. The answer is that God created the world in time, because such was his will from all eternity. But Richard is not a pure voluntarist; he seeks to show that God's will is not arbitrary, but that it was also reasonable so to will:

Cum ergo queritur, aut fuit causa in Deo, quare non prius fecit mundum, verum videtur quod in ipso fuit causa. Hec enim videtur causa, quia scilicet Ipse solus est eternus. Unde sua eternitas et sua incommutabilitas videtur causa quare non fuit mundum ab eterno.   (B f. 104A)

There is one more objection which deals with the problem of an eternal God creating a world in time. Richard mentions the problem that a creation in time seems to imply a change in God, to which he replies that notions like movement and action apply to God in a different way (B f. 104B).[15]

There is a rather interesting interruption in the flow of objection and reply in the form of a long diatribe against 'someone who is very long-winded about himself as well as about the opinions of others', in fact Maimonides (B f. 104D). Incensed as he is by Maimonides' treatment of Aristotle's arguments for the eternity of the world, he does not

[14] For a discussion of this work and its author see ch. v, pp. 94–105. The present argument for the most part only in Va ff. 94D–95D.
[15] This is one of the standard arguments for the eternity of the world. Richard could have found it in the anonymous commentary on the Metaphysics (Va f. 95B) or in Maimonides, *The Guide for the Perplexed*, ii. 14, ed. and tr. M. Friedländer (New York, 1904), p. 175. Most 13th-c. theologians, and Richard among them, used Maimonides extensively in their theology of creation.

seem to see that many of the propositions he attacks do not represent Maimonides' opinion at all, but his explanation of the way in which Aristotle and others argued. He attacks, for instance, the statement that before the world had been made, its existence was either possible, or necessary, or impossible, without seeing that Maimonides had prefaced this statement with the words: 'The Aristotelians in more recent times . . . argue thus'.[16] The excursus ends on a note of dire warning by Richard to his pupils:

Ecce, vide cui credas, et pro modulo meo consulo precipue minus litteratis, aut caute, aut omnino huius miseri scriptum non aspicere, nam multa falsa et frivola asseruntur in illo. (B f. 104D)

There are two arguments which Richard must have considered particularly challenging; they are the only ones he chooses from the confusing wealth of the Oxford commentary and carries over in the abbreviation. Their common characteristic is that they present efforts to come to grips with Aristotle's penetrating analysis of the beginning of the world in the eighth book of the *Physics*.[17] He gives them in two different formulations, first as he finds them in the anonymous commentary on the *Metaphysics*, then as in Grosseteste's essay *De finitate motus et temporis*. He is not, however, completely dependent on his sources, most of the answers are his own.[18]

Richard found Aristotle's argument, based on the analysis of motion, formulated in two different ways in the anonymous commentary on the *Metaphysics*; more specific, following Aristotle almost to the letter, and more general, as an analysis of change in general and not just motion. The latter runs as follows: if there is a first change, called B, there must be a first changeable thing, called A. A must be prior to B. So, we first have A, being able to be changed by change B, and then A, being changed by change B. So, before change B occurs, another change has already taken place in A. Therefore, change B is not the first change; and from there we can regress infinitely.[19]

Richard's refutation of this analysis is based on the presupposition that creation is something unique and cannot simply be called the first

---

[16] Maimonides, *Guide*, ii. 14 (ed. Friedländer, p. 174).

[17] Aristotle, *Physica*, 250^{b}11–251^{b}28.

[18] The arrangement of the two arguments differs in B and V, the main difference being that in B the refutation follows the objection, whereas in V the two are separated by the *responsio*, see pp. 53–4.

[19] Both formulations can be found in Va ff. 94D–95A, B f. 104C and V f. 132A–B. For a transcription of Va and B see Gal, 'Commentarius', pp. 221–2.

change.[20] What can be created ('creabile') is only prior to what is created in our way of looking at it ('secundum modum intelligendi'), not in reality. Also, if we must call the creation of the first creature the first change, then that change does not come under the category of motion. After these first shots he argues more specifically that in the act of creation there are not two changes; change B and a change of disposition in A, because unlike in natural changes there is no time sequence in creation; everything happens at once. Whereas in natural changes a real distinction can be made between the changeable thing (A), the act of change (B), and the changed thing, in God's creation of the world the distinction between *creabile, creari, creatum esse* is merely notional. So, there are no two changes, and we cannot regress infinitely.[21]

He then proceeds to give Grosseteste's formulation of Aristotle's argument and his refutation as given in *De finitate*, introducing it with the words: 'Potest et aliter formari ratio Aristotelis sic'.[22] This is the only argument which he copies completely, both objection and reply, without adding any of his own observations or criticisms. Moreover, he repeats it in the abbreviation, although very little other material from the *Hexaemeron* or any other essay of Grosseteste is preserved in that work.

The second way in which Aristotle had approached the issue of the eternity of the world was through an analysis of the notion of time. Richard gives the analysis as he finds it in the anonymous commentary on the *Metaphysics*: if there was a first moment of the world and of time, then it is true that at that moment the world existed, and that before that moment it did not exist. These two propositions are either true at the same moment or not. They cannot be true at the same moment, because contradictory statements can never be true at the same moment. Therefore, the statement that the world does not exist must

---

[20] This is the line taken by Maimonides, *Guide*, ii. 17 (ed. Friedländer, pp. 178–81), and in his wake by almost all 13th-c. theologians, Rohls, *Wilhelm von Auvergne*, p. 163.

[21] 'Sciendum etiam quod non sunt due transmutationes, scilicet B et illa que ab hac dispositione transmutabile ad hanc dispositionem transmutari, quia creari est creatum esse, eo quod non est successivum. Unde hec dispositio transmutabile est terminus initialis B transmutationis. Non est ergo B finis alicuius transmutationis sed est medium quoddam secundum modum intelligendi inter creabile et creatum. Sunt etiam omnia ista tria: creabile, creari, creatum, unum et idem secundum subiectum et differunt solum secundum rationem, quia illa creatura non erat creabilis, non potuit scilicet creari, antequam crearetur. Deus potuit eam creare, sed in illa que nihil erat non erat aliqua potentia' (V f.133A, B f. 104C).

[22] Grosseteste, *De finitate*, ii (ed. Dales, pp. 257–9); B ff. 104D–105A, V ff. 132B–C, 133A–B.

be true in another, i.e. earlier moment, than the statement that the world exists. Since two moments are always connected by an intermediate period of time, time must have existed before the world existed. So, there was time before time; and since time and movement are inextricably linked, there was movement before movement, from which it can be concluded that they both have existed from all eternity (B f. 104A, V f. 132C, Va f. 95B). Richard also mentions Grosseteste's formulation of this analysis (B f. 105A).[23]

His reply is pieced together from his two sources and his own reflections. He first remarks, in the words of the anonymous commentator, that the sentence: it is true that something exists now and that before now it did not exist, has a different meaning when used to describe the act of creation. In a normal context we use in both parts the measure of time; here the negative part refers to the eternal now (*nunc eternitatis*), whereas the positive part refers to the first moment in time (*primum nunc temporis*). Between these two moments there is no intermediate period of time (B f. 104A, V f. 133B, Va f. 95D).[24]

Some try to defuse Aristotle's objection by maintaining that in the first moment of time being and non-being can exist simultaneously. They come to this conclusion by arguing as follows: if a thing is prior only in nature to another thing, the two can exist at the same moment in time; in creation the non-being of the first creature is prior only in nature to its being, so they can be true together. Richard disagrees with this: 'Nam non-esse nec est prius tempore nec simul tempore cum illo' (B f. 104A, V f. 132C).[25] The further explanation of this sentence in the Oxford commentary is very opaque, and perhaps that is why he leaves it out in the abbreviation, where, instead he quotes Grosseteste's refutation: when we speak of creation there is no before and after in time, but only a relation between time and eternity; the non-being of the world is measured in eternity, its being in time. And he adds:

Esse vero mundi mensurabatur ipso primo nunc temporis, et quamvis eternitas sit simul cum nunc temporis, non tamen propter hoc simul fuerunt non-esse mundi et esse mundi, quia non-esse mundi mensurabatur eternitate sine tempore.   (V f. 133B)

Both Richard and Grosseteste agree that in the act of creation we are dealing with an event in which time and eternity touch each other, and

---

[23] Grosseteste, *De finitate*, ii (ed. Dales, pp. 260–1).
[24] A transcription of Va and B in Gal, 'Commentarius', p. 224.
[25] The argument with which Richard disagrees in Va f. 95D.

cannot, therefore, apply the rules of an all-temporal event. In the Oxford commentary Richard pursues this problem somewhat further in a later question of the first distinction where he wonders whether, given a creature, time has to be postulated. The problem arises in connection with the angels who, once created, do not change and do not, therefore, offer any measure of time. He solves this problem by invoking the conventional division in three measures of duration: eternity for God, who has no beginning and no end, time for creatures who have both beginning and end, and *aevum* for creatures who have a beginning but no end (B f. 105C–D).

These are the main outlines of Richard's treatise on creation; the central position of Aristotle's arguments in favour of the eternity of the world in it is obvious. They are the only ones he bothers to repeat, when summarizing Bonaventure's commentary. How important it was according to Richard, to be very precise on this point, also emerges from the way he dismisses Bonaventure's summary of Aristotle's analysis, and substitutes his own (V ff. 131D–132A).[26] Aristotle's attack is much more damaging than Bonaventure makes it out to be, and to meet this formidable challenge Richard first wants to be sure that he has the best possible formulation of of what Aristotle exactly says.

And here for once he found Grosseteste extremely helpful. In the *Hexaemeron* he had warned that Aristotle could not be made into a Catholic, that he seriously threatened the Christian notion of creation. On this point Richard agreed with Grosseteste. Richard also approved of the way in which Grosseteste had met the challenge. It is significant that, although he already has a good formulation of Aristotle's arguments from the anonymous commentator, he still feels compelled to include the Bishop's summary and to repeat it in the abbreviation. There he also formulates the *responsio* in terms which echo Grosseteste's words both in *De finitate* and in the *Hexaemeron:*[27]

Mundus eternus non est, nec motus, vel tempus, nec aliqua creatura. Et causa erroris multorum circa hoc fuit quod non poterant intelligere eternitatem sine extensione. Hoc autem non est intelligere eternitatem, sed falso imaginari. (V f. 133A)

[26] Bonaventure's formulation in *Commentaria*, ii. 1. 1. i. 2 (*Opera omnia*, ii. 19–20).

[27] 'Sciendum est autem quod illud quod decepit antiquos ut ponerent mundum sine inicio, fuit precipue falsa ymaginacio, qua coacti sunt ymaginari ante omne tempus tempus aliud, sicut ymaginatur fantasia extra omnem locum locum alium, et extra omne spacium spacium aliud, et hoc usque in infinitum', Gross. *Hex.* 1. viii. 5, p. 61; see also *De finitate*, i (ed. Dales, p. 256).

Where Grosseteste uses dialectical methods Richard is quite willing to follow him.

(vi) *Conclusion*

The study of Richard Rufus's introduction to his commentary on the Sentences made it clear that he did not find Grosseteste's way of approaching the faith very helpful since he could not share his predecessor's mental outlook. Now that we have seen how he uses the *Hexaemeron* in practice, this impression is more than confirmed.

Grosseteste had wished theological teaching and theological method to be traditional, based on the Bible, using allegory as its explanatory tool. His interest in natural philosophy was motivated by that purpose: to sharpen those tools. These methodological principles were, moreover, based on a philosophy of participation of Neo-platonic colouring, a philosophy in which the boundaries of sacred and profane, of God and man were fluid, where nothing was too clearly distinguished, too rigorously defined, a world of unity above all else. The intellectual expression of that deep conviction was his use of the allegory of light: light as the unifying force of the universe was at the origin of all existing things, and even now everything participates in the form of light.

And it is in the treatment of light that the divergence between Grosseteste and Richard Rufus becomes most obvious. Light has nothing mystical for Richard, it does not evoke a higher reality, nor was it at the origin of the world, nor does it unify the world. For Richard light is an object, a physical phenomenon which can, like all others, be studied and classified: accident or substance, corporeal or incorporeal, form or matter. Such questions are the questions of Aristotle, of a philosophy of autonomous nature. Richard is moving to a view of the world marked by clear boundaries and distinctions, in which everything is defined and classified, in which the natural and the supernatural, God and man have their places assigned to them, and nature has an autonomy of its own.

This need to draw the line is also obvious in Richard's worrying over the generation of the animal soul. He wants to find out exactly how far this is an autonomous, natural process, as Aristotle had maintained, and how far God intervenes and what direction that intervention takes. Grosseteste had settled the whole question with a grand gesture: all souls are created, man and animal. But he did so, less because he found the question positively interesting or important—his treatment is rather lackadaisical and superficial—but because he was not so worried about assigning areas of competence; those things did not matter too much in his philosophy.

It need now cause no surprise any more that Richard has no place for allegory in his commentary. Allegory only functions in an intellectual atmosphere in which God and world, sacred and profane, are intermingled. Richard, with most theologians of his days, has broken with that pattern of thought. His way of thinking is dialectical, he wants to solve problems, to reach clarity, where Grosseteste had been quite happy to leave an area of uncertainty, and of mystery.

Since, however, he was a theologian and a friar, he could not possibly push his desire for clear-cut distinctions to its logical conclusion. The world might have a certain autonomy, but in the end it was completely dependent upon God; no Christian could ever think otherwise. The concern to hold on to this essential truth explains, I think, his strong emphasis on God's will in the generation of animals, and even more, his preoccupation with creation and the problem of the eternity of the world. Where the easy link forged by the Neoplatonic philosophy of participation was weakening, a new link between God and creation had to be forged. And that could be done if one gave full emphasis to the notion of creation, the notion that everything in existence was ultimately caused to be by God. Richard saw very well that Aristotle, congenial though he might be in many ways, went too far with his defence of the eternity of the world. This was autonomy gone too far; here his philosophy became a threat to the substance of Christianity. And this is the one point on which Richard profoundly agreed with Grosseteste, and where he gives him all due honour. It is an important point, because it shows that in the end, despite a deep difference of outlook, both were driven by the same motive, the concern for the integrity of the Christian faith.

CHAPTER 8

Free will in God and Man

(i) *The Problem of Free Will*

ALTHOUGH the problem of free will, man's capacity to decide freely
and without coercion upon a certain course of action, seems a philosophical problem, touching theology only in some of its repercussions,
such as its relation to God's omniscience, it is a fundamental question
in any Christian anthropology, especially in connection with the
doctrines of redemption, grace, and justification.

Plato had affirmed that man followed reason in his practical
decisions, that evil acts were the result of ignorance. Once man had
fully understood the good, he could not but act upon that insight.[2]
Aristotle developed a more elaborate theory of choice in the *Nicomachean Ethics*. He realized that understanding the good was a
necessary, but not sufficient stimulus to do the good, that another step
had to be taken to forge a link between deliberation and act. To bridge
the gap he introduced 'desire' as a necessary element in the process of
choice: man desires the good he has discerned. He defines 'choice' as
a 'deliberate desire of things in our own power', thus uniting the intellectual and the newly introduced affective element in the process of
choice.[3]

But this theory was still far removed from the Christian understanding of the source of man's actions. There was nothing specifically

---

[1] The more accurate translation of the Latin term *liberum arbitrium* would be 'free
choice' or 'free decision', see. e.g. W. G. Thompson, 'The Doctrine of Free Choice in
Saint Bonaventure', *FS* xviii (1958), 1 n. 1, and Thomas Aquinas, *Summa theologiae*, ed.
T. Sutton (Blackfriars edn., xi, 170), p. 237 n. a. I shall continue to use the less accurate,
though more current English term 'free will' for man's unique indeterminacy as regards
contingents, because it sounds less contrived. I am well aware of the fact that this translation stresses the volitional element too much at the cost of the intellectual.

[2] J. Lebacqz, *Libre arbitre et jugement* (Museum Lessianum, section philosophique,
xlvii, 1960), pp. 11–12.

[3] Aristotle, *Ethica Nicomachea*, 1113ᵃ11; Lebacqz, *Libre arbitre*, pp. 12–13; J. Korolec,
'L'*Éthique à Nicomaque* et le problème du libre arbitre à la lumière des commentaires
parisiens du xiiiᵉ siècle et la philosophie de la liberté de Jean Buridan', in Zimmermann
(ed.), *Auseinandersetzungen*, pp. 332–3.

human about Aristotle's notion of 'desire', a movement which was shared by all living beings. What distinguished man from the animal for Aristotle was the intellect, which channelled man's desire to direct it to its proper objects. The conception of the will as the second specifically human faculty, equal to the intellect, and as the foundation of man's moral actions, is a specifically Christian contribution to the ethical debate.[4]

Especially Augustine, when he reflected afterwards on his own conversion experience, stressed the supreme importance of the will in the direction of man's activities. He had experienced in his own personal struggle how, already won over intellectually by the truth of the Christian faith, he remained unable to free himself from the shackles of carnal desire and to embrace the truth which he had discerned so clearly:

Ita certum habebam esse melius tuae caritati me dedere quam meae cupiditati cedere; sed illud placebat et uincebat, hoc libebat et uinciebat.[5]

The eighth book of the Confessions is probably the most eloquent Christian testimony to the importance of the will as equal and perhaps superior to the intellect in man's choice of his actions.

The will is the source of man's freedom, and it is the freedom of the will, even with regard to the dictates of the intellect, which elevates man above the animals and makes him the principle of his own actions. The fact that the Christian tradition so highly exalts the freedom of the will, and the ensuing reality of free choice, is attributed by Gilson to the high view Christianity takes of man's dignity as a being who participates in the divine power. Man is created in the image of God and shares in God's creative power and in his freedom.[6]

Another reason for Christian theologians to stress man's freedom of will and choice was probably to accommodate the existence of evil. God could not possibly be held responsible for sin and suffering, neither could Christians postulate the existence of a principle of evil, as the Manichees did; that would make a mockery of God's omnipotence. The only possible source of evil left was man's freedom to choose, even to choose evil. Augustine certainly had this in mind when he reflected on man's free will in his treatise *De libero arbitrio*, which

---

[4] G. Wieland, *Ethica—Scientia practica: die Anfänge der philosophischen Ethik im 13. Jahrhundert* (BGPhThMA, n.s. xxi, 1981), pp. 281, 286–7; Lebacqz, *Libre arbitre*, p. 13.

[5] Augustine, *Confessiones*, viii. 5 (ed. Knöll, p. 179).

[6] É. Gilson, *L'Esprit de la philosophie médiévale* (2 vols., Paris, 1932), ii. 101–2.

was directed against the Manichees, and opens with the words: 'Tell me, I ask you, whether God is perhaps the source of evil.'[7]

The third reason for the emphasis of the Christian tradition on man's capacity to choose freely was that man's actions can only be morally significant if they are free. Thomas Aquinas puts this very succinctly in his *Quaestiones disputatae de Veritate*, where he argues that the Christian faith requires the existence of a free will in man, since without it we could not talk about merit or demerit, about due reward or punishment.[8]

Thus the fact of free will was never a matter of serious debate. Discussion concentrated on the nature of free will, whether it had to be defined in terms of its goal, as Anselm was to do ('potestas servandi rectitudinem voluntatis propter ipsam rectitudinem'), or in terms of its potentiality, as Peter Lombard did in the *Sentences* ('facultas rationis et voluntatis, qua bonum, gratia assistente eligitur, vel malum, eadem desistente').[9] Another point of debate was whether the possibility of choosing evil belonged to the essential nature of the free will. The most widely discussed point was probably the determination of the exact relation between intellect and will and the act of free choice itself, a problem which, of course, had not been dealt with in classical philosophy, since it could only emerge after the will had been accepted as a second faculty distinguishing man from all other living things.[10] Finally there was the grave theological problem how to reconcile man's free will with God's continuing concern for his creation, more in particular with his foreknowledge, with predestination and with grace. All these questions are dealt with in one way or another, in both Robert Grosseteste's and in Richard Rufus's treatment of the notion of *liberum arbitrium*.

(ii) *Robert Grosseteste on Free Will in God and Man*

It need cause no surprise that Robert Grosseteste interested himself in the problem of man's free will so much that he went out of his way to devote a long treatise to it. Even by medieval standards he took a very

---

[7] M. Huftier, 'Libre arbitre, liberté et péché chez saint Augustin', *RThAM* xxxiii (1966), 194; Wieland, *Ethica*, p. 283.

[8] 'Respondeo dicendum quod absque omni dubitatione hominem arbitrio liberum ponere oportet. Ad hoc enim fides astringit, cum sine libero arbitrio non possit esse meritum vel demeritum, justa poena vel praemium', Thomas Aquinas, *Quaestiones disputat de veritate*, xxiv. 1, resp.

[9] Lottin, *Psychologie*, i. 13, 29 n. 2.

[10] Ibid. i. 222; Wieland, *Ethica*, pp. 284–5; Korolec, 'Problème', pp. 334–6.

high view of human dignity.[11] When meditating on the words 'let us make man in our own image' (Gen. i. 26), he explains that man has been created as the highest possible imitation of the divinity itself.[12] He is anxious to point out that this does not mean that man was created in the image of the Incarnate Word, or after the likeness of Christ's humanity, but in the likeness of God, three and one, as the sacred author himself makes clear when he repeats 'in the image of God created he him' (Gen. i. 27). Created in the image of the triune God man imitates him in everything: 'In omnibus que divinitatis sunt, imitatur, ut dictum est, propinquissima imitacione homo Deum'.[13] Grosseteste draws far-reaching conclusions from this principle, such as that man shares in a certain sense God's creative power:

Licet enim multa predicentur de Deo que non predicantur de homine, utpote quod creator est, quod eternus est et huiusmodi, tamen homo participat eternitate et creandi quadam imitatione vicinius et similius omni creatura carenie racione. Cum enim gracie Dei inspiracione efficimur nova creatura, cum simus in hoc Dei coadiutores et cooperatores, sumus quoddam huius creacionis initium, et operacionis que creacio est gerimus manifestissimum imitatorium vestigium.[14]

Such a view must lead Grosseteste to consider man's free will, through the exercise of which he participates in God's supreme freedom, to which creation, the act of God's pure disinterested love, especially testifies. And Grosseteste does, indeed, draw that conclusion in his treatise on free will, where he asserts bluntly that man's free will is God's image and likeness, because it is in his free will that man most closely resembles God, who creates everything freely through his Word:

Est enim liberum arbitrium Dei similitudo et imago. Ergo cum Deus sit suo verbo omnia faciens, huius similitudinem erit in libero arbitrio, quod est eius imago, reperire, scilicet quod universum quoddam faciat suo verbo ... Item: cum ita sit Deus summe bonus, patet, quod nihil est in eo, cuius aliquod vestigium non reperiatur in aliqua creatura. Ergo et huius vestigium, quod est omnia suo verbo facere, est in aliqua creatura reperire. Sed constat, quod in nulla, nisi haec sit in libero arbitrio. Est ergo hoc ibi reperire.[15]

[11] Dales, 'Medieval View', pp. 569–71.
[12] Gross. *Hex.* VIII. xvii. 3, p. 242; McEvoy, *Philosophy*, p. 385.
[13] Ibid. VIII. xvii. 4, p. 242.
[14] Ibid.; McEvoy, *Philosophy*, p. 399 n. 114.
[15] Gross. *Lib.* xxi, pp. 237–8. In one of his sermons he distinguishes man from the rest of creation through his reason and free will: 'Homo autem una est de creaturis, et in quantum homo, rationalis est et liber arbitrio', *Sermon 'Ex rerum initiatarum'*, ed. S. Gieben, 'Robert Grosseteste on Preaching', *Collectanea Franciscana*, xxxvii (1967), 122.

In Grosseteste's universe every creature referred to its Creator and participated in his goodness, as we have seen, but as a vestige. Only man can be called God's image.[16] Grosseteste's view of human dignity and his anthropology are founded on the conviction that the most important statement that can be made about man is that he has been created in God's image and after his likeness.[17] And if this likeness is foremost in man's capacity of free choice, then his long deliberation on the subject is more than justified, it is an essential part both of his anthropology and of his theological symbolism.

Grosseteste's treatise on free will has come down to us in two versions. I shall refer only to the longer version, given as the main text in Baur's edition, since this is the one used by Richard Rufus. The treatise has a very lucid structure. Grosseteste first asks himself whether free will can exist. He proves that man's possibility of free choice is not incompatible with God's foreknowledge (chs. i–viii), with the predestination of the saints (ch. ix), with divine grace (ch. x), with the necessity of fate (ch. xi), with God's intention to create the best of all possible worlds (ch. xii), and with the domination of sin (ch. xiii–xiv). The comparison of man's free will and God's foreknowledge takes up more than half of the treatise and is, in fact, a thoroughgoing discussion of the problem of contingency in the universe. Having disposed of all these possible threats, he gives positive proof of the existence of free will (ch. xv).

In the next chapters he enquires into the nature of free will; and the first question is whether the concept *liberum arbitrium* can be used univocally for God, man, and the angels (ch. xvi). In Grosseteste's case the answer cannot be in doubt. Given the fact that he has exalted free will as man's highest likeness to God, he must at least assume a certain analogy: man's freedom and God's freedom are alike at least in some important points. This also determines the answer to the next question whether the ability to sin is an essential part of man's free will (ch. xvii). It cannot be, if man's free will is essentially a participation in God's freedom. He adopts, therefore, as the most accurate Anselm's definition of free will as the capacity to preserve the rightness of the will for the sake of that rightness. He then wonders whether this

---

[16] 'Unde etsi in aliis creaturis eluceat aliqua Dei similitudo, non tamen elucet in illis Dei imago, quia imago est summa et propinquissima similitudo. Naturalis igitur capacitas omnium que sunt in Deo per maxime propinquam imitacionem est in homine Dei imago', Gross. *Hex.* VIII. vii. 4, p. 229; see also Grosseteste, *Dictum 60*, ed. Gieben, 'Traces', p. 156.

[17] McEvoy, *Philosophy*, pp. 380–6.

definition sufficiently covers the indeterminacy (*vertibilitas ad utrumque*) of the will which is an essential part of free will.

The problem is that this inclusion seems to entail the inclusion of the power to choose between good and evil. And if that were true, then God could not be said to possess free will. Grosseteste solves this problem by showing that there are many indifferent things between which man can choose and that the power to choose between good and evil is only accidental:

Vertibilitas voluntatis ad utrumque oppositorum in se consideratorum potest dici potestas peccandi et non peccandi per accidens loquendo, quia est potestas eligendi illud oppositum, cui accidit esse divinae voluntati contrarium, et illud oppositum, cui accidit esse divinae voluntati beneplacitum. Auctores itaque, qui dicunt potestatem peccandi et non peccandi esse quiditatem et essentiam liberi arbitrii per accidens loquuntur. Qui vero hoc abnegant per se loquuntur.[18]

Thus he can accept that even in God there is a certain indeterminacy, although this does not imply that God would ever change his mind. God has the power 'volendi absque initio et ab aeterno quod non vult, et non volendi absque initio et ab aeterno quod vult. Est igitur in Deo voluntatis utriusque oppositorum potestas.'[19] He can also now accommodate Peter Lombard's definition of free will as a faculty of reason and will through which man chooses good and evil: Lombard speaks essentially of indeterminacy, and only accidentally of the choice between good and evil.[20]

In this connection he also broaches the question which vexed his predecessors and contemporaries most of all, to which capacity of the soul free will had to be related: reason or will. His answer is surprising, he maintains that the source of both reason and will is the substance which we call free will. Just as in a ray of the sun, light and heat are different and yet the same, because they flow from the same source, so reason and will are different and yet one in their one root, free will.[21] This leaves us slightly in the dark as to which capacity enjoys priority, but that question is solved next when he comes to speak about true liberty.

---

[18] Gross. *Lib.* xvii, p. 226, quoted by Richard Rufus (B f. 167C).

[19] Ibid. xvii, p. 223 (B f. 167B–C).

[20] Ibid. xvii, p. 225.

[21] Ibid. xvii, pp. 227–8 (B f. 160D). See Lottin, *Psychologie*, i. 195 for a transcription of B.

Grosseteste maintains that true liberty is moral liberty.[22] It consists in a perfect identification of the self with the good, and it requires full power over the will: 'Commensuratio itaque eius, quod est bene esse ad potestatem et voluntatem propriam ordinatam vera libertas est'.[23] In order to distinguish different kinds of liberty he divides the being of a rational nature in two: willing and understanding. And it is the will which comes first, because man's eternal happiness does not so much consist in the perfection of his intellect as in the fulfilment of his yearning: 'In velle enim primo et per se proprie consistit beatitudo, in "aspicere" autem non.'[24]

Three kinds of liberty can be distinguished in man: *libertas a necessitate*, through which man is absolutely free to will as he wills without any external pressure; *libertas a peccato*, which is the freedom to opt for actions that contribute to final salvation, and *libertas complaciti*, with which man chooses to enjoy the highest good.[25] Having considered which of these three forms of liberty was enjoyed by man in paradise (ch. xix), he turns to the question who is the efficient cause of free will and decides that it is God, despite the possibility of the will's corruption (ch. xx).

In the last chapter (ch. xxi) he wonders whether God in some sense moves man's free will, a question left undecided. In that connection he also mentions the classic problem whether man can freely reach out to some meritorious good which, in accordance with the Church's teaching, he denies. The treatise ends with a number of questions which are only jotted down but not answered, to avoid boredom, as he puts it.

(iii) *Proofs of the Existence of Human Freedom of Will*

Richard Rufus spills just as much ink over the treatment of man's free will as Grosseteste. In his Oxford commentary on the *Sentences* he deals with it in great detail in the appropriate place, the twenty-fourth and twenty-fifth distinctions of the second book; in the abbreviation he confines himself to repeating Bonaventure's words and adding two additional short comments. Although Richard must have attached

[22] L. Baur, *Die Philosophie des Robert Grosseteste, Bischofs von Lincoln* (†1253) (BGPhMA, xviii. 4–6, 1917), pp. 278–9.
[23] Gross. *Lib.* xvii, p. 229 (B f. 167C). D. Sharp, 'The Philosophy of Richard Fishacre (d. 1248)', *The New Scholasticism*, vii (1933), 294–5 attributes this definition, mistakenly, to Richard Fishacre.
[24] Gross. *Lib.* xviii, p. 231.
[25] Ibid. xviii, pp. 233–4.

some importance to the topic considering the vast amount of space he needs to look at it from all sides, he has not much to add of his own, either in the way of questions or of answers. A familiar pattern, observed in other parts of his commentary, repeats itself. To a large extent he uses Grosseteste and Fishacre, commenting on their answers where he disagrees with their conclusions. And though he has both Grosseteste's *De libero arbitrio* and Fishacres's commentary in front of him, he clearly quotes Grosseteste through Fishacre in some places.[26]

Although Richard puts the question whether man possesses free will after the problem of its definition, following Fishacre in this,[27] I shall keep here to the more logical order. As we saw, the problem of the existence of free will can be approached from two sides, negatively by enquiring into the forces which seem incompatible with it, and positively. Richard skips the discussion of the relation between God's foreknowledge and man's free will, because he has covered that earlier in the first book, hardly using Grosseteste's extensive discussion of the subject.[28] He does, however, consider the claims of predestination, grace, fate and temptation. Grosseteste is his main guide throughout: he reproduces for each question the relevant chapter from *De libero arbitrio* without adding much of his own (B ff. 161B–162B). Sometimes he mentions Fishacre's answer, only to reject it.[29] Sometimes he adds a few lines in which he indicates his approval of Grosseteste.[30]

Occasionally he slightly adjusts Grosseteste's solution by contrasting him with an authority like Anselm, as in the question whether temptation does not force man sometimes to act against his free will. Grosseteste considers the case of someone who lies to save his life: is this lie not forced upon him rather than the consequence of a freely taken decision? He distinguishes between the will to do something and the act of doing so. Man can never be forced to will something, but he can be forced to act against his will. Thus it is possible that an act

---

[26] Compare e.g. B f. 167C–D with Fishacre (Ba f. 133D, O f. 206C–D) and Gross. *Lib.* xvii, p. 229.

[27] Fishacre first deals with the definition, the capacities, and the name of free will (Ba ff. 128B–130A, O ff. 198B–200D), before asking whether it exists at all (Ba ff.130A–131B, O ff. 200D–202D). Richard Rufus, too, deals first with name and definition (B ff. 160B–161B) and then wonders about its existence (B ff. 161B–162C).

[28] 'In primo libro distinctione 38 habitum est de quibusdam quomodo non repugnent libero arbitrio, scilicet de prescientia dei etc.' (B f. 161B).

[29] Compare e.g. B f. 161C with Ba f. 130B, O f. 201A, or B f. 162C with Ba f. 128D, O ff. 198D–199A.

[30] Compare B ff. 161D–162A with Gross. *Lib.* x, p. 202.

which, considered in itself is voluntary, does not flow from the will to perform that act in a particular case.[31] Rufus does not accept this dichotomy. He comments that, if a man both wants to live and not to lie, and wants the former more than the latter, then obviously it is his will rather to lie than to die; the act of lying is a consequence of the will to lie. He corroborates this statement with a quotation from Anselm's treatise on free will (B f. 162B).[32]

Despite these comments it is clear that Rufus follows Grosseteste completely; and he, in his turn, is dependent upon Anselm and Bernard. Other psychological forces, opposing the exercise of free will, like ingrained habits or moral conditions, both of which are considered by Aristotle, or motives, or the influence of a man's character upon which Augustine reflects, are neglected both by Grosseteste and by Richard Rufus, although they are considered by many other contemporary theologians.[33]

In giving positive proofs for the existence of free will, on the other hand, Richard deviates considerably from Grosseteste, especially in the proof from reason. Grosseteste's arguments have a psychological slant. First he argues from the notions of reward and punishment: man can only be rewarded or punished for his actions if they are not necessary but voluntary. Then he appeals to man's feeling of shame: why should man be ashamed of his actions, or why should he recoil from witnesses to his evil deeds, unless they are in his own power? Man's conscience would not accuse him if he were not master over his own actions. And why should man rejoice in his good deeds, if not for the reason that he has done them voluntarily and without force, and could just as well not have done them?[34] Grosseteste's aversion to dialectics and his preference for psychological or historical arguments comes to the fore once again.

Rufus first quotes some authorities, just as Grosseteste does and then asks what the cause of human actions can be (B f. 162B–C). Although the outline of this argument is borrowed from Damascene's proof of man's free will, Richard freely embroiders upon it.[35] Following Damascene he distinguishes four kinds of efficient causality: two *cause per se* —nature and intellect—and two *cause per*

---

[31] Ibid. xiv, pp. 211–12.
[32] Anselm, *De libertate arbitrii*, v–vi, ed. F. S. Schmitt (*Opera omnia*, i, 1946), pp. 216–18.
[33] Baur, *Philosophie*, pp. 264–5.
[34] Gross. *Lib.* xv, pp. 212–13.
[35] John Damascene, *De fide orthodoxa*, xxxix. 2, (ed. Buytaert, pp. 148–50).

accidens—chance and fortune. Man's actions cannot be caused by nature, since man is distinguished from all other beings by his reason and intellect; nor by chance, because man is not erratic in his actions; nor by fortune, since man acts intentionally and according to plan. Therefore, they must be caused by the intellect: not God's, since evil and unjust actions cannot be attributed to him but man's; not speculative reason, since actions are always about singulars ('operationes sunt circa singularia'), but practical reason, in which there is no necessity, since we speak of necessity only when cause and effect are always the same. The conclusion is that practical reason, using free will, is the principle of all actions of man.

The second argument starts equally from a premiss formulated by Damascene i.e. that all things that are generated are indeterminate (*vertibile*).[36] The indeterminacy of inanimate and irrational things shows itself in their corporeal changes, that of rational beings in their power to choose. Richard adds that this follows from the fact that the rational soul is immortal and incorruptible, hence unchanging in its essence. So its indeterminacy must lie in the will (B f. 162C). He concludes his proof by quoting two further arguments from Damascene, in which man's power to take counsel with himself is seen as an indication for the existence of free will (B f. 162C).

The tone of Rufus's argument is very different from Grosseteste's. Rufus does not rely on introspection, his reasoning is dialectical: by taking logical steps he shows that the existence of free will in man must necessarily follow from the two premisses that we can distinguish four kinds of efficient causality and that all generated things are indeterminate. The fact that he found the outline of his arguments in Damascene's *De fide orthodoxa* does not make this less remarkable; what matters is that Damascene's logic attracted him more than Grosseteste's introspection.

(iv) *Free Will in Relation to the Capacities of the Soul*

Before the middle of the thirteenth century the centrepiece of any debate on free will was formed by a defintion of its nature in relation to intellect and will.[37] Following tradition Richard devotes much attention to this problem as well. To begin with he quotes from Fishacre's solution extensively, adding a few quotations from Damascene and

---

[36] Ibid. xli. 1, p. 152.
[37] Lottin, *Psychologie*, i. 12, 221–3.

Anselm.[38] Fishacre begins his argument by stating that only intellectual creatures have free will. So free will must be rooted in that which distinguishes the intellectual from the sensitive: the intellect itself and rational knowledge. The most characteristic feature of an intellect is that it can reflect upon itself. The root of free will, therefore, must lie in this capacity of the intellect to reflect on itself. The two operations, however, are not identical. The exercise of free will is more limited: it is the capacity of the intellect to reflect on itself at the moment it proposes to act.

To clarify this Fishacre gives a survey of the structure of a human act: the intellect proposes to itself a certain act; a vague desire (*voluntas incompleta*) to act on that proposal arises; then the soul is roused to reflect on that desire and to judge whether or not it will follow its promptings, which is the act proper to the capacity of free choice. Once a positive decision has been reached, the first hesitant movement of the will is completed; now there is *consensus*.[39] There can be no doubt that in Fishacre's eyes reason takes the lead and guides the will. The act of free will is the intellect's judgment on that vague, first desire to do something. It is only after the judgment of reason that the will can run its full course. With approval Fishacre quotes the intellectualist definition of free will given by Boethius: 'Liberum arbitrium est liberum de voluntate iudicium'.[40]

Richard Rufus disagrees heartily with Fishacre. His main objection is that the intellect does not sit in judgment upon the will. And he quotes Grosseteste to show that the will is independent of reason in its willing:

Nec tamen ipsa ratio aliquam necessitatem inducit (B: indici) voluntati ad eligendum vel fugiendum quod ipsa ratio sic iudicaverit, sed relinquit voluntati liberum sententiam iudicii rationis sequi aut abnuere.   (B f. 160D)[41]

On this point Richard is in line not only with Grosseteste, but also with the so-called Franciscan tradition, that the will's incentive to act lies only in itself.

[38] Fishacre's treatise in Ba f. 128B–D, O f. 198B–D, most of it edited in Lottin, *Psychologie*, i. 114–16. For Richard Rufus see B f. 160B–D, edited by Lottin, op. cit., i. 190–2; the additional quotations are from John Damascene, *De fide orthodoxa*, xxxvi. 8 (ed. Buytaert, p. 135) and Anselm, *De concordia praescientiae et praedestinationis et gratiae Dei cum libero arbitrio*, iii. 11, ed. F. S. Schmitt (*Opera omnia*, ii, 1946), pp. 278–84.

[39] Lottin, *Psychologie*, i. 113, 115–16, 192.

[40] Boethius, *Commentarii in librum Aristotelis Περὶ Ἑρμηνείας editio secunda*, iii. 9, ed. C. Meiser (Leipzig, 1880), p. 196. See also his *De consolatione philosophiae*, v. 2, ed. L. Bieler (CC xciv, 1957), pp. 90–1.

[41] Lottin, *Psychologie*, i. 194. Cf. Gross. *Lib.* xvii, p. 226.

Rufus also criticizes Fishacre's unclarity in his description of the capacities of the soul. He himself introduces a new division to describe the soul's relation to its acts: we must distinguish capacities, dispositions, and use or operation.[42] Richard tries to square these new concepts with the terms he inherited, like *instrumentum* from Anselm and *facultas* from Peter Lombard. He seems to be inclined to equate *instrumentum* with *potentia* or capacity, *facultas* and *motus* with *habitus* or disposition, and *usus* with *actus* or act.[43] A certain amount of confusion, however, remains. Some try to describe free will as a capacity of the soul, like Anselm.[44] Richard prefers to follow Peter Lombard and to describe free will as a disposition of the intellect and the will, which in their turn are defined as capacities of the soul.[45]

This definition raises the problem of the unity of free will. Free will, thus defined, seems to consist of two different dispositions, rooted in two different capacities of the soul. Looking for a way out Richard turns to Grosseteste, who sees free will as the source of both intellect and will, but he objects that, even if this were true, it would still be possible for one substance to have several dispositions (B f. 161A). Neither would it be possible to define free will as a *motus intellectus practici*, since the merits which man earns by acting freely extend over all the capacities of the soul; so free will could be a disposition of the entire soul (B f. 161A), a solution Richard found in the work of Philip the Chancellor.[46] His own solution is that free will is one disposition, both of the intellect and the will, since both the intellect and the will

[42] I gratefully accept Anthony Kenny's translation of the terms *potentia*, *habitus*, and *usus*: capacity, disposition, act(ion). His arguments are to be found in Thomas Aquinas, *Summa theologiae*, ed. A. Kenny (Blackfriars edn., xxii, 1964), pp. xx–xxii.

[43] In the Oxford commentary Richard defines a disposition as *motus instrumenti*(B f. 160D; Lottin, *Psychologie*, i. 195). There he also says that Lombard, whose definition of free will is *facultas rationis et voluntatis*, sees it as a *habitus instrumenti*. The triad *instrumentum*, *habitus* or *motus*, *usus*, as used in the Oxford commentary (B f. 160D; Lottin, *Psychologie*, i. 194), is in the abbreviation replaced by a new triad: *potentia*, *habitus*, *actus* (V f. 242B; Lottin, *Psychologie*, i. 186).

[44] 'Ergo, ut dixi, apud Anselmum dicitur liberum arbitrium instrumentum' (B f. 160D, Lottin, *Psychologie*, i. 195).

[45] 'Nescio ergo an possit intelligi intransitive quod hic dicitur facultas rationis et voluntatis . . . Aut aliter, ut supra dictum est, voluntas dicitur tripliciter, similiter et ratio: instrumentum, habitus et usus. Hic ergo forte accipitur facultas, tam voluntas quam ratio, ut habitus; voluntas autem et ratio pro instrumento, et sic pateret quomodo se habet hec facultas ad voluntatem et rationem, nam sicut habitus vel motus ad instrumentum qui ab ipso egreditur . . . hec facultas potest intelligi instrumentum instrumenti' (B f. 160D; Lottin, *Psychologie*, i. 194).

[46] Lottin, *Psychologie*, i. 195–6; the quotation from Philip the Chancellor can be found in the *Summa de Bono*, Oxford, Magdalen College, MS 66, f. 33C.

can be said to choose. This does not seem to solve the problem of its unity and Richard is aware of it:

Numquid ergo est liberum arbitrium plures motus et diversi? Respondeo: et unus et diversi. Nam unus est motus rationis et voluntatis, ultimus scilicet et principalis. Iudicat enim ratio et eligit voluntas; eligit nichilominus et ratio: nam consentit ratio voluntati eligenti et non contrariatur ei.   (B f. 161A)[47]

It is not quite clear whether free will is in the end a disposition of the intellect or of the will, but later on he explains that, although its unity is ultimately based on the fact that the essence of the soul is one, and that we speak of capacities only when we relate the soul to its operations, it must be admitted that the possibility to choose freely is mainly rooted in the will (B f. 160B).[48]

In the abbreviation Richard counters a difficulty which he did not deal with in his first commentary. It arises from the definition of free will as a disposition. Dispositions add something new to the thing of which they are the disposition, and they also can be rather easily lost. Bonaventure, who also speaks of free will as a disposition, is clearly embarrassed by this and goes to great trouble to show that in this case neither applies.[49] Richard, however, freely admits that free will is a disposition essentially different from the soul: 'Liberum arbitrium est habitus naturalis, sed tamen aliud per essentiam a potentia et a substantia' (V f. 243A).[50] The reason is that dispositions directed at objects outside the substance of which they are the disposition always add something to that substance. Richard does not seem to consider the problem that they can also be lost, whereas man can never lose his capacity to choose.

This curious oversight leaves one wondering how well versed Richard really was in the new terminology of *potentia*, *habitus*, and *actus*. He certainly did not have a perfect understanding of the concept of *habitus* (B f. 131B).[51] We also saw how in his discussion of free will in the Oxford commentary, he was not at all sure how to reconcile an inherited terminology with these new concepts. In the abbreviation he has at least decided that the Anselmian *instrumentum* is the same as *potentia*. Nevertheless, it is clear that the new way of thinking in ethics

[47] Lottin, *Psychologie*, i. 196.
[48] Ibid. i. 197.
[49] Bonaventure, *Commentaria*, ii. 25. I. 5 (*Opera omnia*, ii. 602–4).
[50] Lottin, *Psychologie*, i. 188.
[51] As we saw above, p. 184, Richard saw no contradiction in describing light as a substance and as a disposition at the same time.

has not yet fully penetrated Richard's thinking; he is obviously not so well acquainted with the *Nicomachean Ethics* as he is with Aristotle's physical and metaphysical works.[52] This is rather surprising, as Grosseteste had finished his translation of the *Ethics* by the time Richard started his lectures on the *Sentences*.

The next major subject Richard broaches in the twenty-fourth distinction is the scope of free will and its efficient and final causes. On this topic Richard does not get much help from Grosseteste, who touches upon it rather lightly in the last chapter, more as an after-thought.[53] Although this is the chapter in which he sings the praises of free will as God's image in man, he refrains from the question how far it is autonomous, or whether God can move man to choose evil actions. He merely asserts, as he must, that man left to his own devices cannot will any good and meritorious deed.

That leaves Rufus in the hands of Fishacre. Indeed, Rufus has very little to add to Fishacre's digressions on the subject (B ff. 162C–163D).[54] There are a few differences on minor points. Fishacre believes that human actions are either good or bad; and since good actions are always initiated by grace, man turns to evil, when left to himself (B f. 162C = Ba f. 128D, O f. 199A).[55] Rufus maintains that there is a class of indifferent actions, neither good nor bad, like eating and drinking, which man can freely choose without God's assistance (B f. 162C–D).[56] This does not imply that man can perform any action without God's help. God has a hand in all man's actions; it is God who sustains man in all he does and in all he is; if he took his hands from him for one moment, he would be reduced to nothing. But as a rule he does not influence man's will, except to arouse it to reach out to the good and to will meritorious acts.[57]

[52] H. Lio, 'De elementis traditionalibus justitiae in primaeva schola franciscana', *FS* x (1950), 446 comes to the same conclusion after a survey of Richard's views on justice.
[53] Gross. *Lib.* xxi, pp. 237–40.
[54] Compare with Fishacre in Ba ff. 128D–129D, O ff. 198D–200C and Ba f. 131B–C, O ff. 202D–203A.
[55] 'Quamvis actiones alique sint in se indifferentes, tamen respectu agentis et ipsi agenti nulla actio, nulla voluntas est indifferens. Igitur in actionem nudam non potest liberum arbitrium ex se, sed necessario cum exit in aliquem actum, exit in eum formatum adiutorio gratie, vel deformata sine gratia adiuvante' (B f. 162C = Ba f. 128D, O f. 199A).
[56] 'Nescio, sed puto quod potest in actus aliquos nec meritorios nec demeritorios et in aliquos demeritorios sine gratia' (B f. 162C). It should be emphasized that both Fishacre and Rufus are considering here the exercise of man's free will *in statu viae.*
[57] 'Solum ergo in operatione meritoria liberi arbitrii facit nos velle et facere hoc, et vult nos velle et facere hoc. Et hic proprie dicitur coagere et nos eius coadiutores.

This last exception is underlined once more in Richard's own solution. He agrees with Fishacre, but adds a long appendix to stress the fact that through grace alone man can reach the good:

Est ergo gratia que faciat ut benefaciamus, prebendo vires efficacissimas voluntati. Deus enim operatur in nobis velle et ut velimus . . . Tamen sine illo vel operante ut velimus vel cooperante cum volumus, ad bona pietatis opera nihil valemus. (B f. 163C)

This, of course, is good Augustinian doctrine, but perhaps Richard puts this emphasis on man's complete dependence on God here to balance his earlier remarks, where he had advocated a greater autonomy for man than Fishacre.

(v) *Freedom in God and Man*

In the twenty-fifth distinction Richard turns to questions that envisage freedom as such: 'In hac distinctione agitur de libertate arbitrii communiter. Et potest describi hec libertas multipliciter' (B f. 166B). Two sets of problems require his attention: the definition and the distinctions of liberty, and the comparison of liberty in God and man.

On the first topic Richard has very little to add to the reflections of Grosseteste and Fishacre. He takes over Grosseteste's division of liberty in *libertas a necessitate, consilii*, and *complaciti* without any comment,[58] and he adds two other possible divisions taken over from Fishacre.[59] Richard himself proposes another way of distinguishing liberty by opposing it to the notion of slavery. The highest freedom is enjoyed by a being who owes his power and domination to no one but himself and to whom everything else is subjected, whereas he is subjected to no one. Others can only approach that freedom by subjecting themselves to this being. The more they do so of their own will, the freer they are (B f. 167D).

The comparison of liberty in God and man can only begin after it has been decided whether the ability to sin is an essential part of man's free will. Richard finds in Grosseteste and Fishacre everything he needs, and he agrees with the former that the ability to choose between

Generaliter tamen sine illo nulla creatura potest agere eo quod potentiam naturalem activam in quolibet conservat et in nobis voluntatem instrumentum. Non tamen, ut dixi, facit nos velle quicquid volumus' (B f. 163A–B).

[58] Gross. *Lib.* xvii, pp. 229–30 (B f. 167C–D); xviii, pp. 233–4 (B f. 169A).
[59] Compare Fishacre in Ba ff. 133D–134B, O ff. 206C–207C with B f. 167D and in Ba f. 135A, O f. 208C with B f. 169A.

good and evil is an accident belonging to the essential property of indeterminacy (B f. 167B–C).[60]

A question of far greater interest is the linguistic problem whether we can speak of free will in God and man univocally. Grosseteste responds, and Rufus repeats, that nothing, of course, can be predicated univocally of God and man, but, since man is in many ways such a close image of God—and here he is referring to man's free will—we can use the same words, not univocally, but certainly with the closest possible resemblance:

... creatura rationalis ita propinquum vestigium est similitudo ... Creatoris quod meretur idem nomen participare, non quidem univoce sed propinqua, imitatoria similitudine, sicut bonum, iustum, verum et similia.   (B f. 167B)[61]

Our language must reflect the fact that free will is that creative capacity in man in which he most closely resembles his creator and participates in his creative power. Since we can contemplate the exemplar in the image, as we can see what the seal is like by looking at the imprint in the wax, the intellect must use one word and one definition for free will in God and man (B f. 167B).[62]

Rufus's comment is that we can hardly speak of a comparison between God and man; any comparison is almost non-existent. And if liberty can be called a power or capacity, and if it is true also that compared with God's power ours is non-power, then man's liberty, compared with God's, is no more than slavery. If we can speak of liberty in man at all, it exists only in so far as man submits voluntarily to God's power and liberty.[63] In one sentence Richard strikes at the heart of Grosseteste's theology. If there is no point of comparison, no positive relation between God and man, but only a negative one, then the linguistic and metaphysical basis for a theology of participation has disappeared. If compared with God's liberty man's liberty is mere slavery, then we can no longer see in man his Maker, and the

---

[60] Gross. *Lib.* xvii, pp. 220–6. Fishacre seems to admit that the ability to choose evil is essential for the free will, because almost every choice is between good and evil (Ba f. 135B–C, O f. 209B).

[61] Gross. *Lib.* xvi, p. 218.

[62] Ibid.

[63] 'Mihi videtur quod omnis comparatio Creatoris et creature vix est comparatio et fere non est. Sed est comparatio sine comparatione et ideo, cum libertas sit potestas, et omnis nostra potestas ad suam comparata est non-potestas, erit nostra libertas ad suam comparata vere servitus, et ideo solum consequenter dicenda libertas eo quod sue potestati et libertati libere et voluntarie subiecta' (B f. 167B).

contemplation of visible things does not lead to a higher spiritual reality. The difference in outlook between Rufus and Grosseteste is perhaps nowhere more neatly summarized than in these few words; they are clear indicators of a new attitude to man's relation with God, in which the boundaries are far more clearly drawn.[64]

There is one aspect of God's freedom which Grosseteste does not consider, but it is taken up by Fishacre. It is the question whether God has any power over the past. Richard Rufus is fascinated by this question, which he develops far beyond Fishacre's rather short treatment (B ff. 166C–167A; Ba f. 133C, O f. 206A–B). That God has power over the past could mean two different things, according to Fishacre: it could mean that God is able to undo the past; in that sense God has no power over the past, a conclusion with which Richard Rufus agrees.[65] It could also mean that God has the power to revive or reproduce things which have passed away, and in that sense the question deserves careful consideration. It is here that Richard Rufus becomes alert, because, formulated in this sense, it adds a new aspect to the problem of generation and corruption, one of Rufus's favourite subjects.

Fishacre sets up the solution with a distinction of three kinds of being. Some beings pass away and are reduced to nothing, like the animal and vegetative soul, or like time, movement and light. Some are reduced to pure matter, and some return to their seminal principles in matter. Nature is able to reproduce these things again from their seminal principles but only things of the same sort, not the same individuals, and only at a certain fixed moment in time, not at any time. Before that moment no man can reproduce them, unless he is a saint performing a miracle, or an angel.[66] Only God can reproduce the same individuals, since in a certain sense one could speak here of a

---

[64] Richard Fishacre on the other hand agrees with Grosseteste on this important point; he quotes all the relevant passages with approval but warns that, although there is a close likeness between freedom in God and man, nevertheless 'in se divisa sunt secundum essentiarum diversitatem' (Ba f. 133C, O f. 206A–B).

[65] This aspect of the question had been debated many times since the discussion between Peter Damiani and Desiderio of Monte Cassino. In scholastic theology its usual place was in the questions on God's omnipotence; see A. Kenny, *The God of the Philosophers* (Oxford, 1979), pp. 100–9.

[66] I am not too sure what Fishacre is trying to say here. But when he speaks about the reproductive force of nature, he might be thinking of spring when all the flowers etc. which seemed dead start growing again, not the same flowers as last year's, but of the same sort. Saints and angels could, of course, make flowers grow before the appointed time, e.g. in the middle of winter, to which many miracle stories testify.

new creation. To reproduce the first two kinds of beings, those which are reduced to nothing or to pure matter, would be an even bigger miracle, but Fishacre is not sure if it is possible at all. However, if it is possible, then only God is able to do so, since he can do everything that is possible (Ba f. 133C, O f. 206A–B).

Rufus shows that this solution is riddled with mistakes. It is absolutely false to think that animal and vegetative souls are reduced to nothing (B f. 166C).[67] And in the case of time, movement, and light, it is highly doubtful. It is equal nonsense to assume that something can be reduced to pure matter. In fact, everything that passes away is reduced to its seminal principle in matter. Moreover, there is no doubt that, even if some things were reduced to nothing, God could reproduce them; he would do it the same way as he did in the beginning. God can also reproduce an individual after it has returned into its seminal principle; that is exactly what he will do in the resurrection of the flesh (B f. 166C).[68]

Having answered Fishacre, Richard undertakes an inquiry of his own. The first step is to show that it is not possible for nature to reproduce the same individual.[69] There are two reasons, as Richard shows with an example. Assume that air, called B, is generated from fire, called A. In B the form of A is still present, because nothing is reduced to nothing. As a general rule anything which reproduces itself would, if possible, like to reproduce itself completely. Unfortunately A is only present in B potentially, it is not part of the actual, generating thing B; therefore, if B generates fire, it generates a fire different in number from A. The second reason why B must generate an individual different from itself is matter; matter prevents anything from reproducing itself completely. But if there were an agent which had in

[67] Richard has discussed the reason earlier: 'Si omnino in pure nihil, iam ipsius transmutatio non est corruptio sed in pure nihil redactio. Esset enim secundum hanc positionem in generabilibus corruptio forme eiusdem in pure nihil redactio et consimilis forme generatio esset eiusdem creatio et ita generatio est vel esset omnino creatio, quod non ponitur' (B f. 144C); see also above pp. 175–80.

[68] Richard Rufus's comments are given in the form of interjections between quotations from Fishacre. I have separated them for the sake of clarity. The passage also is a welcome confirmation of my earlier conjecture (see above p. 180) that Richard regards the seminal principles as the generic forms which, with prime matter, are the common link in any sort of substantial change.

[69] Earlier on Richard has remarked that nature can neither reproduce the same individual nor the same sort of thing: 'Et non potest universaliter tale preteritum natura reparare, nec idem specie, nec numero' (B f. 166D). The phrase 'idem specie' is not further explained.

itself no passivity at all, it could reproduce the same individual. God is such an agent, but in nature it is not possible.[70]

But even so, it is by no means sure that God could reproduce any individual that has passed away; what about movement and time? The answer depends on the definition of time. If the instant is seen as the substance of time, then that substance is subject to the same pattern of past, present, and future as any other thing. And if so, then God not only can reproduce time; he is, in fact, doing so, reproducing the same instant again and again.[71] If, however, becoming is the essence of time, then God cannot reproduce the past, just as he could not possibly bring it about that in the same respect as something is false, it is also true.[72] Richard prefers the latter alternative, although he does not clearly say so and keeps the first in mind in the next question.

Fishacre thought that time, movement, and light could be reduced to nothing. Rufus is not so sure. Things which have being cannot be reduced to nothing. But if time's essence is becoming, then it is reduced to nothing, because 'becoming' is contrary to 'being'. On the other hand, if the substance theory of time has any justification, then it looks as if time cannot be reduced to nothing. So far the argument is clear, but from here it seems as if Richard has gone astray. First he seems to suggest that time is essentially a privation, a privation of the fullness of life all at once, in other words a privation of eternity, and a privation of immutability. And since privations come from nothing, it is fitting that they should be reduced to nothing. So time could well be reduced to nothing. But then he seems to change tack by suggesting that futureness and pastness are something in the potentiality of matter, which seems to imply that time is not reduced to nothing.[73] He is more certain about light in a medium; if it falls on a dark object, it

[70] 'Generans enim generat aliud propter materiam et non generat aliud nisi propter materiam. Unde si esset agens, nullo modo patiens, et faceret de B aere ignem, posset indifferenter vel A ignem vel alium de ipso B facere. Hoc ergo potest Deus et natura non, quia generans physice partem sue substantie communicat generato' (B f. 166D).

[71] 'Et si instans est tota substantia temporis, non solum hoc potest Deus sed et facit ut idem numero sit semper, secundum esse solum fore et preteritum esse' (B f. 166D).

[72] 'Si autem ipsum fieri et succedere sit substantia et quiditas ipsius temporis, non potest Deus facere preteritum redire, sicut non potest facere ut istud sit verum quod non est, nec potest facere ut eo sit aliquid falsum quo ipsum est verum, non est enim veritati contrarius' (B f. 166D).

[73] 'Futurum et futuritio videtur aliquid esse in potentia materie et presens aliquid in actu et forma materie. Preteritum vero videtur dicere non aliquid et ens in actu materie sed forte aliquid in potentia materie' (B f. 167A).

either returns to its source, or it is, somehow, preserved in the object, but it is not reduced to nothing (B f. 167A).

(vi) *Conclusion*

Free will and its powers are a subject which apparently did not offer much of a challenge to Richard Rufus. For the greater part he is fully satisfied with the answers he found in the works of Robert Grosseteste and Richard Fishacre. No doubt this lack of originality is partly due to the fact that most of the problems concerning man's freedom of choice had been known for a long time and every possible solution had been tried. Already Anselm calls the discussion about the relation between human free will and God's foreknowledge, his predestination, and grace a 'very famous question'.[74] The exciting new speculations on human freedom and its roots in reason and will, which were to hold theologians in the second half of the century spellbound, had not yet been voiced in Richard's days, and he himself was either too unoriginal or lacked the tools to embark on a new quest himself.[75]

The reason for this stagnation is twofold. For Grosseteste man's free will remained a challenging topic, because it was the capacity through which man most closely resembled his Maker in creative power. And from that point of view, despite the fact that it had been studied so many times before, it deserved to be studied again and again, since it revealed so much about God himself. Richard's thinking moves along very different lines; he does not believe in symbolical theology; no comparison can be made between God and man since God is the Other. Once that has been admitted, the study of man's free will loses the peculiar attraction it had for Grosseteste, although, of course, it remains the foundation of morality. So Richard uses Grosseteste, rejecting at the same time the framework from which the Bishop's interest arose in the first place. Where Grosseteste is dialectical and philosophical, Richard uses him freely; where he adheres to vanishing modes of theological thought, Richard goes a new way, as in the proof of the existence of free will.

But there is another reason why Richard treats the problem of free will in a rather lack-lustre manner. Whereas in the theology of creation he had to face Aristotle's challenge to traditional Christian doctrine, here he did not come across such a challenge. Although he uses terms like *potentia*, *habitus*, and *actus*, he is clearly not yet familiar

[74] G. R. Evans, *Anselm and Talking about God* (Oxford, 1978), p. 179.
[75] Lottin, *Psychologie*, i. 225.

with Aristotle's *Nicomachean Ethics*, which in the years to come were to revolutionize much of the Church's moral teaching. He has only the old questions before him, to which all possible answers seem to have been given; there is no new impulse to rethink the problem.

It is not that Richard is unwilling to meet new challenges, where they are presented to him. We have seen—for instance in the question of God's power over the past—how new insights in natural philosophy stimulated his thought, even if the answer is unsatisfactory. Unfortunately the problem of God's relation to the past has no bearing upon the question of man's free will, but lead him back to an area of inquiry in which he feels at home, processes of change, of generation and corruption, the whole world of Aristotle's physics and its relation to the Christian view of the world. With eagerness he turns to meet the challenge, where he sees it, but in the treatment of free will he remains faithful to Augustine and Anselm, and nothing points to the great changes to come.

CHAPTER 9

The Reasons for the Incarnation

(i) *The History of the Question*

THE last subject of this enquiry is purely theological; it is a question which did not become part of normal scholastic debate before the second quarter of the thirteenth century, and Robert Grosseteste was among the first in a long series of theologians to try to come to grips with it. It is a problem connected with the reasons for the Incarnation. Usually it was put in hypothetical form: whether God would have become man, even if man had not sinned.[1] So far theologians had been perfectly satisfied with the answer of the Bible, from which it was abundantly clear that God had become man to redeem man from his sin: 'Christ Jesus came into the world to save sinners' (1 Tim. i. 15). Strenuous efforts had been made to show the rationality of that answer. The most lasting one had been Anselm's theory of the redemption, which departed from the notion that both God's mercy and justice have to be saved. Thus he came to the conclusion summarised here in the words of Boso:

... tu multis et necessariis rationibus respondens ostendisti restaurationem humanae naturae non debuisse remanere, nec potuisse fieri, nisi solveret homo quod Deo pro peccato debebat. Quod debitum tantum erat, ut illud solvere, cum non deberet nisi homo, non posset nisi Deus, ita ut idem esset homo qui Deus. Unde necesse erat, ut Deus hominem assumeret in unitatem personae, quatenus qui in natura solvere debebat et non poterat, in persona esset qui posset.[2]

The meaning of the Incarnation did not, however, exhaust itself in the salvation of mankind and its restoration to its former happiness, because God's grace does not merely return to man what he has lost; it is superabundant, brimming over, and goes beyond anything man can expect: 'Where sin abounded, grace did much more abound' (Rom.

---

[1] I shall not discuss whether the question makes sense in this formulation. For doubts about its meaning see J.-F. Bonnefoy, 'La question hypothétique: *Ultrum* [sic] *si Adam non peccasset* ... au XIIIᵉ siècle', *Revista Española de Teologia*, xiv (1954), 327–68.

[2] Anselm, *Cur Deus homo*, ii. 18, ed. F. S. Schmitt (*Opera omnia*, ii, 1946), pp. 126–7.

v. 20).[3] This awareness that the coming of Christ had given back far more to mankind than it had lost had always been a theme of reflection for the Eastern Fathers; they had always regarded the Incarnation not only as a remedy for the Fall, but also as an opportunity for man to participate in the divine life.[4] But although this perspective offers the possibility to speculate on the absolute predestination of Christ, it is not necessarily connected with it and, indeed, the Greek Fathers never put the question in this way.[5]

The theme was introduced into the stream of Western theology by Rupert of Deutz in the early twelfth century; a curious coincidence, since Rupert was one of the first and most ardent opponents of new methods in theological thinking and teaching. As early as 1117 he had travelled to France for a debate with William of Champeaux and Anselm of Laon on the value of using philosophical concepts in the explanation of the Bible. Rupert resisted any attempt to clarify obscure passages in Scripture with the help of dialectics; only spiritual reading and meditation were safe guides in man's search for truth. Rupert confessed himself ignorant of all these new-fangled methods, but even if he had known about them, he says, he would never have used them, since they do not nourish the holy and simple divine truth: 'Quidquid extra hanc Scripturam sanctam cogitari, vel argumentando potest configi, sicut expers rationis est, ita nullatenus pertinet ad laudem vel confessionem omnipotentiae Dei.'[6] Despite his avowed traditionalism, Rupert departed from the simplicity of the Bible on the subject of the Incarnation and was the first to put the highly speculative question whether God would have become man, even if man had not sinned. He did so in his treatise *De gloria et honore Filii hominis.* Since the glorification of the Son of Man was the purpose of creation, according to Rupert, he answered the question in the affirmative, and added that it would be absurd to think that the coming of God into the flesh could be dependent on man's sin.[7]

[3] R. Haubst, *Vom Sinn der Menschwerdung* (Munich, 1969), p. 97.

[4] Ibid. p. 71; E. Longpré, 'Robert Grossetête et le B. Jean Duns Scot. Le motif de l'Incarnation', *La France franciscaine*, Documents, iv (1939), 15–16.

[5] Haubst, *Menschwerdung*, p. 101.

[6] Chenu, *Douzième Siècle*, pp. 323–4; A. Forest *et al.*, *Le Mouvement doctrinal du XIᵉ au XIVᵉ siècle* (A. Fliche/V. Martin (eds.), Histoire de l'Église depuis les origines jusqu'à nos jours, xiii, 1951), p. 153; Evans, *Old Arts*, pp. 43, 60–79 points out that Rupert, despite his methodological traditionalism, pointed the way for important new developments.

[7] Haubst, *Menschwerdung*, p. 117; Bonnefoy, 'Question hypothétique', pp. 331–2; J. McEvoy, 'The Absolute Predestination of Christ in the Theology of Robert Grosse-

The mysterious Honorius of Autun, living at approximately the same time as Rupert, argued for the same conclusion. His point of departure was God's immutability: from all times God had decided to deify man, and this could only happen by way of the Incarnation. The only consequence of man's sin is that the God incarnate, Jesus Christ, in his human nature now also participated in the punishment for sin, which is death.[8] In fact, Honorius connects the birth of Christ with man's divinization, and Christ's passion and death with man's redemption.

It seems odd that such a speculative question originated with a man who, on all occasions, pledged his loyalty to the ways of the Fathers, to the traditions of allegorical exegesis and symbolical theology. At first sight one would have expected this problem to come up in the Schools, in the brain of some clever young master who wished to sharpen his wits on such a tricky issue for which biblical evidence is scarce to say the least. There is no shred of evidence however, that the issue was ever dealt with in the schools before the thirteenth century.[9]

A closer look may explain why it was a traditional monk who first broke this new ground. Theologians like Rupert thought in symbols; to them, every creature, every word of Scripture, was transparent, an icon of a higher reality. The search for that wisdom was founded on the belief that everything that exists participates in that higher reality and is striving to be united with it. Every symbol has two characteristics: it is the finite shadow of an infinite form, and, therefore, it is incomplete and yearning for unity to be restored. Grosseteste thinks the same way, as we have seen.[10] In such a view of the world the Incarnation can become an almost rational event: in Christ creation is united with its Creator in a personal union; symbol and symbolized, sign and signified coincide in one man. He is the symbol *par excellence*, from which all other symbols take their meaning, because in him the totality of infinity has taken a finite expression.[11] The unity for which all creation is ceaselessly yearning is achieved in one person, the God-man Jesus Christ. In such a way of looking at Christ's coming, sin can

teste', in *Sapientiae doctrina. Mélanges . . . Hildebrand Bascour O.S.B.* (RThAM, numéro spécial, i, 1980), pp. 220–1.

[8] Haubst, *Menschwerdung*, pp. 117–18; Bonnefoy, 'Question hypothétique', pp. 332–3; McEvoy, 'Absolute Predestination', pp. 221–2.

[9] Haubst, *Menschwerdung*, p. 118.

[10] See above pp. 127–30.

[11] Dunbar, *Symbolism*, p. 254.

hardly be a consideration. Man's fall has, no doubt, marred the beauty of the universe and dulled its striving for completion, but it is hardly possible that it can either delay or, for that matter, cause the unification of everything in Christ.

But despite this foundation in tradition and in an essentially symbolical view of the world, the question is also interesting as a sign of the change of times, since it is at the same time an expression of the new mood of questioning curiosity and daring speculation so typical of the twelfth century. As such it need cause no surprise that the issue aroused the interest of Robert Grosseteste, who was both a staunch defender of the traditional modes of thought in theology and an explorer of new methods in science and philosophy.

(ii) *Robert Grosseteste: The Completion of the Universe*

Grosseteste broaches the subject in the course of his treatise *De cessatione legalium*.[12] Parts of the argument he develops there can also be found in the sermon *Exiit edictum* and in the *Hexaemeron*.[13] The main question of the *De cessatione* is at what moment the ceremonial precepts of the Law ceased to be binding. It was not a treatise directed against the Jews, as is often thought, but written for students with an interest in the mentality of the Judaeo-Christians.[14] The first line of the work contains the programme: 'Fuerunt plurimi in primitiva ecclesia qui astruerent sacramenta veteris legis simul cum sacramentis nove legis observanda esse' (Ox f. 158A).

The central theme is worked out in the first and last parts. In the first part Grosseteste looks at the arguments of those who maintained that the Law is eternally binding, ceremonially as well as morally, and in the last part he answers the question at what moment the ceremonial precepts of the Law were finally superseded. The link between those two problems is Christ; his coming into this world is, therefore, the subject of the middle section. First, Grosseteste proves by means of a careful analysis of the relevant passages in the prophets that not only the time, place, and manner of Christ's coming were

[12] The first part (Ox ff. 158A–169A) was edited by B. Ryves (London, 1658); the hypothetical question (Ox ff. 176A–178B) by D.Unger, 'Robert Grosseteste, Bishop of Lincoln (1235–1253) on the Reasons for the Incarnation', *FS* xvi (1956), 3–18; a summary of the contents of the whole work in O. Gratius, *Fasciculus rerum expetendarum et fugiendarum*, ed. E. Brown (2 vols., London, 1690), ii. 246–7. An edition of the whole work is currently being prepared.

[13] The relevant passages of the sermon *Exiit* have been edited by Unger, op. cit. pp. 18–23; Gross. *Hex.* i. xiii. 1 and ix. viii. 1–3, pp. 69–71, 275–6.

[14] Smalley, 'Biblical Scholar', p. 81.

foretold in the Old Testament, but also his suffering and death.[15] And having established the certainty of Christ's coming with scriptural arguments, he also shows that the events of Christ's life and death can be established by reason. It is in this section that he discusses the problem whether God would have become man, even if man had not sinned.

In so far as the Incarnation was God's answer to man's fall, Grosseteste felt no need to go over the arguments once again; all the expositors of the Bible, especially Augustine, Gregory, and Anselm had proved that in this respect God's act was reasonable, even necessary. But there also seemed good reason to think that the Incarnation had already been foreseen in the foundation of the world and was to become true quite independently of man's—accidental— disobedience.[26] Although Grosseteste is quite modest about the possibility of proving this, he is also very confident that he can give 'rationes efficaces', convincing reasons, to show that God's coming into this world had been foreseen from all eternity.[17]

The impressive series of arguments in favour of Christ's absolute predestination can be grouped under five headings.[18] An important consideration is man's justification, which means far more than mere redemption from sin. Even if man had not sinned, he would have been in need of justification. God is, of course, perfectly able to justify man without any mediation through Christ but, in fact, he has chosen to act otherwise. Quoting St Paul (1 Cor. i. 30, Rom. v. 18) Grosseteste shows that Christ is not just man's redeemer, but also has become man's justification. If Christ had only come to die for our sin, his part in God's plan would have been ridiculously small, which is most unfitting.[19]

Moreover, through his justification, man is exalted to the dignity of adopted son, a favour which God would have granted to man, even if man had not sinned. To be called sons of God a mere unity of wills is not sufficient, that would be the unity of unequals, the unity of mere

---

[15] For an excellent example see above p. 125 n. 15.

[16] Grosseteste, *De cessatione*, i–ii (ed. Unger, pp. 3–4); quotations from *De cessatione* have been checked in Ox.

[17] Grosseteste, *De cessatione*, iii (ed. Unger, p. 4); on Grosseteste's reticence see McEvoy, 'Absolute Predestination', pp. 221–4.

[18] As done by McEvoy, op. cit., pp. 213–18.

[19] Grosseteste, *De cessatione*, xi–xvi (ed. Unger, pp. 7–9); Haubst, *Menschwerdung*, p. 119; McEvoy, 'Absolute Predestination', p. 214.

obedience; sonship implies unity of nature. To achieve that unity God had to become man.[20] In these first arguments Grosseteste's starting-point is the notion that in the Incarnation God gave back far more to man than man had ever lost in the fall. He emphasizes again and again that Christ's coming brought man so much more than forgiveness of sins and he wonders, quite reasonably, whether God would not have bestowed all these gifts upon man all the more, if man had not sinned.

The instruments through which man's absorption into God's nature is achieved are the sacraments, especially the Eucharist and marriage. These sacraments derive their significance from the Incarnation. It is not fitting to assume that man would have missed these means to achieve unity with God, if he had not sinned; neither is it reasonable to suppose that the fall of man could be the cause of the sacraments and their high dignity.[21]

An assumption underlying the arguments so far is that evil can never be the cause of good: the grace of sonship, the Church, and the Eucharist cannot be the consequence of sin. Grosseteste was fully aware of this assumption and elaborated on it: sin and punishment are a privation of being; it is unthinkable that a privation could be the cause of such a good as the capability of receiving the Word: 'Sed quis dicat hanc unibilitatem esse essentie negationem, vel privationem? Si igitur essentia est, nullo modo est eius causa essentie defectio' (Ox f. 176B).[22]

If then sin cannot be the cause of the Incarnation something good must be, and now Grosseteste comes into his own. It is, indeed, God's goodness which is one of the main reasons for the Incarnation. With this theme he opens his reflections, and he returns to it, as if to stress it, after he has dealt with the misapprehension that evil could possibly be the cause of any good. The created universe could never have been so good, so perfect, if the Word had not become flesh, because the naked flesh is not adorable. But the flesh assumed by the Word is adorable, not because of itself, but because of its union with the Word. Since there can be no doubt that Christ's flesh is part of the created world, all creation shares in the glory bestowed upon Christ's human nature. There is no way creation could have reached such a state of

[20] Grosseteste, *De cessatione*, xvii–xviii (ed. Unger, pp. 9–10); Haubst, *Menschwerdung*, pp. 119–20; McEvoy, 'Absolute Predestination', pp. 214–15.

[21] Grosseteste, *De cessatione*, xxi–xxii, xxxiii–xxxv (ed. Unger, pp. 11, 15–16); McEvoy, 'Absolute Predestination', p. 215.

[22] Grosseteste, *De cessatione*, v–vii (ed. Unger, p. 5); McEvoy, 'Absolute Predestination', p. 214.

perfection and glory without the Incarnation.[23] So, either the Word would have become flesh anyway, or creation is now much better off than if man had not sinned. Grosseteste does not say so here, but he implies again that the latter conclusion would be unfitting, since from evil can come no good.

The same theme is approached from a different angle. Again the point of departure is the glorious state to which the universe has been exalted by Christ. Then Grosseteste argues: God is the highest Good, better than anything we can think of. Therefore, he must make everything as good as possible, which means that he must fill all that exists with all the good it is capable of. The fact of the Incarnation proves that human nature is capable of receiving the Word and being exalted by that union. So, if God is the highest Good, the Incarnation must take place, quite apart from man's sin.[24] The presupposition of this argument is obvious: the possible good that God can do, he must necessarily do. Elsewhere he puts it more explicitly:

Cum igitur melius sit tam rerum universitatem quam humane generationis seriem . . . uniri, quam ista unitione privari, possibile quoque sit et Deum sic perficere, et ista sic perfici, manifestum videtur esse, quod huius . . . perfectionem necesse sit esse.   (Ox ff. 177D–178A)[25]

The determinist overtones of this simple rule reveal once more Grosseteste's roots in Neoplatonism. It certainly forges a strong link and bridges the gap between creator and creation. If all the good which man can see around him is to be regarded not simply as a gift of God— as any theologian would admit—but also as the best God can do, and as such offers an exhaustive survey of God's capacities, then creation becomes no less than a mirror of the divine mind and man's knowledge of God through the contemplation of creation becomes quite accurate. The reason for Grosseteste's confidence, both here and in the *Hexaemeron*, that man is able to ascend to his Creator through the contemplation of the miracles of creation, is now obvious.

That perfect symmetry between the ideas in the divine mind and their realization in the world is also tacitly assumed in Grosseteste's

---

[23] Grosseteste, *De cessatione*, viii (ed. Unger, p. 6): 'Cum igitur caro Christi extra universitatem creature omnino numeranda non sit, habet creature universitas in carne Christi adorabili gloriositatem supra estimationem maiorem quam habere posset Verbo Dei numquam incarnato' (Ox f. 176B).

[24] Ibid. iv (ed. Unger, pp. 4–5); McEvoy, 'Absolute Predestination', pp. 213–14.

[25] Grosseteste, *De cessatione*, xxxii (ed. Unger, p. 15).

last and most impressive argument for the absolute predestination of Christ, that he is the perfection of the universe, the unification of all creation. Clearly this is the heart of the matter for Grosseteste; three times he returns to the theme of Christ as the final purpose of creation: here, as the climax of a long series of arguments, in his Christmas sermon *Exiit edictum*, and in the *Hexaemeron* twice.[26] All the scattered parts of the universe are yearning to be reunited, and that unity can only be achieved by something that unites all the different parts in itself, as the heart unites all the members of the body.[27] This being so, Grosseteste begins his search for such a principle that unites everything in itself.

First he discusses the possibility of an angel's being such a principle. This cannot be, since angels have nothing in common with the material world. Neither could it be a creature lower than an angel or a man, since it would lack the dignity of rational nature.[28] Man, however, has a very special position. Because he is a rational, intelligent being he shares the same nature with the angels, and through his body he is united with all lower grades of being. Man's body consists of the four elements, through which it shares in the nature of all lifeless, material things and of the heavenly bodies. Moreover, the human soul has not only a rational part, but also a sensitive part, through which it participates in the nature of the animals, and a vegetative part, through which it shares in the soul of plants. Finally in man himself body and soul are united in the unity of a person. The best summary of this view of man as microcosm is given in the *Hexaemeron*, but the argument is the same everywhere:

Angelus enim et anima sunt unum in natura racionalitatis et intelligentie. Anima autem racionalis et caro humana uniuntur in unitatem persone in quolibet singulari homine. Caro autem humana habet in se materialiter omnia huius mundi elementa. Anima eciam humana participat unitate virtute nutribili cum plantis et sensibili cum brutis.[29]

The whole cosmos is summed up in man, but that unity is not yet perfect, since God is excluded from it. Since Creator and creature can never be united in one nature or species, that unity can only be

[26] Grosseteste, *Exiit edictum*, viii–xvi (ed. Unger, pp. 20–3); id., *Hex.* I. xiii. 1, IX. viii. 1–3, pp. 69–71, 275–6.
[27] Id., *De cessatione*, xxvi (ed. Unger, p. 13).
[28] Ibid.
[29] Id. *Hex.* IX. viii. 2, p. 276; also id., *De cessatione*, xxviii (ed. Unger, pp. 13–14), and 'Exiit edictum', viii, p. 20).

achieved as a unity in one person. So, if God assumes human nature in the unity of a person, the universe has finally reached that perfection of which it is capable:

Si igitur assumat Deus hominem in unitatem persone, reducta est universitas ad unitatis complementum. Si vero non assumat, nec universitas ad unitatis complementum sibi possibile deducta est.   (Ox f. 177D)[30]

The image of the circle is best suited to describing the perfect unity achieved through the Incarnation: 'Hoc ... facto habeat universitas plenissimam et decentissimam unitatem, redacteque sint per hoc omnes nature in complementum circulare' (Ox f. 177D).[31] A chain already links everything from the angels, created first, to man, created last. If God becomes man, the ends of the chain are linked, since in assuming human nature he becomes one in nature with both angels and man.[32] The circle of human generation is completed, too, in the Incarnation. From Adam a line goes from father to son until Jesus, and Jesus begot Adam.[33] So, in whatever way we look at it, in Christ the circle is closed, he is the jewel linking the two halves of a gold ring:

... cum assumit humanam naturam in unitatem persone, tunc est circulus creaturarum firmissime Creatori coniunctus, cum ipse Creator per unitatem personalem assumpto homine in unitatem persone, sit eidem circulo insertus, factusque decor et honor huius circuli tamquam gemma aurei anuli.[34]

The last remark shows how central the place of the Incarnation was in Grosseteste's view of the world, so central that it could not be made dependent on an accidental event like man's fall from grace. It also reveals from what source that belief sprang forth, where he says that through the Incarnation God is inserted in the circle of creatures. This is the tradition in which there was no sharp dividing line between natural and supernatural, human and divine, the realms of nature and grace, in which unity is praised and sought for above all else; in fact, the same tradition as Rupert of Deutz belonged to. All creation refers to a higher reality; it is incomplete in itself and yearning for unity and perfection. Left to itself it is a mere shadow, a vestige. Man is the highest perfection to which creation can reach; he is not just a vestige, he has been created in the image of God, and he shares in God's

---

[30] Grosseteste, *De cessatione*, xxix (ed. Unger, p. 14).
[31] Ibid. xxx (ed. Unger, p. 14).
[32] Ibid.
[33] Ibid. xxxi (ed. Unger, pp. 14–15).
[34] Grosseteste, 'Exiit edictum', xiv (ed. Unger, p. 22).

creative powers.[35] Man is exalted even above the angels, who, although they are more perfect, are appointed to minister to man.[36] In man, moreover, all creation from angels to the elements is summed up in the unity of a person. Looking at these two aspects of man Grosseteste is virtually compelled to take the next step: the union of God and man, of Creator and creature; only then has the quest for unity come to rest.

Grosseteste acknowledges the logic of this almost inevitable conclusion earlier on in the *De cessatione*, where he remarks that all creation can signify the Incarnation; it has been written into the very nature of things to crave for that completion which only the Word can give by assuming flesh:

Potest autem creatura huius mundi Dei Filium incarnatum designare. Non caret enim creatura huius mysterii omni similitudine, qua potest hoc mysterium liquido designare. Deus igitur, qui omnia facit congruentissimo ordine, sic ordinavit huius mundi sensibilis creaturas, quas propter hominem ipse condidit, ut suis formis et speciebus quasi quibusdam litteris significantibus denuntiarent homini salvationis sue beneficium per Filium eius incarnatum.   (Ox f. 164B–C)

The Incarnation thus becomes an event that is rational and sensible and accessible to human reason; it is in the nature of things. In this cosmic view of Christ, man's sin does not really figure; Christ's role as the redeemer is secondary and inferior to his role as the head of creation. Theoretical and unbiblical as the question may be, it fits perfectly into Grosseteste's essentially symbolic way of thinking and of looking at the world.

(iii) *Richard Fishacre: The Divine Pedagogy*

Both Richard Fishacre and Richard Rufus discuss the hypothetical question on the Incarnation at length, and both are influenced by Grosseteste's arguments. One might even suppose that the question only occurred to them because of Grosseteste's treatise on the matter. Fishacre's treatment has some odd features; he uses by and large the same arguments as Grosseteste and seems to agree with his conclusion, but there is no sign of any literary dependence. Fishacre

[35] See above pp. 203–5.

[36] 'Licet enim angelus maior sit homine per incorruptibilitatem et per actum fruendi Deo et per confirmacionem a principio perseverandi in precepto felicitatis bono, unde tamen ministrat homini vicem optinet velud minoris et subiecti', Gross. *Hex.* VIII. xv. 2, p. 240.

begins by stressing that the circle of being is completed only when the highest and the lowest nature have been conjoined:

Cum natura suprema sit Deus, infima terra, tunc primo videtur circulus creaturarum completus et perfectus, cum unitum fuerit supremum infimo. Nec est aliter completum universum, quia antequam extrema claudantur, semper est possibilis additio et perfectum est, cui non est possibilis additio.[37] Ergo decuit ad completionem universi terram Deo et e contrario uniri. Quod factum est cum Dei Filius carnem est unitus secundum illud Ioannis 1: 'Verbum caro factum est' (John i. 14). Item primum increatum est Deus, ultimum creatum est homo. Tunc igitur circulus creature est perfectus, cum Deus homo factus est. Et nisi hoc fieret, perfectio universi non fuisset. Et tunc est verum uno modo quod dicitur Ysaias 44: 'Ego primus, quia Deus et novissimus, quia homo' (Isa. xliv. 6).[38]   (Ba f. 154C, O f. 240B)

Not only the universe as a whole, but also the constituent parts would be incomplete without the Incarnation. Fishacre's way of proving this is rather complicated: man is a microcosm, he contains all created nature. And in man all parts of nature have been greatly enhanced in nobility through the Word, when it assumed human nature. Otherwise they would have remained imperfect:

Iterum non tantum universum mansisset incompletum, sed et singula quelibet pars universi. Quippe non nihil nobilitatis et proinde perfectionis sortitur terra ex hoc quod nobiliori elemento utpote aqua vel aeri vel igni unitur in mixto corpore.[39] Magis autem cum unitur celo, magis cum spiritu vegetabili, quia secundum Augustinum ignobilissimus spiritus nobilissimo corpore est nobilior.[40] Magis cum sensibili, magis cum rationali. Igitur si possibile fuit terre vel insita potentia, ut Deo uniretur, scilicet summo Spiritui, quod res iam facta probavit, patet quod terra non infimo sue nobilitatis fuisset, nisi hoc contegisset. Similiter de aqua, et sic de singulis que omnia tunc primo uniuntur [?] perfecta cum Deus homini est unitus, cum in homine sit omnis creatura, unde et dicitur microcosmus.   (Ba f. 154C, O f. 240B)

The tacit assumption is, of course, just as in Grosseteste's arguments, that God must do the best he can do, as is equally obvious in a later argument:

Item magne bonitatis indicium est quod voluit nobilitare corporalem creaturam per unionem cum spiritu irrationali, maior cum spiritu rationali,[41]

---

[37] 'et perfectum . . . additio' om. Ba.
[38] The Vulgate has: 'Ego primus et ego novissimus, et absque me non est Deus'.
[39] 'corpore' om. Ba.
[40] 'secundum Augustinum' om. Ba.
[41] 'cum . . . maior' om. O.

maior cum spiritu creato rationali, maxime cum spiritu increato. Igitur ut summe potentie, sapientie, bonitatis relinqueret vestigium, hec fieri oportebat.   (Ba f. 154D, O f. 240C)

At the end of this series of arguments Fishacre draws his readers' attention to the fact that, so far, everything he has said about the fittingness of the Incarnation would apply equally if man had not sinned:

Attende quod hee rationes omnes non tantum probant Deum decere humanitatem assumere, sed etiam quod sive homo peccasset, sive numquam peccasset, quod hoc eum facere decuisset.   (Ba f. 154D, O f. 240D)

Fishacre also wonders why in the New Testament so much emphasis is put on the redemption, but hardly anything is said about the completion of the universe as a possible reason for the Incarnation. With a homely comparison he makes that perfectly clear to his clerical students. Many clerics are more grateful to their bishop for a benefice they have received than to God for his creation, for their soul, and for the grace they have received in the sacraments, because as a result of man's sin a gift is appreciated all the more when given to fewer people. Since the sacred authors know about man's misery, they stress, with subtle pedagogy, the redemption, given to man only, and refer only casually to the completion of the universe, which benefits all creation (Ba f. 155A, O ff. 240D–241A). Just like Grosseteste, Fishacre sometimes prefers a psychological to a speculative solution.

In the end Fishacre leaves his hearers with two possible accounts and does not choose between them. It could be that God, foreknowing man's fall and his manner of repairing it, has given man the capacity of being completed by the Incarnation, which he would not have done if man had not sinned. He warns that even looking at the cause of the Incarnation from this angle man's sin is not the cause, but only the occasion; the real cause is God's goodness, for he knows how to use the bad to reach the good. It could also be that God has granted to man the capacity to be perfected by the Incarnation quite apart from original sin, just in order to complete the universe. If the first is true, man's restoration is the prime cause; if the second, the completion of the universe.

The striking feature of Fishacre's argument is that he is so near Grosseteste in outlook. As with his predecessor unity is the keyword: the Incarnation is essential because in Christ, the God-man, all creation is united and brought to perfection. Although, of course, they recognize the abyss which separates God from man—Grosseteste more clearly than Fishacre, as appears from his emphasis on the fact that the union of God and man in Christ is personal, not natural—their main concern is to discover how God and man can be brought together in an all-embracing unity. Both accept the capacity of man to be united with his Creator as a natural thing, and even more, both are convinced that man and, indeed, all creation must be united with God, otherwise the whole world would be incomplete. The perfection of creation lies outside itself, a thought very dear to all theologians in the Platonic tradition.

(iv) *Richard Rufus: The Redemption from Sin*

Richard Rufus reflects on the reasons for the Incarnation in iii. 1 of his Oxford commentary. First he speaks about its fittingness in general, the appropriateness of the time of its occurrence, its possibility. Then he looks at the arguments of Anselm, and finally he tackles the problem posed by Grosseteste whether God would have become man if man had not sinned (B ff. 196C–197C). Richard follows the arguments as given in the *De cessatione*; he did not consult the sermon *Exiit edictum* or the *Hexaemeron* on this point.

The structure of his solution is as follows: summary of Grosseteste's first series of arguments (B f. 196C. 45–196D. 18),[42] followed by a succinct statement of his own views (B f. 196D. 18–43); summary of the second series (B ff. 196D. 43–197B. 33),[43] with a short commentary (B f. 197B. 33–42); summary of the passage where Grosseteste shows how well his arguments fit into the theme of Christ as the Head of the Church (B f. 197B.42–55),[44] immediately followed by Fishacre's explanation of the emphasis of the New Testament on the redemption (B f. 197B. 55–197C. 5). He concludes with a characteristic phrase: 'Ecce, de omnibus hiis non curo', and quotes five passages from the Fathers to strengthen his own position (B f. 197C. 5–14).

Richard never changes the order of Grosseteste's arguments, nor does he seem to listen to them very well. The interruptions are outbursts in which Richard voices his fundamental disagreement with Grosseteste's opinion, but hardly reactions to the arguments just quoted, except in the most general sense. His disapproval is most

---

[42] Grosseteste, *De cessatione*, iv–x (ed. Unger, pp. 4–7).
[43] Ibid. xi–xxx (ed. Unger, pp. 7–14).
[44] Ibid. xli–xlii (ed. Unger, p. 17).

emphatic after he has quoted Grosseteste's glorious vision of the
unification of the universe in the God-man:

> Et si oporteret hic aliquid asserere, magis putarem quod [Deus] non fuisset
> homo, nisi peccasset homo, et ambo ab eterno fuerunt prescita a Deo. Nam ait
> Augustinus de verbis apostoli omelia 73 prope finem: 'Quare venit in
> mundum? Peccatores salvos facere, alia causa non fuit quare veniret in
> mundum. Non enim de celo ad terram merita nostra, sed peccata duxerunt.
> Hec est causa cur veniret, peccatores salvos facere.[45]   (B f. 197B)

And after quoting Fishacre's explanation of the apparent omissions of
the authors of the New Testament he adds once more:

> Ecce, de omnibus hiis non curo. Nam ut predixi, magis consentit anima mea
> in contrarium. Ait enim Augustinus de hoc super primam Ioannis omelia 6:
> 'Ideo venit in carnem ut moreretur pro nobis'.[46]   (B f. 197C).

So convinced was Richard that the redemption was the only reason
for God to become man that he could not be bothered to tackle
Grosseteste's arguments one by one, they seemed absurd, in any case
not cogent: 'Nescio de omnibus hiis nec definio. Sed forte mihi
videntur omnes predicte rationes non cogere, sed longum esset ad
singular respondere' (B f. 197B).

Richard's attack on Grosseteste is more general and it can be
because he singles out Grosseteste's most central positions for attack.
He does so after his survey of the first series of Grosseteste's
arguments, before he had even heard everything Grosseteste has to say
for himself. Richard simply denies that the universe is not perfect
without the Incarnation. When the Word became flesh, neither a new
nature, nor a new person came into being since the universe consists
of natures and persons, it was complete before the Incarnation.[47] That
is not to say that there has been no change. Richard admits that man
and the whole of creation are now better off than before. But that
higher degree of well-being must not be understood as the completion
of something imperfect; the universe was perfect before, there was no
necessity for God to become man apart from sin, and even man's
redemption from sin is not necessary for the completion of the

---

[45] Augustine, *Sermones*, clxxiv. 7(8) (PL xxxviii), col. 944.
[46] Augustine, *In epistolam Ioannis ad Parthos*, vi. 13 (PL xxxv), col. 2028.
[47] 'Nam incarnato Verbo nec natura nova facta est que non fuit, nec persona que
prius non erat. Ergo si universitas ex hiis solis, scilicet naturis et personis, integra
consistit, integra esset et perfecta universitas, etsi Deus homo non fuisset' (B f. 196D).

universe, only fitting to restore order in God's kingdom.[48] The essential perfection of creation is in no way marred or damaged by original sin. Richard stresses that not sin but only God's goodness is the cause of the Incarnation:

Melior tamen est nunc tota universitas et meliores singule partes, quam si Deus homo non esset. Sed hec melioritas de integritate universi forte non est, nec tamen huius melioritatis causa fuit peccatum, sed bonitas Redemptoris. Occasio tamen fuit hoc illius et sine illo integra et perfecta fuisset universitas. Melior tamen est nunc, quia maior et addita est gratia redemptionis super gratiam creationis. Nec fuit gratia redemptionis de integritate universi necessitate, sed post peccatum fuit de regni ordinatione necessaria.　(B f. 196D)

Richard wants to make it crystal clear that neither the Incarnation nor, indeed, the redemption is necessary for the completion of the universe.

With the same brevity, he counters Grosseteste's second best argument that since man has a capacity to receive God, that capacity must be used, if God is the highest Good. He begins by clarifying Grosseteste's notion of 'capable'. It means, according to Richard, that all creation has a natural desire to be completed by God, in other words that the Incarnation is an event in the order of nature which could be expected by all those who look at creation from the correct angle:

Nec videtur quod natura humana vel universitas tota fuit capabilis huius tanti boni, sub hoc sensu ut capabile dicat naturalem inclinationem et desiderium, scilicet quod Deus esset homo.　(B f. 196D)

This is, I think, a possible interpretation of Grosseteste's meaning. If so, it is nonsense, according to Richard. Grosseteste makes the fundamental mistake of mixing up the orders of nature and grace; the Incarnation belongs to the latter. It is neither natural, nor necessary; it is an act of love, of pure grace. Man's reason has no access to such a mystery:

Omnino istud naturale non est, sed gratia gratiarum et naturam excellens. Unde licet huius gratie sic capax fuit natura humana, non propter hoc esset

---

[48] Richard may well have referred here to Anselm's remark that the right order in God's kingdom requires that man is punished for his sin, e.g. *Cur Deus homo*, i. 12 (ed. Schmitt, p. 69): 'Deum vero non decet aliquid inordinatum in regno suo dimittere . . . Non ergo decet Deum peccatum sic impunitum dimittere', and also i. 20 (ed. Schmitt, p. 86): 'Aliter aliquatenus inordinatum maneret peccatum, quod esse non potest, si Deus nihil relinquit inordinatum in regno suo'.

imperfecta universitas, quamvis non esset hec unio. Si autem naturalem inclinationem haberet humana natura ad hanc unionem, hec ei a Deo indita esset, et tunc imperfecta esset universitas, si hec unio non esset, hec enim inclinatio semper esset et otiosa. Melior est universitas sic quam illo modo et non est quelibet melioritas de necessitate et perfectione universi, sed de superfluente largitate Creatoris, qui pro malo reddit bonum et post malum bona restaurat meliora. (B f. 196D)

In this last paragraph Richard counters three of Grosseteste's main arguments at the same time. First he maintains that the capacity of human nature to receive God is not natural, but an act of grace. Because it is an act of grace and not in the nature of things, Richard can maintain that creation is perfect in itself and has no innate desire to move on to a higher plane or to be completed by God. And between the lines he does something far more ominous, he removes the foundation of Grosseteste's confidence and optimism by denying that God must realize all the good he is capable of. Richard admits that God could have given man the natural inclination to be perfected by the Word, but he has chosen not to do so. On the other hand, Richard leaves us in no doubt that in itself that capacity is a good thing. So, there is at least one good thing God is capable of that he has kept from man for reasons of his own. In other words Richard breaks down the perfect symmetry between the ideas in the divine mind and their realization in the world and broadens the gap between God and man. Where Grosseteste saw necessity or at least fittingness, Richard sees mere contingency: the contingent sin of man elicited the contingent grace of the Incarnation.

Thus, although Richard Rufus follows Grosseteste far more to the letter than Fishacre did, his refutation reveals a completely different attitude both to God and man, different both from Grosseteste and Fishacre. The Incarnation is the supreme union between human and divine, between natural and supernatural. As such it fitted perfectly into Grosseteste's theology, where unity was the key word. To him it was an almost natural event, an event of which traces could be detected in all creation in advance, and especially in man; it was the final act of the cosmic drama. Man's sin gave perhaps a new urgency to that final denouement, but made no fundamental change. Such a vision is incomprehensible to Richard Rufus; he seems genuinely disturbed by it, since from his point of view the Incarnation is more like the first act of a completely new play, the second creation, in

which the second Adam, Jesus Christ, played the principal part. The
coming of God into this world is the grace of graces, to be praised by
all Christians, but it is not the keystone of an unfinished vault, the last
scene of a cosmic drama; creation is perfect in itself, it has a
consistency of its own, it is 'at unity in itself' (Ps. cxxi. 3 Vulg., tr.
Coverdale). Where Grosseteste is in search of unity, Richard looks for
clarity, he wishes to define and distinguish and clearly indicate the
lines that separate God and man, nature and grace.[49]

Thus he safeguards not only the autonomy of creation, but also
God's sovereign freedom. That latter concern is clearly on his mind
when he tries to sever the link between God and man which results
from the simple rule that God must, of necessity, realize all the good
he is capable of. This mild form of determinism enables man, as we
saw, to penetrate into the depths of God's mind by way of his creation.
Man is able to keep God to his word. If this perspective is given up, as
Richard does here, and exchanged for a more contingent view of the
universe, God becomes more removed from man's sight, and man
himself becomes at the same time more autonomous, but also more
dependent on God's gracious revelation of himself.[50]

Such a move to a more contingent universe, in which the abyss
separating God and man has become very much deeper, makes the
Incarnation an incomprehensible event, 'what no eye has seen, nor ear
heard, nor the heart of man conceived, what God has prepared for
those who love him' (1 Cor. ii. 9). No reasons could possibly be found
for it; it is the fully unexpected new beginning God wants to make with
man. That is the conclusion Richard comes to; in no way could man
have foreseen what was going to happen: 'Omnino istud naturale non

---

[49] The same concern is very well expressed by Eudes Rigaud, archbishop of Rouen
(1248–1275/6), who lectured on the *Sentences* at Paris from 1245 to 1247. On the
completion of the universe as a reason for the Incarnation he says: 'Ad aliud dicendum,
quod nullo modo intelligendum quod universum non fuisset completum, esto etiam
quod Deus non fuisset unitus creaturae, nec hoc desiderabat ipsum universum, nec
Deus se ad hoc astrinxerat, nec etiam Christus dicendus est de universo, sed supra
totum universum. Unde, etsi non esset facta illa unio, non esset universum (in)com-
pletum, quia non caput eius quantum ad primam completionem ipsius universi, nec
ipsa congruitas quam adducit spectat ad necessitatem universi' (ed. I. Bissen, 'De
motivo Incarnationis, disquisitio historico-dogmatica', *Antonianum*, vii (1932), 335.

[50] The same move towards a more contingent view in Eudes Rigaud's treatment of
the hypothetical question, (ed. Bissen, p. 335): '. . . dicendum quod ratio diffusionis sive
bonitatis non exigit quod facit omnia bona quae potest, sed illud solum tenet in
diffusione aeterna; de creatura nihil valet, nam potuit facere meliorem istum hominem
vel illum et minus bonum, et in hoc nulla est iniustitia. Sufficienter autem manifestatur
diffusio sive bonitas aeternaliter in generatione Filii et temporaliter in creatione mundi.
Potuit etiam plures mundos facere, sed tamen non oportet.'

est, sed gratia gratiarum et naturam excellens'; '. . . non est quelibet melioritas de necessitate et perfectione universi, sed de superfluente largitate Creatoris'. The world is better off through the Incarnation, but it was an act of God's gracious love, in no way necessitated by being already written into creation. The line separating nature and grace also separates creation and redemption. Whereas the Incarnation seems to make Grosseteste more aware of the unity underlying everything, on Richard it has the opposite effect; it makes him more aware of the distinction between necessary and contingent, between nature and grace, between creation and redemption. The former had been governed by the laws of nature, the latter is the realm of grace and love. Grosseteste sees creation brought to perfection by Christ; for Rufus, Christ is the beginning of a new creation. Their different answers to the hypothetical question reveal a different sensitivity. Grosseteste was trying to preserve a unity of sacred and profane, the precious inheritance of earlier generations. Richard was aware that that unity had been irrevocably lost, that new ways had to be found to formulate God's concern for the world, a world that had become much more aware of its independence or autonomy. His answers are perhaps unsatisfactory, but in his emphasis on God's sovereign freedom and in his description of man's relation to God as a relation of pure grace, a new vision arises and the first chords are being struck of a theme that before long was to become central to Oxford theologians.

Conclusions

PERHAPS the most significant change in European culture of the High Middle Ages was the 'redrawing of the boundaries between the sacred and the profane', or even the effort to disentangle the sacred from the profane, the natural from the supernatural.[1] The causes of this fundamental change in outlook are many, a milder climate, population growth, an increase in the volume of trade and industry, a curbing of the internecine feudal warfare; all this resulted in a new feeling of self-confidence. Man became less dependent on the blows of fate; apparently the whimsical forces of nature and the anarchy and lawlessness of society could be curbed. There was a new mood, a new optimism about man's possibilities. Raoul Glaber was one of the first to give voice to that new mood, when he wrote that after the thousandth year after the Lord's passion, it was as if the world had cast off its old weariness and veiled itself in a white garment of new churches. The new mood manifested itself in a higher appreciation of man, nature, and society, of visible reality in general; perhaps life on earth was not so desperate after all. With the growth of this new awareness, the feeling that the visible world was not quite real, but a stage, or a shadow cast by an invisible, but far more real, light began to vanish and lose its fascination.

In the Crusades Christendom, for the first time, took the initiative in the incessant struggle against Islam; the days when the Saracens were only just kept at bay, as at Poitiers, were over. The Investiture Contest was the beginning of an effort to reformulate the division of authority between clergy and princes; for the first time since the days

---

[1] P. Brown, 'Society and the Supernatural: a Medieval Change', in id. *Society and the Holy in Late Antiquity* (London, 1982), p. 305. Various aspects of this fundamental change have been discussed in Part II of M. Bloch, *Feudal Society* (London, 1961), pp. 59–120; in the title-essay of R. Southern, *Medieval Humanism and Other Studies* (Oxford, 1970), pp. 29–60; and in W. Von den Steinen, *Der Kosmos des Mittelalters* (2nd edn., Berne etc., 1967); C. Morris, *The Discovery of the Individual 1050–1200* (London, 1972); A. Murray, *Reason and Society in the Middle Ages* (Oxford, 1978); B. Ward, *Miracles and the Medieval Mind* (London, 1982). For the theological repercussions see Chenu, *Douzième siècle*, and Evans, *Old Arts*. New aspects of monasticism and spirituality are discussed by C. Bynum, *Jesus as Mother. Studies in the Spirituality of the High Middle Ages* (Berkeley, 1982).

of the Roman Empire, the possibility of an independent secular government emerged, though it took some centuries to take shape. At first it seemed as if the better organized of the two, the Church, would take possession of all authority, secular and divine.[2]

Christian piety, too, changed dramatically and took on a new warmth and humanity; the image of Christ and of things supernatural took completely new forms. One only has to compare the awe-inspiring *Pantocrator* of Cefalù, last eruption of a great tradition, with the humane and mild *Beau Dieu* of Amiens, or look at the fearsome angels with their huge wide eyes in Beatus' commentary on the Apocalypse and then call to mind the smiling angel of Rheims. Obedience to strict rules, formulated in the penitentials, made place for emphasis on personal experience. Intention became just as important as the moral act itself. The notion of conscience, that most inner self of man in which, struggling with his God, he had to make the right decisions about his life, was quickly developed. In this struggle man was very much helped by a new appreciation of Christ's life and death. Gone were the days when Christ was seen as the remote King on the Cross; now all attention was concentrated on the man Jesus who, like us, 'is compassed with infirmity' (Hebr. v. 2), who had been tempted and had begged his Father that this cup might pass from him, who had suffered a painful and lonely death.[3] So literal was the desire to follow Christ in his life on earth that Francis could say to Brother Leo during a journey in the middle of winter that the best thing that could happen upon their arrival was that they should be thrown out of one of their own friaries, and that the porter would set the dogs on them after beating them; that would be perfect happiness.

Such a fundamental change in outlook made itself felt in theology as in every other human activity. Early medieval theology had been built on the tacit assumption that the boundaries separating heaven and earth were fluid, that every creature had self-evident transparency and that the miraculous was almost palpably present. It was an outlook admirably suited to the experience that the world as such had little to offer and only invited escape from its dangers and dreariness. Neoplatonic philosophy with its emphasis on the unity of heaven and earth, its contempt for the purely material, its hierarchy of natures in

---

[2] R. Southern, *Western Society and the Church in the Middle Ages* (The Pelican History of the Church, ii, 1970), pp. 34–41.

[3] Id., *The Making of the Middle Ages* (London, 1973) pp. 218–22.

which every lower nature was appreciated not for itself but only in the measure of its participation in the perfection of the higher, was an appropriate intellectual expression of this deep feeling. It offered a rational possibility of ascending from the drudgery and darkness of the material world to the world of spirit and light.[4] Christians had quickly found a way of expressing their faith in the terms of Neoplatonism; this synthesis, which in the West was forged mainly by Augustine, served subsequent generations well until the twelfth century, because their day-to-day experiences were basically the same as those of men in late Antiquity.

If all visible things are mainly valued as symbols, the appropriate method of scholarly discourse, theological and otherwise, is the allegorical method, a technique which lays bare the transparency of nature and of human speech by revealing that behind the visible and the letter another world is opening up that is far more real and stable than anything man can see. The figure of speech that nature must be read like a book sums up this attitude.

In such an outlook all knowledge becomes more or less religious. It was one of Augustine's most cherished views that knowledge must be wisdom and that knowledge without love was pointless. Secular knowledge lost its independence completely, because it could not open that perspective man was looking for. The Bible was the only reliable guide in man's search of a way out of this exile, because there man was taught to look at visible things so as to discover their hidden meaning. Science and liberal arts are useful if they prepare the ground for that discovery; they can be plundered as the wealth of Egypt was by the Israelites.

With the growing awareness of man's capabilities in the eleventh and twelfth centuries, this synthesis broke down. The lack of interest in visible reality as such, which had been so characteristic of most thinkers and writers of the early Middle Ages, did not correspond to the overwhelming new experience that the world was worth while and that nature had a value of its own, that it was not just a sign pointing upwards to a reality beyond the grasp of man. And just as man tightened his grip on reality around him, likewise thought about God and about the world became more precise and more tightly organized. Scholars gradually learnt how to marshal their own thoughts; they found new pleasure in the logical works of Boethius and through him made their first acquaintance with Aristotle. Logic and dialectics were

---

[4] E. R. Dodds, *Pagan and Christian in an Age of Anxiety* (Cambridge, 1965), pp. 2–36.

the new and powerful instruments that enabled intelligent and confident men to get a firmer grasp on the rich, yet confusing, world that surrounded them. Where allegory had thrived on vagueness and equivocation, dialectics prospered on sharp distinctions and definitions. In theology the allegorical Bible commentaries gradually took second place after the *quaestio*, in which the basic tenets of faith were subjected to a penetrating, intellectual analysis.

In the second half of the twelfth century the pace of this movement quickened, as more and more works of Aristotle were poured out over Europe. The *Prior* and *Posterior Analytics* offered a complete method of scientific thought, a possibility for scholars to reach, with the help of natural reason only, heights of knowledge that had been shrouded in mystery before. But the works of Aristotle offered far more than new forms of thought: they also gave a survey of the natural world and its workings that was unparalled hitherto. Moreover, Aristotle had not regarded the world as dependent for its being on a higher reality; his world was a closed universe, perfect in itself, its centre of gravity was in man and in nature itself, and there was no need to appeal to outside forces. Aristotle's God, after setting everything in motion, was now engrossed in the contemplation of his own perfection, but in no way influenced the present course of events in the world. Such an outlook fitted the mood of confidence in the twelfth and thirteenth centuries.

But there were problems. Christians define their faith as 'the substance of things hoped for, the evidence of things not seen' (Hebr. xi. 1); any treatise on faith started from that definition. Yet it contained an implicit admission that the centre of gravity was outside visible reality, that nature was not a closed system and man not self-sufficient. All theological problems of the time arose from that fundamental clash of interests. Allegory could be easily disposed of and theological questioning be adapted to the Aristotelian model of science, but in the end every theologian had to find a way of defining the difference between insight and faith. Nature might be self-consistent, but it went too far to uphold its complete independence, as Aristotle did when he maintained that the world had neither beginning nor end. Man's soul might in its vegetative and sensitive functions be a part of the rest of living nature, and far more closely linked to the body than had been thought acceptable before, yet its rationality and immortality were unique and must be God's creation. The mystery of the Eucharist could be explained in terms of Aristotle's philosophy of substantial change; in the end, however, its miraculous character had to be preserved. Yet despite all problems and all wrangling between the different schools of thought, the outcome was that the boundaries between God and man, between nature and grace, knowledge and wisdom, insight and faith, were more sharply formulated. Instead of the fluidity that had marked the previous era, the actions of both God and man were more narrowly circumscribed; man had become more autonomous, God more sovereign. God's intervention and his concern for man were never denied, of course, but they were more rigorously defined in contrast to the areas of man's own competence.

It is necessary to draw this picture of the background to the theological controversies of the thirteenth century to bring out in full relief the contributions that Robert Grosseteste and Richard Rufus made to the debate. We have seen that a deep difference in outlook separates the two men, and it would perhaps be attractive to regard Grosseteste as a staunch defender of tradition and Richard Rufus as a theologian who swam with the tide. But that would be far too simple. Grosseteste was very much aware of the fact that a new age had dawned upon him and that new challenges had to be faced. He knew both Aristotle's methodological works and his natural philosophy: he commented both on the *Posterior Analytics* and on the *Physics*. Richard Rufus on the other hand, though fascinated by Aristotle's view of nature, often shrank from the consequences of the daring positions he discovered in the works of the Philosopher and fell back on the safe authority of the Saints, as in the question of God's knowledge of the world, where he says after an analysis of the relevant passage of the *Metaphysics*: 'Observe, I do not define anything in such an important matter but leave it to cleverer men to judge. If I had seen a clear statement in the works of the Saints, I should have felt safer in saying something more positive on the subject.' (B f. 78B).

Both men reacted to the new challenges that were presented to them, yet in a very different way. Grosseteste thought that the best answer was to try to preserve the inheritance of the Fathers in all its essentials and to pick and choose parts from the Aristotelian synthesis to bolster up tradition. We have seen that he firmly rejected dialectics as an appropriate method in theological discourse, and refused to approach theology from a logical point of view, but clung to the Bible as the organizing principle of theological learning. Allegory remained the best way of disclosing the mystery of God expressed in the letter of Scripture, since it respected the mystery and was *fidei congruens*.

The basis of that methodological traditionalism was formed by Grosseteste's firm conviction that all reality was one. He refused to draw a clear line between heaven and earth, between God and man, everything participated in a higher form; a continuity that stretched from the highest Source to the lowest emanation, a continuity guaranteed by the first corporeal form, light, in which every being participated. Man had a very special place in Grosseteste's cosmos, as he of all created beings resembled his Maker most closely, especially in his free will in which he reflected God's creative power, but also because in man the unity of all creation was summed up. Creation was united in man, but Grosseteste saw an even more embracing unity, the union of Creator and creation in the God-man Jesus Christ. The unity of everything, even God and man, was so self-evident to him that he could wonder whether it must not be the case that from all eternity God had decided to unite heaven and earth in Christ, so that God might be all in all, and that man's sin played only a subordinate part in this momentous decision. The Incarnation was the jewel in the golden ring of the universe, the crown on Grosseteste's system.

Within this essentially Neoplatonic outlook Grosseteste found a way to accommodate some of the insights he had gained in his younger days, when he had occupied himself with the new learning. His programme became not to change the method of theology but to strengthen the foundations of the traditional method, to ensure the objective basis of the allegorical ascent. By strengthening the letter he hoped to curtail the arbitrariness of much traditional allegorization and to give new vigour to its application. The book of nature and the book of Scripture were the two entrance doors to that reality of which Grosseteste wished to catch a glimpse. In Aristotle he found a wealth of new and—in his eyes—very accurate information on natural phenomena that enabled him to outline the properties of natural things much better than his predecessors; by thus revaluing the symbol, he hoped to get a firmer grasp on the thing symbolized. The same concern drove him to linguistics, to find the most accurate text of the Bible by comparing the Vulgate with the Septuagint, the Vetus Latina, and Aquila. Knowledge of nature and of the text of Scripture was far more important than logical precision.

Modern scholars have often tried to construct a tradition of Oxford theology on the basis of Grosseteste's work. They have remarked how Oxford theologians on the whole tended to cultivate the Augustinian heritage and always nourished a suspicion of Aristotle. Other points of interest seemed to be the interest in linguistics and mathematics and, of course, the doctrine of the absolute predestination of Christ. Thus Duns Scotus could be seen as the heir of a rich and unbroken tradition, distinct from that of Paris. The study of Richard Rufus's works and the manner in which he uses Grosseteste's theological thought shows that no such simple and unbroken continuity ever existed.[5] We have seen that Richard Rufus, unlike Grosseteste, had received most of his education at Paris, he was a master of Arts of that university, and did not forget his Parisian experience when he started teaching at Oxford. In his first commentary on the *Sentences* he mentions several times, not without pride, that he had found such and such a thing while he was studying at Paris. His Parisian roots are also obvious from the manuscripts in which his works have been preserved: the collection of disputed questions now in Assisi was drawn up in Paris and used there by Bonaventure when he prepared himself to lecture on the *Sentences*. Nevertheless, this collection also contained questions by other English scholars; but the collection now in Toulouse, which was composed for one of the Italian *studia generalia*, is purely French, giving a survey of Franciscan teaching at Paris before 1250. How important the achievements of theological speculation at Paris were for Richard is most clearly shown by the fact that, when he finally became *lector* to the Oxford convent in 1256, he did not bother to write his own course of lectures, but made a summary of Bonaventure's lectures on the *Sentences* instead and limited his own contribution to some additional remarks.

But far more than his Parisian experience separates Richard Rufus from his predecessor Grosseteste. I have tried to argue in the second part of this work that Richard failed to understand Grosseteste's deepest concern and carry out the programme the Bishop had mapped out for his successors, because their outlooks were fundamentally different. The intellectual break in European culture is mirrored in the misunderstanding between these two scholars.[6] One

---

[5] Catto, 'Theology and Theologians', pp. 471, 475, 480, 487–8, 491, 493, 495 also comes to the conclusion that the Parisian influence on early Oxford theologians was much more important than Grosseteste's.

[6] Richard's troubles with Grosseteste were far from unique. A similar misunderstanding, arising from the clash of views which marks epochs of great cultural change, can be observed in the life of Gerald of Wales. He was severely criticized by some of his contemporaries for his interest in the natural world and was urged to move on to theology and especially to expand the allegorical element in his writing, a desire to

wonders whether Grosseteste's work would ever have become the starting-point of a new tradition, as his theology was the expression of a way of looking at the world that had been lost and could not be revived. Even if it is true that some theologians in the fourteenth century took a renewed interest in Grosseteste and borrowed some of his views, they did not try to revive the mentality from which these views sprang.

In any case the difference in outlook between Richard Rufus and Grosseteste is obvious from the beginning. In the prologue to his commentaries on the *Sentences* Richard had to ask questions about the methods of theology. We have seen that, out of deference to Grosseteste's authority as the Bishop of the diocese in which the university was situated and as an old friend of the Franciscans, he tried to argue that only Bible exposition was real theology and that lectures on the *Sentences* only provided footnotes to the sacred text. But Richard did not know how to go on from there, since he had no feeling for the narrative style of the sacred authors, who expressed eternal truths in the words of a simple story. He had been trained as a dialectician and his approach to theological problems betrayed his early training. The only thing he could do to appease his order's protector and to make sense of his own work was to find a way of proving that even the Author of Scripture often speaks like a dialectician and uses scientific language when trying to explain the hierarchy of being to us. Allegory as a method of discovering truth had become obsolete to him. The fact that Richard's two main theological works are commentaries on the *Sentences* is in itself sufficient proof that his way of looking at God and the world was different from Grosseteste's. Even when he defended in theory the idea that the Bible was the only source of theological specu-lation, he did not act upon that insight in practice.

The difference in outlook that becomes visible in the discussion of theological method is equally obvious where Richard uses Grosse-teste's commentary on the work of creation. We have seen that Richard carefully avoided all the passages where Grosseteste left the level of the letter and moved on to discuss the meaning hidden behind the words. He also left out all the passages where Grosseteste had tried to bring out the features of the symbol more clearly by discussing linguistic problems or the properties of things. Richard was no linguist. He did not know any Greek, nor was he interested in

which he gave way. See R. Bartlett, *Gerard of Wales, 1146-1223* (Oxford, 1982), pp. 144–53.

mathematics as a way of outlining the properties of things; he solved theological problems by applying logical rules.

The reason for this difference in method is that Richard could no longer believe in such an all-embracing view of reality in which everything was connected with everything else, and a continuity existed linking God with the lowest nature; he sought to analyse and distinguish, to assign areas of competence both to God and man. This shift in perspective can perhaps best be approached by comparing Richard's treatment of light with Grosseteste's imaginative speculations on it. As I have said many times, light was for Grosseteste the expression of his unitary view of reality, the form pervading all being, the unifying force in the universe. For Richard light had no such mystical fluidity; he regarded it as a purely physical phenomenon in the natural world, one among many, an object that could be classified and studied: a substance or an accident, corporeal or incorporeal. Not once did he speculate on light as a fundamental metaphysical force giving coherence to the universe.

Richard's treatment of light is a clear sign that his concern was to disentangle the natural and the supernatural and to consider natural phenomena on their own merits and not as symbols of something else. The same experience of the autonomy of nature governs Richard's treatment of the soul, the principle of life. He was heavily influenced by Aristotle's naturalist description of the generation of the soul. We have seen in some detail how much ink he spilt over the generation of the animal soul to decide how far this was an autonomous, natural process, and how far God exerted his influence over it.

Even more obvious is the strength of this new way of analysing reality in Richard's treatise on the soul of man. The central truth about man's soul was for him no longer that it had been created in God's own image and was, therefore, the highest resemblance of the Trinity. We have seen that he skipped very lightly over that issue, merely repeating some pious clichés. A consequence is that the relation of the soul to the body is no longer such a problem; it is quite conceivable that the soul is the form of the body without any mediating nature. The central problem is rather how to relate the soul to God, its undoubted origin. Richard saw the new problem, but hesitated over the answer; he posited a complicated plurality of forms to account on the one hand for the soul's divine origin, on the other hand for its equally obvious participation in the rest of nature. Even more telling is that the debate on the origin of the soul invited Richard

to reflect on what he must have seen as a related, but certainly fundamental problem of natural philosophy, the process of substantial
change, whereas for Grosseteste it was an opportunity to voice some
thoughts on the Trinity, so beautifully reflected in the soul's memory,
reason, and will.

The distinction that Richard tried to make between the natural and
the supernatural is openly proclaimed in the discussion of free will.
Man's unique capacity to choose freely between two opposite
alternatives was for Grosseteste the supreme testimony to the soul's
close resemblance to God, because in his free will man imitated God's
creative power. Richard rejected this view very forcefully, there can be
no comparison between Creator and creature: 'Mihi videtur quod
omnis comparatio Creatoris et creature vix est comparatio et fere non
est, sed est comparatio sine comparatione' (B f. 167B). Compared with
God's creative liberty, man's liberty is slavery. In these terse words
Richard demolished the foundations of any philosophy of participation. If what Richard says is true, nothing visible can be the symbol
of an invisible reality, because there is no point of comparison. Even
theologians in the symbolic tradition would, of course, have admitted
that in comparison between God and man the disproportion is always
far greater than the proportion, but a proportion there was. Richard
goes one step further by denying any proportion at all; nature and God
are separate, perhaps independent realities, in any case their link
becomes problematic.

The problem is obvious in Richard's treatise on the Incarnation, the
coming of God in the flesh. Grosseteste had seen the Incarnation as an
event that was, somehow, in the logic of things; the whole of creation
proclaimed God's coming; it was the fulfilment of the desire for unity
that pervaded all being. Therefore the Incarnation was to be expected
quite independently of man's fall. In this cosmic view the Incarnation
as such is important, the decisive moment is the union of God and
man; the subsequent life, suffering, and death of Christ take second
place. Richard could not possibly find any reason for the Incarnation,
certainly if man's sin was not taken into account. Neither necessity,
nor fittingness was a concept applicable to God's coming in the flesh,
because God was in heaven and man on earth, and no one could
expect a union. The event of the Incarnation, when it happened
against all human reason was, therefore, pure grace, *gratia gratiarum*. If
one could speak of a reason at all, it was that Christ had come to die for
man's sin; Richard's attention was held not by the union, but by the

redemption. By focusing on Christ's life on earth and on his suffering and death Richard gives theological expression to the new mood of piety that had caused thousands of men and women to leave their houses and follow Christ in his life on earth, sharing his poverty, *nudus nudum Christum sequi.*

It is always easier to destroy than to build up. A new way of looking at God and nature made Richard turn away from Grosseteste's grandiose effort to pour new wine into old bottles. But it proved easier to break down than to reintegrate. Richard clearly faltered when he tried to redefine the link between God and man which for him was, of course, as much a matter of faith as it had been for Grosseteste. In matters of pure philosophy Richard was self-confident; his description of the process of substantial change, his definition of seminal principles, his reflections on light or the animal soul, show that in philosophy he knew his way about and had a good reading knowledge of Aristotle, although it is also quite clear that he had not yet mastered him. He could not handle Aristotle's concept of *habitus*, nor had the Philosopher ever maintained that forms could exist by themselves outside the concrete things of which they were the forms. Richard must have picked this up in one of Aristotle's Arab or Jewish commentators.

It is where he has to make the connection with theology that he begins to hesitate. How could the link between God and man be re-established in a world that had become aware of its autonomy and independence and had found a philosopher to give voice to that awareness? That was the main problem Richard faced, and he did not find any coherent answer. So great was his uncertainty about the task that faced him that it became, as we have seen, a mark of his literary style: 'Nescio', 'In hiis non definio.' His confusion can also be seen in his answer to the question whether theology can be called a science in the Aristotelian sense. After much toing and froing, he finally came to the rather meagre conclusion that even in the Bible demonstrations are sometimes used and that, therefore, in so far as this scientific mode of speaking has penetrated into the Bible, we may call theology a science, a conclusion which both shows a deep misunderstanding of the literary genre of the Bible and undervalues the new contribution of speculative questioning to theological reflection. The complicated plurality of forms he postulates in the human soul is another example of the problems in which he found himself.

Nevertheless, Richard did more than just muddle along. Although he does not argue about it very much, he gained, as far as I can see, one central new insight formulated between the lines of his exposition on the reasons of the Incarnation, when he maintains that the relation between God and the world is purely contingent, by denying that God must of necessity realize all the good he is capable of, at least in relation to his creation. God could have given man the natural capacity to receive the divine nature. In his wisdom, he has chosen not to do so, but to give it as a grace, although that capacity in itself is a good thing. Thus Richard freed God from the shackles that bound him to creation in the theology of Grosseteste and in most of the Platonic tradition. God was free and sovereign, everything he did was good, but the good things we see do not exhaust the richness of God's nature. For Richard there was no longer a perfect symmetry between the ideas in the divine mind and their reflection in the world, and so the possibility of analogy was diminished, perhaps even excluded.

The same conception of the link between God and man can be seen in Richard's account of the production of animal souls. He is very insistent on the role the divine will plays in the generation of all living things, in other words God's free love and grace. In this connection Richard's emphasis on the act of creation must also be mentioned. The world might be autonomous and self-consistent up to a point, but in its origin even nature itself comes from God's hands and is the result of a free and gracious decision on his part. Richard defended this insight both against Aristotle, who had held that the world was eternal and fully autonomous, and against extreme Neoplatonists, like Avicenna, who admitted that the world was created by God, but regarded creation as an eternal process, thus establishing a relation of necessity between God and the world. Richard defended, with all Christian theologians, the temporal creation of the eternal God, but not all theologians in his class went so far as he did in drawing the consequence that the only way of conceiving a relation between the eternal and the temporal is to see it as contingent, that no comparison or analogy can exist in this relation. In Richard's theology the keyword to define the link between God and man is not participation or analogy, but grace. God and the world are held together by two clasps: the grace of creation and the grace of the Incarnation (B f. 196D).

In stating an emphatic conclusion like this I am perhaps already making too much of a system out of some statements that are scattered throughout Richard's works. Certainly they would have to be checked in other passages, where he is not dependent on Grosseteste. Richard himself had no pretensions to offer a final solution; he digested a great amount of new learning and asked new questions and so gave voice to a new way of looking at God and the world. But when it came to answers, he just tried to cope and in the end often fell back on the authority of the Fathers; they were the guardians of faith, and that faith had to be preserved above all else. That was the basic instinct that kept him going, when intellectually he was no longer able to absorb and digest all the learning that was presented to him.

Perhaps the Oxford Franciscans had a fair estimation of his intellectual capabilities, after all, and were not so wrong when they decided to give the post of *lector* to their convent to Thomas of York instead of to Richard Rufus in 1253. For us, however, he becomes all the more interesting, since in his work we can feel more of the struggle to come to grips with the challenges presented by a new world than in the polished masterpieces of his contemporaries like Bonaventure and Thomas Aquinas. And perhaps when judging a theologian the difference is not so important. The object of their search is so far beyond all human speech that they all have to realize that in the end their words are vain and fatuous. Aquinas knew about it at the end of his life, Richard somewhat earlier:

Man's condition is miserable. In this life we can know nothing completely, nothing in a way that is satisfactory. And when it is so fatuous, then it is also presumptuous to assert anything in this ambiguous darkness. However, to have doubts about some particular issue need not be in vain. (As f. 277C)

Richard asserted very little and had many doubts which he could not solve, but in some points he showed a way to the Franciscans of a later generation.

Bibliography

(i) *Manuscript Sources*

For MSS discussed in some detail references to the relevant pages are given in brackets.

Assisi, Biblioteca comunale, MS 138 (pp. 64–81).   (= As)
Assisi, Biblioteca comunale, MS 176 (pp. 40–4).   (= A)
Assisi, Biblioteca comunale, MS 186.
Berlin (West). Staatsbibliothek Preussischer Kulturbesitz, MS
    Cod. theol. qu. 48 (pp. 45–7).   (= Be)
Bruges, Bibliothèque publique de la ville, MS 497 (pp. 108–9).
Cambridge, Pembroke College, MS 87 (p. 106 n. 30).
Erfurt, Bibliotheca Amploniana, MS qu. 290 (pp. 96–7).
London, British Library, MS Royal 8 C. iv (pp. 91–3).   (= L)
London, British Library, MS Royal 12 F. xix, (p. 111).
Naples, Biblioteca nazionale, MS VII. C. 19 (pp. 85–6).   (= N)
Oxford, Balliol College, MS 57.   (= Ba)
Oxford, Balliol College, MS 62 (pp. 20–5).   (= B)
Oxford, Balliol College, MS 196 (pp. 17–18).
Oxford, Bodleian Library, MS Bodley 681 (p. 19).
Oxford, Bodleian Library, MS Digby 2 (p. 109).   (= Di)
Oxford, Bodleian Library, MS Digby 24 (pp. 107–9).   (= D)
Oxford, Bodleian Library, MS Digby 55.
Oxford, Bodleian Library, MS Lat. theol. c. 17.   (= Ox)
Oxford, Corpus Christi College, MS 293B (p. 110).   (= C)
Oxford, Magdalen College, MS 66.
Oxford, New College, MS 285 (pp. 95–6).   (= Ne)
Oxford, Oriel College, MS 43.   (= O)
Oxford, Oriel College, MS 64.
Padua, Biblioteca Antoniana, MS 152 (p. 93 n. 50).
Paris, Bibliothèque nationale, MS lat. 14069 (p. 109).
Paris, Bibliothèque nationale, MS lat. 16149.
Paris, Bibliothèque nationale, MS lat. 16406 (pp. 86–90).   (= P)
Paris, Bibliothèque nationale, MS Nouv. acq. lat. 338 (pp. 105–7).
Prague, Library of the Metropolitan Chapter, MS M. lxxx
    (pp. 97–8).   (= Pr)
Todi, Biblioteca comunale, MS 33 (pp. 18–19).
Toulouse, Bibliothèque municipale, MS 737 (pp. 81–4).   (= T)

Trier, Staatsbibliothek, MS 162.

Troyes, Bibliothèque municipale, MS 1245.

Vatican City, Bibliotheca Apostolica Vaticana, MS Borghese 362
(pp. 44–5). (= Bo)

Vatican City, Bibliotheca Apostolica Vaticana, MS lat. 782.

Vatican City, Bibliotheca Apostolica Vaticana, MS lat. 4538
(pp. 94–5). (= Va)

Vatican City, Bibiliotheca Apostolica Vaticana, MS lat. 12993
(pp. 40–4). (= T)

(ii) *Printed Sources*

The full title of some editions is given in the list of secondary works.

Adam Marsh, *Letters*, ed. J. Brewer, Monumenta Franciscana, i (RS 1858), pp. 77–489.

Albert the Great, *De anima*, ed. C. Stroick (*Opera omnia*, vii/1, 1968).

——, *Liber de natura et origine animae*, ed. B. Geyer (*Opera omnia*, xii, 1955).

Alexander of Hales, *Quaestiones disputatae 'antequam esset frater'* (Bibliotheca Franciscana Scholastica Medii Aevi, xix–xxi, 1960).

Anselm, *Opera omnia*, ed. F. S. Schmitt (6 vols., Seckau etc, 1938–61).

Aristotle, *Analytica Posteriora. Translatio Jacobi*, ed. L. Minio-Paluello and B. G. Dod (Aristoteles Latinus, iv/1–4, 1968).

——, *Metaphysica. Translatio anonyma sive media*, ed. G. Vuillemin-Diem (Aristoteles Latinus, xxv/2, 1976).

Augustine, *Confessiones*, ed. P. Knöll (CSEL xxxiii, 1896).

——, *Contra Faustum*, ed. J. Zycha (CSEL xxv, 1897), pp. 249–797.

——, *De civitate Dei*, ed. B. Dombart and A. Kalb (CC xlvii–xlviii, 1955).

——, *De diversis quaestionibus lxxxiii*, ed. A. Mutzenbecher (CC xlivA, 1975), pp. 1–249.

——, *De doctrina Christiana*, ed. J. Martin (CC xxxii, 1962), pp. 1–67.

——, *De Genesi ad litteram*, ed. J. Zycha (CSEL xxviii/1, 1894), pp. 1–456.

——, *Enarrationes in Psalmos, i–l*, ed. E. Dekkers and I. Fraipont (CC xxxviii, 1956).

——, *In epistolam Ioannis ad Parthos* (PL xxxv), cols. 1977–2062.

——, *Sermones* (PL xxxviii–xxxix).

Avencebrol, *Fons vitae*, ed. C. Bäumker (BGPhMA i/2–4, 1895).

Averroes, *Commentarium magnum in Aristotelis De anima libros*, ed. F. S. Crawford (Corpus commentariorum Averrois in Aristotelem versionum Latinarum, vi/1, 1953).

Basil of Caesarea, *Hexaemeron, Eustathius, ancienne version des neuf homélies sur l'Hexaéméron de Basile de Césarée*, ed. E. Amand de Mendieta and S. Rudberg (Texte und Untersuchungen zur Geschichte der altchristlichen Literatur, lxvi, 1958).

Boethius, *Commentarii in librum Aristotelis Περὶ Ἑρμενείας editio secunda*, ed. C. Meiser (Leipzig, 1880).
Boethius, *De consolatione philosophiae*, ed. L. Bieler (CC xciv, 1957).
Bonaventure, *Commentaria in quatuor libros Sententiarum* (*Opera omnia*, i–iv, 1882–9).

Conciliorum oecumenicorum decreta, ed. J. Alberigo *et al.* (3rd edn., Bologna, 1973).
Councils and Synods with other Documents Relating to the English Church, II: A.D. 1205–1313, ed. F. Powicke and C. R. Cheney (2 vols., Oxford, 1964).

Eckhart, Meister, *Collatio in libros Sententiarum*, ed. J. Koch (Die lateinischen Werke, v, 1936), pp. 1–26.
Hugh of Saint-Victor, *Liber de sacramentis Christianae fidei* (PL clxxvi), cols. 173–618.

Inventario dell'antica biblioteca del S. Convento di S. Francesco in Assisi compilato nel 1381, ed. L. Alessandri (Assisi, 1906).

John Blund, *Tractatus de anima*, ed. D. Callus and R. W. Hunt (Auctores Britannici Medii Aevi, ii, 1970).
John Damascene, *De fide orthodoxa. Versions of Burgundio and Cerbanus*, ed. E. Buytaert (Franciscan Institute Publications, Text Series, viii, 1955).
John Duns Scotus, *Ordinatio* (*Opera omnia*, i–, 1950–).
John of La Rochelle, *Tractatus de divisione multiplici potentiarum animae*, ed. P. Michaud-Quantin (Textes philosophiques du Moyen Âge, xi, 1964).

Maimonides, *The Guide for the Perplexed*, ed. and tr. M. Friedländer (New York, 1904).
Matthew Paris, *Chronica majora*, ed. H. R. Luard (7 vols., RS, 1872–83).

Peter Abelard, *Sic et non*, ed. B. Boyer and R. McKeon (Chicago, 1977).
Peter Comestor, *Historia scholastica* (PL cxcviii), cols. 1049–722.

Robert Grosseteste, *Commentarius in mysticam theologiam*, ed. U. Gamba (Milan, 1942).
—, *Commentary on Ecclesiasticus, xliii. 1–5*, ed. J. McEvoy, 'The Sun as *res* and *signum*', pp. 62–91.
—, *De cessatione legalium* (part), [ed. B. Ryves] (London, 1658).
—, *De cessatione legalium* (part), ed. D. Unger, 'Robert Grosseteste', pp. 3–18.
—, *De finitate motus et temporis*, ed. R. C. Dales, 'Robert Grosseteste's Treatise', pp. 253–66.
—, *De libero arbitrio*, ed. L. Baur, *Die philosophischen Werke*, pp. 150–241.
—, *De luce*, ed. L. Baur, *Die philosophischen Werke*, pp. 51–9.
—, *Dictum 60: 'Omnis creatura speculum est'*, ed. S. Gieben, 'Traces', pp. 153–8.

—, *Epistolae*, ed. H. R. Luard (RS, 1861).

—, *Hexaemeron*, ed. R. C. Dales and S. Gieben (Auctores Britannici Medii Aevi, vi, 1982).

—, *Quaestio de modis subsistendi*, ed. O. Lewry, 'Robert Grosseteste's Question', pp. 19–21.

—, *Questio de fluxu et refluxu maris* or *Questio de accessu et recessu maris*, ed. R. C. Dales, 'The Text', pp. 459–68.

—, *Sermon 'Ex rerum initiatarum'*, ed. S. Gieben, 'Robert Grosseteste on Preaching', pp. 120–41.

—, *Sermon 'Exiit edictum'*, ed. D. Unger, 'Robert Grosseteste', pp. 18–23.

Roger Bacon, *Compendium studii theologie*, ed. H. Rashdall (British Society of Franciscan Studies, iii, 1911).

Statuta antiqua universitatis Oxoniensis, ed. S. Gibson (Oxford, 1931).

Summa theologica 'Alexandri' (5 vols., Quaracchi etc., 1924–79).

Thomas Aquinas, *Summa theologiae, 1a. 75–83*, ed. T. Sutton (Blackfriars edn., xi, 1970).

—, *Summa theologiae, 1a2ae. 49—54*, ed. A. Kenny (Blackfriars edn., xxii, 1964).

Thomas of Eccleston, *Tractatus de adventu fratrum minorum in Angliam*, ed. A. G. Little (Manchester, 1951).

William of Auvergne, *De universo* (*Opera omnia*, i, 1674), pp. 593–1074.

William of Shyreswood, *Introductiones in logicam*, ed. M. Grabmann (Sitzungs-berichte der Bayerischen Akademie der Wissenschaften, philosophisch-historische Abteilung, 1937).

(iii) *Secondary Works*

Abate, G. and Luisetto, G., *Codici e manoscritti della Biblioteca Antoniana* (Fonti e studi per la storia del Santo a Padova, Fonti, i–ii, 1975).

Alszeghy, Z., 'Abbreviationes Bonaventurae. Handschriftliche Auszüge aus dem Sentenzenkommentar des hl. Bonaventura im Mittelalter', *Gregorianum*, xxviii (1947), 474–510.

Baldwin, J., *The Scholastic Culture of the Middle Ages 1000—1300* (Lexington, 1971).

Bale, J., *Index Britanniae scriptorum*, ed. R. Poole and M. Bateson (Anecdota Oxoniensia, Mediaeval and Modern Series, ix, 1902).

—, *Scriptorum illustrium maioris Brytanniae . . . catalogus* (2 parts in one vol., Basle, 1557–9).

Barbet, J., 'Notes sur le manuscrit 737 de la bibliothèque municipale de Toulouse', *Bulletin d'information de l'Institut de Recherche et d'Histoire des Textes*, v (1956), 7–51.

Bartlett, R., *Gerald of Wales, 1146—1223* (Oxford, 1982).

Baur, L., *Die Philosophie des Robert Grosseteste, Bischofs von Lincoln (†1253)* (BGPhMA xviii/4–6, 1917).

— (ed.), *Die philosophischen Werke des Robert Grosseteste, Bischofs von Lincoln* (BGPhMA ix, 1912).

Bea, A., 'Deus auctor Sacrae Scripturae. Herkunft und Bedeutung der Formel', *Angelicum*, xx (1943), 16–31.

Bethmann, L., 'Dr. Ludwig Bethmann's Nachrichten über die … Sammlungen von Handschriften und Urkunden Italiens, aus dem Jahre 1854', *Archiv der Gesellschaft für ältere deutsche Geschichtskunde*, xii (1874), 201–426, 474–758.

Beumer, J., 'Biblische Grundlage und dialektische Methode im Widerstreit innerhalb der mittelalterlichen Scholastik', *FnSn* xlviii (1966), 223–42.

——, 'Robert Grosseteste von Lincoln, der angebliche Begründer der Franziskanerschule', *FnSn* lvii (1975), 183–95.

Bissen, I., 'De motivo Incarnationis, disquisitio historico-dogmatica', *Antonianum*, vii (1932), 314–36.

Bloch, M., *Feudal Society* (London, 1961).

Bonnefoy, J.-F., 'La question hypothétique: *Ultrum* [sic] *si Adam non peccasset* … au xiiie siècle', *Revista Española de Teología*, xiv (1954), 327–68.

Boyle, L., 'Robert Grosseteste and the Pastoral Care', *Mediaeval and Renaissance Studies*, viii (1979), 3–51.

Brinkman, H., *Mittelalterliche Hermeneutik* (Tübingen, 1980).

Brown, P., 'Society and the Supernatural: a Medieval Change', in id. *Society and the Holy in Late Antiquity* (London, 1982), pp. 302–32.

Bynum, C., *Jesus as Mother. Studies in the Spirituality of the High Middle Ages* (Berkeley, 1982).

Callebaut, A., 'Alexandre de Halès O.F.M. et ses confrères en face de condamnations parisiennes de 1241 et 1244', *La France franciscaine*, x (1927), 257–72.

Callus, D., 'Introduction of Aristotelian Learning to Oxford', *Proceedings of the British Academy*, xxix (1943), 229–81.

——, 'Robert Grosseteste as Scholar', in id., (ed.), *Robert Grosseteste, Scholar and Bishop* (Oxford, 1955), pp. 1–69.

——, 'The Subject-Matter of Metaphysics According to Some Thirteenth-Century Oxford Masters', in P. Wilpert (ed.), *Die Metaphysik im Mittelalter* (Miscellanea mediaevalia, ii, 1963), pp. 393–9.

——, 'The *Summa theologiae* of Robert Grosseteste', in R. W. Hunt *et al.* (eds.), *Studies in Medieval History Presented to Frederick Maurice Powicke* (Oxford, 1948), pp. 180–208.

——, 'Two Early Oxford Masters on the Problem of Plurality of Forms, Adam of Buckfield, Richard Rufus of Cornwall', *Revue néo-scolastique de philosophie*, xlii (1940), 411–45.

Catto, J., 'New Light on Thomas Docking O.F.M.', *Mediaeval and Renaissance Studies*, vi (1968), 135–49.

——, 'Theology and Theologians 1220–1320', in id. (ed.), *The Early Oxford Schools* (The History of the University of Oxford, i, 1984), pp. 471–517.

Cenci, C., *Bibliotheca manuscripta ad Sacrum Conventum Assisiensem* (Il miracolo di Assisi, iv/1–2, 1981).

——, *Manoscritti francescani della Biblioteca nazionale di Napoli* (Spicilegium Bonaventurianum, vii–viii, 1971).

Charles, E., *Roger Bacon: sa vie, ses ouvrages, ses doctrines* (Paris, 1861).

Chenu, M.-D., *Introduction à l'étude de S. Thomas d'Aquin* (3rd edn., Publications de l'Institut d'Études Médiévales, xi, 1974).

——, *La Théologie au douzième siècle* (3rd edn., Études de philosophie médiévale, xlv, 1976).

Conlan, W., 'The Definition of Faith according to a Question of MS. Assisi 138', in J. R. O'Donnell (ed.), *Essays. . . A.C. Pegis* (Toronto, 1974), pp. 17–69.

Coxe, H., *Catalogus codicum MSS. Collegii Corporis Christi* (Oxford, 1852).

——, *Catalogus codicum MSS. Collegii Novi* (Oxford, 1852).

Crombie, A., *Robert Grosseteste and the Origins of Experimental Science, 1100–1700* (Oxford, 1953).

Crowley, Th., *Roger Bacon. The Problem of the Soul in His Philosophical Commentaries* (Louvain etc., 1950).

Cruz Pontes, J. da, 'Le problème de l'origine de l'âme de la patristique à la solution thomiste', *RThAM* xxxi (1964), 175–229.

Dales, R. C., 'The Influence of Grosseteste's Hexaëmeron on the Sentences Commentaries of Richard Fishacre O.P. and Richard Rufus of Cornwall O.F.M.', *Viator*, ii (1971), 271–300.

——, 'A Medieval View of Human Dignity', *Journal of the History of Ideas*, xxxviii (1977), 557–72.

——, 'Robert Grosseteste's Treatise *De finitate motus et temporis*', *Traditio*, xix (1963), 245–66.

——, 'The Text of Robert Grosseteste's *Questio de fluxu et refluxu maris* with an English Translation', *Isis*, lvii (1966), 455–74.

Davy, M.-M., *Les Sermons universitaires parisiens de 1230–1231* (Études de philosophie médiévale, xv, 1931).

De Poorter, A., *Catalogue des manuscrits de la bibliothèque publique de la ville de Bruges* (Catalogue générale des manuscrits des bibliothèques de Belgique, ii, 1934).

Destrez, J., *La Pecia dans les manuscrits universitaires du XIIIᵉ et du XIVᵉ siècle* (Paris, 1935).

Distelbrink, B., *Bonaventurae scripta . . . critice recensita* (Subsidia Scientifica Franciscalia, v, 1975).

Dod, B.G, 'Aristoteles Latinus', in N. Kretzmann *et al.* (eds.), *The Cambridge History of Later Medieval Philosophy* (Cambridge, 1982), pp. 45–79.

Dodds, E. R., *Pagan and Christian in an Age of Anxiety* (Cambridge, 1965).

Doucet, V., 'Commentaires sur les Sentences. Supplément au répertoire de M. Frédéric Stegmüller', *AFH* xlvii(1954), 88–170.

[——], 'Prolegomena', *Summa theologica 'Alexandri'*, iv (1948), v–ccccxvi.

Dunbar, H., *Symbolism in Medieval Thought* (New Haven, 1929).

Easton, S., *Roger Bacon and His Search for a Universal Science* (Oxford, 1952).

Ebbesen, S., 'Roger Bacon and the Fools of His Times', *Cahiers de l'Institut du Moyen Âge Grec et Latin*, iii (1970), 40–4 (90–4).

Ehrle, F., 'Zu Bethmanns Notizen über die Handschriften von St. Francesco in Assisi', *Archiv für Litteratur- und Kirchengeschichte des Mittelalters*, i (1885), 470–507.

Emmen, A., 'Einführung in die Mariologie der Oxforder Franziskanerschule', *FnSn* xxxix (1957), 99–217.

Evans, G. R., *Anselm and Talking about God* (Oxford, 1978).

——, *Old Arts and New Theology* (Oxford, 1980).

Fabricius, J. A., *Bibliotheca Latina mediae et infimae aetatis* (6 vols., Hamburg, 1734–46).

Felder, H., *Geschichte der wissenschaftlichen Studien im Franziskanerorden bis um die Mitte des 13. Jahrhunderts* (Freiburg i. B., 1904).

Forest, A., *et al.*, *Le Mouvement doctrinal du XIe au XIVe siècle* (A. Fliche and V. Martin (eds.), Histoire de l'Église depuis les origines jusqu'à nos jours, xiii, 1951).

Gal, G., 'Commentarius in *Metaphysicam* Aristotelis, Cod. Vat. lat. 4538, fons doctrinae Richardi Rufi', *AFH* xliii (1950), 209–42.

——, 'Opiniones Richardi Rufi Cornubiensis a censore reprobatae', *FS* xxxv (1975), 136–93.

——, 'Robert Kilwardby's Questions on the *Metaphysics* and *Physics* of Aristotle', *FS* xiii (1953), 7–28.

——, 'Viae ad existentiam Dei probandam in doctrina Richardi Rufi OFM', *FnSn* xxxviii (1956), 177–202.

Gieben, S., 'Robert Grosseteste on Preaching', *Collectanea Franciscana*, xxxvii (1967), 100–41.

——, 'Traces of God in Nature According to Robert Grosseteste', *FS* xxiv (1964), 144–58.

Gilson, É., *L'Esprit de la philosophie médiévale* (2 vols., Paris, 1932).

——, 'Pourquoi saint Thomas a critiqué saint Augustin', *Archives d'histoire doctrinale et littéraire du Moyen Âge*, i (1926–7), 5–127.

Gratius, O., *Fasciculus rerum expetendarum et fugiendarum*, ed. E. Brown (2 vols., London, 1690).

Gründel, J., *Die Lehre von den Umständen der menschlichen Handlung im Mittelalter* (BGPhThMA xxxix/5, 1963).

Haren, M., *Medieval Thought. The Western Intellectual Tradition from Antiquity to the 13th Century* (London, 1985).

Haubst, R., *Vom Sinn der Menschwerdung* (Munich, 1969).

Hayes, Z., *The General Doctrine of Creation in the Thirteenth Century* (Munich, 1964).

Henquinet, F. M., 'Autour des écrits d'Alexandre de Halès et de Richard Rufus', *Antonianum*, xi (1936), 187–218.

——, 'Un brouillon autographe de S. Bonaventure sur le commentaire des Sentences', *Études franciscaines*, xliv (1932), 633–55.

——, 'Le commentaire d'Alexandre de Halès sur les Sentences enfin retrouvé', in *Miscellanea Giovanni Mercati*, ii (Studi Testi, cxxii, 1946), pp. 359–82.

——, 'Eudes de Rosny, O.F.M., Eudes Rigaud et la Somme d'Alexandre de Halès', *AFH* xxxiii (1940), 3–54.

——, 'Frère Gérardin de San Giovanni in Persiceto, O.F.M., usager du manuscrit Toulouse 737', *AFH* xxxi (1938), 522–8.

——, 'Les questions inédites d'Alexandre de Halès sur les fins dernières', *RThAM* x (1938), 56–78, 153–72, 268–78.

——, 'Un recueil de questions annoté par S. Bonaventure', *AFH* xxv (1932), 553–5.

——, 'Trois petits écrits théologiques de saint Bonaventure à la lumière d'un quatrième, inédit', in *Mélanges Auguste Pelzer* (Louvain, 1947), pp. 196–216.

Hödl, L., 'Die sakramentale Busse und ihre kirchliche Ordnung im beginnenden mittelalterlichen Streit um die Bussvollmacht der Ordenspriester', *FnSn* lv (1973), 330–74.

Huftier, M., 'Libre arbitre, liberté et péché chez saint Augustin', *RThAM* xxxiii (1966), 187–281.

Humphreys, K. W., *The Library of the Franciscans of Siena in the Late 15th Century* (Studies in the History of Libraries and Librarianship, iv, 1978).

Hunt, R. W., 'Notable Accessions. Manuscripts', *Bodleian Library Record*, ii (1941–9), 226–7.

James, M. R., *A Descriptive Catalogue of the Manuscripts in the Library of Pembroke College, Cambridge* (Cambridge, 1905).

——, *Lists of Manuscripts Formerly Owned by Dr. John Dee* (Transactions of the Bibliographical Society, Supplements, i, 1921).

Kenny, A., *Aquinas* (Oxford, 1980).

——, *The God of the Philosophers* (Oxford, 1979).

Knowles, D., *The Evolution of Medieval Thought* (London, 1962).

Köpf, U., *Die Anfänge der theologischen Wissenschaftstheorie im 13. Jahrhundert* (Beiträge zur historischen Theologie, xlix, 1974).

Korolec, J., '*L'Éthique à Nicomaque* et le problème du libre arbitre à la lumière des commentaires du xiiie siècle et la philosophie de la liberté de Jean

Buridan', in A. Zimmermann (ed.), *Die Auseinandersetzungen an der Pariser Universität im XIII. Jahrhundert* (Miscellanea mediaevalia, x, 1976), pp. 331–48.

Lampen, W., 'De fr. Richardo Rufo, Cornubiensi, O.F.M.', *AFH* xxi (1928), 403–6.

Lang, A., *Die theologische Prinzipienlehre der mittelalterlichen Scholastik* (Freiburg i. B., 1964).

Lebacqz, J., *Libre arbitre et jugement* (Museum Lessianum, section philosophique, xlvii, 1960).

Leff, G., *Paris and Oxford Universities in the Thirteenth and Fourteenth Centuries* (New York, 1968).

Lelandus, J., *Commentarii de scriptoribus Brittannicis*, ed. A. Hall (Oxford, 1709).

Leonii, L., *Inventario dei codici della comunale di Todi* (Todi, 1878).

Lewry, O., 'Grammar, Logic and Rhetoric 1220–1320', in J. Catto (ed.), *The Early Oxford Schools* (The History of the University of Oxford, i, 1984), pp. 401–33.

——, 'The Miscellaneous and the Anonymous: William of Montoriel, Roger Bourth and the Bodleian MS. Digby 2', *Manuscripta*, xxiv (1980), 67–75.

——, 'Robert Grosseteste's Question on Subsistence: an Echo of the Adamites', *MS* xlv (1983), 1–21.

Libera, A. de, 'La littérature des *abstractiones* et la tradition logique d'Oxford', in O. Lewry (ed.), *The Rise of British Logic* (Papers in Mediaeval Studies, vii, 1985), pp. 63–113.

Lindberg, D., *Theories of Vision from Al-Kindi to Kepler* (Chicago etc., 1976).

Lio, H., 'De elementis traditionalibus justitiae in primaeva schola franciscana', *FS* x (1950), 164–85, 286–312, 441–58.

Little, A. G., *Franciscan Papers, Lists and Documents* (Manchester, 1943).

——, 'The Franciscan School at Oxford in the 13th Century', *AFH* xix (1926), 803–74.

——, *The Greyfriars in Oxford* (Oxford Historical Society, xx, 1892).

——, 'The Lamport Fragment of Eccleston and Its Connexions', *EHR* xlix (1934), 299–302.

—, and Pelster, F., *Oxford Theology and Theologians* c. A.D. *1282–1302* (Oxford Historical Society, xcvi, 1934).

Lohr, Ch., 'Medieval Latin Aristotle Commentaries', *Traditio*, xxiii (1967), 313–413; xxiv (1968), 149–245; xxvi (1970), 135–216; xxvii (1971), 251–351; xxviii (1972), 281–396; xxix (1973), 93–197; xxx (1974), 119–44.

Long, R. J., 'Richard Fishacre and the Problem of the Soul', *The Modern Schoolman*, lii (1975), 263–70.

——, 'The Science of Theology According to Richard Fishacre', *MS* xxxiv (1972), 71–98.

Longpré, E., 'Robert Grossetête et le B. Jean Duns Scot. Le motif de l'Incarnation', *La France franciscaine*, Documents, iv (1939), 1–16.

Lottin, O., 'L'influence littéraire du chancelier Philippe sur les théologiens préthomistes', *RThAM* ii (1930), 311–26.

——, *Psychologie et morale aux XIIe et XIIIe siècles* (6 vols., i–iv: Louvain etc., v–vi: Gembloux, 1942–60; 2nd edn., i: Gembloux, 1957).

McEvoy, J., 'The Absolute Predestination of Christ in the Theology of Robert Grosseteste', in *Sapientiae doctrina. Mélanges . . . Hildebrand Bascour O.S.B.* (RThAM, numéro spécial, i, 1980), 212–30.

——, *The Philosophy of Robert Grosseteste* (Oxford, 1982).

——, 'The Sun as *res* and *signum*: Grosseteste's Commentary on Ecclesiasticus ch. 43, vv. 1–5', *RThAM* xli (1974), 38–91.

Macrae, E., 'Geoffrey of Aspall's Commentaries on Aristotle', *Mediaeval and Renaissance Studies*, vi (1968), 94–134.

Madan, F. and Craster, H., *A Summary Catalogue of Western Manuscripts in the Bodleian Library at Oxford* (7 vols., Oxford, 1895–1953).

Maier, A., *Codices Burghesiani Bibliothecae Vaticanae* (Studi e Testi, clxx, 1952).

Mandonnet, P., 'Thomas d'Aquin, novice prêcheur (1244–46)', *Revue thomiste*, n.s. vii (1924), 243–67, 370–90, 529–47; viii (1925), 3–20, 222–49, 393–416, 489–533.

Mare, A. de la, and Barker-Benfield, B. (eds.), *Manuscripts at Oxford* (Oxford, 1980).

Mazzatinti, G. and Alessandri, L., 'Assisi. Biblioteca del convento di S. Francesco', in G. Mazzantinti (ed.), *Inventari dei manoscritti delle bibliotheche d'Italia*, iv (1894), pp. 121–41.

Meier, L., *Die Barfüsserschule zu Erfurt* (BGPhThMA xxxviii/2, 1958).

——, 'De schola Franciscana Erfordiensi saeculi xv', *Antonianum*, v (1930), 57–94, 157–202, 333–62, 443–74.

Menestò, E., 'Codici del sacro convento di Assisi nella biblioteca comunale di Poppi', *Studi medievali*, 3rd ser. xx (1979), 357–408.

Mercati, G., 'Codici del convento di S. Francesco in Assisi nella Biblioteca Vaticana', in *Miscellanea Ehrle*, v (Studi e Testi, xli, 1924), pp. 83–127.

Mersch, E., 'L'objet de la théologie et le "Christus totus" ', *Recherches de science religieuse*, xxvi (1936), 129–57.

Michel, A., 'Trinité, ii: la théologie latine du VIe au xx_e siècle', *Dictionnaire de théologie catholique*, xv (1950), pp. 1702–1830.

Moorman, J., *A History of the Franciscan Order from Its Origins to the Year 1517* (Oxford, 1968).

Morris, C., *The Discovery of the Individual 1050–1200* (London, 1972).

Murray, A., *Reason and Society in the Middle Ages* (Oxford, 1978).

Mynors, R. A. B., *Catalogue of the Manuscripts of Balliol College Oxford* (Oxford, 1962).

[Parkinson, A.], *Collectanea Anglo-minoritica, or a Collection of the Antiquities of the . . . Gray Friers* (London, 1726).

Patterson, S., *Paris and Oxford University Manuscripts in the Thirteenth Century* (B. Litt. thesis, Oxford, 1969).

Pelster, F., 'Die älteste Abkürzung und Kritik vom Sentenzenkommentar des hl. Bonaventura', *Gregorianum*, xvii (1936), 195–223.

——, 'Der älteste Sentenzenkommentar aus der Oxforder Franziskanerschule', *Scholastik*, i (1926), 50–80.

——, 'Beiträge zur Erforschung des schriftlichen Nachlasses Odo Rigaldis', *Scholastik*, xi (1936), 518–42.

——, 'Cod. 152 der Bibliothek von S. Antonio in Padua und seine Quästionen', *RThAM* ix (1937), 23–55.

——, 'Literargeschichtliche Probleme im Anschluss an die Bonaventura-ausgabe von Quaracchi', *Zeitschrift für katholische Theologie*, xlviii (1924), 500–32.

——, 'Neue Schriften des englischen Franziskaners Richardus Rufus von Cornwall (um 1250)', *Scholastik*, viii (1933), 561–8; ix (1934), 256–64.

——, 'Der Oxforder Theologe Richardus Rufus O.F.M. über die Frage: "Utrum Christus in triduo mortis fuerit homo" ', *RThAM* xvi (1949), 259–80.

——, 'Quästionen des Franziskaners Richardus Rufus de Cornubia (um 1250) in Cod. VII C. 19 der Nationalbibliothek Neapel und Cod. 138 der Stadtbibliothek Assisi', *Scholastik*, xiv (1939), 215–33.

——, 'Roger Bacon's *Compendium studii theologiae* und der Sentenzenkommentar des Richardus Rufus', *Scholastik*, iv (1929), 410–16.

——, 'Zu Richardus Rufus de Cornubia', *Zeitschrift für katholische Theologie*, xlviii (1924), 625–9.

——, 'Zwei ehemalige Turiner Handschriften aus dem Kreise um Alexander von Hales', *Scholastik*, xii (1937), 519–46.

Pinborg, J., 'Magister abstractionum', *Cahiers de l'Institut du Moyen Âge Grec et Latin*, xviii (1976), 1–4.

——, 'Bezeichnung in der Logik des XIII. Jahrhunderts', in A. Zimmermann (ed.), *Der Begriff der Repraesentatio im Mittelalter* (Miscellanea mediaevalia, viii, 1971), pp. 238–81.

——, *Logik und Semantik im Mittelalter* (Stuttgart, 1972).

Pitseus, J., *Relationum historicarum de rebus Anglicis* (Paris, 1619).

Podlaha, A., *Soupis rukopisů knihovny metropolitní kapitoly pražské* (2 vols., Prague, 1910–22).

Pollard, G., 'The *Pecia* System in the Medieval Universities', in M. Parkes and A. Watson (eds.), *Medieval Scribes, Manuscripts, and Libraries, Essays . . . N. R. Ker* (London, 1978), pp. 145–61.

Possevinus, A., *Apparatus sacer ad scriptores . . . conscriptos* (2nd edn., 2 vols., Cologne, 1608).

Rijk, L. M. de, *Logica modernorum* (2 parts in 3 vols., Assen, 1962–7).

Rodulphius, P., *Historiarum seraphicae religionis libri tres* (Venice, 1586).

Rohls, J., *Wilhelm von Auvergne und der mittelalterliche Aristotelismus* (Münchener Universitätsschriften, v, 1980).

Rose, V., *Die Handschriften-Verzeichnisse der königlichen Bibliothek zu Berlin, XIII: Verzeichnis der lateinischen Handschriften, ii/1* (Berlin, 1901).

Ross, D., *Aristotle* (5th edn., London, 1956).

Russell, J. C., *Dictionary of Writers of Thirteenth Century England* (Bulletin of the Institute of Historical Research, Supplements, iii, 1936).

Samaran, Ch. and Marichal, R., *Catalogue des manuscrits en écriture latine portant des indications de date, de lieu, ou de copiste* (Paris, 1959–).

Sbaralea, J., 'Supplementum et castigatio ad scriptores . . . a Waddingo . . . descriptos', L. Wadding, *Scriptores* (q.v.), part ii.

Scheffczyk, L., *Creation and Providence* (London etc., 1970).

Schneyer, J. B., *Repertorium der lateinischen Sermones des Mittelalters für die Zeit von 1150–1350 (Autoren R—Schluss)* (BGPhThMA xliii/5, 1973).

Schum, W., *Beschreibendes Verzeichnis der Amplonianischen Handschriften-Sammlung zu Erfurt* (Berlin, 1887).

Seeberg, R., *Die Theologie des Johannes Duns Scotus* (Studien zur Geschichte der Theologie und der Kirche, v, 1900).

Sharp, D., *Franciscan Philosophy at Oxford in the Thirteenth Century* (Oxford, 1930).

——, 'The Philosophy of Richard Fishacre (d. 1248)', *The New Scholasticism*, vii (1933), 281–97.

Smalley, B., 'The Biblical Scholar', in D. Callus (ed.), *Robert Grosseteste, Scholar and Bishop* (Oxford, 1955), pp. 70–97.

——, *The Study of the Bible in the Middle Ages* (2nd edn., Notre Dame, 1970).

Southern, R., *The Making of the Middle Ages* (London, 1973).

——, *Robert Grosseteste. The Growth of an English Mind in Medieval Europe* (Oxford, 1986).

——, *Medieval Humanism and Other Studies* (Oxford, 1970).

——, *Western Society and the Church in the Middle Ages* (The Pelican History of the Church, ii, 1970).

Spade, P., 'Robert Fland's *Consequentiae*: An Edition', *MS* xxxviii (1976), 54–84.

Stegmüller, F., *Repertorium commentariorum in Sententias Petri Lombardi* (2 vols., Würzburg, 1947).

Synan, E., 'The *Introitus ad Sententias* of Roger of Nottingham O.F.M.', *MS* xxv (1963), 259–79.

Tanner, Th., *Bibliotheca Britannico-Hibernica* (London, 1748).

Thompson, W. G., 'The Doctrine of Free Choice in Saint Bonaventure', *FS* xviii (1958), 1–8.

Thomson, S. H., *Latin Bookhands of the Later Middle Ages, 1100–1500* (Cambridge, 1969).

Unger, D., 'Robert Grosseteste, Bishop of Lincoln (1235–1253) on the Reasons for the Incarnation', *FS* xvi (1956), 1–36.

Van Steenberghen, F., *Aristotle in the West. The Origins of Latin Aristotelianism* (2nd edn., Louvain, 1970).

—, 'La controverse sur l'éternité du monde au XIIIᵉ siècle', in id., *Introduction à l'étude de la philosophie médiévale* (Philosophes médiévaux, xviii, 1974), pp. 512–30.

—, 'La philosophie de la nature au XIIIᵉ siècle', *La filosofia della natura nel Medioevo*, Atti del terzo congresso internazionale di filosofia medioevale (Milan, 1966), pp. 114–32.

—, *Die Philosophie im XIII. Jahrhundert* (Munich etc., 1977).

Von den Steinen, W., *Der Kosmos des Mittelalters* (2nd end., Berne etc., 1967).

Wadding, L., *Scriptores ordinis minorum*, ed. J. Sbaralea (Rome, 1806).

Ward, B., *Miracles and the Medieval Mind* (London, 1982).

Warner, G. and Gilson, J., *Catalogue of Western Manuscripts in the Old Royal and King's Collections* (4 vols., London, 1921).

Weisheipl, J., 'The Interpretation of Aristotle's Physics and the Science of Motion', in N. Kretzmann *et al.* (eds.), *The Cambridge History of Later Medieval Philosophy* (Cambridge, 1982), pp. 521–36.

—, 'Repertorium Mertonense', *MS* xxxi (1969), 174–224.

Wieland, G., *Ethica—Scientia practica: die Anfänge der philosophischen Ethik im 13. Jahrhundert* (BGPhThMA, n.s. xxi, 1981).

Willotus, H., *Athenae orthodoxorum sodalitii Franciscani* (Liège, 1598).

Wilson, C., *William Heytesbury: Medieval Logic and the Rise of Mathematical Physics* (Publications in Medieval Science, iii, 1956).

Wilson, E. F., *The Stella Maris of John of Garland* (Cambridge, 1946).

Wlodek, S., 'La génération des êtres naturels dans l'interprétation de Thomas Sutton', in A. Zimmermann (ed.), *Die Auseinandersetzungen an der Pariser Universität im XIII. Jahrhundert* (Miscellanea mediaevalia, x, 1976), pp. 349–60.

Wood, A., *Historia et antiquitates universitatis Oxoniensis* (2 parts in one vol., Oxford, 1674).

—, *The History and Antiquities of the University of Oxford*, ed. J. Gutch (2 vols., Oxford, 1792–6).

Zimmermann, A., *Verzeichnis ungedruckter Kommentare zur Metaphysik und Physik des Aristoteles aus der Zeit von etwa 1250–1350* (Studien und Texte zur Geistesgeschichte des Mittelalters, ix, 1971).

Index

Medieval authors have been listed under their Christian names

accident 175, 183–4, 186
action, human 209–10, 211, 214–15
Adam Marsh 1, 4, 5–9, 10 n., 30–1, 62, 118, 138
Adam of Bocfeld 103, 104 n.
Adam of Whitby 97, 104
Agnellus of Pisa 117
Albert the Great 85, 167 n., 185 n., 187
Alexander of Hales 30 n., 65, 74–5, 76–7, 80, 81, 86–7, 89–90, 91, 93, 124, 145 n.
Alghazel 73
Alszeghy, Z. 18–19
Ambrose 125, 155
analogia entis 145, 216–17, 228, 237, 250, 252
 see also participation
Anaxagoras 178
angels 87, 229
 taking human form 62
 composition 66–8
 movement 83, 183 n.
 creation 155, 188–9
 influence on spontaneous generation 165–8
 soul 171
Anselm of Canterbury 35, 50, 51–2, 69, 147, 203, 205, 208–9, 211–13, 220–1, 222, 226, 234, 236 n.
Anselm of Laon 223
Apostles' Creed 124
Aquila 133, 246
Aristotle 68 n., 69, 95–100, 103–4, 108, 111, 113–14, 187, 214, 221, 243, 247
 potentiality of the mind 35–8
 eternity of the world 52–7, 191–3, 195–8, 200, 220, 244, 252
 God's knowledge 66, 100–3, 244
 substantial change 84
 philosophy of science 123–4, 126–7, 130–1, 133, 151, 244, 251
 natural philosophy 130–3, 137, 161, 169, 181, 199, 244, 246
 generation of the soul 161–2, 164, 167, 172–3, 244, 249
 soul and body 175, 244

light 182–6
free choice 201–2, 209
 see also Richard Rufus of Cornwall; *work*, general; influence of Aristotle *and* Robert Grosseteste, *and* Aristotle
aspectus-affectus 71, 79
Assisi, Sacro Convento, library of the 40–4, 65–6
 catalogue of 1381: 10–13, 17–18, 43, 61, 64–5
auctoritates, appeal to 29, 56, 70, 103, 125–6, 188–90, 234, 245, 253
Augustine 35, 52, 69, 71, 102, 125–6, 128, 132, 134, 137, 140–1, 156, 158, 161, 166, 171, 174, 182–4, 188–9, 191, 193, 202–3, 209, 221, 226, 235, 243
Avencebrol 168
Averroes 35, 56, 66, 75, 79–80, 88, 98–9, 174–5, 183, 186, 191
Avicenna 53, 99, 178, 191, 252

Bale, John 11, 13, 17
baptism, manner of administration 63
Bartholomaeus Anglicus, *De proprietatibus rerum* 114
Basil of Caesarea 52, 135, 152, 154, 157–8, 189, 193
beatitude see heaven
Beatus, commentator on the Apocalypse 242
Bede, Venerable 90, 125, 155
Benedictus Hectoris 109
Bernard of Chartres 30 n.
Bernard of Clairvaux 209
Boethius, Anicius Manlius Severinus 128–9, 211, 243
Boethius of Dacia 34
Bonaventure 9, 65–6, 72, 73–4, 80, 253
 commentary on the *Sentences* 17–19, 25, 26 n., 40, 61, 63 n., 70
 see also Richard Rufus of Cornwall; *work*, abbreviation of Bonaventure; comparison with Bonaventure

Callus, D. 120 n.
Cambridge, university of 9
Cathars 191
Catto, J. 23 n., 27 n., 138 n.
causality 55, 103, 146, 148, 166
  material 144, 193
  efficient 165 n., 169, 194, 209–10
  formal 169
celestial bodies 160, 165–8
change, substantial 164, 171, 175–81, 218–
    19, 244, 250, 251
  moment of 83–4
choice 201–2
  see also free will
Christ, Jesus, his human nature after
    death 32–3, 112
  conception 57–9
  resurrection 87
  creator of the world 156
  redeemer 222, 224, 226, 231, 233, 235–9,
    250–1
  final purpose of creation 223–5, 227–8,
    229–32, 233–4, 237–9, 246
  man's justification 226
  hypostatic union 229–30
  second Adam 238–9
  see also Incarnation
Clement VI, Pope 44–5
Conlan, W. 86
contingency and necessity 146–7, 205,
    209–10, 228, 232, 236–9, 252
creation 34, 127, 132, 218
  time of 22, 155–6
  instantaneous or successive 125–6,
    188–90
  doctrine of 191, 198, 200, 244, 252
  ex nihilo 193
  first and second creation 237–9
  see also eternity of the world
Crusades 241

dator formarum see forms
Davy, M.-M., 2 n., 105, 106 n.
Dee, John 110
Democritus 184
demonstration 123, 125–8, 143, 146–9, 151,
    248, 251
Desiderio of Monte Cassino 217 n.
desire 201–2, 211
determinism *see* contingency and neces-
    sity
disposition (*habitus*) 184, 186, 212–13,
    220–1, 251

Doucet, V. 65 n., 77, 79, 86 n.
dualism 191

Easton, S. 5 n., 7, 34 n.
Ebbesen, S. 33 n., 107 n.
Elias of Cortona 2–4, 105, 117
emanation 191, 193
equivocation 129, 244
eternity of the world 52–5, 77, 192–200,
    244, 252
  eternal creation 191, 193, 252
  see also Aristotle, eternity of the world
  and creation
Eudes of Châteauroux 86, 90, 105–6
Eudes Rigaud (Odo Rigaldi) 65, 73 n., 81,
    86, 238 n.
Eustace of Normanville 30–1
Eustathius 158

Felder, H. 2 n.
forms, generic/universal 82, 176, 177–80
  and seminal principles 82, 180, 218 n.
  plurality of substantial 162, 172–3, 249,
    251
  spiritual 163, 184
  separate existence 164–5, 178, 251
  specific/singular 176, 178–9
  dator-formarum-theory 178
  hidden in matter 178
  individual 179–80
  incorporeal 184
  substantial 184
Francis of Assisi 4, 242
Frederick II, Emperor 25–6
freedom, human 205, 207, 215–17
  divine *see* God, freedom
  see also free will
free will 121
  in Greek philosophy 201–2
  Christian concept 202–3
  in God and man 205, 215–17, 250
  relation to reason and will 206–7,
    210–14
  and merit 207, 212, 214–15
  proof of its existence 209–10

Gal, G., 94 n., 100, 104 n.
generation and corruption 161, 168, 178,
    217–19, 221
  see also change, substantial
genus see forms, generic/universal
Geoffrey of Aspall 95, 103, 104 n.
Geoffrey of Cornwall 11

Gerardinus of San Giovanni in Persiceto 81
Gérard of Abbeville 86
Gerard of Parma 42
Gilson, E. 202
God, proof of his existence 48, 50, 68–9
  his knowledge 51–2, 66, 73–5, 85, 100–2, 244
  existence of ideas in him 104, 128, 160, 228, 237, 252
  author of theology 139–40
  creator of souls 162–5, 168, 170–2, 249
  freedom 165–6, 205–6, 216–20, 238–9, 245, 252
  will 165–6, 168–9, 194, 200, 206, 252
  relation to the world 168, 181, 199–200, 216–17, 238–9, 252
  creator of the world 191–200, 252
  power over the past 217–19
Gregory of Naples 105–6
Gregory of Nyssa 126
Gregory the Great, Pope 226
Gründel, J. 18
Guerric of Saint-Quentin 65
Guiard of Laon 65, 105–6

habitus see disposition
Haymo of Faversham 3, 12, 106 n.
heaven, man's state in 71–3, 89–90
  blessedness of virgins in 93
heaven and firmament 126, 190
Henquinet, F. M. 65, 74–5, 81, 86
Henry of Harclay 119 n.
Herbert of Auxerre 97 n.
Honorius of Autun 224
Hugh Cote 7 n.
Hugh of Saint-Victor 19, 23, 27, 29, 30, 131, 143–5, 173, 174, 190
hylomorphism 163–4

illumination, divine 147–8
Incarnation 121, 250–1, 252
  Anselm's theory 222
  consequence of original sin 222, 234–9
  proof from Scripture 222, 225–6
  absolute predestination of Christ 223–4, 228–9, 247
  as completion of the universe 223–5, 227–34, 237–9, 246
  and symbolical theology 224–5, 230–1
  and the sacraments 227
individuation, principle of 77, 178–9, 180
intellect 35–8, 78–9, 162, 164, 211–13

Investiture Contest 241
Islam 241

James I, King 91
James of Viterbo 20, 26 n.
John, papal legate 5
John Blund 99
John Boston 91
John Damascene 58, 154, 158, 174, 182, 184, 209–10
John Duns Scotus 119, 131 n., 180, 247
John Ioli 10
John of Garland 91, 109
John of La Rochelle, 65, 73 n., 77, 81, 86, 90, 145 n.
John of Parma 2 n., 4, 6
John of Reading 2, 4
John of Saint-Gilles 105–6
John of Salisbury 30 n.
John of Wales 138
John Peckham 95
John Wyclif 119
Josephus, Flavius 126

knowledge, theory of 35–8

Lambert of Auxerre 97 n.
Lateran Council, Fourth 124
Lawrence of Cornwall 23
Leland, John 11–13
Leo, Brother 242
Lewry, O. 80 n., 107 n., 109
Libera, A. de 107 n., 112
liberum arbitrium see free will
light 158–9, 219–20, 251
  diffusion of 83–4, 182–3
  philosophy of 181, 187, 246, 249
  accident or substance 182, 183–4
  corporeal or incorporeal substance 184–7
Little, A. G. 3, 5–7, 17–18, 31, 34 n.
Lottin, O. 88
Lumley, John 91
Lyons, Council of 25

McEvoy, J. 80 n., 120
Magi, star of the 76
Maimonides 35, 55, 194–5, 196 n.
Mandonnet, P. 2 n.
Manichees, 139 n., 140, 202–3
Martin de S. Cruce 10
Mary, mother of God *see* Christ, Jesus, conception

matter, double meaning 67–8
  in souls 163–4
  active principle in nature 165
  in substantial changes 176–7, 179–80,
    217–19
  separate existence 178
  uncreated first principle 192
Matthew of Aquasparta 66 n.
Matthew Paris 117
merit *see* free will
Merlin 62
Michael Scotus 98
mind, potentiality of the 35–8
Moses 192
Mynors, R. A. B. 35 n.

necessity *see* contingency and necessity
Neoplatonism 160, 174, 181, 187, 191, 193,
    199–200, 228, 234, 242–3, 246, 252
  see also participation *and* symbolical
    theology
Nicholas Lakmann 45, 47
Nicholas Rufus 3
Norwich, cathedral library 11, 19

Origen 125
original sin 161, 171, 222–4, 226–7, 233,
    235–7
Oxford, provincial chapter OFM at 4
Oxford, university of 5–6, 8, 29–30, 63, 80–
    1, 84, 117, 119, 122, 137–8, 143, 246–7

Paris, university of 29–30, 63, 80–1, 84,
    105–6, 122, 124
participation 132, 134, 136, 160–1, 168–9,
    181, 191, 199–200, 204–5, 216, 224–5,
    243, 246
  see also analogia entis and Neoplatonism
    and symbolical theology
pecia 21–3, 41–3, 65
Pelster, F. 31, 32–4, 35 n., 70–7, 86, 87–90,
    93
Peter Abelard 68 n.
Peter Comestor 8, 26, 138, 166 n.
Peter Damiani 217 n.
Peter Lombard, *Sentences* 8, 18, 26, 90, 124,
    138, 142–3, 154, 203, 206, 212
Peter of Aquila 45
Peter of Tewkesbury 118
Philip the Chancellor 105–6, 212
Pinborg, J. 32 n., 107, 111–12
Plato 192, 201
Plotinus 23, 191

Poitiers, battle of 241
Porphyry, tree of 109
predication 77
premisses 123–4, 126–7, 146
principia per se nota see premisses
Proclus 96–7
prophecy (*divinatio*) 87
punishment, eternal 70–1

Radulphus Brito 34
Ralph of Colebruge 30–1
Raoul Glaber 241
resurrection, of all flesh 89–90, 91
  of Christ *see* Christ, Jesus, resurrection
Richard Fishacre 27, 71, 75, 80, 104, 107
    111, 139, 207 n.
  subject matter of theology 28–9, 144
  commentary on the *Sentences* 85, 93,
    119, 124, 137, 152–4, 160, 208
  theology and Scripture 140, 142–3, 150
  theology as a science 146
  use of allegorical method 157
  animal soul 162 n., 163–4
  creation 189
  free will 210–15
  God's power over the past 217–20
  reasons for the Incarnation 231–4
  see also Richard Rufus of Cornwall;
    work, general; comparison with
    Richard Fishacre
Richard of Barton 106 n.
Richard of Draughton 106 n.
Richard of Mediavilla 10 n.
Richard Rufus of Cornwall;
  life
    sources 1–3, 11–13
    birth 1, 12
    denunciation by Roger Bacon 1–2, 5,
      31–4
    entrance OFM 2–4, 105–6
    studies at Oxford 4–5, 31, 84, 103, 138–
      9, 143, 247
    delay of inception 5–9, 253
    encounter with Bonaventure 9, 63, 247
    lecturer at Oxford 9–10, 62–3, 247
    judgement of posterity 10–13
  work
    general;
      rediscovery 17–19, 64
      comparison with Robert Grosseteste
        27–8, 53–4, 119–21, 138–9, 142–
        3, 144, 145–6, 149, 150–1, 152–
        60, 163, 165, 168–9, 170, 180–1,

182, 187, 188–90, 192, 194, 195–
200, 208–10, 211, 214, 215–17,
220, 234–9, 247–51, 252
comparison with Richard Fishacre
27–9, 140, 142–3, 144–5, 146,
150, 152–4, 157, 160, 163–4, 189,
208, 210–12, 214–15, 217–19,
220, 234
dialectic theologian 31–4, 84, 113–14,
150–1, 154–60, 188–90, 199–200,
209–10, 247–9
influence of Aristotle 35–9, 52–5, 56–
7, 66, 68, 84, 100–3, 113–14, 150–
1, 161, 169, 175, 181, 183–7,
193–8, 199–200, 220–1, 245, 251
literary style 49–50, 56, 69–70, 72,
245, 251
survey of authentic works 113–14
ignorance of Greek 157–8
Oxford commentary on the *Sentences*;
manuscripts 20–5, 70, 91–2
time and place of origin 25–30
author 30–9, 61–2
abbreviation of Bonaventure;
manuscripts 40–7
comparison with Bonaventure 47–9,
51–5, 57, 59, 60, 62–3, 82–3, 89,
143, 193, 198, 207, 213
author 47–61
comparison with Oxford commentary 49–60, 145 n., 149 n., 165 n.,
167 n., 176–8, 180 n., 183–6,
195–8, 207, 213
time and place of origin 62–3
disputed questions;
general:
manuscripts 64–5, 79–80, 81, 247
comparison with Oxford commentary 67, 68–9, 72, 83–4, 176–
8, 180
comparison with abbreviation 81–
2, 176–8
on the acquisition of knowledge 35–
9, 77, 80
on the divine intellect 66
on the composition of angels 66–8
treatise on God and the soul 68–9,
76, 253
on man's state in heaven 71–3
on seminal principles 81–2, 176–8,
180
on the moment of change 83–4,
183 n.

lost works 114
attributed works;
university sermon 2 n., 105–6
disputed questions 70–1, 73–81, 85–
6, 86–90, 92–3
commentary on the *Metaphysics* 94–
105, 194–7
Abstractiones 107–13
Richardus Sophista 107–8, 113
Rijk, L. M. de 107
Robert Cowton 119
Robert Grosseteste 7, 22, 65, 71, 79, 80, 91,
191
influence on Oxford theologians 99,
103, 118–20, 137–9, 150, 246–8
reform of the Church 117–18, 137
relations with OFM 117–18, 138, 248
conflict with Oxford theology faculty
122, 124, 137–8, 142–3, 150
theological conservatism 124–30, 154–
6, 181, 199, 230–1, 245–6
and Aristotle 126–7, 130–3, 137, 162–3,
192, 245–6
reform of allegorical method 130–7,
152, 157–8, 246
linguist 133, 157, 246
mathematician 159–60, 168, 187
creation of animal souls 162–3, 199–200
seminal principles 165 n.
anthropology 169–70, 203–5, 229–31,
246
philosophy of light 181–2, 199, 249
creation doctrine 192, 194, 196–8
free will 203–7
Incarnation 222, 225–31, 237–9, 246
see also Richard Rufus of Cornwall;
work, general; comparison with
Robert Grosseteste
Robert Holcot 119 n.
Robert Kilwardby 100, 104
Rodulphius, P. 11, 13
Roger Bacon 1–3, 5, 7, 9, 11–13, 31–4, 39,
62, 103, 104 n., 107, 112, 124, 138, 187
Roger of Nottingham 10, 34
Rupert of Deutz 223–4, 230

Saracens 241
Sbaralea, J. 12–13
Schneyer, J. B. 106 n.
seminal principles 81–3, 103, 165, 168, 170,
171, 180, 217–18, 251
senses *see* soul, human, movement of the
senses

Siger of Brabant 34
Simon of Hinton 138
Smalley, B. 119, 124 n., 125 n., 130, 131 n., 225 n.
soul, animal 249, 251, 252
    generation or creation 161, 162–5, 217–18
    matter and form 163–4
    spontaneous generation 166–8
    mode of generation 165–8
soul, human 69
    powers of the sensitive soul 73
    composition 78–9, 229
    movement of the senses 87–9
    generation or creation 161–2, 171–2
    Christian concept 161–2, 172–3, 175, 244
    plurality of substantial forms 162, 172–3, 249, 251
    spiritual form 163
    matter and form 163–4
    created in God's image 169–70, 204–5, 249
    not created in seminal principle 171
    relation to the body 173–5, 229, 249
    and free will 210–12
    capacities (*potentiae*) 212–14
    see also intellect *and* will, human
Southern, R. W. 80 n., 120 n., 122 n.
species see forms, specific/singular
spontaneous generation *see* soul, animal, spontaneous generation
Streveler, P. A. 107 n.
substance 175, 183–4, 186
Summa 'Alexandri' 9, 17, 64, 75, 145 n.
syllogisms in theological discourse *see* demonstration
symbolical theology 127–9, 132–3, 136, 139, 181, 220, 224–5, 231, 242–3, 246
    see also participation *and* theology, allegorical method

Tanner, Th. 10 n., 12–13
theology,
    subject-matter 27–9, 47, 131, 143–5
    and logic 31–4, 243–4

as a science 46–7, 122–4, 126–7, 145–51, 244, 248, 251
and Scripture 122–4, 126–30, 137, 139–43, 150–1, 199, 223, 243, 248, 251
    allegorical method 127–37, 150–1, 157, 181, 199–200, 223, 243, 245
    see also symbolical theology
Thomas Aquinas 25, 44, 46–7, 149 n., 178, 203, 253
Thomas Bacon 6–7
Thomas Docking 138 n.
Thomas of Eccleston 1–4, 9, 11–13, 31, 62, 105
Thomas of York 5, 7–9, 26 n., 31, 253
time, creation and 196–8
    nature of 198, 219
transubstantiation 177, 244
Trinity, persons in the 24
    notiones 50–1
    creator of the world 156
    man created in the image of the 169, 180, 249

universals 77
univocation 129

Virgil 166 n.

Walter Burleigh 97, 111
Walter of Château-Thierry 65, 76–7, 80, 81
Weisheipl, J. 5 n.
will, human 78–9, 165 n., 194, 202, 206–7, 208–9, 211–13, 215
    divine *see* God, will
William Grey 20
William Heytesbury 108–9
William of Alnwick 119 n.
William of Auvergne 105–6, 168 n.
William of Auxerre 97 n., 124
William of Champeaux 223
William of Melitona 9, 65, 81
William of Moerbeke 96
William of Montoriel 107
William of Nottingham 4–5, 8–9
William of Ockham 108
William of Shyreswood 33